FILIP ČAPEK

ARCHAEOLOGY, HISTORY, AND IDENTITY FORMATION OF ANCIENT ISRAEL

TRANSLATED BY
VÁCLAV KOUTNÝ

KAROLINUM PRESS
PRAGUE, 2024

KAROLINUM PRESS
Karolinum Press is a publishing department of Charles University
www.karolinum.cz

© 2024 by Filip Čapek
Translation copyright © 2024 by Václav Koutný
Photographs copyright © 2024 by David R. Moulis
Originally published in Czech as *Archeologie, dějiny a utváření identity starověkého Izraele*, 2018, by Vyšehrad, Prague
First English edition
Designed by Jan Šerých
Set and printed in the Czech Republic by Karolinum Press

ISBN 978-80-246-5417-1
ISBN 978-80-246-5525-3 (pdf)
ISBN 978-80-246-5526-0 (epub)

We are able to see that biblical interpretation, historical investigations, and archaeological research can successfully dialogue even in the absence of consensus about the "facts."
—Andrew Vaughn and Ann Killebrew

CONTENTS

List of Figures and Tables		11
Abbreviations		13
Acknowledgements		15
1.	**Introduction**	**17**
2.	**Origins (Late Bronze Age to Late Iron Age I)**	**24**
2.1	Iron Age I Developments	27
2.1.1	Northern Highlands	28
2.1.2	Southern Highlands and Shephelah	30
2.2	Iron Age I Social Organisation	32
2.3	Summary—When and How Israel and Judah First Emerged?	32
3.	**The Difficult Tenth Century (Late Iron Age I to Iron Age IIA)**	**34**
3.1	Closely Watched Chronology	34
3.2	Less United, Less Visible?	37
3.2.1	Western Border Processes—Sorek and Elah Valleys (Shephelah Region)	37
3.2.1.1	Khirbet Qeiyafa: The First Trace of Judah?	38
3.2.1.1.1	Location, Geographical Context, and Identification	38
3.2.1.1.2	Settlement—Urban Planning Concept	39
3.2.1.1.3	Stratigraphy and Dating	39
3.2.1.1.4	Ethnic Identification	40
3.2.1.2	Beth-Shemesh: Late-Canaanite and Judean Traces	43
3.2.1.2.1	Location, Geographical Context, and Identification	43
3.2.1.2.2	Boundaries and Ethnicity	43
3.2.1.2.3	Stratigraphy and Food Habits	44
3.2.1.2.4	Pottery and Architecture	45
3.2.1.3	Tel Batash: Late-Canaanite, Philistine, and Judean Traces?	47
3.2.1.3.1	Location, Geographical Context, and Identification	47
3.2.1.3.2	Boundaries and Ethnicity	47
3.2.1.3.3	Stratigraphy, Pottery, and Food Habits	48
3.2.1.3.4	Tel Batash IV and a Newly Emerging Ethnic Group	49
3.2.1.4	Preliminary Summary	51
3.2.1.4.1	Complexity	51
3.2.1.4.2	Pottery	52

3.2.1.4.3	General Scheme Problems (Modelling Demographic Trends)	53
3.2.1.4.4	Continuity	53
3.2.1.4.5	Including Biblical Texts in Reconstructing Historical Context	54
3.2.1.4.6	Is There a Key to the Origins of the Kingdom of Judah?	54
3.2.2	Far Up North—the Land of Saul	56
3.2.2.1	It All Started in Shechem	57
3.2.2.2	Fall of New Canaan, Gibeon, and Saul	57
3.2.2.3	Re-dating Saul and Shoshenq I, and the Egyptian-Philistine Transposition	59
3.2.2.4	Khirbet Qeiyafa—the Northern Scenario	60
3.2.2.5	What about Jerusalem and the United Monarchy?	61
3.2.2.6	The Northern Trail—a Provisional Critical Evaluation	62
3.2.3	It Was Jerusalem, After All—the Southern Variant	65
3.2.3.1	Shoshenq I—a Campaign with Another Purpose	65
3.2.3.2	Archaeology of Jerusalem—New and More Conservative	65
3.2.3.3	Decisive Role of Benjamin	68
3.2.3.4	They Were Truly Philistines	69
3.2.3.5	What Is Israel and What Is Judah?	70
3.2.3.6	North and South—Separate But Concurrent	71
3.2.3.7	Southern Trail—a Provisional Critical Evaluation	71
3.3	Summary	73
4.	**The First True Unification and the First True Division (Iron Age IIA–B)**	76
4.1	Big and Little Histories	76
4.1.1	The Neo-Assyrian Empire	77
4.1.2	Arameans	77
4.1.3	Ancient Dominoes	78
4.2	First Unification to First Independence	81
4.2.1	Writing—an Indicator of Territorial State Formation?	82
4.2.2	Developments in the First Half of the Ninth Century BCE and the Rise of the Omride Dynasty	83
4.2.3	Israel and Judah: Unification according to the Northern Scenario	88
4.2.4	Traditions: Original and Transformed	89
4.2.4.1	From Abraham to Saul	90
4.2.4.2	From David to the End of the Golden Era	93
4.2.4.3	Israel's Presence in the Traditions of Judah—How, When and Why?	95
4.2.5	The Chronicles of the Kings—a Special Case	98
4.2.5.1	The Case of Jehu and Joash	108
4.2.5.1.1	The House of Ahab and the House of Omri	108
4.2.5.1.2	The Double Patronymic	112
4.2.5.1.3	Inventing Unity, Creating Disunity	115
4.2.6	Ninth-Century BCE Jerusalem	116
4.3	Summary	118

5.	**First Independence (Iron Age IIB–C)**	120
5.1	Ancient Dominoes	120
5.2	Transformations in Judah—the First Half of the Eighth Century BCE	123
5.3	Judah in the First Half of the Eighth Century BCE and Biblical Texts	125
5.3.1	Judah in the First Half of the Eighth Century BCE—Critical Reading	126
5.3.2	Biblical Texts—the Eighth Century BCE and the Prophetic Traditions	132
5.3.3	Biblical Texts—the Eighth Century BCE and Bethel	134
5.4	Summary	138

6.	**The Last Long Century (Iron Age IIC)**	142
6.1	Ancient Dominoes	143
6.2	Historical Crossroads, Intersections, and Cul-de-Sacs	151
6.2.1	Ahaz: Consolidation, Reforms, and Construction Efforts under Assyrian Supervision	152
6.2.2	Hezekiah: Reforms and Unwise Politics Ending Well	158
6.2.3	Manasseh: Bad Reputation, Bad King?	165
6.2.4	Josiah: *David Redivivus*, Monotheism, and Policies	169
6.2.4.1	The Extent of the Territory	170
6.2.4.2	Religious Reform and Death	172
6.2.5	Jehoiakim and His Successors according to Biblical Texts	177
6.3	Summary	179

7.	**The End and a New Beginning (Neo-Babylonian and Persian Periods)**	182
7.1	Ancient Dominoes	183
7.2	Intellectual Processing of the Defeat and Shaping the New Israel	185
7.2.1	Myths of the Empty Land and the Mass Return	187
7.2.2	The Archaeology of Judah and Jerusalem in the Neo-Babylonian Period	189
7.2.3	Three Perspectives on the Exile and the Myth of the Empty Land	190
7.2.4	Those Who Remained . . .	193
7.2.5	The Myth of the Mass Return	195
7.2.6	Who Is and Who Is Not Israel?	198
7.3	Summary	202

8. Conclusions — 204

Bibliography	211
Ancient Personal Names Index	241
Hebrew Bible/Old Testament	243
Other Ancient Textual Sources	247
Modern Authors Index	248
Place Names Index	253

LIST OF FIGURES AND TABLES

Fig. 1. The interrelationship between the three variables of interpretation
Fig. 2. The relationship between references and their contexts
Tab. 1. High, low, and modified conventional chronologies (overview)
Fig. 3. Factors contributing to the Late Bronze Age city-state system collapse
Tab. 2. City-state destructions that are dated to the Late Bronze Age or Iron Age I
Fig. 4. Urbanisation changes from the Late Bronze Age to Iron Age IIA
Tab. 3. Estimated extent of built-up area and total population in the Iron Age I (according to Lehmann 2003)
Fig. 5. Topographic plan of Khirbet Qeiyafa (courtesy of Khirbet Qeiyafa Excavation)
Fig. 6. Relative chronology: upper and lower limits in Khirbet Qeiyafa
Tab. 4. Stratigraphy of Khirbet Qeiyafa, Beth-shemesh, and Tel Batash
Tab. 5. Ratio of pig bones found in Ekron, Ashkelon, and Tel Batash
Fig. 7. Possible interactions in the Shephelah in the Late Bronze Age and the Iron Age I and IIA
Fig. 8. The Saulide Kingdom according to biblical and archaeological sources (Finkelstein 2013)
Fig. 9. The Formation of Israel and its gradual retrospective depiction in the Hebrew Bible
Fig. 10. Development of the area around Jerusalem from the fourteenth to eleventh century BCE (according to Sergi 2017a)
Fig. 11. Reconstruction of the northern origin of the oldest David-related stories (based on Fleming 2013)
Fig. 12. Historical patterning using the examples of Jezebel, Athaliah, Jehu, and Joash
Fig. 13. Diagram of the standardised biblical fiction relating to the division of the kingdoms
Fig. 14. Reconstruction of the relationship between the chronicles of the kings of Israel and Judah
Fig. 15. Dynastic construction in 1 Kgs 15
Fig. 16. Four formation stages of the kingdoms of Judah and Israel
Fig. 17. Intertextual links between Josh 6:26 and 1 Kgs 16:34, with a secondary reference to 1 Kgs 16:24
Fig. 18. The Nimshide dynasty as part of the wider Omride family (according to Lamb 2007 and Baruchi-Unna 2017)
Fig. 19. Dynasty of Nimshidides/Jehuites with double patronymics in the Books of Kings
Fig. 20. Judean kings and their mothers, according to the Books of Kings
Fig. 21. Joash of the Nimshide dynasty as the ruler of Jerusalem and Samaria (according to Frevel 2016)
Fig. 22. Judean kings in the first half and early second half of the eighth century BCE
Fig. 23. Prophetic books referring to the eighth century BCE
Tab. 6. Original and revised stratigraphy of Tel Arad (Aharoni 1981 and Herzog 2002)
Fig. 24. Rosette stamped handles distribution map (according to Koch and Lipschits 2013)
Fig. 25. Fictitious and real (retroactive) timelines of Josiah's reform
Tab. 7. Historical patterning of Judean kings in the eighth and seventh centuries BCE
Fig. 26. The exodus from Egypt and the return from Babylonian exile as mirror events
Fig. 27. The triple conflict of the Babylonian diaspora upon its return to Judah

ABBREVIATIONS

AASOR   Annual of the American Schools of Oriental Research
ABC   Assyrian and Babylonian Chronicles (Grayson)
ADPV   Abhandlungen des Deutschen Palästina-Vereins
AfO   Altorientalische Forschungen
AHI   Ancient Hebrew Inscriptions—Corpus and Concordance (Davies)
AIL   Ancient Israel and Its Literature
ANEM   Ancient Near East Monographs
ANET   Ancient Near Eastern Texts Relating to the Old Testament (Pritchard)
ANES   Ancient Near Eastern Studies
AOAT   Alter Orient und Altes Testament
ArOr   Archiv orientální
ATSAT   Arbeiten zu Text und Sprache im Alten Testament
BA   The Biblical Archaeologist
BAR   British Archaeological Reports/Biblical Archaeology Review
BASOR   Bulletin of the American School of Oriental Research
BN   Biblische Notizen
BVB   Beiträge zum Verstehen der Bibel
BWANT   Beiträge zur Wissenschaft vom Alten und Neuen Testament
BZAW   Beihefte zur Zeitschrift für Alttestamentliche Wissenschaft
CBQ   Catholic Biblical Quarterly
CUSAS   Cornell University Studies in Assyriology and Sumerology
CHANE   Culture and History of the Ancient Near East
COS   The Context of Scripture (Hallo—Younger)
CV   Communio viatorum
DB   Darius' Besitun Inscription (Schmitt)
EA   El-Amarna Correspondence (Rainey)
ESHM   European Seminar in Historical Methodology
FAT   Forschungen zum Alten Testament
FRLANT Forschungen zur Religion und Literatur des Alten und Neuen Testaments
HBS   Herders Biblische Studien
HeBAI   Hebrew Bible and Ancient Israel
HS   Hebrew Studies
HSS   Harvard Semitic Studies
HThKAT Herders Theologischer Kommentar zum Alten Testament
IEJ   Israel Exploration Journal
IJRHSC International Journal of Research in Humanities and Social Studies
JAEI   Journal of Ancient Egyptian Interconnections
JAJSup Journal of Ancient Judaism—Supplements
JANES   Journal of the Ancient Near Eastern Society
JANEH   Journal of Ancient Near Eastern History
JANER   Journal of Ancient Near Eastern Religions
JAS   Journal of Archaeological Studies

JBL	Journal of Biblical Literature
JETS	Journal of the Evangelical Theological Society
JHS	Journal of Hebrew Scriptures
JNES	Journal of Near Eastern Studies
JNSL	Journal of Northwest Semitic Languages
JSJ	Journal for the Study of Judaism
JSOT	Journal for the Study of the Old Testament
JSS	Journal of Semitic Studies
JTS	The Journal of Theological Studies
JSOT	Journal for Studies of the Old Testament
KUSATU	Kleine Untersuchungen zur Sprache des Alten Testaments und seiner Umwelt
LAS	Leipziger Altorientalistische Studien
NEA	Near Eastern Archaeology
NEASB	Near East Archaeological Society Bulletin
NSAJR	New Studies in the Archaeology of Jerusalem and Its Religion
OBO	Orbis Biblicus et Orientalis
OJA	Oxford Journal of Archaeology
OLA	Orientalia Lovaniensia Analecta
ORA	Orientalische Religionen in der Antike
OTS	Old Testament Series
PEQ	Palestine Exploration Quarterly
RB	Revue Biblique
SAAS	State Archives of Assyria Studies
SCJ	Stone-Campbell Journal
SHCANE	Studies in the History and Culture of the Ancient Near East
SJOT	Scandinavian Journal of the Old Testament
SR	Studies in Religion
TA	Tel Aviv
TAD	Textbook of Aramaic Documents (Porten—Yardeni)
UF	Ugaritische Forschungen
VT	Vetus Testamentum
VTSup	Vetus Testamentum Supplement Series
WMANT	Wissenschaftliche Monographien zum Alten und Neuen Testament
WO	Die Welt des Orients
WUB	Welt und Umwelt der Bibel
ZAW	Zeitschrift für Altestestamentliche Wissenschaft
ZDPV	Zeitschrift des deutschen Palästina-Vereins

ACKNOWLEDGEMENTS

The creation of this book would have been impossible without discussions with and advice from my colleagues at the Protestant Theological Faculty of Charles University; consequently, I want to thank Prof. Martin Prudký, Assoc. Prof. Petr Sláma, Assoc. Prof. Jan Rückl, David Cielontko, Ph.D. and David R. Moulis, Ph.D. (for visual aids, maps, and overview tables). Apart from these Czech and Slovak scholars, many of my colleagues and friends from the archaeology institutes of Tel Aviv University and the Hebrew University of Jerusalem made essential contributions which assured the successful completion of this book. They were gracious enough to discuss with me individual chapters, topics, and issues arising from them, be it remotely or during conferences, research visits, and archaeological fieldwork (in Ramat Rahel, Tel Azekah, Khirbet Qeiyafa, Jerusalem, Nahal Refa'im and Tel Moza). I owe a special debt of gratitude to Professor Oded Lipschits for both his long-standing friendship and for the long-term and highly beneficial collaboration between our institutions; furthermore, I would like to thank Prof. Ze'ev Herzog, Prof. Yuval Gadot, Omer Sergi, Ph.D., Ido Koch, Ph.D., Sabine Kleiman, Ph.D., Helena Roth, M.A. and Shua Kisilevitz, Ph.D.; last but not least, I wish to express my gratitude to Prof. Yossi Garfinkel and Prof. Amihai Mazar; both from the Hebrew University. The institutes of the universities mentioned were kind enough to provide many of the visual aids and overview materials included in this book. Comments by the readers, Prof. Petr Charvát and Assoc. Prof. Petr Chalupa, made numerous sections of the book more precise. I also want to thank Jáchym Šenkyřík, M.A. and Ondřej Zeman for the indices and editorial processing and Václav Koutný and Julia Bailey for their work on the English translation of this book, which was first published in 2018. Many thanks also to Caleb Harris for his final very thorough editing of the updated text and for his valuable additions and comments. The translation features the most recent literature, even though some amendments were, unfortunately, impossible to implement in a complete and satisfactory manner; this especially concerns Christian Frevel's exquisite text *Geschichte Israels* (German 2016, 2nd edition 2018), published in English roughly at the same time the present book goes to press—consequently, the original German text is referred to in this book.

My greatest thanks go to my wife Kateřina and my children, Maruška, Jonáš, Matěj, and Barbora, for their great patience with my frequent absences from home because of reasons linked to the subject of the book.

Prague, January 2024

1. INTRODUCTION

> *Neither archaeologists nor biblical scholars have access to the whole truth, due not only to the limits of reliable information but also to their own inevitable subjectivity. History writing is about the present, as well the past.*
> —William Dever

The origins of ancient Israel are shrouded in mystery, with many—often unforeseen—variables which influence the decision-making processes used in methods of reconstructing its early days and even scholars' understanding of the nature of the object of this search itself. In this respect, there are different assignments for archaeologists, historians, biblical scholars, and theologians—although their efforts often overlap and complement each other. Essentially, each of the professions must focus on three areas of inquiry and their relationship to each other: firstly, non-written material culture; secondly, literature of the ancient Levant; and thirdly, biblical texts, which present an important and very extensive resource for examining the past.

The first area of inquiry involves inspecting, analysing, and evaluating material culture, discovering specific pieces of information, and proposing interpretations. Unlike in the case of biblical testimony, which mostly comes from a later period of time and expresses the specific perspectives and desires of its later authors or editors, it seems that with material culture we basically stand on firm ground. However, even here we will encounter countless pitfalls, as this book will often demonstrate, which will make it impossible to find a simple solution to the mystery of Israel's creation and the formation of its identity. This search will lead us to more questions and interpretive crossroads than answers. What was there at the beginning; what was Israel? Was it a late eleventh or early tenth-century BCE state in the north, near the ancient city of el-Jib (the biblical Gibeon)? Or should the origins be sought more to the south, in the region of the Shephelah? There, the tenth century BCE saw the formation of a political entity in the valleys of the Judaean Mountains which also extended to their southwest, that some identify as the Kingdom of Judah even then. What is its relation to Jerusalem? And if Israel was created even earlier, at the end of the Late Bronze Age in the thirteenth century BCE, as suggested by the Merneptah Stele (COS 2.6), how was Israel then related to the later city-states and states in the region? What is the relation between

Late Bronze Age city-states, such as Jerusalem (presumably), and Iron Age territorial states? Is there a connection to be found? Or maybe Israel was not created until much later. Perhaps it became an independent political entity in the ninth century BCE, with the Kingdom of Judah being brought to life even later in connection with Neo-Assyrian influence over the Southern Levant in the second half of the eighth century BCE. As will be shown throughout this book, solutions to the mystery of Israel's creation greatly depend upon defining this object of study. This issue will be a topic of discussion, as well as the issue of the transformations of the name "Israel," which was not used to describe only one single entity, as it had numerous bearers during the more than five hundred years of history under discussion.

The second area of inquiry is tied to ancient non-biblical texts. In this area, knowledge is not obtained from the evidence of human activity in architecture, farming, or cult. There are no ramparts, walls, palaces, temples, religious items, or small objects of material culture for daily use. Rather, this area of inquiry centres upon written records, and those describing the origins of Israel are especially scarce. The domain of epigraphers, the literature of Israel's early reconstructed history, is only fragmentary, with more complete documents first appearing in the ninth century BCE. These documents shed their own light on the origins of Israel and, secondarily, on the Kingdom of Judah.

The third area concerns Old Testament texts. Separating these texts from non-biblical textual evidence is crucial, due to the nature of the perspective(s) presented and advocated by biblical materials in their own specific historical contexts. Biblical texts are distinct entities which should be separately investigated and analysed, before engaging these in direct confrontations with material culture and non-biblical textual evidence. In terms of synchronicity, the existence of a direct link between a historical event and a biblical text referring to it is both an ideal—and often unprovable—reality, and a trap set for laypeople and scholars alike who neglect critical approaches to biblical interpretation. The biblical textual corpus is similar to the ancient tell. It is an entity with multiple layers that must be identified within their specific

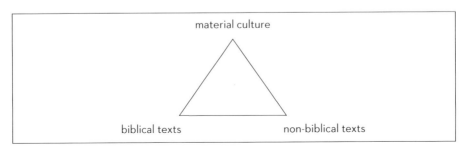

Fig. 1. The interrelationship between the three variables of interpretation

times and places; only afterwards can the data acquired be confronted with the other variables of interpretation—i.e., material culture and non-biblical texts.

Continuity and discontinuity are two words which play a key role in the study of Israel's history. Firstly, they aptly describe all reconstructions of the course of history. These are characterised by observable links and connections, but also turns and shifts due to puzzling data, as well as missing evidence for various events or even entire periods. Furthermore, continuity and discontinuity will be shown to be tools of interpretation used in the formation of ancient Israelite identity. Constituted mainly in retrospect, this identity was formed in various ways: by establishing an independent concept of the history of Israel and the neighbouring nations, justifying the origins of Israel, taking root in a specific geographic area, and often by very strict religious and cultural self-determination. This identity was construed against the flow of historical continuity, and historical "facts" are treated accordingly. Very simply put, the biblical discussions concerning Israelite identity are not about the exact manner in which events took place, but about the way they should have taken place to make sense to a very specific group of text authors and, consequently, also readers. In the process of identity formation everything is subordinated to this assignment. This includes seemingly objective and unquestionable facts—such as chronological lists which ostensibly catalogue the reigns of kings, lists of territories that they controlled, and also genealogical overviews (Oeming 1990).

Biblical texts place a characteristic emphasis on the formative role of the past in the formation of the identity of ancient Israel. The past is uniquely adapted and documented in this literature to carry weight and relevance for the present day (cf. Sláma 2017). Past events provide varying perspectives on the present, which shows a primary reason why the biblical writers included the material that they did in these great Old Testament compositions. This includes material such as the distant origin stories which have no apparent historical value, the patriarchal traditions, the exodus from Egypt, the occupation and settlement of Canaan, and even the monumental Deuteronomistic History. Finally, this explains the monotheising tendency present within biblical texts, though monotheism was not a primary feature of Israel's religion for the majority of the history depicted throughout these biblical texts (cf. Herzog 1999; Rollston 2003; Heiser 2008; Mastin 2010; Stern 2010; Stavrakopoulou and Barton 2010; Sugimoto 2014; van Oorschot and Witte 2017; Becking 2020).

In all the founding and historicising myths and texts linked to ancient Israel, it is necessary to differentiate between the idealised depiction of history they present and the actual reconstructible historical reality—examples of where this is necessary include events such as the formation of the United

Monarchy or the mass exodus and mass return of the Judeans to the land in the Neo-Babylonian and Persian periods. Confronting these two aspects, both of which are of considerable importance and have crucial roles to play, shows that the biblical depictions of these events function to serve the purposes of their authors' in their own present times.

When considering Israel and its sacred scriptures, the Old Testament/Hebrew Bible, it is immediately surprising that so much space is dedicated to the origins, the travels, the nomadic patriarchs, the utopian cult area on Mount Sinai, the period of the Judges, and other such topics which appear to be outside of the area of interest and influence of the nascent Israel. However, modern research has convincingly proven that all these topics are construed through exilic and postexilic perspectives. That is, they are seen through the lens of authors writing from the sixth to fourth century BCE; a reflection which moves from the oldest to the newest and current. This chronological depiction of history explains the present and justifies its connections to everything that came before. The Creation of the world, the promise of land, the establishment of an independent kingdom, the cult of the Jerusalem Temple, and the choosing of the People are all described based on the following rule: the greater the importance of an early period to a later one, the more detailed its description.

Anticipating Israel's later settling and existence in a specific land, the wandering of the patriarchs occurs in an important geographical context, and so its toponymical logic cannot be considered random. There is a similar intention to the cult, which eventually finds its true and—according to biblical authors—only legitimate place in the Jerusalem Temple, after numerous temporary homes. A special position is also assigned to the topic of the kingdom; firstly, the idealised depiction of one in a golden age; and later, a kingdom that is more real and consequently subject to deterioration. Likewise, the land, cult, and political existence of Israel are also central topics and points in a specific time and place in the history of nascent Judaism, which is why they are discussed at such length.

As described by Rolf Rendtorff (2001, 297-301), professor of Old Testament at the University of Heidelberg, the past explains the present, and the present gives weight to the past. The best way to understand the significance of the present is to retell the past for the sake of the present and the continuity of a specific community—in this case, Israel (cf. Deut 6:20; 26:5ff; Josh 4:6-8; 24:2-15; Judg 6:7-11). It is no coincidence that Rendtorff's approach—building on the legacy of Gerhard von Rad (1901-71; see also Oeming 2001), another Heidelberg scholar and one of the most important Old Testament scholars in twentieth-century Europe—reminds one of Jan Assmann's (2000; 2003) concept of mnemohistory. The latter author, an Egyptologist and professor from the same university town, bases his study of collective memory also on von

Rad's (1947; 1961) studies of the Book of Deuteronomy and Old Testament historiography. Paraphrasing Assmann (1992; 2000), biblical texts may be said to contain a connective structure, which lends itself to accepting and forming an identity, and to establishing a connective memory. Part of this connective memory is differentiation (*Entdifferenzierung* in German), in which a distinction is made between the binding past and the present, which then reinforces counter-present recollection (ibid., 2000).

Drawing a line between a historical event (i.e., when, if at all, "it" happened) and a reference to it, no matter how transformed, is one of the principal tasks of not just biblical studies, but also archaeology and history. The interdisciplinary dialogue between these branches also examines the reference itself regarding its historical, religious, and ideological background (i.e., when it was written). There is another element investigated: the reference's function in the community of ancient audiences and readers (i.e., why and how it was written in this, and not any other, manner). In summary, critical research examines two basic historical contexts: firstly, the item to which reference is made; and secondly, the position from which reference is made. If we do not differentiate between the two contexts, we are at risk of plunging into (neo)fundamentalism and a superficial or naïve reading of not only biblical but ancient texts in general.

Frequently considered by many to be very ancient, the Old Testament Book of Hosea may serve as an example for this. In truth, the book itself is highly unlikely to feature any more comprehensive texts that were written in the second half of the eighth century BCE—i.e., directly in the time linked to the eponymous prophet. The book is not an on-site report on what the prophet said and did, but a text with later origins (secondary context), which retrospectively refers to the "original" period (primary context), by retrojecting present opinions into the past; the factual analysis of such views may then be used to trace the reasons for the writing of the book (the "why"). A graphic representation of these references is given below.

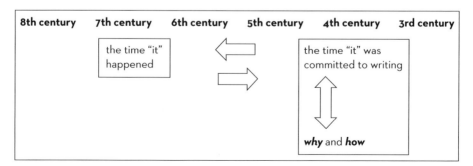

Fig. 2. The relationship between references and their contexts

Consequently, navigating ancient texts is a very complex matter, requiring erudition and competence among scholars and interpreters. This is further complicated by working with material culture and texts outside the Bible—but cognate in nature—which makes the whole enterprise even more daunting.

The chapters in this book are ordered according to a major segment of the chronology of historical periods in the Southern Levant. The default chronology used in the majority of the book is the modified conventional chronology, as introduced and further refined for the Iron Age I and IIA by Amihai Mazar and Christopher Ramsey (2008; for a reaction, see Finkelstein and Piasetzky 2010; Finkelstein 2013; for Vieweger's criticism, see 2006, 54-56, cf. also Boaretto et al. 2019). Instances where a different chronology is used by some scholars will be brought to the reader's attention, including what this means for the interpretation of the related topic.

Tab. 1. High, low, and modified conventional chronologies (overview)

	High chronology	**Low chronology**	**Modified conventional chronology (MCC)**
Late Bronze Age I IIA IIB (III)	1550–1400 BCE 1400–1300 BCE 1300–1250 BCE	1550–1400 BCE 1400–1300 BCE 1300–1130/1071 BCE	1550–1400 BCE 1400–1300 BCE 1300–1200 BCE
Iron Age I	1250–1000 BCE	1130/1071–920/900 BCE	1200/1140–970 BCE (964–944 BCE)
Iron Age IIA	1000–930 BCE	920/900–845 BCE	970–840/830 BCE
Iron Age IIB	930–721 BCE	845–722 BCE	840/830–732/701 BCE
Iron Age IIC	721–586 BCE	722–586 BCE	732/701–605/586 BCE
Neo-Babylonian Period	587/586–539 BCE	587/586–539 BCE	587/586–539 BCE
Persian Period I II	539–450 BCE 450–333 BCE	539–450 BCE 450–333 BCE	539–450 BCE 450–333 BCE

This book attempts to provide a critical reading of Israel's history, which was written by a highly diverse collective of Old Testament "authors." There will be neither a harmonising reading, which takes the picture painted by texts as a given fact, nor a reading complementing biblical texts with "missing" archaeological and epigraphic data, to prevent any tension between biblical texts and history; more options will be offered to the reader, often as theories and hypotheses about alternate ways to understand biblical narratives on historical as well as theological levels. In connection with this search for the identity of ancient Israel, this effort to comprehend these old texts may be described as an analysis of memory traces, either visible, hidden, or somewhere between these two positions. As a biblical scholar cooperating with archaeologists and historians, the author of this book is an expert on biblical texts and theologian first, and an archaeologist second. Consequently, he may view the texts in a less "biblicist" manner than his fellow archaeologists and historians, but on the other hand, he is certain to have less knowledge of, and experience in, the archaeological field.

The following pages have a dual purpose: To reintroduce the basic state of research in recent decades, and secondly, the book aims to draw the reader's attention to new hypotheses and reconstructions based on the interdisciplinary dialogue between biblical studies, archaeology and history. These newly proposed interpretations are founded upon ongoing archaeological research in Israel, in which scholars and students from the Protestant Theological Faculty of Charles University take part, in cooperation with Tel Aviv University and the Sonia and Marco Nadler Institute of Archaeology.

2. ORIGINS (LATE BRONZE AGE TO LATE IRON AGE I)

*If historical (verifiable) truth should be our only concern,
the history of ancient Israel should not only be very short
(written on ten pages or so), but it would also be utterly boring.*
—Hans Barstad

Attempts to determine the very origins of Israel are destined to fail if we expect to discover a clearly defined state with borders, evidence of centralised administration, and existing literature. These origins are often sought in the period between the Late Bronze Age IIB (1300–1200 BCE) and Iron Age I (1200–970 BCE). However, none of these three aspects have been identified conclusively throughout these periods. There is no founding charter, nor any clear indication that "something" emerged in the southern Canaan area that could be termed *Israel*. The word itself exists courtesy of the late thirteenth-century BCE Merneptah Stele (see COS 2.6), but there are various interpretive pitfalls when attempting to select an entity corresponding to that name which is identifiable in terms of territory and politics. There is an even older occurrence of the designation *Israel* on a fragment of a statue base, now housed in Berlin; the fragment dates to the time of Ramesses II (1279–1213 BCE), the father of Merneptah (1213–1203 BCE), but no certain conclusions can be drawn from reading it (see discussion in Görg 2001; Wood 2005; Hoffmeier 2007; van der Veen, Theis, and Görg 2010). Do we seek a nation, a specific state, or something else entirely? The hieroglyphic name *Israel* from the stele itself is a word for a group of people whose region cannot be directly and unequivocally determined; as such, it seems to originate more from the context of localising Late Bronze Age Canaanite city-states based on the Amarna correspondence (Mynářová 2007). In this early period, a connection of the name *Israel* with a state, a state-like entity, or a Canaanite city-state may be ruled out with a high degree of probability (cf. Frevel 2016, 57).

Seeking Israel at the end of the Late Bronze Age means reconstructing, or rather constructing, an identity in the time when Canaanite city-states were collapsing throughout the area. Differing from region to region in severity, the collapse happened gradually and was caused by various circumstances. The least likely explanation—which is probably impossible to be considered a determining factor—is that there is an "Israelite" trace, as depicted in biblical texts written centuries later, mainly the Book of Joshua. Championed by the first generations of archaeologists, this interpretation continues to be advocated by some contemporary archaeologists, historians, and theologians of a fundamentalist and conservative persuasion, who do not differentiate the ideological basis of biblical texts from the historical, with the latter working for the former (for more, see chapter I). It is not the aim of this book to confirm such a setting in history; this possibility has already been convincingly disproven by critical research, which is why it should suffice to refer the reader to the literature included in the bibliography.

A lively debate is taking place as to the reasons for the gradual collapse of Canaanite city-states, and the role of specialised scientific disciplines continues to grow: archaeozoology, palynology, dendroarchaeology, climate archaeology, as well as the use of radiocarbon method, which all further hone the accuracy the dating of the period under discussion (Langgut, Gadot, and Porat 2013; Cline 2014; Langgut et al. 2015; Regev et al. 2017). There are a number of factors which contributed to this collapse each of which impacted multiple key aspects of these societies, the most common of which are the following:

It follows that this collapse was not a one-off event, but a longer process which occurred throughout the late thirteenth to second half of the twelfth century BCE. Moreover, some sites were not destroyed, and so the settlement system did not collapse everywhere (cf. Finkelstein 2013; Gadot 2017; Dever 2003; 2020); other sites were resettled quickly after the destruction; while yet others were temporarily abandoned (e.g., Lachish VII and VI). Selected destructions dates are presented in the following table.

Fig. 3. Factors contributing to the Late Bronze Age city-state system collapse

Tab. 2. City-state destructions that are dated to the Late Bronze Age or Iron Age I

Site	Time of destruction
Azekah S2–5b/T2–3b	ca. 1140 BCE
Aphek X	ca. 1230 BCE
Ashdod XIV	ca. 1200 BCE
Beth-shean VII	sometime after 1150 BCE
Beth-shemesh IVB (or 6)	ca. 1200 BCE
Bethel 1	ca. 1200 BCE
Hazor XII	sometime after 1250 BCE
Lachish VII Lachish VI	ca. the first half of the twelfth century BCE ca. 1130 BCE
Megiddo VIIB Megiddo VIIA	second half of the thirteenth century BCE second half of the twelfth century BCE
Gezer XV	ca. 1200 BCE
Tell Balata (Shechem) X	ca. 1200 BCE (possibly 1150 BCE)
Beit Mirsim C	late thirteenth century BCE
Timnah / Tel Batash VI	ca. 1200 BCE

The end of Canaanite city-states—or the majority of these—was a key development. This becomes most apparent when comparing total city areas in the Bronze Age and the subsequent settlement in the Iron Age I and early Iron Age IIA. The main shift concerns the architecture, since the monumental elements typical of the Bronze Age vanish almost entirely. The evidence includes the absence of massive fortification walls or their significant reduction (see, e.g., Gezer XV and Tel Zayit IV), and there are apparent changes in pottery as well. However, despite the provable population decline and the documented destruction of numerous sites, the area of southern Canaan did not remain uninhabited. These developments were regionally determined: some locations were more affected by the decline in population and settlements than others (Frevel 2016, 68–70). In certain areas, such as the Philistine Pentapolis on the Coastal Plain and on the borders of the western Shephelah, the city-state system survived, only under a different local hegemon (see below). Still, an overall urban shrinkage is apparent and well documented. Tel Arad, built in the Bronze Age on nine hectares of land, was reduced to a fort of a mere half hectare in the Iron Age. Similar trends are observable in Megiddo and Hazor, where the original areas of the tells and the adjoining settlements shift from double (e.g., Hazor with eighty hectares) to single digits.

What happened in southern Canaan after the collapse of city-states in the Late Bronze Age? This question, which is closely linked to the search for Israel's origins, can be divided into three queries. The first and second focus

on examining notional pre-histories; without them, we cannot talk about the origins of Israel and Judah as two independent and, in certain periods, intimately connected political entities. The third query will be discussed in detail in the following chapter. The queries are as follows:
1. What was the general situation in the area of southern Canaan after the collapse of the city-state system (2.1)?
2. In what way was the area settled, and what was its social organisation (2.2)?
3. When and how did Israel and Judah first appear (3)?

2.1 IRON AGE I DEVELOPMENTS

The end of the city-state system in the Late Bronze Age brought about major developments in terms of settlement, administration, social relations, and agriculture. Viewed through a slightly simplifying "textbook" lens, the period was typified by the disappearance of cities (urban shrinkage) and a reduction in city populations (deurbanisation), while rural settlements and villages grew and developed. An intensive transition to agriculture, pastoral farming, and local barter trade also characterised the period. At the turn of the Iron Age I and Iron Age IIA, this trend gradually changed in two ways: sites that saw a decline in urban culture were reurbanised, and entirely new settlements were established.

The Iron Age I settlement transformation is linked to a shift in agriculture, moving from surplus to self-sufficient (subsistence) agriculture. Long-distance trading involving strategic commodities as well as luxury items which was characteristic of the Late Bronze Age ceased or occurred in a limited capacity, as evidenced by the pottery assemblages discovered (cf. Gadot, Lipschits, and Gross 2014). The morphology of these assemblages changed to simpler pottery types which were intended almost exclusively for everyday use. Some types of pottery vanished completely, and decorativeness (use of decor and colours) was minimal. However, such a dramatic disruption of the urban settlement was not seen in such localities as Kinneret in the

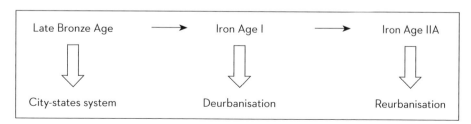

Fig. 4. Urbanisation changes from the Late Bronze Age to Iron Age IIA

area of the Galilee, Megiddo and Yokneam in the Jezreel Valley, and, to the southwest, Beth-shean and Tel Rehov (see below).

2.1.1 NORTHERN HIGHLANDS

Starting in the south, in the territory above Jerusalem, and extending to the Jezreel Valley, the area of the northern highlands is likely to have been controlled by the city-state of Shechem (*Tell Balata*; cf. EA 254 and EA 289), and it saw a settlement increase in the Iron Age I. The number of settlements exceeds that of the Late Bronze Age many times over, since the indigenous seminomadic population mixed with the Canaanite urban population who were arriving from lowland areas affected by the city-state collapse. There was also a third (and possibly fourth) group co-creating a new compound ethnic population in the northern highlands: *Apiru* is the name given to the group of migrants of varying origins recorded as early as the Amarna documents (for more, see EA 285–290), while in fourteenth- and thirteenth-century BCE Egyptian texts there is also mention of *Shasu* (the name means "the travelling" or "shepherds"), although as this group is sometimes also referred to as *Apiru*.

The sedentarisation (of seminomadic groups) and resedenterisation of the population coming from Canaanite city areas brought about a shift in the way of life and forms of subsistence. The region was typified by smaller rural settlements of up to one hectare, almost half of which were founded on previously uninhabited sites (Frevel 2016, 83); these localities had one settlement phase and then vanished again. Somewhat larger settlements, created mainly for strategic reasons near water sources, were the rudiments of key cities of the Kingdom of Israel in the ninth century BCE (e.g., Taanach, Samaria, and Tirzah). The only documented northern location that might have been an administrative centre in the Iron Age I is Shiloh, uncovered in the 1980s. Its destruction dates to 1050 BCE (Finkelstein, Bunimovitz, and Lederman 1993; Finkelstein 2020c; cf. Dever 2003).

When observing the developments in the northern highlands, we must keep in mind that most of the area observed is situated on the West Bank. That is, a location where recent decades have seen minimal standard archaeological research with proper institutional backing (Finkelstein and Na'aman 1994; Zertal 2000–2008). The information at our disposal is therefore limited and so partial findings are continuously reinterpreted and old excavation reports are perused, without any new data becoming available. The only place where the ^{14}C absolute dating method has been used is Shiloh and Stratum V therein (dating to the second half of the eleventh century BCE; see above). Other localities have been dated using pottery that shows a strong continuity with the Bronze Age which makes exact dating difficult. This brings into play another question: what is the relationship between Egypt's withdrawal from Canaan and the destruction and later reemergence of the local urban culture (Schipper 2012)? In contemporary studies, localities have tended to be revisited in an interpretative sense, reconsidered, with their significance reevaluated. The authors of some of these more recent papers (e.g., Gadot 2017) claim that the urbanisation of the highlands was greater than has previously been suggested, and so it was also more in line with the settlement trend of the preceding periods.

In the Iron Age I, subsistence agriculture was used in the northern highlands, dependent on the local production. Rural settlements have characteristic houses with four rooms (or sections) divided according to their respective functions. The self-sufficiency of the settlements is corroborated by the higher number of silos discovered in the villages; the numerous silos constructed outside buildings contrast with the significantly lower number of these structures in the Bronze Age, at which time centralised storage was used. The volume of produce stored proves "that these are self-sufficient agricultural villages where the uncertainties of rural life—drought, noxious pests, poor yields—would have necessitated large-scale storage facilities" (Dever 2003, 115).

Corn and other agricultural produce was stored in reinforced containers or collared rim jars (henceforth CRJ), which, along with cooking jars, are sometimes interpreted as evidence typical of Proto-Israelite or Israelite culture (Faust 2012, 230-54). These containers are smaller in comparison with those from the Bronze Age The reason for this difference is functional, not ethnic. Smaller volume allowed for easier manipulation and met the needs of the specific settlements; these were understandably much lower in line with the population size (cf. Pfoh 2009) as compared to the central storehouses of Canaanite cities, which gathered produce from the wider surroundings.

In the Iron Age I, the northern highlands were a region where the various ways of life of diverse southern Canaanite groups intersected. The mechanisms triggering change included the collapse of the city-state system at the end of the Late Bronze Age and the resulting search for more convenient and safer places to live. Referring to the northern highlands, some scholars use the phrase *melting pot* (Dever 2010), in which the participating groups become a new entity with, putatively, new specific characteristics (see above) that may be termed *Israelite* or *Proto-Israelite*. However, the fact that these shared aspects are proven to show continuity with Canaanite culture speaks against such an identification. The evidence—including texts that would clearly demonstrate the genesis of a unique new ethnic group or an embryonic political formation, endogenous or exogenous, named *Israel* at the turn of the Late Bronze Age and Iron Age I—is unconvincing or outright lacking (this idea is advocated in, e.g., Redford 1992; Hasel 1994; 2003; Miller 2004; Dever 2010; also cf. chapter 1).

2.1.2 SOUTHERN HIGHLANDS AND SHEPHELAH

The area of the southern highlands, which comprises the Judaean Mountains, and the Shephelah which is located to the west and southwest, paint a rather different demographic picture. The mountains show a trend similar to that of the northern highlands: compared to the Late Bronze Age, more new settlements were created after the collapse of the city-state system when the area was mostly inhabited by migrating shepherds, though not as many as north of Jerusalem (see 2.1.1). South of Jerusalem, there was no significant increase in population (Sergi 2017b). However, there was a different and highly complex settlement situation in the Shephelah. The older theory which claimed that the Shephelah was practically uninhabited and that "the countryside was almost completely deserted" (Finkelstein 1996) in the Iron Age I, is now in stark contrast with the most recent research findings in numerous localities (see table below).

Estimates of populations which have been acquired from recent or ongoing archaeological campaigns in several sites in the area (Tel Azekah, Lachish, Tel Burna, Tel Zayit, Khirbet Qeiyafa, Yarmuth, Tel Batash, Bethshemesh, Tel Gezer, and others) show that the most important process "in the entire region of Shephelah is the continuous founding and refounding of local centers at the very same sites from the Middle Bronze Age II to the Iron Age II" (Koch 2017b, 183). Situated at the meeting points of several ancient cultures, the individual localities in the Shephelah also underwent very different developments. Consequently, the model demonstrable elsewhere (urbanisation—deurbanisation—reurbanisation) applies only in a limited capacity here (cf. Sergi and Koch 2023).

The events at the turn of the Late Bronze Age and early Iron Age I are sometimes described, rather schematically, as the creation of a power vacuum (a similar theory is used for the late seventh century BCE in a largely identical area; see 6.1). It is likely that no such thing ever happened. Granted, Egypt's influence in southern Canaan had grown weaker, but very soon after, or immediately, Philistia became the new hegemon over the area of the Coastal Plain and on the western borders of the Shephelah, particularly around the entrances to the Sorek and Elah Valleys (for discussion see Maeir 2023). The exact determination of the cultural and power interactions is linked to the dating, which is hotly debated (see, e.g., Webster et al. 2017). One can also assume that the waning influence of the twentieth Egyptian dynasty strengthened the ambitions of the local Canaanite city-states, which started vying for power. Comprising the destruction of numerous settlements by unknown actors, the events of the time may be compared to uncoordinated movements on a chess board; the pieces used break the "rules of the game," so some predictable events do not occur, while other, unexpected ones do take place instead. Some archaeologists (e.g., Bunimovitz and Lederman 2017) have likened the events in the Shephelah to swinging on a swing: a cycle in which the influence of one culture was gradually replaced by a series of newly arriving and originating cultures.

Regional developments did not only involve cities—some of which were abandoned, while others were rebuilt after destruction, and still others gained influence as local hegemons (especially Ekron and Gath)—but also the countryside. Unlike in the more sparsely populated Judaean Mountains, in the late Iron Age I there are dozens of villages documented in the Shephelah (Bunimovitz and Lederman 2008), which formed the economic hinterlands around cities. The amount of documented built-up area is considerable, as demonstrated in the following table outlining the estimated total population, which is significantly higher than that of Jerusalem.

Tab. 3. Estimated extent of built-up area and total population in the Iron Age I (according to Lehmann 2003)

Region	Built-up area in the Iron Age I (hectares)	Estimated total population
Shephelah	39.9	5,985–11,970
Southern highlands (south of Jerusalem)	18.1	2,715–5,430
Area north of Jerusalem (including Jerusalem)	7.9	1,185–2,370
Total	65.9	

The specific feature of the region is the presence of Philistine culture, which is partially adopted by the late-Canaanite population. Though this process also works in reverse. Interpreting the mutual influence between these two populations is one of the key aspects in determining possible ethnic developments and defining the creation of new political entities (see 3.2).

In similar fashion to the northern highlands, one may claim that the area of the southern highlands was predominately inhabited by the late-Canaanite population, which had the greatest influence on the material culture, evident from its considerable continuity. The shifts in pottery were especially functional (volume changes) and economical (a decrease in the luxurious types). The situation was more complex in the transition area between the Shephelah and the Coastal Plain: there, the indigenous population—in cities and the countryside—was confronted with a new ethnic group, the Philistines. However, even here, the most important characteristic of the area is the continuity with the earlier traditions of Canaanite culture and the presence of some traditions adopted from Egypt, especially concerning small objects (including scarabs, amulets, and jewellery) and pottery (Ben Dor Evian 2011; 2017). Consequently, it is impossible to find specific ethnic features that could be termed Israelite or Proto-Israelite in this area in the context of the eleventh century BCE.

2.2 IRON AGE I SOCIAL ORGANISATION

The population pattern allows one to attempt to reconstruct the organisation of society. There was no central administration in the highlands area; Shiloh is the only place that could be considered an administrative centre. In the late Iron Age I, the highlands population was more of a multifaceted and highly diverse unit oriented on immediate and specific life necessities than, sociologically speaking, a homogenous community (cf. Frevel 2016, 80). In their efforts to depict the society in a more specific manner, numerous reconstructions (e.g., Halpern 1981; Brooks 2005) lean on biblical texts, especially the Book of Judges; however, the book comes from a much later time and presents a paradigmatically ideal, romanticised picture of the origins, rather than a reliable historical description. The same caveat applies to the claim that society was egalitarian, documented by simple unadorned pottery and the syntax of house architecture (esp. Faust 2012; 2015; contra Pfoh 2009; Berlejung 2010). Highland settlements and villages were small and inhabited by several families, forming tribes led by elders. It is likely that other hierarchic structures, characteristic of a more complex social organisation, did not develop until the turn of the Iron Ages I and IIA, in relation to reurbanisation.

The situation is different in two types of areas in the Shephelah: mainly in the immediate vicinity of late-Canaanite cities, which did not collapse or were briefly abandoned and then resettled; and around Philistine cities. Constant developments—especially the eastward expansion of Philistine cities into the Shephelah, but also their temporary withdrawal due to intercity competition (Ekron versus Gath in particular)—brought about complex changes that, in terms of ethnic identification, are difficult to interpret clearly based on material culture analysis (Lipschits and Maeir 2017). The model of synekism is sometimes used for the Shephelah (cf. Soja 2008): rural settlements create support for the cities, which in turn offer the rural population opportunities for trade, work, and protection from danger (Faust and Katz 2011; Bunimovitz 1998; contra Koch 2017b).

2.3 SUMMARY—WHEN AND HOW ISRAEL AND JUDAH FIRST EMERGED?

The above description of the Iron Age I in southern Canaan offers a brief overview of multiple processes which took place during the collapse of the city-state system and thereafter, at the end of the twelfth and during the eleventh centuries BCE. Concerning the search for the origins of Israel and Judah as specific political entities, it can be argued that there is no reliable data to support the identification of these states as a single whole or separate units. Connecting the rural population in the highlands to the Israel of the Merneptah Stele, the historical continuity theory is legitimate, but remains speculative (Frevel 2016, 89; for a defence of the theory, see Hasel 1994; 2003).

The same applies to the supposedly oldest occurrence of the name *Israel* in biblical texts—the Song of Deborah in the Book of Judges (see Judg 5:2ff)—which is likely to have originated in the ninth or eighth centuries BCE, at the time of the Omrides (Knauf and Guillaume 2016, 98). The text establishes an identity or ethnicity retrospectively, using a tribal and "genealogical roofing" (ibid.) from the time when the northern Kingdom of Israel already existed, but also from later exilic and postexilic times—i.e., from the sixth to fourth century BCE. There can be no doubt that the book underwent a complex editing process, but searching it for historically accurate information on the very origins of Israel in the Late Bronze Age and Iron Age I is a highly disputable endeavour. As depicted in biblical texts, the origins of Israel are a "collage of distinct images, not all from the same setting or date" (Fleming 2013, 270). According to one such notion, peculiar but understandable in respect to establishing the ancient identity of Israel (see the basic trajectory: nomad → herder → settled farmer → tribal leader → king), "the Israelite writers imagine their forebears to have lived differently from themselves" (ibid. 271). Generally, as described in the texts, the origins of Israel are largely a retrospective construct, and must be treated as such (cf. Frevel 2016, 91).

The Iron Age I is a period during which late-Canaanite culture continued to develop in a strong continuity with Late Bronze Age traditions. The most crucial developments did not concern customs, cult, or ethnic transformations; rather, they related to the socioeconomic realm. The changes were functional answers to impulses that were both political (city-state system collapse) and environmental (decrease in precipitation, droughts etc.), which is clear from archaeological materials (including pottery, settlements, and storage methods). Signs of transformations, which can be considered political in nature, did not appear until the end of the period—i.e., at the moment of transition to the Iron Age IIA. A primary substrate, the Iron Age I promised the future existence of new political entities (cf. Cline 2024) that would be established gradually and—most importantly—independently, as will be demonstrated in the following chapter. Without the Iron Age I, the new processes of the Iron Age IIA would have never taken place.

3. THE DIFFICULT TENTH CENTURY (LATE IRON AGE I TO IRON AGE IIA)

Archaeology is partly the discovery of the treasures of the past, partly the meticulous work of the scientific analyst, partly the exercise of the creative imagination.
—Colin Renfrew and Paul Bahn

The period termed the Iron Age IIA (970–840/830 BCE, according to the modified conventional chronology) is one of the most debated eras in relation to Israel's history. Almost two centuries of the Iron Age I were followed in southern Canaan by a new phase of urban settlement (reurbanisation) and a significant increase in the area settled; this applied mainly to the region of the northern highlands (although cf. Gadot 2017) and, with a caveat, its southern part (for a description of Jerusalem and Hebron, see 3.2.3). However, the trend described is more complicated and cannot be generalised to the whole locality. Contrary to the population decrease or temporary abandonment of cities in most areas, there is archaeological evidence supporting the continuity of urban culture in Galilee, the Jezreel Valley (for "New Canaan"; see Finkelstein 2013), the Coastal Plain settled by the Philistines, and in some late-Canaanite settlements in the western Shephelah (Panitz-Cohen, and Mullins 2016; Sergi and Kleiman 2018). The development of inland cities, which were probably rural in nature for most of the Iron Age I, is linked to the renewal of long-distance trading, a growing barter trade, and more extensive agriculture. According to demographic calculations, the total population increases (Dagan 1992; Ofer 1993; Finkelstein 1988; Lehmann 2003), and so does the area settled.

3.1 CLOSELY WATCHED CHRONOLOGY

In accordance with biblical chronology (also termed high or conventional chronology), past research used southern Canaan in the late Iron Age I and the first half of the Iron Age IIA as a setting for the "United Monarchy," with Jerusalem as the capital; this period signified the "golden age" of Israel as a territorial state. At its peak, Israel stretched from the Sinai Peninsula in the south to Lebanon, possibly as far as the Euphrates River (cf. 2 Sam. 8). Generally, it can be argued that, until the 1970s, biblical texts supported archaeological work and vice versa. From the 1980s, the historicity of the United Monarchy as a political entity documentable using archaeology has been cast into doubt, especially when using the high chronology for reconstruction. A full discussion of the issues within the debate over chronology would provide enough material for a stand-alone book (for a summary, see Handy 1997; Frevel 2016), which is why only basic context will be given here, as well as some lesser-known realities from the history of research.

Here in particular the concept of "Solomonic archaeology" needs to be revised, as it is based on intuitive speculations and unverified hypotheses. This concept was first elaborated not by an archaeologist in Israel, but by the Australian scholar Gregory J. Wightman. The impulse for change came from the results of renewed excavations in Lachish in 1973, during which a team led by David Ussishkin from Tel Aviv University newly dated the six-chambered gates in Stratum IV to the ninth century BCE, ruling out their "Solomonic" origins (cf. Ussishkin 2004a). Wightman (1985) then described the development at length in his extensive dissertation at the University of Sydney. In this and several later studies, the author uses a remarkably detailed pottery analysis to propose a more exact dating of Hazor X/IX: specifically, as an extension of Stratum XI, including the chamber gate from a later time, the ninth century BCE. For Samaria, the author suggested dating the second construction phase to the time of Ahab—i.e., the same period as Hazor X/IX. As for Gezer (Field III, Stratum 6), Wightman made reference to 1 Kings 16:24 when dating the extension of the south wing of the outer wall, including the six-chambered gate, also to the ninth century BCE. Therefore, specific strata in all three sites were re-dated to almost a century later (cf. Wightman 1990).

The fourth locality, Megiddo, is a peculiar case. There, the author distinguished three phases: VB (960–950 BCE), IVB (late tenth century BCE), and IVA (mid-ninth century BCE). According to Wightman, Megiddo was only a small fortress in the VB phase, extended by the construction of Palace 6000. In the IVB phase, the west administrative wing was constructed, as was a two-chambered wall further west of the new wing, and there was also an overall extension, with older buildings enclosed by new ones. The phase was also said to have seen the destruction of Megiddo linked with Shoshenq I (the biblical Shishak, 946–924 BCE), supported by a fragment of the pharaoh's victory stele found near Palace 6000 (although it was not found in a clear stratigraphic context). Massive fortification walls and the six-chambered gate linked to them architectonically were constructed in the IVA phase— i.e., the Omride dynasty period in the second half of the ninth century BCE.

The gradual shift in the perception of the United Monarchy was crucially influenced by linking and confronting the archaeological sites discussed above with the biblical text of 1 Kgs 9:16, which claims that Solomon built Hazor, Megiddo, and Gezer. Wightman (1990) elaborated the "low chronology" (ibid., 19) not because he doubted the existence of the United Monarchy, which he considered a historical fact, but based on pottery analysis, which he used to propose a change in the dating of the stratigraphic sequence. The historicity is not disputed; the argument concerns attributing construction activities linked with Solomon and the mid-tenth century BCE to a later period and different rulers of the already separate entities of Israel and Judah. Though Solomon is ruled out as the main instigator of the monumental construction efforts, biblical narratives still carry weight in the author's eyes; the only change involves attributing the building activities to a specific ruler. Politically, Wightman associates Gezer with Judah and links the wall and gate construction with Asa (912–871 BCE), or even with Jehoshaphat (870–846 BCE). Unlike the understandable attribution of Samaria, Hazor, and Megiddo to the Omride dynasty, the author ignores the possibility of Gezer being part of the northern kingdom, since he puts his faith in the biblical text regarding the borders of the existing kingdoms of Judah and Israel.

The revision of the concept of Solomonic archaeology and low chronology, which stems from it, was predictably criticised by scholars such as Dever (1990), but even by Israel Finkelstein, the man who would later champion the very same chronology. Considering Wightman's conclusions to be insufficient and misleading, Finkelstein (1990) instead argued that individual pottery phases cannot be attributed to the rulers of Israel, since this leads interpretation down the rabbit hole of ambiguity. Finkelstein added that the methodology is flawed if there are doubts about the historical reliability of biblical texts regarding Solomon (1 Kgs 9:16), while the text is elsewhere tied uncritically to a specific stratigraphic sequence. This methodological flaw is only exacerbated by the dating "evidenced" by biblical texts (Samaria) being used to legitimise the putative chronological shift in other localities (Megiddo, Gezer, and Hazor). In Finkelstein's view, Wightman relied too heavily on archaeological evidence in Samaria, which caused him to misunderstand the biblical text; while in Gezer and other sites, the opposite happened—a biased interpretation of the historical source led to a misinterpretation of archaeological data (Finkelstein 1990, 117).

Despite these reservations, which carry traces of professional rivalry, Wightman must be considered the first proponent of low chronology, a postulate with a far-reaching impact on notions of Israel and Judah's origins in the Iron Ages I and IIA. Originally based on pottery analysis, low chronology would be later corroborated in many aspects and refined using the radiocarbon method, which would determine an absolute time horizon. In terms of the northern kingdom, assigning the strata to the ninth century BCE is considered a consensus of sorts; even Finkelstein, originally a dissenter, still uses this consensus in his work to this day (for discussion see Boaretto 2019). The contributions of the new postulate are no less valuable even though, over the years, the historical reconstructions proposed by Wightman proved to be inaccurate, his reading of biblical texts biased, selective, and sometimes almost naïve. The debate among the supporters of the high, low, and modified chronologies continues, and it will be described in more detail below.

3.2 LESS UNITED, LESS VISIBLE?

If there was no United Monarchy in the region under discussion in the Iron Age IIA, then what was there in its place? From the outset, it must be noted that presenting the birth of the Kingdom of Judah and the northern Kingdom of Israel is a highly demanding task, and that, in this regard, the tenth century BCE is indeed a difficult century, as stated in the title of this chapter. The following subchapters will introduce three reconstructions of the nascent Judah and Israel in the Iron Age IIA: the first concerns the area of Shephelah and three localities within it, whose interactions can be used to note processes leading to the ethnogenetic developments on the borders between late-Canaanite and Philistine localities (3.2.1); the second focuses on Israel as a possible polity in the area of Gibeon and Bethel in the northern highlands (3.2.2); and the third, which is in many aspects opposed to the second, involves Jerusalem and the land of Benjamin in the north (3.2.3).

3.2.1 WESTERN BORDER PROCESSES—SOREK AND ELAH VALLEYS (SHEPHELAH REGION)

The western Shephelah and three localities within it constitute an area that can serve to document the highly complex process by which new ethnic and political realities were established. Specifically, the three areas are Khirbet Qeiyafa in the Elah Valley and the two cities Beth-shemesh and Tel Batash which are located to the north of the first locality in the Sorek Valley. Located within kilometres of each other, the three sites are associated geographically and also in terms of their cultural, religious, and political evolution. This evolution has inspired a notion, championed by many who base their claims on biblical texts and their harmonisation with the available material culture, that the three cities were Judean settlements at the turn of the Iron Ages I and IIA. According to this theory, the sites themselves evidence the existence of Judah as a state provable in accordance with traditional biblical chronology. However, the matter is much more complex, as will be explained presently.

The following line of reasoning will start with localities uncovered later and then move to sites where archaeological research started earlier; its aim is to examine the degree of connection between the areas, their mutual fea-

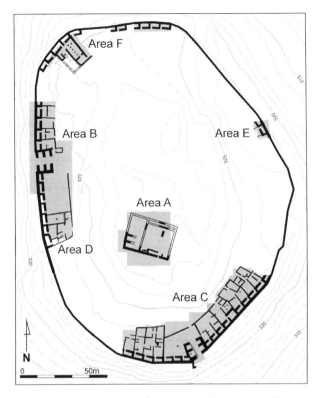

Fig. 5. Topographic plan of Khirbet Qeiyafa (courtesy of Khirbet Qeiyafa Excavation)

tures, and their demonstrable discrepancies. Firstly, there will be an examination of excavation reports, prepared by the campaign directors: whether finished (Tel Batash) or still in the process of publication (Khirbet Qeiyafa and Beth-shemesh). In conclusion, these localities will be discussed jointly, with emphasis on the origins of early Judah as a territorial state separate from Israel. This distinction is made even though numerous scholars still do not differentiate between the two entities, or they consider everything "Israelite" without further categorisation. However, in this historical period, such an interpretation is unjustified if the focus is on Judah and the south (cf. chapters V and VI).

3.2.1.1 KHIRBET QEIYAFA: THE FIRST TRACE OF JUDAH?

3.2.1.1.1 LOCATION, GEOGRAPHICAL CONTEXT, AND IDENTIFICATION

Khirbet Qeiyafa is situated 328 metres above sea level, on the right bank of the Elah Valley which connects the Judaean Mountains with the Coastal Plain. At 2.3 hectares, it is a relatively small settlement surrounded by 700 metres of fortification walls. Research at this site was carried out in 2007-13 under the direction of Yosef Garfinkel from the Hebrew University of Jerusalem and Saar Ganor from the Israel Antiquities Authority. Over seven seasons, one of which also included Czech representatives, a total of six areas (A-F) were uncovered, with the most important being Area C and the connected Areas B and D. Two four-chambered gates in Areas B and C were a crucial discovery. The gates are followed by chamber walls which run along the entire length of the settlement.

Due to the discovery of the second gate, the campaign directors identified the locality as the biblical area of Shaaraim (meaning in Hebrew "gates"), referred to in 1 Sam 17:52, Josh 15:36, and 1 Chr 4:31-32. The first of the texts gives relatively exact coordinates for the site: doubtlessly in the Elah Valley, and likely between Sokoh, Azekah, and Ephes-dammim on one side, and the Philistine cities of Gath and Ekron on the other.

3.2.1.1.2 SETTLEMENT—URBAN PLANNING CONCEPT

According to Garfinkel and Ganor, the nature of the settlement resembles that of other localities in ninth-century BCE Judah. Individual buildings directly adjacent to chamber walls are documented in Beer-sheba, Tell en-Nasbeh, and Tell Beit Mirsim. The site is a fortified settlement with analogies in Arad Stratum XI, Beer-sheba Stratum VI, and Lachish Stratum IV—all likewise dating to the ninth century BCE. In the preceding period of the tenth century BCE, which comprises the settlement strata of Arad XII, Beer-sheba VII, and Lachish V (cf. also Tel Batash IV), the cities had no fortifications, but they were settlements which were enclosed by the rear sides of buildings.

3.2.1.1.3 STRATIGRAPHY AND DATING

Iron Age IIA settlements were uncovered in all areas of the site (Khirbet Qeiyafa IV), without any evidence of prior life in the settlement; the only exception is a tiny quantity of Middle Bronze Age pottery found in Stratum V. Clearly, though there are other strata coming after it, Stratum IV is dominant and defines the entire locality. The excavation directors themselves comment on this fact, stating that Khirbet Qeiyafa is "in a way a one period Iron Age IIA site" (Garfinkel and Ganor 2010a, 72). Further interpretation of the site under discussion is heavily influenced by two aspects: the dating of Stratum IV and the question of the ethnic composition of Khirbet Qeiyafa (see below). When considering the nature of the settlement and the possibility of urban planning, we could be forgiven for thinking that this is a ninth-century BCE locality. However, both relative and absolute chronology date this stratum to an earlier time: between the late eleventh and mid-tenth century BCE.

As elaborated by Hoo-Goo Kang and Yosef Garfinkel, relative chronology is derived from pottery analysis. The upper limit is based on the absence of debased Philistine pottery (the Mycenaean type MYC IIIC:1b) known from Tell Qasile X, Tel Miqne IV, and Ashkelon XIV, and the absence of non-Philistine CRJ type pottery. Both pottery types are connected to the late Iron Age I and the first half of the eleventh century BCE, when Khirbet Qeiyafa had not yet been inhabited. By contrast, the site featured local as well as Late-Philistine ("Ashdod") pottery, which the authors proposed should be classified as the Ashdod I type (LPDW, short for late-Philistine decorated ware). Garfinkel and Kang (2011) dated both types to the late eleventh and tenth centuries BCE. The lower limit is based on the absence of several pottery types: firstly, LPDW of the Ashdod II type, which was uncovered in Gath 4 (dated to 830 BCE) and Ekron, among other sites; secondly, the pottery attributed to the strata of Lachish V, Tel Batash IV, and Arad XI; and thirdly, Cypro-Phoenician pottery (BoR, short for black on red; see Schreiber 2003). According to the campaign directors, the dating of the area-dominant Stratum IV as being from the Iron IIA is evident owing to these upper and lower limits.

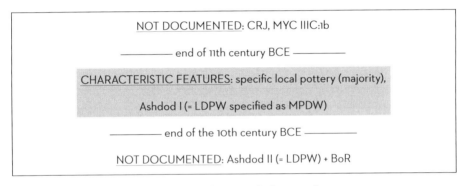

Fig. 6. Relative chronology: upper and lower limits in Khirbet Qeiyafa

Absolute dating stems from the analysis of Stratum IV olive pits, carried out in the Oxford Radiocarbon Accelerator Unit (Garfinkel and Kang 2011; Garfinkel et al. 2012; Garfinkel et al. 2015). The calibrated average points to 1051–969 BCE (77.8% probability) or 963–931 BCE (17.6% probability). Both results confirm that the locality—as an already fortified settlement—precedes other ninth-century BCE Judean sites. Based on these findings, the excavation directors are adamant that the transition between the Iron Ages I and IIA should be re-dated to the turn of the eleventh and tenth centuries BCE, in accordance with high chronology and the biblical depiction of early Judah ruled by King David (ca. 1000–965 BCE) and King Solomon (ca. 965–930 BCE).

3.2.1.1.4 ETHNIC IDENTIFICATION

According to the archaeologists conducting the excavation, the surprising identification of the site as belonging to the early Iron Age IIA demands the reevaluation of some current knowledge. Firstly, the transitional process between the Iron Ages I and IIA must be considered nonhomogeneous, and individual phases and localities have to be thoroughly distinguished. Khirbet Qeiyafa proves the establishment of a new socioeconomic unit in the area and the existence of fortified settlements in the tenth century BCE. The campaign directors consider the site a Judean fort, interpreting it as a locality in the zone bordering the influential Philistia; in their view, this explains the massive fortifications and, possibly, the sudden abandonment of the site, which was not destroyed but merely ransacked, and remained uninhabited for another six hundred years until the Persian period (Garfinkel, Kreimerman, and Zilberg 2016, 94–98). But can we truly consider the area Judean? That is the principal question of this interpretation. According to Garfinkel and Ganor, ethnic identification is based on the following arguments:

- Geographic position: This argument stems from biblical texts and the traditional assessment of Judah's surface area (again based on biblical texts).
- The locality being named Shaaraim in the Judean city list (cf. 1 Sam 17:52; Josh 15:36; in Hebrew, the toponym is in the dual number, and so it refers to two gates, which were indeed discovered in the area; for different view see Levin 2012).
- The absence of pig bones, which are frequently documented in the Philistine city of Ekron, in Ashkelon, and in the border town of Tel Batash; by contrast, there are also none in the nearby Beth-shemesh (Kehati 2009; Bunimovitz and Lederman 2008; Faust, Lev-Tov 2011).
- The absence of an iconic cult: Neither figurative depictions nor artefacts that could serve as cult objects are documented in the area. In the 2011 season, a basalt altar was discovered in Khirbet Qeiyafa that is similar to the Tel Rehov altar, but without silhouettes of naked women (cf. Mazar, Panitz-Cohen 2008). All cult objects present were desacralised; according to Garfinkel (2009), an example of this is the seventy-centimetre-long massebah in Area B, which was incorporated into the wall by its wider (base) part, facing downward. In the author's view, there is an analogous phenomenon in Beer-sheba, where the altar was removed during Hezekiah's or Josiah's presumed religious reform (cf. Aharoni 1972; 1974a; 1974b; 1975a; 1975b; Herzog 2010; Moulis 2019; 2021; Kleiman S. 2023; for more, see 6.2.2).
- Pottery: Local pottery differs from Philistine painted pottery, which is scarcely represented. Furthermore, over 700 one-, two-, or three-thumbed jar impression handles were discovered in the area.
- Petrography has confirmed that the materials used to produce pottery were locally sourced; the excavation directors consider the large quantities of thumbed storage jars to be proof of the existence of an early Judean administration. These thumb impressions are further interpreted as

predating the *lmlk* impressions which are known from the late periods of the Kingdom of Judah (Shai and Maeir 2003; see discussion in chapter 6).
- The concept of urban planning, which was also documented in other Judean areas (see above)
- The orientation of the main gate: The southern gate in Area C opens to the Elah Valley and Jerusalem. It is worth noting that this gate was not found to have a massive stone threshold with a step preventing it from opening outwards. By contrast, such a threshold was discovered in Area B, which faces the Philistine cities of Gath and Ekron.
- One ostracon: A shard of local origin, made of clay from the adjacent Elah Valley and featuring approximately fifty letters, was found in Area B of Stratum IV in 2008. Most epigraphers consider the text to be very difficult to reconstruct and have even expressed doubt regarding its definite identification (Finkelstein and Sass 2013; Rollston 2010; 2011; 2017). On the other hand, Misgav, Garfinkel, and Ganor (2009) use their own newly proposed classification to interpret the ostracon as late-Canaanite and, at the same time, as the oldest Hebrew inscription from the turn of the Iron Age I and IIA. Ada Yardeni (2009) considers the ostracon text to be Semite and possibly Hebrew, since it contains several Hebrew words or verb stems (specifically, the stems '-b-d, '-s-h, š-p-ṭ and m-l-k). The most elaborate interpretation of the text was submitted by Gershon Galil (2009), who provided the following translation:

1' do not do (it), but worship . . .
2' Judge the slave and the widow / Judge the orph[an]
3' and the stranger. Plead for the infant / plead for the poor and
4' the widow. Avenge (the pauper's vengeance) and the king's hand.
5' Protect the needy and the slave / suppo[rt] the stranger.
(Ibid., 196)

Contrary to Galil, who claims the text was dictated by a teacher or father to, respectively, a student or son, Misgav, Garfinkel, and Ganor (2009) consider it to be the work of an experienced scribe. In their view, scribes already had a certain social standing in the place where they lived, and the area where the ostracon was written was "a royal fortress from the early days of the United Monarchy." Consequently, the letter found near the gate "testifies to the presence of literate administrators in the city, despite its modest size" (ibid., 256).

According to the archaeologists excavating at Khirbet Qeiyafa, the above arguments serve as evidence for a different form of Judean history and an earlier transition between Late Iron Age I and Iron Age IIA which accords with high chronology. Despite the controversy arising from this interpretation (see Schroer and Münger 2017; Garfinkel, Kreimerman, and Zilberg 2016; Na'aman 2010; Finkelstein, Fantalkin 2012; Čapek 2012; 2019b), and the rather offensive and absolute manner in which the authors present their claims, it is clear that the locality provides new information about the Shephelah, which is an area crucial to understanding the early development of the urban settlement. This new data therefore amends earlier notions concerning the notion that there was urban planning at the turn of the Iron Ages I and IIA (see 3.2.1.1.2). The next two sites, Beth-shemesh and Tel Batash, which will be discussed individually, shed a different light on the events in the area under discussion. As these are localities with a significantly longer settlement continuity, they may be used to describe the developments in the Shephelah in broader cultural, ethnic, and political contexts.

3.2.1.2 BETH-SHEMESH: LATE-CANAANITE AND JUDEAN TRACES

3.2.1.2.1 LOCATION, GEOGRAPHICAL CONTEXT, AND IDENTIFICATION

The locality was first identified by Edward Robinson in the mid-nineteenth century. Archaeological work in Beth-shemesh, located close to the eponymous modern city, started in 1911–12 under the auspices of the Palestine Exploration Fund (Mackenzie et al. 2016), and was renewed in 1928 by Haverford College, Pennsylvania. The site was interpreted as Canaanite (Stratum III; First City), Philistine (Stratum II; Second City), and, from the late eleventh century BCE, as a city populated by Israelites and controlled by Philistines (Stratum I; Third City).

Newer excavations were led first by Bar-Ilan University (1990–95) and later by Ben-Gurion University of the Negev (1995–96). From 1997, the baton was picked up by Zvi Lederman and Shlomo Bunimovitz, both working at the Institute of Archaeology of Tel Aviv University. The most recent campaign has provided crucial new knowledge regarding the nature of the Beth-shemesh settlement in the Iron Ages I and IIA, which is now considered to be much more difficult to interpret than was suggested by the results of the preceding expeditions (Bunimovitz and Lederman 2016).

3.2.1.2.2 BOUNDARIES AND ETHNICITY

An ancient city located 240 metres above sea level, on the left bank of the Sorek Valley, Beth-shemesh is situated at the intersection of the Canaanite, Philistine, and Israelite/Judean cultures (for a differentiation, see 3.2.1.2.4). Eleven phases of settlement have been identified in Beth-shemesh so far, taking place between the twentieth and seventh centuries BCE. The rich archaeological records on the life of Beth-shemesh offer valuable knowledge of mutual cultural relationships and of ethnogenesis in the western Shephelah. Contrary to popular belief—that the formative process of Judah/

Israel must be sought in the Judaean Mountains (as a representative example, see Miller 2004)—Bunimovitz and Lederman propose two theses: firstly, that the process is likely to have had a different starting point; and secondly, that the process of ethnic identification itself must be defined along several lines. The authors make the following comments on the subject of ethnicity:
1. Ethnicity is not only the "sum of former cultural differences"; such a definition is too vague.
2. Ethnicity is the result of a long process of inclusion and exclusion. Anthropologically speaking, the process consists of two aspects: competition, which stimulates the formation of a specific group; and the separation of powers, which has a specific nature, expressed by characteristic ethnic markers shaped during this process.
3. Ethnicity stems from the action of a group; this action is best observed from a long-term perspective—i.e., as a "long stratigraphic sequence."
4. Most settlements in the mountain area were short term or merely single-period settlements. Consequently, no sequence for observing a long-term perspective can be found there.
5. Though current research on Israel's origins is more precise and erudite, it still holds true that, since the 1980s, "no new archaeological information has been introduced into the discussion" (Bunimovitz and Lederman 2008).

3.2.1.2.3 STRATIGRAPHY AND FOOD HABITS

Due to its stratigraphic richness, Bunimovitz and Lederman consider Beth-shemesh a very opportune place for comprehending the possible ethnogenesis of Israel. Comparing the settlement strata makes it clear that Beth-shemesh Levels 6 and 5 are from the same period as Tel Batash Stratum V (see the overview below). In the latter locality, situated a mere few kilometres down the Sorek Valley, there is evidence of pork consumption. By contrast, no pig bones have been found in Beth-shemesh (Hesse, Brown, and Griffith 2016; see the table in 3.2.1.3.3).

Differences in food habits in these localities deserve particular attention. Returning to the Late Bronze Age and Iron Age I, three facts must be noted:
1. In Late Bronze Age Canaanite settlements in the Shephelah and on the Coastal Plain, pigs were consumed in small quantities (2–8%).
2. The coming of the Philistines changed the situation considerably; particularly in Philistine settlements, pork consumption spiked (18–20%).
3. However, analysis of over 6,000 bones discovered in Beth-shemesh proves that there, consumption fell to zero in the same period.

As pointed out by Bunimovitz and Lederman, these findings do not mean that the locality should be immediately and unequivocally identified as Isra-

Tab. 4. Stratigraphy of Khirbet Qeiyafa, Beth-Shemesh, and Tel Batash

Period	Khirbet Qeiyafa	Beth-shemesh	Tel Batash
Twelfth century BCE	uninhabited	Level 6 1150–1100 BCE	VIA
Eleventh century BCE	IV (late)	Level 5 1100–1050 BCE	V
Tenth century BCE	IV	Level 4 1050–950 BCE	IVA-B continuity? (see discussion below)
Ninth century BCE	uninhabited	Level 3 950–750 BCE	uninhabited
Eighth century BCE	uninhabited	Level 2 750–701 BCE	IIIA-B
Seventh century BCE	uninhabited	Level 1 650–635 BCE	II
Sixth century BCE	uninhabited		IIA (early, only isolated remnants)

elite (see discussion in Sapir-Hen et al. 2015). According to the authors, the issue of mutual cultural interactions in the Shephelah, including alimentary habits, is more complex and should be treated as such; consequently, it will be discussed here as well (see 3.2.1.3.3).

3.2.1.2.4 POTTERY AND ARCHITECTURE

Dating from the second half of the twelfth century BCE, Level 6 Beth-shemesh pottery is akin to that of the lowland areas, such as Tel Batash, Gezer, and Tell Qasile on the Yarkon River. The pottery is different to that from "Proto-Israelite" locations such as Gilo and Khirbet Raddana, since there is a complete absence of CRJ-type vessels, and different to assemblages found in Philistine regions. Beth-shemesh has no monochrome pottery, and bichrome pottery only constitutes 5% of the pottery assemblage (similar situations have been documented in other areas bordering Philistia—for example, Aphek and Gezer). This absence is in stark contrast with Ashdod, Ekron, and the nearby locality of Tel Batash, in which bichrome pottery accounts for 30% of the assemblage.

According to Bunimovitz and Lederman, these ratios in pottery traditions prove that contact between Beth-shemesh and the Philistine culture was scarce. Furthermore, they confirm the continuity of the Canaanite cultural tradition in an area attributed to Israel by the biblical tradition as early as before the rule of the Judges (see Josh 19:41, where the place is referred to in Hebrew as ʿÎr Šāmêš, "the city of [the god] Shemesh"; also 21:16; 1 Sam 5-6; for a critical analysis of directly linking literary traditions and history, see 3.3).¹ The authors conclude that the material culture of Beth-shemesh pottery is "intriguing—even puzzling—since it raises the question of how to identify Israelite remains in the archaeological record" (Bunimovitz and Lederman 1997, 44).

Another argument against the direct ethnic attribution of Beth-shemesh to Israel arises from the architecture of the locality; specifically, the pillars in Iron Age I buildings. In this epoch, monolithic stone pillars were used in the highlands, but there is evidence of wooden pillars in Beth-shemesh. According to the campaign directors, this construction element is closer to the Canaanite tradition (Bunimovitz and Lederman 1997). Only later architecture, dating from the tenth century BCE, can be typologically assigned to the Israelite tradition; this concerns Area B, where massive fortification walls were uncovered atop the remains of eleventh-century BCE settlements in the "New City." The walls and the whole Area B complex have been recently interpreted as a state administrative centre built after 950 BCE (Bunimovitz and Lederman 2016, 281–388).

The discoveries made at Beth-shemesh prove that it is extremely difficult to determine the ethnicity of Shephelah inhabitants in the Iron Age I and early Iron Age IIA. Consequently, Bunimovitz and Lederman warn against drawing hasty conclusions and using alimentary habits as evidence of the locality being settled by Israel. Possible ethnogenetic connections should be considered in a wider context of culture and religion as a process of mutual long-term influence, likely triggered by Philistine territorial expansion. The indigenous population of late-Canaanites reacted by profoundly transforming their social, cultural, religious, and symbolic boundaries; avoiding pork consumption was part of the transformation, as inferred from the bones discovered in Beth-shemesh and from the locality's comparison with Tel Batash (see the comparison table in 3.2.1.3). Gradually, this habit became a commonly shared value not just in the Shephelah, but also in the highlands. Interpreted using a "long stratigraphic sequence," the slow process of Israel's ethnogenesis may be described with the following scenario:

> Instead of conceiving the process as taking place in the central hill country and later encompassing the peripheries of that region, we would reverse the direction of at least part of it: from the western frontier with the Philistines, where the indigenous population was forced to redefine its identity as a result of daily existential competition with the Philistines, inland into the relatively sheltered mountain area that slowly succumbed to the Philistine pressure. According to this interpretation of the finds from Tel Beth-Shemesh within the Iron Age I cultural and historical context of Shephelah,

---

1 Biblical quotations are taken from the New Revised Standard Version Updated Edition (NRSVUE).

the emergence of a social and symbolic boundary at the western periphery of the hill country had a profound impact on its core. Israelite identity seems to have been forged to some extent under the Philistine hammer.
(Bunimovitz and Lederman 2008, 28)

A similar observation may be appended to this concept of the ethnogenetic process: the opposite direction mentioned above may be substantiated by the written culture documented from the southern Coastal Plain and the westernmost parts of the Shephelah, but not from the Judaean highlands (see the texts discovered in Qubur al-Walayda, Gath, Tel Zayit, Khirbet Qeiyafa, Beth-shemesh, Gezer, and Izbet Sartah). The advanced administrative relations in the area testify both to the development of cultural traditions and—indirectly—to the crucial role of late-Canaanite and Philistine cultures in the formation of a new ethnic group at the foothills of the Judaean Mountains (cf. Finkelstein 2010; Finkelstein and Sass 2013).

3.2.1.3 TEL BATASH: LATE-CANAANITE, PHILISTINE, AND JUDEAN TRACES?

3.2.1.3.1 LOCATION, GEOGRAPHICAL CONTEXT, AND IDENTIFICATION
Situated 132 metres above sea level, Tel Batash is located on a broad, open, fertile alluvial plain in the Sorek Basin, seven kilometres downstream of Beth-shemesh and a mere six kilometres away from Ekron (*Tel Miqne*), which was one of the five cities of the Philistine Pentapolis (Kelm and Mazar 1982). The locality, which was promptly identified as the biblical town of Timnah (cf. Judg 14; Josh 15:57), was discovered in 1871 by the French archaeologist and Orientalist Charles Clermont-Ganneau. There was further interest in Tel Batash in the 1940s, when a new investigation of the area was carried out by Benjamin Mazar and Jacob Kaplan.

A substantial contribution to the understanding of the locality's history was made by an archaeological campaign that started in 1977 and took place over twelve seasons in total. Conducted by the Hebrew University of Jerusalem in cooperation with a consortium of American academic institutions, the excavations were led by Amihai Mazar and George Kelm. A total of twelve layers of settlements, dating between the eighteenth and fourth centuries BCE, were uncovered in Tel Batash.

3.2.1.3.2 BOUNDARIES AND ETHNICITY
Tel Batash is a textbook example of a place where various cultural influences intersect. In the Iron Age I, it was a town on the border between the Philistine and Canaanite cultures. Many scholars (e.g., Mazar, Panitz-Cohen 2001) claim that, in the Iron Age IIA, the town was exposed to the cultural influence of Israel, under which it remained for a time. Previously, the Philistine city

of Ekron had been the regional hegemon, and this assumption is based on three aspects: the analysis of material culture; the size comparison of both localities mentioned (Ekron had fifty acres, while Tel Batash only had six); and the existence of a road from Tel Batash leading through the Sorek Valley to Ekron. However, assigning the area unequivocally to the Canaanite, Philistine, or Israelite culture is a more complex issue. For instance, Amihai Mazar is convinced that the relations between these ethnic groups cannot be precisely determined (Panitz-Cohen and Mazar 2006). From the material culture available, he surmises that the city was likely subject to Ekron, and that the majority Philistine population lived there alongside indigenous Canaanites until the advent of the Iron Age II.

3.2.1.3.3 STRATIGRAPHY, POTTERY, AND FOOD HABITS
Dating from the late Iron Age I, the settlement at Stratum V bears a marked similarity to the material culture found in coinciding layers in Gezer and Beth-shemesh. In all three locations, pottery of the Canaanite tradition mingles with Philistine bichrome pottery; however, there is a marked difference in proportion. While Philistine pottery constitutes a substantial 34% in Tel Batash, it only accounts for 5% in Gezer and Beth-shemesh. The higher ratio in Tel Batash can be interpreted as proof of strong Philistine cultural influence. An analysis of the bones discovered in Tel Batash shows an increase in pork consumption after the Philistines arrived; 8% pig bones here contrasts with none found in the nearby town of Beth-shemesh.

Regarding the background of the Tel Batash campaign documentation, it should be noted that the chapter entitled "Faunal Remains from Tel Batash" from the excavation report was included by the editors in the third volume and only covers a single page (see Panitz-Cohen, and Mazar 2006, 311). Animal bone data was never contrasted critically with stratigraphy. The bones were analysed by Brian Hesse from the University of Alabama, but the results of the analysis were never provided to the editors of the report. However, Hesse himself included them in two studies (Hesse 1990; Hesse and Wapnish 1997).

Finding the key to a possible ethnogenesis grows even more complicated when comparing this locality with other demonstrably Philistine areas: those show even greater pork consumption, which seems to confirm Amihai Mazar's theory of high ethnic diversity in Tel Batash. For instance, there was a total of 18% pig bones in the coastal city of Ashkelon in the Iron Age I, and the same percentage is documented in Ekron. In the Iron Age IIA, the trend decreased slightly to 10% in Ekron and markedly in Tel Batash, where only 0.9% such bones were found. Exact data from Ashkelon in the period observed is not currently available (cf. Stager, Schloen, and Master 2008). However, preliminary calculations suggest that pigs accounted for less than 1% of the bones discovered (from personal correspondence with Daniel Master).

3. THE DIFFICULT TENTH CENTURY (LATE IRON AGE I TO IRON AGE IIA)

Tab. 5. Ratio of pig bones found in Ekron, Ashkelon, and Tel Batash

Period	Ekron	Ashkelon	Tel Batash
Late Bronze Age	8%	4%	5%
Iron Age I	18%	18%	8%
Iron Age IIA	10%	<1% (?)	0.9%

The table shows some important facts that have already been mentioned in part (see 3.2.1.2.3). Firstly, it turns out that pigs were consumed as early as the Bronze Age—i.e., even before Philistine dominance in the area. Secondly, consumption clearly grew considerably in the Iron Age I; the increase is mostly interpreted as evidence of the growing influence of Philistine culture. Thirdly, it is apparent that consumption decreased slightly in Ekron and dramatically in Tel Batash in the Iron Age IIA. The latter site was on the outermost part of Philistia, adjoining a location inhabited by the indigenous Canaanite population; furthermore, the area comprises Beth-shemesh, which had an almost identical percentage of pork consumption to that of Tel Batash in the Iron Age IIA. Taking both facts into account, it is conceivable that there was a continual, multidirectional cultural influencing process between the Canaanite (or already according to some Israelite) and Philistine populations (for discussion see Bunimovitz and Lederman 2016; Niemann 2013; Yasur-Landau 2012; Lipschits-Maeir 2017; Koch 2020; 2021). Consequently, Tel Batash is solid proof of influences intersecting. On the other hand, this is also the reason why it is difficult to clearly identify the ethnicity of the site in the period observed.

3.2.1.3.4 TEL BATASH IV AND A NEWLY EMERGING ETHNIC GROUP

There is a certain irony to the fact that it is Tel Batash Stratum IV that is chronologically ambiguous, since this stratum is crucial to our comprehension of the early Iron Age IIA in the context of the nascent Judah/Israel (Mazar, Panitz-Cohen 2001, 273). Tel Batash IV is different to the preceding "Philistine city" (Stratum V) in many aspects. The pottery is characterised by red slip hand-burnished ware, which is completely dissimilar to both the Philistine and Canaanite traditions (for discussion see Gitin 2015a; Gitin 2015b; Herzog and Singer-Avitz 2015). The same pottery is documented in Lachish V-IV, Gezer VIII, Tell Qasile IX-VIII, Beer-sheba VIII-VI, Arad XII-XI, and in the north, in Megiddo VA-IVB, Taanach IIa, Yokneam XIV, and Tel Rehov VI. The pottery type succeeds Iron Age I painted pottery assemblages, and so it is considered typical of the transition between the Iron Ages I and IIA, which, according to modified conventional chronology, took place as early as the tenth century BCE (cf. Zimhoni 1997b, 172–74). Many scholars, including archaeologists from the last campaign in the area, link this shift in

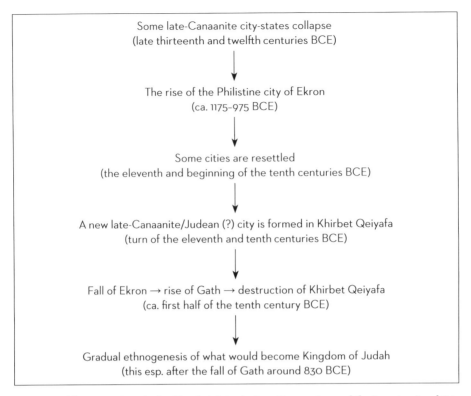

Fig.7. Possible interactions in the Shephelah in the Late Bronze Age and the Iron Age I and IIA

material culture to the origins of Judah or Israel as a specific socioeconomic and ethnic entity. Some urban planning aspects of Tel Batash IV are similar to Judean settlements like Beer-sheba VII: both sites are enclosed, unfortified settlements.

The growing influence of Judah/Israel is also evidenced by calculations of the populated area of the Philistine cities of Ekron and Ashdod in the tenth and ninth centuries BCE, and the analysis of pottery from Ekron IV and Ashdod XA–B. Ekron's total area in the mid-tenth century decreased from 50 to 7–10 acres, while Ashdod grew from 20 to 50 acres. Most explain this contradictory trend as a result of the growing pressure of Judah/Israel on the eastern border of Philistia, leading to a population plunge in the border city of Ekron, with people moving to the more distant city of Ashdod (Mazar, Panitz-Cohen 2001, 278). However, it must be noted that there is another interpretation of these demographic changes: they may have been the result of Egypt's invasion, during which Siamun (979/978–960/959 BCE) of the 21st Dynasty conquered Gezer (e.g., Redford 1992; Kitchen 2001; cf. 1 Kings 9:16). Still, it seems more likely that, at the time of Tel Batash Stratum IV, Ekron indeed began to decline due to the westward expansion of an ethnic group that had been significantly shaped by Philistia on its eastern border. Should the ethnic group be classed as late-Canaanite, Israelite, or Judean? That question will be discussed in detail later.

For the sake of completeness, two more interpretative options must be mentioned. The first stems from low chronology, which does not envisage that the changes are linked to the tenth century BCE; consequently, it does not attribute them to Judah/Israel's expansion on Philistia's eastern border, nor to Egypt's putative attempt to renew its influence in Canaan (Ahlström 1993). According to some scholars, change came from the north, along with the Arameans, in the ninth century BCE (see discussion in Mazar 2005; Sharon et al. 2007; Mazar and Ramsey 2008; Finkelstein and Piasetzky 2010). The second possibility is that the changes in Ekron were not caused externally by interaction with another ethnic group, but by the competition among the Philistine cities themselves. Ekron's decline in the mid-tenth century BCE may be linked to Gath, which was in its ascendancy during the same period and may have been responsible for the disappearance of Khirbet Qeiyafa (cf. Čapek 2019b) and the considerably smaller settlement of Tel Azekah (see Lipschits and Maeir 2017; Gadot, Kleiman, S., and Lipschits 2018).

3.2.1.4 PRELIMINARY SUMMARY

The three localities introduced provide important information on the evolution of, and shifts in, late-Canaanite culture, which gradually gave birth to a new ethnic group. In the small-scale analysis above, material culture discovered in Khirbet Qeiyafa, Beth-shemesh, and Tel Batash evidences the rapid changes in the political, territorial, and cultural landscape of the Shephelah in the neighbouring Elah and Sorek Valleys at the turn of the Iron Ages I and IIA. Similar situations are documented for other sites in the same area (cf. Čapek 2012; 2019b). Though the localities discussed are not very far from each other, unlocking their interrelationships is a highly complex task. There is no simple answer to the question of at what point Judah can be discussed as a tangible object of archaeological study; instead, it turns out that the issue is extremely intricate, and that every argument presented (be it based on pottery analysis, urban planning concepts, food habits, cult, etc.) has an—at least—equally valid counterargument. As illustrated by the points below, it is crucial to be cautious and critical when positing basic theses on the formation and origins of Judah—specifically regarding this entity, in the context of the western Shephelah.

3.2.1.4.1 COMPLEXITY
Attributing the areas of the Shephelah under discussion to an ethnicity or political unit stems from the combination a myriad of data—from architec-

ture and pottery to the remains of animal bones and other small material culture objects. Every possible conclusion is grounded in more or less substantiated evidence interpreted in a fundamentally variegated context; this also concerns the ideas about the formation of early Judean history, emerging on the frontier between the late-Canaanite and Philistine cultures. The line of reasoning provided shows that even the formation of this new entity itself (or entities in general) was not a one-way process; furthermore, the process was varied in different areas. Consequently, the formation of Judah and Israel are treated separately in this book (see chapter 4).

3.2.1.4.2 POTTERY

Comparison of the strata of Khirbet Qeiyafa IV, Tel Batash IV, and Beth-shemesh 4 has led some researchers (mainly those from the first of these localities) to conclude that these areas were concurrently inhabited by the same ethnic group—specifically, Judeans. But was it really the same group, the same *ethnos*? Were the inhabitants of these settlements in contact with each other; did they know about each other; did they communicate and trade with each other? A comparison of pottery assemblages provides no clear answer. In Khirbet Qeiyafa, 692 examples of thumbed jar impressions have been documented. Consequently, it is surprising that a much smaller number has only been found in Tel Batash (see the overview in Kang and Garfinkel 2015; Garfinkel 2017) and none (!) were found in the nearer city of Beth-shemesh, even though the assumption is that these two areas were populated by the same ethnic group—late-Canaanites or Judeans—at the same time (the mid-tenth century BCE).

If the impressions are interpreted as evidence of early Judean administration and centralisation (Garfinkel and Kang 2011; Garfinkel, Kreimerman, and Zilberg 2016), it is perplexing that their distribution is so scarce even in the immediate surroundings (very important settlements, no less). The most likely explanation is that the impressions were marks of local potters and had nothing to do with an organised circulation of pottery marked for local purposes. The absence of provable distribution clashes with the existence of early Judean *lmlk* impressions, which have a clearly demonstrable function and are documented for numerous areas (e.g., Azekah, Lachish, Beth-shemesh, Tel Batash, Maresha, and Gath). According to some researchers, there is further evidence supporting pottery-based ethnic identification, namely the cooking pots and baking trays found in both Khirbet Qeiyafa and Beth-shemesh (Kang and Garfinkel 2009, 127; Garfinkel, Kreimerman, and Zilberg 2017, 74), which are not documented in the nearby Philistine city of Gath. This correspondence is posed as proof of the Judean origins of both areas; however, other scholars refute the identification, claiming that only Beth-shemesh is provably Judean and not before the mid-tenth century BCE (cf. Maeir 2017, 139–44; cf. Römer 2017a).

Conceding that pottery is not or cannot be a fully sufficient indicator of distinctive ethnic groups, there may be a chronological explanation for the disconnection of the settlements. The collapse of Khirbet Qeiyafa dates to 960 BCE (Garfinkel, Streit et al. 2015), and according to new dating, Beth-shemesh Stratum IV was inhabited from a later point, in the mid-tenth century BCE, so there might have been no interaction between the sites at all (cf. Bunimovitz and Lederman 1997; 2016). However, this line of reasoning brings us beyond the capabilities of both relative and absolute chronologies, since the localities might have been inhabited concurrently for a decade or two, but, equally, that might not have been the case (cf. Koch 2017b, who dates Beth-shemesh IV to the first half of the tenth century BCE, and, by contrast, Khirbet Qeiyafa IV to the second half of the same century).

3.2.1.4.3 GENERAL SCHEME PROBLEMS (MODELLING DEMOGRAPHIC TRENDS)
Due to the ongoing research in the Shephelah, the schemata used to interpret the origins of Judah have undergone a thorough revision. Earlier theses were put to the test and some claims—for example, that the Shephelah had been an uninhabited or peripheral area with no urban settlements—had to be corrected considerably (Koch 2017c; Čapek 2023; cf. also Maeir 2023). The same care must be exercised when analysing the results of demographic calculations, even though they present a very enticing instrument for interpreting ethnic and cultural interactions. The recently conducted and renewed campaigns in Khirbet Qeiyafa and Beth-shemesh have provided new findings on the possible ethnogenesis of Judah. However, these must be seen as preliminary. Especially when considering the former site, a one-stratum city inhabited for a short time, it is necessary to include the broader context offered by other localities. Inhabited for centuries and, according to some, the Judean royal residence of King David (Athas 2005), Beth-shemesh provides far more data in a wider time frame, which offers the opportunity to posit a new, more detailed interpretative scheme to gain insight into the dramatic cultural, religious, and political shifts occurring in the western Shephelah in the late Iron Age I and early Iron Age IIA (cf. Fleming 2012).

3.2.1.4.4 CONTINUITY
Material culture in the localities discussed shows continuity with respect to the traditions passed on in the area, firstly, the continuity of the local late-Canaanite culture; and secondly, the continuity of Egyptian influences, provable especially by the artefacts discovered which document the local imitation of Egyptian models (scarabs, amulets, bullae, and conical seals). In the Shephelah, late Iron Age I and early Iron Age IIA material culture shows continuity with the pottery traditions of the Late Bronze Age (in morphology and typology), albeit with local characteristics. The same applies to reli-

gion—for example, in the area of funerary customs and rituals. Sometimes, the postulate of a new "ideology of simplicity" is interposed between the Late Bronze Age and Iron Age (especially Faust 2004; 2012). However, the graves which have been discovered do not corroborate this distinction; the skeletal remains uncovered prove that the society was stratified.

3.2.1.4.5 INCLUDING BIBLICAL TEXTS IN RECONSTRUCTING HISTORICAL CONTEXT

When searching for the history of early Judah, it is important to consider the role in to be played by biblical texts in scholarly interpretation- many of which make reference to the region of the Shephelah. A differentiating approach should be the starting point, both for identifying the genre of, and the period described by, the texts. The fact that the localities are mentioned in the texts and that the narratives are rooted in a specific geographical context (e.g., Judg 14–16) is not enough to corroborate the historicity of the subject matter. Contrary to the continuity of material culture, which is provable by the corresponding chronological context, these texts are much more recent and must be evaluated as such. The historical continuity they present is a retrospective religious construct; its value must be interpreted through the lens of theology, anthropology, and sociology, in order to evaluate where it belongs and has meaning. By contrast, introducing texts, demonstrably written in a different time, into the reconstruction of historical periods that preceded them by some hundreds of years requires the utmost care. As will be shown in the following chapters, referring to "vague memories" is an almost limitless source of uniquely conceived, but highly vulnerable, historical reconstructions (see, e.g., 3.2.2 and 3.2.3).

3.2.1.4.6 IS THERE A KEY TO THE ORIGINS OF THE KINGDOM OF JUDAH?

When and where should we seek the origins of the Kingdom of Judah? That remains an open question. Accepting the reverse evolution theory—from the lowlands and foothills to the mountains—the area of the Shephelah and the Beer-sheba Valley (along with its localities, such as Tel Masos, Tel Beer-sheba, and Tel Arad) are among the likely candidates. See the highly thought-provoking description of the formative process of Judah by Herzog and Singer-Avitz (2004):

> The heart of the emerging monarchy in Judah should be relocated from the hill country to the lower land regions. Such redefining of the centre of the emerging Kingdom of Judah in the lowland should not surprise us, since a dominant role of the highland is quite anomalous. The hillside and lowland regions are pointedly more urbane than the highlands. This phenomenon was generalized by Braudel: "The mountains are as a rule a world apart from civilizations, which are an urban and lowland achievement."
> (Ibid., 235)

Discussing the first of the theories describing the establishment of the Kingdom of Judah, it must be said that, as a territorial state – i.e., an organised entity with a social structure and, at least partially, centralised administration and economy—this political unit is not documentable until approximately the ninth century BCE, or even later (cf. Frevel 2016). Apart from the absence of unequivocal proof of monumental architecture, the arguments against dating the Kingdom of Judah to the Iron Age IIA and the tenth century BCE in the area of the Shephelah include the existence of the local hegemon in Gath. Gath reigned supreme over the area until the second half of the ninth century BCE, which, according to numerous scholars, would prevent another territorial state from establishing a new administrative centre mere kilometres to the east of Philistine territory (Sergi 2013; Koch 2012; 2017b; or see Knauf and Guillaume 2016).

On the other hand, more optimistic reconstructions which propose an earlier date for the origins of the Kingdom of Judah must be included as well (esp. Sergi 2023). Some scholars claim that state formation may be identified as early as the tenth century BCE, taking into account the localities inhabited in the Shephelah during that period (Faust 2012; 2017b; Garfinkel, Kreimerman, and Zilberg 2016; cf. Mazar 2007). Those include Beth-shemesh in the second half of the tenth century BCE (Level 4), an even earlier Khirbet Qeiyafa (until ca. 960 BCE—i.e., Stratum IV), and, for a time, perhaps also Tel Batash (Stratum IV). However, the latter area is possibly the most complex in terms of ethnic and political identification (Maeir 2017; cf. 3.2.1.3.4). Azekah is another ancient settlement that must be mentioned. The fortress at the site might have been a part of the nascent Kingdom of Judah on Philistia's eastern border even before the destruction of Gath, just like Tel Burna, another fortified settlement to the south (Shai 2017; Šmejda et al. 2017). The small size of the cities may not necessarily be synonymous with the non-existence of the Kingdom of Judah; instead, it expresses ratios and proportions in the shape of settlement patterns and shifts of influence in the region (even within a single political entity; see the conflict between Ekron and Gath, for example). Azekah may serve to prove two points: the existence of a newly established political formation; and the impossibility of constructing too large forts near a powerful neighbour's centre of power (see chapter 5).

A description of the events in the Shephelah must include interactions that, likely, did not merely follow the pattern of the stronger dominating and the weaker conforming. Certainly, whilst it may be an attractive but rather simplifying and mechanistic approach, it provides what seem to be the most conclusive and convincing arguments, though not necessarily the only possible answer in terms of the complexity and multiplicity of the processes. Trying to determine the starting date and exact inception of the Kingdom of Judah using non-written material culture is like measuring the precise moment of transition between the twilight and the dawn: it will always depend on definitions, such as the parameters specifying how much illuminance (units of lux) constitutes light and, on the other hand, how much constitutes twilight. Evidently, as a territorial state, the Kingdom of Judah gradually emerged from the late-Canaanite substrate, undoubtedly under the strong influence of Philistia. According to recent findings, this influence reached as far as the heart of the Judaean Mountains in Jerusalem. In 2012 and 2013, in Areas C and H of the City of David, Ashdod type pottery (LPDW or Philistia 3) was discovered in a clear stratigraphic context from the ninth and eighth centuries BCE; furthermore, petrographic analysis confirmed that the pottery was of local origin (Cohen-Weinberger, Szanton, and Uziel 2017). In 2017, the same pottery type was found in Area E as well (results not yet published) thus proving the close connection between the mountains and the lowlands and the ethnic groups that settled there.

The formation of the Kingdom of Judah as a territorial entity was impacted by other factors, including the establishment of local elites, kinship relationships, patronage, treaty relations, pragmatic agreements, and contracts confirmed with the impressions of private seals or non-epigraphical bullae (Maeir and Shai 2016; cf. also Lipschits and Maeir 2017; but cf. Ben-Yosef and Thomas 2023). Therefore, this kingdom in our view did not become a territorial state with a comprehensive administrative system until the Iron Age IIB (see discussion in chapters 4 and 5).

3.2.2 FAR UP NORTH—THE LAND OF SAUL

Another theory on Israel's origins in the "difficult" tenth century BCE and at the turn of the Iron Ages I and IIA has recently been proposed by the Israel Finkelstein from Tel Aviv University. After several small-scale studies, he presented a detailed reconstruction of Israel as an independent unit in the northern highlands (Finkelstein 2013). His reconstruction does not cover Judah, since, in the author's view, Judah is a much later political entity. When considering the impetus for Finkelstein's book, one cannot help but feel that the great publicity of Khirbet Qeiyafa (see 3.2.1.1)—and the discussion surrounding this site, which Finkelstein joined almost immediately (Finkelstein and Fantalkin 2012)—might have been an impulse for its publication. In the 1990s, he considered the United Monarchy to be "a short-lived exception in the history of the highlands" (Finkelstein 1999b, 48), and later he refuted this possibility outright; however, after 2007 and the first interpretation of Khirbet Qeiyafa as a site which revealed the early roots of the Kingdom of Judah, he proposed the existence of a polity north of Jerusalem, which also disproves the existence of any similar formation in the south (Finkelstein 2011a; 2011b; Finkelstein and Fantalkin 2012). Hyperbolically, one might say that, after even Yosef Garfinkel stopped trying to find historical basis for the existence of the United Monarchy and took the Judean path exclusively,[2] Finkelstein wagered on the northern scenario, following earlier studies (Finkelstein 1996; 1999b; 2006; 2010, 2011a; 2011b) and offering his own entirely contrasting alternative, often based solely on a repolarised line of reasoning.

3.2.2.1 IT ALL STARTED IN SHECHEM

The first Israelite territorial entity termed a Gibeon (or Gibeah) state or Saulide territory by Finkelstein has a pre-history of its own, beginning in the time of the Canaanite city-state of Shechem (*Tell Balata*) at the end of the Late Bronze Age. According to Finkelstein, this political entity is evidenced by material culture as well as information from the Book of Judges 9 regarding Abimelech, the ruler of Shechem. Here is preserved "a memory in the north regarding events that took place before the rise of the northern kingdom" (Finkelstein 2013, 21). Discussion of Abimelech, the pre-monarchic strongman, provokes vague memories from the turn of the eleventh and tenth centuries BCE; at the time, the first Israelite polity was formed in the Gibeon-Bethel Plateau to the north of Jerusalem. In Finkelstein's view, the city-state of Shechem is likely to have been destroyed in a later phase of the Late Bronze Age (ibid., 22; cf. Campbell and Wright 2002, who date the settlement's destruction to 1150–875 BCE). As a consequence, it was Shiloh— "the only Iron I site in the highlands that reveals evidence of public construction" (Finkelstein 2013, 26; cf. a revision of this view in Gadot 2017)—that became the new administrative centre in the area.

3.2.2.2 FALL OF NEW CANAAN, GIBEON, AND SAUL

It has already been mentioned that there were regional differences across the collapse of city-states at the end of the Bronze Age (see chapter 2 and the overview table in 2.1.2). One of Finkelstein's main theses is to use the name "New Canaan" to denote the continuous population of some cities in the north (Megiddo, Kinneret, Yokneam, Dor, Keisan, and Tel Rehov), while other cities collapsed. Some object that this is not a new phenomenon but a general "swansong" of Canaan in the second millennium BCE (Mazar 2013, 353). One way or another, it is clear that, at the end of the Late Bronze Age, some cities were not destroyed, or the devastation was only partial. Later, at the end

---

2 This development occurred in the spring of 2011, when Professor Garfinkel—possibly also based on the many conversations we had at the Hebrew University of Jerusalem—reconsidered the necessity of holding on to Judah and Israel as two parts of the United Monarchy whole, leading him to focus solely on the Kingdom of Judah.

of the Iron Age I, even the surviving cities were destroyed and "the fall of the Canaanite system was terminal" (Finkelstein 2013, 32). Opinions differ as to who or what caused the destruction: some think it was an earthquake; while others claim it was a result of the campaign led by Shoshenq (946–925 BCE). Using the method of radiocarbon dating, Finkelstein concludes that the destruction was not a single event, but a longer, gradual process, and he attributes the destruction of New Canaan to highlands Israelites, who led raids from their territory into the rich fertile valleys (cf. Fleming 2013, 233).

Finkelstein's reconstruction of the oldest territorial entity of Israel is based on three sources. The first is the geography and evident urban planning of the settlements under discussion: chambered walls are key for this source, documented in the highland locations of Khirbet ed-Dawwara, Tell

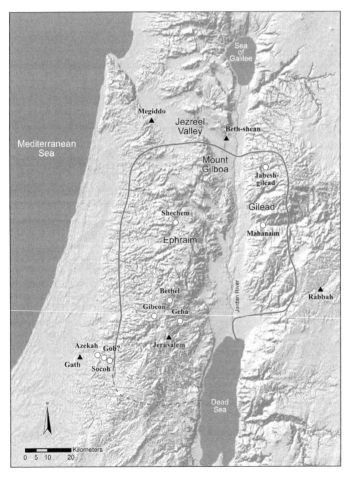

Fig. 8. The Saulide Kingdom according to biblical and archaeological sources (Finkelstein 2013)

en-Nasbeh, et-Tell, and, by all accounts, also in Al Jib, the biblical Gibeon (Finkelstein and Fantalkin 2012, 53; Finkelstein 2012a). In Finkelstein's view, the peculiar accumulation of this fortification type in the Gibeon-Bethel Plateau—an elevated plain with an average height of 800 metres above sea level, located north of Jerusalem—suggests that it was in this area that the centre of a specific territorial entity was located, comprising of the highlands up to the Jezreel Valley in the north and in the east, and reaching beyond the Jordan River to Jabesh Gilead and Mahanaim. The sudden abandonment of the fortified cities in the Gibeon-Bethel Plateau is explained by the second source.

The second source evidencing the existence of Saul's polity is Shoshenq's list, located at Karnak, Egypt (OIP 74), which enumerates multiple areas in the northern highlands. The areas mentioned are Gibeon, Beth-horon, and Zemaraim in the Gibeon-Bethel Plateau; in the north, Sukkot, Tirzah, Mahanaim, Adamah; and in the northern valleys, Taanach, Megiddo, Beth-shean, and Rehob. Since Jerusalem and the areas to the south (up to Arad) and west of this are not mentioned on the list, Finkelstein deduces the political importance of the north and the insignificance, or subordination, of the south to the Egyptians. The sudden abandonment of the settlements in the Gibeon-Bethel Plateau is then due to the Egyptian campaign aiming to weaken Saul's territorial entity, which threatened Egypt's interests in the region. In this, the fate of the area resembles that of the Canaanite city-state of Shechem four centuries earlier, which posed an identical risk to Egypt in the southern Levant and had to be removed (cf. EA 289).

Biblical texts linking Saul's territory to Gibeon are the third source (Finkelstein 2013, 52) as they contain themes that cast a positive light on the Saulides. These texts include the stories in the Jacob cycle, the Book of Saviours which is included in the Book of Judges, and individual texts from the Prophets (e.g., Hos 9:9 and 10:9). Considered to be some of the earliest texts, these pericopae preserve "vague memories" (Finkelstein 2013, 54) of the Saulides. According to Finkelstein, the continuity of these memories and their antiquity are confirmed by the opening chapters of the First Book of Samuel describing the events in Shiloh. As its destruction was dated to the mid-eleventh century BCE, this site precedes the existence of Saul's territorial entity (cf. Na'aman 2023).

3.2.2.3 RE-DATING SAUL AND SHOSHENQ I, AND THE EGYPTIAN-PHILISTINE TRANSPOSITION

Though it may seem that Shiloh and Saul could be assigned to the same historical period, Finkelstein advises against doing so: the Gibeon-Bethel Plateau settlements are from a later time, and Shiloh precedes them. Contrary to biblical chronology, which dates Saul to the end of the eleventh century BCE (ca. 1025–1005), Finkelstein considers Saul a later ruler, who may have ruled concurrently with David; the length of David's rule (some thirty years, 1000–965 BCE) and the rule of Solomon (some thirty-five years, 965–931 BCE; cf. Galil 1996) are not verifiable, since there are no non-biblical synchronisms for them. As deduced by the author, Saul had ruled for a longer time until the coming of Shoshenq I (946–925 BCE), who stabilised his influence over the region by destroying the Gibeon-Bethel Plateau settlements; in doing so, he likely ended the existence of the first Israelite territorial entity some time before 926 BCE—i.e., earlier than the majority consensus suggests (cf. James and van der Veen 2015). Apart from Egypt, this power struggle had another winner: the territory of Tirzah ruled by Jeroboam. In Finkelstein's opinion (see 2013, 61), Egypt's intervention might have included the support of Tirzah as a rival to Gibeon. The fortunes of Saul and his sons came to an end during a battle at Mount Gilboa over the Harod Valley. Though the biblical texts claim the enemies were the Philistines, according to Finkelstein it was actually the Egyptians who had defeated Saul and displayed his and his sons' corpses on the walls of Beth-shean (see 1 Sam 31:10). This historical transposition will be dealt with in detail later (see 3.2.3.4).

3.2.2.4 KHIRBET QEIYAFA—THE NORTHERN SCENARIO

As part of his opposition to theses on the early origins of the Kingdom of Judah in the area of the Shephelah, and Khirbet Qeiyafa in particular, Finkelstein reverses direction by claiming that the site is a part of the territorial entity north of Jerusalem—i.e., Saul's dominion in the Gibeon-Bethel Plateau (Finkelstein and Fantalkin 2012; Finkelstein 2013). He also refutes Khirbet Qeiyafa's link to Jerusalem, since in the tenth century BCE, Jerusalem was an insignificant settlement with limited political power over the surrounding area (see 3.2.2.4). The reasoning for Khirbet Qeiyafa being Israelite, not Judean, is two-fold: the first explanation is provided by the biblical texts of 1 Sam 22 and perhaps also 1 Kgs 15:27, 16:15, and 17 (see 3.2.2.5); and the second is based on the nature of the fortifications, particularly the abovementioned chambered walls.

It is important to note Finkelstein's usage of archaeological evidence (walls, in this case) in his attempt to replace the theory on the formation of the Kingdom of Judah with his own reconstruction. The chambered walls are not passed off as Judean but Israelite, which is supported by other similar fortified settlements in Tell en-Nasbeh, Khirbet ed-Dawwara, and possibly Gibeon as well. Garfinkel proposes the southern origin of Khirbet Qeiyafa as being where the Kingdom of Judah was formed early on (Garfinkel et al. 2012, 368); while others are inclined to consider the locality late-Canaanite (Koch 2012; Čapek 2012; 2019b). However, Finkelstein thinks that this fort belongs to

Saul's Gibeonite territory. In his view, the Khirbet Qeiyafa settlement in the Elah Valley, which was fortified with chambered walls in the same manner as the cities in the Gibeon-Bethel Plateau, was in a buffer zone, defending Saul's territorial entity against Philistine attacks from the nearby city of Gath. Depopulation is then linked to the Egyptian campaign led by Shoshenq I, which left the site either destroyed or abandoned (Finkelstein 2013, 58).

3.2.2.5 WHAT ABOUT JERUSALEM AND THE UNITED MONARCHY?

The "difficult" tenth century BCE impacted Jerusalem in terms of both its appearance and influence. Describing the reverse growth of the nascent Kingdom of Judah, the previous section introduced the possibility that the origins of the Kingdom of Judah and the ethnogenesis of the population of Judah should not be sought in the mountains, but elsewhere. Numerous scholars lean towards the opinion that this political and ethnic entity was formed in the Shephelah amongst the interaction of the late-Canaanite population and the Philistines in the late Iron Age I and early Iron Age IIA (Bunimovitz and Lederman 2017; Herzog and Singer-Avitz 2004; cf. Garfinkel 2017; Lipschits and Maeir 2017). The link to Jerusalem as the centre of the Kingdom of Judah is considered a later stage of development. However, what was Jerusalem's relationship to the territorial entity in the Gibeon-Bethel Plateau? And is the tradition depicting Saul as the autocrat of the first Israelite territory connected to this city located to the south?

From an archaeological viewpoint, Jerusalem in the Iron Ages I and IIA is one of the most complex areas in the southern Levant. The stratigraphy (more than 20 strata in some areas) is ambiguous due to the gradual settlement of the area from the Chalcolithic onwards, as well as the position of the "City of David" on the steeply sloping hillsides of the Kidron and Tyropoeon Valleys, and this ambiguity has led to heated debates (see especially Finkelstein et al. 2007; Na'aman 1996b; Mazar 2010; Regev et al. 2017). The traditional view on tenth-century BCE and Iron Age IIA Jerusalem is determined by biblical narratives and the chronology derived from them. According to this view, Jerusalem was the capital of the United Monarchy, and it comprised a temple, royal palace, and all other buildings that emphasised the kingdom's importance. But there are other perspectives in research: in the period observed, the city was small and had a very limited influence over the surrounding areas. Jerusalem is sometimes likened to a cow town, or to a medieval castle (*Burg* in German), whose influence does not extend far beyond the surrounding settlement, which houses the closest necessary economic infrastructure. In Finkelstein's view, tenth-century BCE Jerusalem was "no more than a small, poor highlands settlement without monumental construction," (Finkelstein 2013, 43) and so its influence must have been minimal. Additionally, Finkelstein thinks that it is important to take into account that "the expansion of Judah to the territories of the Shephelah and Beer-sheba Valley did not take place before the second half of the ninth century BCE" (ibid).

According to Finkelstein, it is impossible to determine "whether Saul ruled also in Jerusalem" (ibid., 54). Since Saul came from the land of Benjamin (following the biblical tradition of the geographical distribution of Israel's tribes; see 1 Sam 9:1–3), which also incorporated the Gibeon area, the main place of dominion was located to the north of Jerusalem. It is from here, the "northern polity in the highlands of Benjamin and Ephraim, with its hub in the area of Gibeon/Gibeah" (Finkelstein 2013, 47), that Saul's entire territorial entity was administered, including its southern outpost: the Khirbet Qeiyafa fortress in the Elah Valley. If the territory comprised Jerusalem as well, which is impossible to know (see above), it was a less important part of the political entity and lagged behind in terms of development.

It is only in a footnote—as if outside of his main line of reasoning—that Finkelstein contemplates the United Monarchy as an idea rather than a reality of the tenth century BCE. In his view, the space for such a state might have been created during Egypt's intervention in Gibeon and the defeat of the northern territorial entity located there. Creating a situation in which the leaders of Jerusalem "could have taken over the ex-Saulide territories in the hill country (and the western Gilead?)," this "could have been the historical seed behind the memory in late-monarchic Judah of a great 'united monarchy' in the time of the early Davidides" (ibid., 60; for the author's later understanding of the United Monarchy as a political concept born under Jeroboam II in the north, see Finkelstein 2020b).

3.2.2.6 THE NORTHERN TRAIL—A PROVISIONAL CRITICAL EVALUATION

The reconstruction of the first Israelite territorial entity administered from the Gibeon-Bethel Plateau—accompanied by a thesis about interactions not only with Egypt, but also with another polity, Tirzah—although admirably sophisticated and supported by numerous arguments, also carries interpretation risks and raises some questions. In the 1990s, Finkelstein completely refuted Iron Age I and IIA reconstructions similar to the one he has begun advocating recently. Moreover, some of his claims are mainly counter-interpretations to other reconstructions. This is especially true regarding Khirbet Qeiyafa and its attribution to a specific political unit: in Finkelstein's view, it was a part of Saul's territory in the north, not a fortress of the Kingdom of Judah, which did not yet exist at the time.

Finkelstein's selective reading of geographical data in biblical texts is also a debatable approach: this is illustrated, for example, by his claim that the text of 1 Sam 17, depicting the famous battle between David and Goliath, cannot be used as proof for identifying Khirbet Qeiyafa as Shaaraim (cf. 3.2.1.1.4). In his view, the language of the text is Deuteronomistic—i.e., it describes seventh-century BCE realities—which is why the identification of the site with the Gob locality (according to Na'aman 2008a; but cf. Levin 2012) should be considered instead. This identification is based on an older tradition (2 Sam 21:15-19), and, by Finkelstein's reckoning, this makes it a more accurate record of David's battles (cf. Dietrich and Naumann 2000; Nitsche 1998; Adams 2009, 60-64; Garsiel 2011). This is a possible conclusion, but two aspects are unclear. Firstly, why restrict the geographical identification to the seventh century BCE? And secondly, why discard the long process of passing on older traditions and earlier sources, which may feature geographical information as well, if a similar phenomenon is quite naturally taken into account and utilised elsewhere (e.g., the Abimelech tradition from the Book of Judges)?

In our view, Finkelstein somewhat selectively connects biblical texts and material culture as the basis for his reconstruction of the first Israelite territorial entity expanding into the area of the Shephelah. In fact, archaeology is the only, albeit ambiguous, source for determining what might have happened in the northern highlands at the turn of the Iron Ages I and IIA. There is no information on Saul outside of biblical texts (cf. Kaiser 2010; 2011), which is also why the reconstruction that assigns Khirbet Qeiyafa, a location far to the south, to the northern territorial entity is highly disputable. Furthermore, if we take a different view on the chambered walls—for instance, that they are a fortification also found in other areas in the Iron Age I, namely Moab and the Negev (Na'aman 2010, 510-11)—it becomes clear that the claims about a political entity in the Gibeon-Bethel Plateau are mainly based on the creative reading of biblical texts. This sidelines some information and highlights other data in favour of the chosen line of reasoning—for example, the story about the sacking of the temple in the time of Shoshenq I, depicted in 1 Kgs 14.

It is interesting to note Finkelstein's treatment of texts that were redacted by Deuteronomistic, and hence pro-Judean, editors (but cf. Finkelstein 2020b). These literary documents come from a much later period, although they also mention Shiloh, whose existence is linked to the mid-eleventh century BCE. In Finkelstein's opinion, the mention of Shiloh in the First Book of Samuel, redacted by the same editors, "could have catered to those Israelites who seem to have constituted a major element in the population of Judah in late-monarchic times" (Finkelstein 2013, 50). Given the possible retention of memories as a solid foundation for the reconstruction of Iron Age I events, this theory is very optimistic. There is also much optimism in reconstructions of Israel's origins in the northern highlands during the period of the Judges, linking to the Abimelech tradition. Finkelstein bases those on older research (esp. Richter 1966), in which the image of Iron Age I society is largely deduced from biblical texts. Granted, the texts certainly play a crucial role in the formation of Israel's identity; however, it is necessary to note that they build the scenery of the early origins through a mainly retrospective constitution of the cultural memory (see chapter 1 and 2.3). The degree to which these texts are historically accurate cannot be determined merely by paraphrasing what they say (Čapek 2019b).

According to Finkelstein, the "proto-Omride" Jeroboam I (933-911 BCE), a vassal of Shoshenq I ruling from the rival city of Tirzah, is the next historically reliable monarch of the Saulide kingdom. But the maximalist conception of the kingdom has two notable prerequisites. The first is historiographic, describing David, Solomon, and Rehoboam as more or less fictitious figures, whose much less structured and less politically important reigns originate in Judah (cf. Frevel 2016, 107). Whilst linked to the first, the second prerequisite is chronological, based on significantly extending the duration of the Iron Age I to the late tenth century BCE (in accordance with low chronology, which dates its end to as late as 920-900 BCE) and on the immediate subordination of Judah to Israel and the Omride dynasty. A strong initial thesis is required to separate this firmly pro-northern variant of history and—from a historical perspective—the supposedly fictitious southern traditions in the texts. This thesis is deduced from an *argument ex silentio*—the absence of Jerusalem in Shosenq's city list.

Despite the above criticism, the proposed formation of the first Israelite territorial entity in the highlands north of Jerusalem is a very powerful postulate. In the form of the "grand synthesis" (Pioske 2014), contemporary research comes to terms with this in various ways (Dever and Burke 2014; Frevel 2016, 112-14; Mazar 2016, 98-103; and earlier esp. Kreuzer 2006). Finkelstein's concurrent readings of the material culture and biblical texts, often as vague memories transformed many times over, offer a multifaceted view

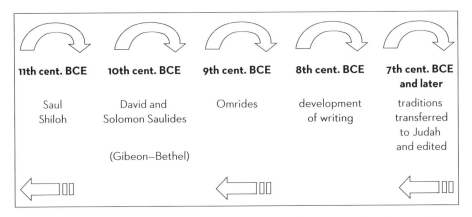

Fig. 9. The Formation of Israel and its gradual retrospective depiction in the Hebrew Bible

of the very origins of Israel; that it was as an independent unit that existed earlier than the realities of the south, namely Jerusalem and the Kingdom of Judah. In the following section, a reconstruction will illustrate the markedly different ways in which essentially the same subject matter—be it material culture or textual evidence—may be read and interpreted.

3.2.3 IT WAS JERUSALEM, AFTER ALL—THE SOUTHERN VARIANT

In many aspects, the third reconstruction of nascent Iron Age IIA Judah and Israel is the antithesis of Finkelstein's theory of the first Israelite polity originating in the area of the Gibeon-Bethel Plateau. An image of Jerusalem serving as the centre of a tenth-century BCE political entity, comprising of the area considered to be a part of Israel by Finkelstein, has been elaborated over the last decade in a very detailed and compelling way by Omer Sergi (2013; 2015c; 2017a; 2017b; 2023), a Tel Aviv University archaeologist and historian who is a generation younger than Finkelstein.

3.2.3.1 SHOSHENQ I—A CAMPAIGN WITH ANOTHER PURPOSE

For the history of southern Canaan, Shoshenq's campaign (946-925 BCE) is something of an Archimedean point, which is used as a basis for many theories. Both the northern and southern interpretations of the origins of Israel and Judah revolve around this 'firm date' marked on the Karnak relief. In Finkelstein's view, the topographical list on the relief and Jerusalem's absence from this list evidence the city's insignificance and confirm the existence of Saul's territorial entity in the Gibeon-Bethel Plateau, which threatened Egyptian interests in the second half of the tenth century BCE. However, Sergi's reasoning completely opposes such an interpretation. He questions Finkelstein's chronological shift in relation to Judean and Israelite kings, and the validity of 're-dating' Saul to more than half a century later (Sergi 2017b, 375). Likewise, he does not take the absence of Jerusalem from Shoshenq I's topographic list to mean that there was no political entity with Jerusalem as the capital. The text of 1 Kgs 14:25-28 (considered historically unreliable by Finkelstein; see 3.2.2.5), and the mentions of the pharaoh's campaign against Jerusalem during the rule of King Rehoboam (933-916 BCE), lead Sergi to deduce that the developments in the region occurred in the opposite manner.

3.2.3.2 ARCHAEOLOGY OF JERUSALEM—NEW AND MORE CONSERVATIVE

As a reminder and for the sake of comparison, let us briefly re-outline Finkelstein's assessment of Jerusalem in the tenth century BCE. In his view, the city had a very limited influence over the surrounding areas and was modest in size, likely no bigger than a typical hill village (cf. Finkelstein and Silberman 2007) and was "no more than a small, poor highlands settlement without monumental construction" (Finkelstein 2013, 43). This view strongly contrasts with Sergi who takes a completely different view on the same locality. Rather, Shoshenq's interest in Jerusalem documented in the biblical text of 1 Kgs 14:25–28, which the author considers a historically reliable source, suggests that the city had relative importance for the Egyptians.

> 25 In the fifth year of King Rehoboam, King Shishak of Egypt came up against Jerusalem; 26 he took away the treasures of the house of the Lord and the treasures of the king's house; he took everything. He also took away all the shields of gold that Solomon had made, 27 so King Rehoboam made shields of bronze instead and committed them to the hands of the officers of the guard who kept the door of the king's house. 28 As often as the king went into the house of the Lord, the guard carried them and brought them back to the guardroom. (1 Kgs 14:25–28)

Sergi bases his notion of the city's importance mainly on reevaluating archaeological evidence; specifically, on the analysis of architecture in Area G of the City of David. In the city, a Stepped Stone Structure, formerly known as the Jebusite ramp, was built above the Gihon Spring. It is likely that the structure supported buildings located above it (Sergi 2017a, 2); however, these did not survive until the present and their relation to the Stepped Stone Structure remains debatable from an archaeological viewpoint. This possibility applies mainly to the Large Stone Structure identified as the Palace of David by Eilat Mazar in 1997 (see also 2006). Yet like many other archaeologists, Sergi does not discuss this debatable link to the Large Stone Structure; instead, he focuses on the construction below and tries to date it as precisely as possible.

Having undergone several construction phases, as evidenced by the different sizes of the material used, the building below is typified by steps, which were probably built to protect the hillside and to increase the load-bearing capacity of the platform above. Houses were then built later in the lower part of the construction which some archaeologists (e.g., Cahill 2003b) have dated to the tenth and ninth centuries BCE, due to corresponding pottery from Jerusalem Strata 14 and 13. According to Sergi, the earlier dating of the Stepped Stone Structure is confirmed by CRJ type pottery, whilst the dating of houses is based on the pottery found in fills adjoining the building (red slip hand-burnished ware and the Iron Ages I and IIA). The reconstruction above shows that the Stepped Stone Structure is either from Iron Age I or early Iron Age IIA—i.e., the turn of the eleventh and tenth centuries BCE—and that the houses are from the subsequent period. In Sergi's view (2017a, 3–4), the monumental construction and the adjoining houses which were built later

3. THE DIFFICULT TENTH CENTURY (LATE IRON AGE I TO IRON AGE IIA)

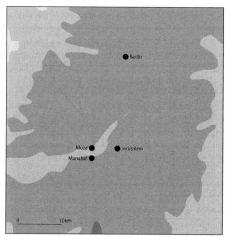
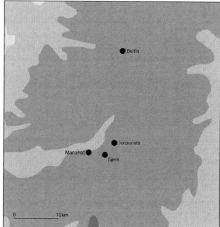
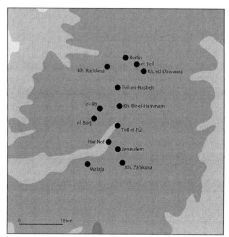

Fig. 10. Development of the area around Jerusalem from the fourteenth to eleventh century BCE (according to Sergi 2017a)

are proof of continuous construction activity above the Gihon spring in the City of David during the period in question.

According to Sergi, there are two reasons for the construction growth of Jerusalem in the City of David at the turn of the Iron Ages I and IIA. The first is pragmatic, a reaction to the general demographic growth in the city and surrounding areas; the other is symbolic. The author considers the Stepped Stone Structure monumental, and monumental architecture is a public expression of political ambition in two ways. Outwardly, this public and magnificent architectural type symbolises the political power and economic wealth of the ruling elite. With respect to the population, the subordination of the lower social classes is made more visible by assigning them work on expensive buildings. This confirms the social stratification—i.e., the dominance of the ruling class (cf. Sergi 2017a, 4). As evidenced by Sergi, the growth of a specific social group's political and socioeconomic capacity also impacts more remote areas. The rise of Jerusalem is reflected in the gradual, and eventually dramatic, increase in rural settlements in the period between the Late Bronze Age and late Iron Age I (according to Kloner 2000–2003; cf. Sergi 2017a, 5–8; 2017b, 373–75). In this period, the settlements developed as follows:

- In the fourteenth and thirteenth centuries BCE, there are settlements in al-Maliha in the Valley of Rephaim, in Moza near Jerusalem, and in the Bethel (Beitin) locality situated to the north.
- In the twelfth century BCE, a settlement is created in Gilo; Bethel and possibly al-Maliha are populated as well.
- In the eleventh century BCE, existing settlements grow and new settlements are established: Khirbat Zaquqa and possibly Khirbet Walaje in the south; and, north of Jerusalem, this applies to Har Nof, Tell el-Ful, Al Jib, Khirbet Bir al-Hamam, Tell en-Nasbeh, Khirbet ed-Dawwara, Khirbet Raddana, et-Tell, and Bethel.

In turn, the growth of settlements is reflected in the architecture of Jerusalem, with the political elite using the intentionally monumental constructions as a symbolic expression of their ambition. The rulers in the capital make it very clear that they control the rural settlements in the north—i.e., the southern part of the Benjamin Plateau up to Bethel, and up to Beth Zur in the south.

3.2.3.3 DECISIVE ROLE OF BENJAMIN

Sergi is convinced that attributing the Benjamin area to Jerusalem from a political and territorial standpoint "was an important stage in the formation of Judah" (Sergi 2017a; 2023; cf. Na'aman 2007b); it is not just important to note the establishment of rural settlements and the corresponding increase in Jerusalem's monumentality, but also their further development, which manifests in the transformation of some northern settlements which are gradually fortified in the Iron Age IIA. This fortification process does not happen at random: it is a reaction to an outside threat, a neighbouring political entity located further to the north. Sergi links the urban planning transformations of the settlements in Khirbet ed-Dawwara and Tell en-Nasbeh, and especially their fortifications, to specific biblical texts:

> 17 King Baasha of Israel went up against Judah and built Ramah to prevent anyone from going out or coming in to King Asa of Judah. 18 Then Asa took all the silver and the gold that were left in the treasuries of the house of the Lord and the treasuries of the king's house and gave them into the hands of his servants. King Asa sent them to King Ben-hadad son of Tabrimmon son of Hezion of Aram, who resided in Damascus, saying, 19

"Let there be an alliance between me and you, like that between my father and your father: I am sending you a present of silver and gold; go, break your alliance with King Baasha of Israel, so that he may withdraw from me." 20 Ben-hadad listened to King Asa and sent the commanders of his armies against the cities of Israel. He conquered Ijon, Dan, Abel-beth-maacah, and all Chinneroth, with all the land of Naphtali. 21 When Baasha heard of it, he stopped building Ramah and lived in Tirzah. 22 Then King Asa made a proclamation to all Judah; none was exempt: they carried away the stones of Ramah and its timber with which Baasha had been building; with them King Asa built Geba of Benjamin and Mizpah. (1 Kgs 15:17–22)

The text describes the events of the late tenth and early ninth centuries BCE; according to biblical texts, this period saw conflict between King Baasha of Israel (910–887 BCE) and King Asa of Judah (912–871 BCE) over the Benjamin Plateau, a buffer zone of both kingdoms. In the ninth century BCE, the need for border protection led to the fortification of Tell en-Nasbeh (biblical Mizpah) with chambered walls, so the settlement would defend Judah's highlands territory against attacks from the north. The processes mentioned are interconnected, and so, as stated by Sergi, "the kings of Jerusalem established their rule over the settlers on the Benjamin Plateau. Accordingly, the Stepped Stone Structure reflects the emergence of Judah as a territorial-political entity between Jerusalem and Benjamin" (Sergi 2017a, 16; contra Finkelstein 2012a).

3.2.3.4 THEY WERE TRULY PHILISTINES

According to Sergi, the reconstruction that prefers Jerusalem as the local hegemon controlling the Benjamin area in the north also better justifies the Philistines' rivalry with the early Kingdom of Judah. Saul's fights against the Philistines are treated by the early pre-Deuteronomistic traditions which are contained in some texts in 1 Sam 9–14. This older, Saulide Israelite tradition (cf. Sergi 2017b, 378)—which was not extended with pro-Davidide editorial amendments (criticising Saul) until later—documents that the Philistines posed the main threat to Jerusalem; this is why there is so much space dedicated to them in the Books of Samuel; this is why Saul, and later David, fight them. In Sergi's view, the primary scope of the Saul narrative is restricted to the closest area north of Jerusalem (i.e., the Benjamin area), and then to the Philistine threat in the Shephelah to the west. Consequently, these original traditions concern "a Judahite, not Israelite, point of view" (Sergi 2017b, 379).

Circumstantial evidence may include the fact that the text which describes the deaths of Saul and his sons at the hands of the Philistines during the battle at Mount Gilboa, which is almost geopolitically inexplicable, reflects a lack of knowledge of the areas further from the centre, and especially Jerusalem (Sergi 2017b, 381; cf. 3.2.2.3). Another explanation may be that Beth-shean—the location to which the dead Saulides were transported and displayed as a deterrent example—remained known in tradition as a Canaanite fortress, and that, in terms of political interactions in the region, the Philistines and their battles with Saul are merely a literary adaptation of the familiar southern status quo. Sergi considers the third possible explanation—that the enemies were Egyptians—to be improbable. This assessment accords with the current archaeological information gathered from Beth-shean: there is no evidence supporting Egyptian presence in the area after 1130 BCE. Granted, some researchers think that the erection of monuments in the New Kingdom period (1550–1077 BCE) outside the temple in settlement Stratum V is evidence for Egyptian presence after Shoshenq's invasion (cf. Mazar 2011); however, there is apparently no other pro-Egyptian evidence of material culture. (A. Mazar 2006).

3.2.3.5 WHAT IS ISRAEL AND WHAT IS JUDAH?

The southern variant proposed by Sergi must overcome another obstacle: in 1 Sam 13–14—i.e., the oldest tradition—why are Jerusalem and Judah missing, while Israel is often featured? In total, this section mentions Israel fourteen times, while there is not a single word about either Jerusalem or Judah. Sergi explains this discrepancy by distinguishing between Israel as a group of people or collective identity, and as a name for a specific political and territorial entity. The first name is broader and older (by all accounts, this is confirmed by the late thirteenth-century Merneptah stele); the second is more specific and, later, related to an Iron Age II polity (e.g., Tel Dan inscriptions and the Mesha stele). Used in the former sense, Israel was the name for the identity of a collective who lived in the highlands area, comprising of the Benjamites, such as Saul and probably also David (Sergi 2017, 382). Later, during the formation of Judah in the ninth century BCE, David and the Davidides adopted a new identity opposed to Israel: the umbrella identity of the Judeans. According to the author, the tradition attributing David to Bethlehem must be viewed in a more critical light. Sergi formulates the reconstruction as follows:

> It may therefore be concluded that both David and Saul originated from clans affiliated with Israel that settled north (Benjaminite clans) and south (Ephrathite clans) of Jerusalem. From an archaeological point of view, by the early 10th century BCE, the entire region from Bethlehem in the south to Bethel in the north [...] came under the political hegemony of the rulers of Jerusalem.
> (Sergi 2017b, 383)

3.2.3.6 NORTH AND SOUTH—SEPARATE BUT CONCURRENT

The formative process of the Kingdom of Judah in the south occurs in tandem with the formation of Israel in the north. Sergi infers the borders and relations of these territories mostly from biblical texts. Documented in 1 Kgs 15:17–22, the conflict between the north and south plays a key role in the thesis about the construction of fortifications in Mizpah (*Tell en-Nasbeh*) and Geba—i.e., two locations in the Benjamin Plateau during King Asa's rule. For its part, Israel was seated in Tirzah (*Tell el-Far'ah*), constructed by Baasha. In all likelihood, the confrontation of the rulers tested the strength of each of their borders. It was probably an "important stage in the formation of Judah as a territorial kingdom under the centralized rule of the House of David" (Sergi 2017a, 17), succeeded by the alliance of Ahab and Jehoshaphat several decades later (cf. 4.2.2).

3.2.3.7 SOUTHERN TRAIL—A PROVISIONAL CRITICAL EVALUATION

In a way, the newest reconstruction of the origins of Israel and Judah proposed by Sergi is a renaissance of the more harmonic—or at least partly harmonising—reading of biblical texts. Undoubtedly, this is also a reaction to Finkelstein's "grand synthesis" (Pioske 2014) oriented towards the north and the Gibeon-Bethel territorial entity, as evidenced above. Sergi largely uses the same documents of material culture, epigraphic material, and biblical texts, but he reaches completely different conclusions. The south, Jerusalem, and the nascent Kingdom of Judah are not phenomena related to a later period— i.e., the ninth century BCE - but quite the contrary; they prove the centralisation of political power as early as the tenth century BCE, or even earlier (Sergi 2015c; 2023).

The reconstruction proposed above is disputable right from the start, if the Stepped Stone Structure and its direct temporal connection to other construction activities in the same part of the City of David (see 3.2.3.2) are considered to be key evidence. The contestable part is the thesis about the continuity of construction throughout the eleventh and tenth centuries BCE, which in Sergi's view is a result of the rise of the Kingdom of Judah. This continuity is questioned by numerous recent and older studies: the Stepped Stone Structure underwent several modifications, and exact dating based on a very limited amount of pottery, gathered from ten different archaeological contexts, is highly controversial (see Kenyon 1974; Shiloh 1984; Finkelstein et al. 2007; Finkelstein 2011b). Based on more data discovered in Area G, current research places the construction phase of the houses in the lower part of the structure to the late Iron Age IIA and the early Iron Age IIB, rather than an earlier phase (see discussion in 4.2.6).

As emphasised by Sergi, the trigger mechanism for the rise in Jerusalem's monumentality was the settlement growth in the Benjamin area to the north (Sergi 2017a; 2017b; 2023). The surviving evidence of this activity, especially the Stepped Stone Structure, is therefore directly linked to events outside Jerusalem. The settlement growth outside the city influences the architecture in terms of its symbolic and pragmatic functions. But is it possible to make such a direct connection between these processes and to include the north under the umbrella of the nascent Kingdom of Judah? Do the events occur in a single territorial entity? What about Shoshenq? Is the text of 1 Kings 14:25-28 enough to emphasise the importance of Jerusalem, despite the city's absence from the Karnak relief? Moreover, one must take into account the history of the formation of this text, which is very distant in time from the "reality" it describes, including issues surrounding its preservation and dissemination (for this cf. Jamieson-Drake 1991; Rollston 2006; Frevel 2016; Ebeling et al. 2017; Richelle 2022).

Sergi's line of reasoning against the northern reconstruction and the supposed Gibeon-Bethel polity is obvious and, in a way, predictable, since it is a reaction to a highly hypothetical reconstruction, in which much solid material evidence is missing or—at the very least—ambiguous in terms of interpretation (e.g., chambered walls in Tell en-Nasbeh; see Zorn 1993). However, the same applies in the case of the southern scenario. For example, Sergi (2017b, 379) bases his hypothesis on the refusal to attribute Benjamin to the northern kingdom tradition, stating that the early Saulide traditions hardly reflect the geographic and political realities of the Kingdom of Israel; however, considering the same textual traditions, this may apply even more appropriately to the Kingdom of Judah.

The analysis of northern settlements plays a specific role in Sergi's line of reasoning, as he paints a very dramatic picture of the furthest area in Jerusalem's sphere of influence. Urban transformations of the settlements and with some turning into forts with chambered walls (especially Tell en-Nasbeh; other localities are very disputable in this regard) may be attributed to one political entity or another as a result of confrontation with the growing influence of the northern kingdom. Based on the available material culture north of Jerusalem—an area which has been essentially void of any new official archaeological research for decades—interactions, relations, and trends may be determined mainly on a hypothetical basis, with the help of biblical texts; however, one must proceed with the utmost caution when using them for such early periods of history.

3.3 SUMMARY

The three reconstructions above which describe the formation of Judah and Israel at the end of the Iron Age I and in the Iron Age IIA attempt to outline the formative processes of these territorial entities in the tenth century BCE, which is a time fraught with interpretative difficulty. Historically, this period begins earlier—in the late Iron Age I—and also ends later, since it overlaps with the ninth century BCE according to modified conventional chronology. Each reconstruction has aspects that are valid and based on sound arguments, but each also has weak, unexplained blind spots. One lacks a connection to Jerusalem, which is quite understandable, since the birth of Judah is sought in an earlier period and a different region: the Shephelah. More closely tied to Jerusalem, the other two reconstructions do not possess a clearer stratigraphic and chronological setting for this administrative centre, existing already or yet non-existent in the late eleventh and tenth centuries BCE. Sergi takes the conservative view, that Jerusalem was a territorial entity with monumental architecture as early as the late eleventh century BCE; while on the other hand, Finkelstein thinks the same place is an unimportant location on the periphery of the northern kingdom, which would not transform into an individual unit until the ninth century BCE.

When searching for the origins of Jerusalem and Israel, one cannot help but wonder if (and how) it is possible to distinguish the centralisation of a specific political power from territorial expansion. Are they concurrent phenomena, or could it be that centralisation comes first and expansion second? Furthermore, is the monumental architecture in Jerusalem (and elsewhere, such as in the localities of the Gibeon-Bethel polity) necessarily synonymous with the aspirations of a local political entity to expand its territory? Should we not reverse the perspective and interpret the monumentality—which is, moreover, less grandiose than that of other Levantine cities and buildings—as the result of an entirely pragmatic decision to provide an ancient city with basic static security (see the Large Stone Structure), as well as water source protection, minimising the risk of conquest? Considering the dynamics of the gradual formation of territorial states in the late tenth and ninth centuries BCE, this perspective seems more logical. Expansion is especially typical of stabilised political units that have existed for long periods of time, as was the case for Israel, Aram Damascus, and other Levantine states in the ninth century BCE.

The manner of appropriately evaluating an interpretation based on a synthesis of material culture and written testimonies is another matter worth discussing. The dating of the former source is relatively, and sometimes also absolutely, secure (it is worth noting that Shiloh is the only locality in the northern highlands where radiocarbon dating has been used; in Jerusalem, until recently, it was only Iron Age I Gilo; for the current state of research, see Regev et al. 2017); the latter is problematic due to the highly complex process of textual development over time. The intentions behind the writing, passing on, and editing of such texts make it clear that these sources are historiographic rather than historically accurate in nature, describing events that were said to have occurred in accordance with certain ideas formulated in a much later period. In our view, this is how the comprehensive narratives about Saul, David, and the division of the United Monarchy should be interpreted (for discussion see Bietenhard 1998; Linville 1998; Vermeylen 2000; Lemaire and Halpern 2010; Čapek 2015; Rückl 2021; Na'aman 2023).

Used as a basis for Finkelstein and Sergi's completely disparate reconstructions, Benjamin is a specific topic that warrants a book of its own. According to biblical texts, this tribe, people, or geographical unit is variously assigned to Judah (1 Kgs 12:21.23; 15:22) or Israel (Judg 5:14), whilst sometimes it stands alone against Judah (Jerusalem) or Israel (Judg 20–21). Archaeological evidence related to Benjamin and the tenth century BCE is ambiguous, to say the least (see the interpretations of the Gibeon-Bethel Plateau fortifications).

Much later, in the sixth century BCE, Mizpah (*Tell en-Nasbeh*) became an important administrative site of the Neo-Babylonian Empire; in this period, the area is termed the territory of Benjamin in the Book of Jeremiah (17:26; 32:44; 33:13). Due to more solid archaeological evidence from the Iron Age IIC and Mizpah in particular, some take this as proof of Benjamin's existence as a separate political entity (as early as Malamat 1950; Zorn 2003; and then Fleming 2013; cf. Lipschits 2005) not only after the collapse of Jerusalem, but also beforehand. That would explain the peculiar resistance of Benjamin to identification as being northern or southern. Research has not yet provided a definitive earliest point of the existence of an independent Benjamin; but is that possible if sources other than biblical texts (e.g., Jer 1:1–3) were to be used?

One also encounters terminological obstacles when discussing the formation of political entities in the Iron Age IIA. What were tenth-century BCE Judah and Israel, if they existed? Were they states or a preceding developmental stage? Research also uses numerous other terms: *polity*, *territorial political entity*, *early state*, and *full-blown state*. Likewise, distinction is also made between unstable and stable forms of governance, depending on the deficit or sufficiency of their institutional and organisational foundations. The former (unstable) comprises of what is known as a *chiefdom* (*Häuptlingstum* in German; see discussion in Országh 2013; Charvát 2013), a term that denotes a one-ruler administration in local tribal communities. David and Saul may fall into this category as their reigns are characterised by strong kinship relationships, the existence of a small elite group, and territorial demarcation (cf. Frevel 2016; Maeir and Shai 2016; for discussion see esp. Hualong 2024).

Sometimes, the term used in this context is *proto-state* (cf. Knauf-Guillaume 2016).

The formation of a full-blown state is based on solid institutional and organisational foundations. A full-blown state is typified by the following: enforcement power, bureaucracy, military protection, an organised justice system, tax collection, public and public-financed constructions, trade, centralised state religion, and social stratification (Frevel 2016, 95). In this case, a greater stability is presumed, and the existence of epigraphic and iconographic material also forms part of a full-blown state. Taking these criteria into account, Israel and Judah cannot be considered full-blown states in the Iron Age IIA, and the terms *polity* (for this see esp. Ferguson and Mansbach, cf. also Mazar A. 2014; Lederman and Bunimovitz 2014; Thomas 2021) or *early state* are more appropriate (for further discussion cf. esp. Hall 2022 and Ben-Yosef and Thomas 2023).

The historical period between the end of the Iron Age I and the Iron Age IIA enables the identification and more detailed description of some aspects of these nascent states; for others, there is mostly a lack of necessary evidence. Consequently, the break point and epochal transition cannot be clearly determined on the basis of material culture. It is self-evident that written documents—especially biblical texts—describe the moment of creation "accurately and in detail" centuries later; it is also self-evident that these texts must be subjected to critical analysis, so they do not become bases for simplistic or unfounded historical reconstructions, if they do contain any historical facts at all. The more documentable early political forms of Judah and Israel in the late Iron Age IIA and Iron Age IIB will be discussed in the next chapter.

4. THE FIRST TRUE UNIFICATION AND THE FIRST TRUE DIVISION (IRON AGE IIA-B)

> *Most of the Bible focuses on forming links to the past. It is up to us to verify their comprehensiveness and to what degree they reflect new attempts by the authors to come to terms with moments of crisis and transition.*
> —Daniel Fleming

The end of the previous chapter stated that the formation of a full-blown state requires solid institutional and organisational foundations, bureaucracy, a justice system, a functioning army, and income sources provided by levying taxes. For Judah and Israel, the kingdoms under discussion, these conditions were not met in the tenth century BCE; consequently, the early Iron Age IIA has been interpreted as the dawn of, or prelude to, the birth of these political entities. The period saw population growth (see 2.1), but territorial states and city-states were not formed until the very end of the tenth century and the subsequent ninth century BCE (i.e., during the continuation of the Iron Age IIA). Additionally, as of the mid-ninth century BCE, all three areas of inquiry are available for the very first time—non-written material culture, ancient Levantine literature, and Old Testament texts (see chapter 1.). The synchronicity with the period is guaranteed for the first two areas; in the case of the third, it is a question to be discussed vis-à-vis the formative and dating processes of biblical traditions.

4.1 BIG AND LITTLE HISTORIES

During the late tenth and the first half of the ninth centuries BCE, new political entities were established and grew in the Levant. This period is typified by the rise of mostly small territorial states and—especially in the region of Syria—by the formation of city-states; it is characterised by the creation of local coalitions for the purpose of expansion, or later, during the rise of new hegemons, of larger regional coalitions to protect and secure the area under their control. The influence of major empires spread in different directions, with dramatic impact on the events in individual territories; this was due to Egypt's withdrawal and the rise of a new hegemon in the form of the Neo-Assyrian Empire, which subjugated almost the entire Near East and, during the seventh-century BCE rule of Esarhaddon (681-669 BCE), conquered Egypt and Cyprus as well. The history of the Southern Levant region is heavily influenced by the Arameans—specifically, the polity of Aram Damascus, Israel's northern neighbour. Consequently, the relations between Assyria and Aram Damascus were also important for the events to the south—i.e., in the northern kingdom and Judah.

4.1.1 THE NEO-ASSYRIAN EMPIRE

Assyria's influence started to spread westwards under Ashurnasirpal II (884-859 BCE), and especially under Shalmaneser III (859-824 BCE). This expansion peaked during the later rule of Tiglath-Pileser III (745-727 BCE), and his successor, Shalmaneser V (727-722 BCE), conquered Samaria, ending the existence of an independent Israel. Assyria did not reach its greatest size until later, during the seventh century BCE. Territories of the Neo-Assyrian Empire were subjected to vassalage, paying tribute, deportation (Radner 2019), and forced changes of rulers in case of resistance, on one hand; and on the other, they were incorporated into the Assyrian economic system and trade, which provided opportunity for development (Hrůša 2015; Lipschits 2018; Gadot and Bocher 2018; Gadot 2022; Koch 2019; 2022). Assyria's influence is obvious, impacting religion, literature, architecture, and culture in general (for more detail, see 5.1).

4.1.2 ARAMEANS

Twelfth-century BCE Assyrian sources use the name "Aram" or "Arameans" for the population living in the area of Syria at that time (Kreuzer 1996; Lipiński 2000; Younger 2016; Sader 2016; Doak 2020). In this period, the balance between the Hittite Empire, Egypt, Babylonia, and Assyria was disturbed, leading to two centuries of instability, chaos, and the gradual establishment of new "ethnic identities" (Bunnens 2016, 273). Similar to those concerning Israel, older theories depict Arameans as exogenous groups coming from the desert and newly settling west of the Euphrates River; however, new research proves otherwise. It was a mixed, multi-ethnic population, comprising immigrants in part, but mostly consisted of former urban populations which were organised tribally and they subsisted on cattle farming and seasonal agriculture (cf. Frevel 2016). Later, once the instability ceased—i.e., in the tenth and ninth centuries BCE—Aramean states were formed in the same area, with their existence proven by non-written material culture as well as relatively copious epigraphic material. These were small states and local kingdoms, such as Arpad, Hamath, Sam'al, *KTK* (Younger 2016), probably Geshur with the cities of et-Tell, Tel Hadar, En Gev, and Tel Dover located east of the Jordan River (see discussion on Geshur's existence in Arav 2013; Blum 2016b; Panitz-Cohen and Mullins 2016; Sergi and Kleiman A. 2018). Furthermore, Aramean states included Damascus, sometimes termed Aram Damascus, Israel's northern and eastern neighbour. At the same time, two new political entities were formed east of the Jordan River: Moab and Ammon (Lipiński 2006; MacDonald 2020), both of which also play an important role in the history of Judah and Israel.

4.1.3 ANCIENT DOMINOES

The importance of Assyria and Aram Damascus to the formation of Judah and Israel is comparable to the influence of Egypt and Philistia in the late Iron Age I and early Iron Age IIA. However, there are changes to the direction from which power and cultural impulses arose. Moreover, this influence is incomparably more demonstrable as it is documented on both the material culture level and in numerous more-extensive Assyrian and Aramean texts. The development of the relational network observable in the area during the late Iron Age IIA and Iron Ages IIB–C is similar to a complex domino effect, where the reasons for shifts develop into numerous expected and even unexpected consequences. If Assyria was on the rise, leading westward campaigns, the influence of Aram Damascus was restrained, and so Israel was able to keep with the polity, if not be a more than a formidable rival; consequently, it could have used dynastic ties forced upon Judah to dictate its power interests further south, in Jerusalem. This first applies to the Omride dynasty, especially the rule of Ahab (871–852 BCE), and later, to the time after the rule of Shalmaneser III (859–824 BCE) — i.e., the final decades of the ninth century BCE, when Shamshi-Adad V (824–811 BCE) made a largely unsuccessful attempt to enforce Assyrian interests throughout the Southern Levant.

Preceding the campaigns of Adad-nirari III (811–783 BCE), which aimed to reconsolidate Assyrian interests in the region, the intervening period saw Damascus gain the upper hand under the rule of Hazael (843/842–803 BCE). Probably after 837 BCE, he exerted pressure in the south, conquering both the area east of the Jordan River up to Sukkot (Tell Deir Alla) and the Jezreel Valley, including Megiddo. During Hazael's rule, the Aramean cities of Dan, Hazor, and Bethsaida were constructed in the north. During the Aramean campaign in the south, the southern part of Tirzah, Beth-shemesh, and Aphek were conquered, whilst Gath may have been as well, around 830 BCE (for more, see 3.2.1.3.4). According to many researchers, Hazael expanded even further south, seeking to take control of the copper trade in Edom and thus secure the raw material resources necessary for confronting Assyria. There is, however, no clear archaeological evidence to support such a widespread influence beyond the layers of destruction, which, of course, need not be attributed specifically and solely to Hazael, but local or regional interactions can be considered, which, of course, are related to overall developments in the southern Levant.

Aramean pressure on Israel showed in the temporary weakness of the latter and in the changes in Judah, which likely resulted from this; these changes were reflected in tensions which were felt during the Omride dynasty, which eventually ceased to exist, as it is generally assumed, due to a coup during the reign of Jehu (841–814 BCE). As suggested by some, this coup was supported by Arameans aiming to subjugate Israel, their neighbour and rival (cf. Frevel 2016, 220). Possibly aided by the Arameans, Jehu carried out the putsch and became king himself (cf. Lamb 2007; Baruchi-Unna 2017; Quine 2020). Equally, one cannot rule out the possibility that the coup might have been assigned secretly by Assyria, an even more powerful state that would use Jehu to secure its influence in the south. This would be indirectly documented by the famous Black Obelisk (COS 2.113F), depicting Jehu in subjugation alongside a text listing tribute paid to Shalmaneser III.

The violent death of Jehoram in 841 BCE and the subsequent power shift in Samaria impacted developments in the south: in Jerusalem, the daughter (or sister) of Ahab, Athaliah (ca. 845–840 BCE), was deposed, and Joash (840–801 BCE) seized power with the support of the local elite, which might have been directly responsible for the queen's murder. Was Joash the first Davidide, as suggested by a simple reading of the biblical text? And is the first territorial self-determination of the Kingdom of Judah linked to these events (cf. Sergi 2013)? Both questions will be discussed later. Furthermore, alternative interpretations will be discussed as well, including claims that Joash was imposed by the northern powers as the first member of the Nimshide dynasty (Frevel 2016, 221), or that he was a continuation of the re-established Omride dynasty (Čapek 2010b; 2016a). Clearly, Hazael's power showed in specific governmental changes in Israel and Judah, whether they were caused by tactical negotiations or direct military interventions.

Aram Damascus's temporary hegemony ended with five campaigns led by Adad-nirari III (811–783 BCE), grandson of Shalmaneser III. Written documents from the period prove that the Assyrians conquered Aram Damascus, as well as Tyre, Sidon, and Arwad, and that Jehu's grandson, Joash, ruling Israel from Samaria, had to pay tribute to Assyria as a vassal from 796 BCE. The description of the vassal king Joash (^{m}ia-'a-su) as a ruler from Samaria (KUR *Sa-me-ri-na-a-a*), carved on the Tell el-Rimah stele, conveys the sovereignty of the Assyrian court, which, however, granted Israel considerable independence (Hasegawa 2019). It was during Joash's reign (802–787 BCE), and later, in the time of Jeroboam II (787–747 BCE), that Israel's territorial expansion reached its peak and the situation likely grew stable in Judah. After the territorial shrinkage during Hazael's reign, the tide began to turn:

Israel newly controlled the Transjordan as well as the Galilee, including the north up to Tel Dan (Stratum II). It was a heyday (cf. Frevel 2016, 230) and also "Israel's swansong" (Finkelstein 2013, 129–41); cities were constructed and heavily fortified (Kinneret II, Hazor VI/IVA, Yokneam XIII, Jibleam X); it was a period of great economic prosperity, thriving international trade, and also cult centralisation (Finkelstein 2013; Kleiman et al. 2017; cf. Hall 2020; 2022), as evidenced by the material culture, as well as the first more extensive evidence of developed writing (Finkelstein and Sass 2013, Rollston 2010; 2017). The final defeat of Damascus by the Assyrians in 732 BCE benefitted Israel in the short term, but only for a decade; then, the same empire inflicted a similar fate on Samaria.

The history of the Kingdom of Judah is strongly influenced by events in the second half of the eighth century BCE. First, the death of Jeroboam II was followed by the short rule of Zechariah and his subsequent murder in 747 BCE at the behest of Rezin of Damascus (754–732 BCE). At that time, Israel came under the influence of Aram Damascus and, together, alongside other Levantine kingdoms, they made vain attempts to stop Assyria from expanding again. Zechariah was the last member of the Jehuite dynasty (or the Nimshide dynasty, or the still surviving Omride dynasty; see discussion in 4.2.5), which exerted influence over whoever ruled Jerusalem. The last king controlled in this manner was Jotham (750–735 BCE), succeeded by Ahaz (732–716 BCE), the latter of whom resisted the pressure to join an anti-Assyrian coalition. In fact, Ahaz did the exact opposite, by becoming a vassal of Tiglath-Pileser III and thus joining a system that would later develop into what would be named *Pax Assyriaca* (cf. 2 Kgs 16:7–20) at the turn of the eighth and seventh centuries BCE. On the one hand, this decision involved Jerusalem in the Syro-Ephraimite War (736–732 BCE) and exposed it to danger from the Philistines and Edom, who took advantage of the new situation; while on the other hand, the independent state of Judah grew stronger.

The truly separate kingdoms of Israel and Judah should be sought, however, at the very end of the ninth century BCE, and especially in the first half of the eighth century BCE. At this time, Judah ceased to be a branch kingdom of Israel, since the influence of Samaria subsided, and was replaced by a ruling dynasty of Judah's own, though its roots probably trace back to the north too (see 4.2.5.1).

The second event with a formative impact on the Kingdom of Judah was the fall of Israel in 722 BCE. Though Judah's journey to independence had begun earlier (possibly under the rule of Amaziah in the early eighth century BCE), it was only in the absence of a stronger neighbour that a new understanding of their "common" history developed. One may assume that the oral and literary traditions of Israel, alongside other cultural and economic influences, spread to the south due to the pre-existing close bond between the two kingdoms (for discussion see Gadot, Kleiman A. and Uziel 2023). However, the fall of Samaria constitutes another turn in biblical reflections upon the past and proided the impetus for the creation of an entirely independent historiography which is documented in Old Testament texts (Kahn 2019; Levin 2019). This historiography features a fundamental transformation of Judean lived experience, endowing the retrospectively viewed past with continuity, coherence, logic, and, especially, the formation of Judah and Jerusalem as the starting point of history.

4.2 FIRST UNIFICATION TO FIRST INDEPENDENCE

The preceding chapter proposes that the tenth-century BCE United Monarchy cannot be documented according to the shape, scope, and form of political power described by biblical texts. On the other hand, we can trace the slow formation of the territorial states of Israel and Judah as independent kingdoms. Some date them to as early as the late eleventh and tenth centuries, at the transition between the Iron Ages I and IIA (see 3.2.2 and 3.2.3), while others consider later dating. This book adopts the latter view—that neither Israel nor Judah can be proved to be territorial states, in the full extent and sense of the word, until the ninth century BCE or, in Judah's case, possibly not until even later.

If there was ever a unification between the two kingdoms, it occurred in the ninth century BCE, with power asymmetry: Israel dominated, and Judah was subordinate to it. And if there was ever an emancipation, it only took place later, in the eighth century BCE. At the time—probably only for a few decades—two independent political entities existed side by side: the kingdoms of Israel and Judah. The latter became independent from the former due to the pressure exerted by Aram Damascus and Assyria on Samaria (see 4.1.3). It is in this light that biblical historiography must be interpreted as well, since it describes events in retrospect with a very specific aim: to produce an extensive record documenting the formation of an independent national identity. Frevel (2016, 149) describes the process in a similar manner, stating that, viewed through the lens of history, the biblical perspective is reversed: Solomon and David do not represent the origins of a kingdom which would serve as a basis for deriving the monarchies of Jeroboam I in the north and Rehoboam in the south. The birth of the kingdoms of Israel and Judah is derived from another provenance—i.e., probably as late as the ninth century BCE in Samaria and the eighth century BCE in Judah (cf. Schipper 2020a).

This notion, which will be explored later, is based on specific historical facts imprinting upon the material culture and literary traditions that were later committed to writing. By critically analysing these, one may deduce if a given political entity could have existed, and to what extent. Thus, it can be stated that the entire complex development of the relations between Israel and Judah from the first unification to the first independence took place in the late Iron Age IIA and Iron Age IIB. Let us now examine this process in greater depth.

4.2.1 WRITING—AN INDICATOR OF TERRITORIAL STATE FORMATION?

One of the features of statehood is the existence of written documentation which indicates that a certain territorial entity is developed enough to organise economic and political matters in a clearly defined territory under its long-term control. This is clearly the reality in the case of Bronze Age Egypt and the concurrent empires in Asia Minor and Mesopotamia. Meanwhile, there are very few written testimonies in Canaan in the Iron Ages I and IIA, a later period which followed the collapse of the city-state system as well as the "global" Egyptian administration, and which is otherwise quite well documented owing to numerous records (see COS 2.2.3; 2.4; 2.5; etc.). From the time of the first reconstructed entities in the area under discussion—i.e., Israel and Judah in the first half of the ninth century BCE—there are virtually no documents, with a few exceptions consisting of short inscriptions numbering in some cases to single digits (Finkelstein and Sass 2013; Rollston 2017).

The texts which are known and their analysis, carried out systematically and in detail by Finkelstein and Sass (2013), show that Hebrew was present as a language used by a specific political entity in the late ninth century BCE at the earliest in Israel, and even later in case of Judah. Late eleventh- and tenth-century inscriptions—such as the Khirbet Qeiyafa ostracon, claimed by earlier research to be the first documents in Hebrew (Puech 2010; Galil 2009, Misgav 2009, cf. Yardeni 2009)—have been most recently interpreted by other scholars as a script which was clearly derived from the Phoenician alphabet, but not provably Hebrew (Rollston 2011; 2016) because the words are generally Semitic terms making it impossible to declare any ostracon to be written in Hebrew.

It was at the turn of the tenth and ninth centuries BCE that the Phoenician alphabetic script—developed from the Proto-Canaanite script—began to be distributed to the inland regions, mainly from the areas of Philistia and the Coastal Plain. The first Hebrew inscriptions in Samaria (AHI 3.001ff) and Kuntillet 'Ajrud (COS 2.47) date to as late as the first half of the eighth century BCE; but due to the general duration of the dissemination of scripts, the existence of early Hebrew forms may be presumed in the first half of the ninth century BCE, since there is archaeological evidence for the Hebrew-type script in Gath and Tel Rehov (cf. Finkelstein and Sass 2013, 198; Mazar,

A. and Panitz-Cohen 2020; furthermore, cf. 4.2.5.1.1). From there, it spread to the inland regions, as well as to the Judaean Mountains and the northern highlands. Based on the claim that written documents are missing due to the limited service life of the material used (parchment, papyrus), the consideration of even earlier distribution in Israel was put in doubt by the results of wet sifting in Megiddo: not a single bulla was found there from the first half of the ninth century BCE. The same applies to Judah. In recent years, a larger number of bullae were found near the Gihon Spring, but these were non-epigraphical bullae—i.e., bullae preceding inscribed bullae—which date to the first half of the eighth century BCE at the earliest (Mendel-Geberovich, Chalaf, and Uziel 2020; Mendel-Geberovich 2023).

There is an ongoing discussion as to the relationship between the Hebrew used in Israel and Judah (Young 1995; Fredericks 1996; Knauf 2006; Rollston 2006; 2010; 2017; Na'aman 2020). In Fleming's view (2013), the differences are not great enough to suggest the existence of two separate political entities. In addition, it should be stressed that the assignment of a dialect to a territory is also unreliable, because the boundaries of the territory itself are not only sometimes quite unclear, but they also shift. According to Rollston, the oldest (eighth-century BCE) Old Hebrew inscriptions were shared across Israel and Judah, whilst Fleming expresses agreement with the idea, stating that "in the end, there is probably too little basis for drawing sweeping conclusions about the relationship of scribal education and practice to the political division between Israel and Judah in the ninth and eighth centuries" (Fleming 2013, 302).

4.2.2 DEVELOPMENTS IN THE FIRST HALF OF THE NINTH CENTURY BCE AND THE RISE OF THE OMRIDE DYNASTY

The history of Israel and Judah preceding the mid-ninth century BCE can only be reconstructed using non-written material culture and biblical texts. Non-biblical texts are rare (see 4.2.1), and archaeological evidence for clearly identifying separate political entities and their structures is inconclusive (cf. Frevel 2016, 193). In the north, a documentable territorial state arose in the time of the Omride dynasty, approximately after 880 BCE. Some researchers, however, place the Gibeon-Bethel polity and the Tirzah territory into an earlier period (see esp. Finkelstein 2013; see 3.2.2.5). In the south, a specific territorial state did not appear until even later, and it was formed under strong northern influence. Some scholars propose an earlier state here as well, formed in Jerusalem and its immediate surroundings, later reaching further, especially to the area of Benjamin in the north, where it rivalled Israel (see 3.2.3). A third possible earlier development, in the Shephelah in the tenth century BCE, must be mentioned as well. Here, some scholars consider to be the area from which the gradual ethnogenesis of Judah from the late-

Canaanite culture emerged due to the interactions of this culture with that of the Philistines which then expanded further into the mountains (see 3.2.1).

Until the early ninth century BCE, the situation in Israel was typified by instability, which impacted the variability in population of the localities which would become the future power centres. This is in contrast with the events in the Jezreel Valley and to its north, in Aramean-controlled territories. The new state first began to take form in the highlands. Considered a historical figure by some, but not by others (see 4.2.3), Jeroboam I (933–911 BCE) is linked by biblical texts to various localities: Shechem, Penuel, and perhaps even Tirzah. However, no ruler until Baasha makes a claim to Tirzah as their capital (see 1 Kgs 15:21, 33). The first of the areas, Shechem (*Tell Balata*)—an important Middle Bronze Age city—was not repopulated until the turn of the ninth and eighth centuries BCE (regarding Shechem Stratum IX, see Campbell and Wright 2002). The same applies to Penuel, whether it is identified as Tell edh-Dhahab al-Gharbi or Tell el-Hammah; the settlements are from a later time, meaning it is necessary to maintain that there is, as yet, no solid evidence for the residence of Jeroboam I (cf. Frevel 2016, 154; cf. Finkelstein 2013, 73).

Meanwhile, there are various interpretations for Tirzah (*Tell el-Far'ah*), an area that, according to biblical texts, was inhabited by Baasha and then Elah, Zimri, and Omri for six years, before he built Samaria. One interpretation is based on biblical chronology, which leads (more or less, by circular reasoning) to the settlement date being set at the late Iron Age I and the early Iron Age IIA. Jeroboam I is a candidate for the potential settlement, since, during his rule, the Middle Bronze Age walls were used to refortify Tirzah after a period in which it was merely a rural settlement. This interpretation is then expanded into a claim about later, ninth-century BCE settlement, with documented unfinished buildings being used as evidence that the power centre moved to Samaria at this time.

By contrast, newer interpretations date the same settlement stratum to a later time, specifically the Iron Age IIB and the eighth century BCE. Detailed analysis of pottery assemblages and architecture further distinguishes a period attributed to the Omride dynasty (Tirzah VIIb) from a later stratum which features a building and palace complex from the Iron Age IIB (Tirzah VIId), likely from the time of Jeroboam II (see an overview of Tirzah research history in Finkelstein 2013, 66–74; Arie 2008). This later dating is also applied to another two important areas more frequently linked to Jeroboam I: Bethel and Dan (Finkelstein and Singer-Avitz 2009; contra Lipschits 2017). In accordance with the general consensus, these areas show greater population in a later period as well, especially in the time of Joash (802–787 BCE) and Jeroboam II (787–747 BCE), which alters the image of Israel's origins considerably (Herzog and Singer-Avitz 2006).

In terms of Israel's development in the late tenth and the first half of the ninth century, the information above means that the nascent state was less monumental, less visible, and that it was only in an embryonic stage. Far less urbanised than the cities then in the Jezreel Valley in the north, the highlands saw a new political entity emerge gradually and, by all accounts, in reaction to the events further to the north, which was controlled by the Arameans, who had the upper hand at that time (see 4.1.3). In retrospect, the kingdom of Jeroboam I appears to have been a small highland state with a moving centre, formed from tribal confederations of peasants and cattle farmers (cf. Berlejung 2010).

If Israel was indeed such a tiny and only nascent territory, it seems logical that it is difficult to provide archaeological evidence supporting the theory of its history which is elaborated by biblical texts, which is the division of what was originally the United Monarchy. By all accounts, it is necessary to revisit the existence of the first rulers, especially Jeroboam I, who is—much like Rehoboam, his Judean counterpart—more of a fictitious figure produced by a stylised ideal history describing the original unity, the first division, and the formation of two independent kingdoms (see 4.2.5).

According to biblical chronology, this was a time of transformation and crisis; the golden age of the United Monarchy came to an end, and the situation changed drastically. It is not a coincidence that the Books of Kings describe the following period as one of constant conflict between Jeroboam I and Rehoboam, later Abijah, and then between Asa of Judah and Baasha of Israel. It is almost inevitable that the new be born from mythical chaos and the archetypal ethnomachy of two nations that used to be one is expressed in political or theological literature.

The Books of Chronicles link the same period to significant construction efforts on the part of Rehoboam, who strengthened his position by building fortified cities in Judah (2 Chron. 11:5-12). However, almost none of these settlements (Bethlehem, Etam, Teqoa, Beth Zur, Sokoh, Adullam, Gath, Maresha, Ziph, Adorayim, Lachish, Azekah, Tzora, Ayalon, and Hebron) are linked to the northern border and Israel, though the northern neighbour is given as the reason for their construction; instead, they are connected to the western and southwestern border of Judah.

If the list of fortified cities is to be linked with a specific period, it correlates more to the late eighth and seventh centuries BCE and Hezekiah and Josiah's building efforts (see 6.2.2 and 6.2.4). Additionally, one cannot ignore the fact that, during Rehoboam's putative rule, cities—with some exceptions—were not yet fortified, and apart from that, some of them, such as Azekah, have not been proven to have been significantly populated, let alone having fortifications being built there at the time (cf. Lipschits, Gadot, and Oeming 2017).

Omri (882–871 BCE) is the first more definite figure in the history of Israel, as the founder of the most influential dynasty, seated first in Tirzah and later moving to the newly established power centre in Samaria (1 Kings 16:23–24). According to biblical testimony, his accession was accompanied by unrest, tension, and the elimination of competition. Later, Omri became more widely known by expanding and resisting the strong northern rivals, mainly the Neo-Assyrian Empire, via his offspring, especially Ahab. The name "House of Omri" (*Bīt-Ḫumrī*) is documented in several Assyrian inscriptions (for more detail, see 4.2.5.1), and during the rule of his dynasty, Israel slowly grew to an imposing size. The time of Ahab, and probably also Jehoram, saw the occupation of Transjordan up to the Moab Plateau, including the cities of Jahaz, Ataroth, and possibly Tell er-Rumeith in the Gilead region in the north (Finkelstein and Lipschits 2010; Finkelstein, Lipschits, and Sergi 2012; for a sceptical perspective, see Frevel 2016, 201–2). In the west, Israel may have expanded as far as the Mediterranean; according to maximalist theories, it controlled a territory stretching from the Philistine border in Tell Qasile on the Yarkon River in the south to the Akko area in the north. Some researchers consider a smaller territory demarcated by Mount Carmel in the north and by the Yarkon River in the south—i.e., the Plain of Sharon, located to the east of the northern highlands (cf. Frevel 2016, 197). It is also possible that access to the sea was restricted only to a narrow strip delineated by Mount Carmel in the north and Wadi az-Zarqa south of Tel Dor, which was either a port of Israel (Finkelstein 2013) or fell within the Phoenician sphere of influence. The latter attribution to Israel is based mainly on pottery analysis and the stratigraphy of the Tel Dor locality (Kleiman 2015; Shochat 2017).

It is difficult to determine the extent of the Omride dynasty's influence in the north, since the material culture is very similar to that of the Arameans (cf. Frevel 2016, 190–91; Finkelstein 2013; Maeir 2016b) and the borders frequently shifted (see 4.1.3). According to Berlejung (2010), the first decades (ca. 880–840 BCE) and then the time from Joash to Pekah (802–732 BCE) saw Israel control the areas of Jezreel, Beth-shean, and part of Galilee, whilst the Arameans ruled there in the meantime. In the mid-ninth century BCE, the Omride dynasty by all accounts controlled Jezreel (Ussishkin and Woodhead 1992; 1994; 1997) and Hazor (X), Megiddo (VA–IVB), and Gezer (VIII). Expansion further north did not take place until later; after Assyrian interests were consolidated during the rule of Adad-nirari III (811–783 BCE), Joash took control of Dan (Stratum IVA/III; for stratigraphy see Biran 1994; Greer 2013; Arie 2008) and Hazor (VIII and VII). This is the furthest that Israel's power reached, with border fortresses being constructed in Har Adir, Tel Harashim, En Gev, and in Ramoth-gilead (Finkelstein 2013, 130). Generally, the northern areas mentioned were controlled by Aram Damascus for most of their joint history rather than Israel (de Hulster, Oeming and Sergi 2016; Berlejung, Maeir and

Schüle 2017; Berlejung, Maeir 2019; Dušek, Mynářová 2019; for a more optimistic view see Zwickel 2019 and Thareani 2016). The biblical historiographic depiction of Jeroboam I's influence reaching as far as Dan must be viewed through the lens of a later period: the eighth century BCE and the eponymous king Jeroboam II (cf. Arie 2008; Greer 2017; Römer 2017; 2020).

Construction efforts were an intrinsic part of the Omride cultural and political identity, which is evident in their typical monumental architecture. This includes particularly impressive raised platforms filled with soil. The construction method that secured the platforms consisted of building chamber walls that were "built typically of ashlars in the header-and-stretchers technique" (Finkelstein 2013, 91) Another such monumental architectural feature was a glacis which supported the walls and was surrounded by a dry moat. Omride dynasty architecture is also typified by six-chambered gates, which were previously attributed to Solomon and were dated to the tenth century BCE by earlier research (Mazar 1992; for more on the dating, see 3.1).

Apart from sophisticated fortifications, Israelite settlements are also characterised by ornamental features, such as Proto-Ionian capitals, which later spread into Judah as well (see 6.2 and 6.2.3); some consider these to be local architectonic forms later adopted by the Assyrians (e.g., Lipschits 2011). The economic potential of Israel, which had access to international trade with the Phoenicians and Arameans, is evident in the number of luxury items found mainly in Samaria. The royal compound with a palace on an elevated platform constructed there is "one of the largest Iron Age buildings known in the Levant" (Finkelstein 2013, 91; see the discussion about which Omride dynasty member resided in the palace in Franklin 2003; 2004; 2008). The artefacts found in Samaria include ivory plaques with Egyptian motifs that decorated furniture (Pienaar 2009; Finkelstein 2013). In summary, it is clear that, during Omride rule, Israel became an independent territorial state with sufficient economic capacity to reform what used to be underdeveloped highlands into a great local power and to expand in all cardinal directions. As a kingdom, Israel was able to resist the Arameans for a time, sometimes taking control of parts of their territory, and, in coalition with other kingdoms, able to impede temporarily Assyria's campaign into the southern Levant.

In comparison to Israel, Judah is a less noticeable political entity in the same period. Unlike the settlements in the north and the west, where the Philistine Pentapolis was located, Judean cities were smaller. In the ninth century BCE, Jerusalem covered some ten hectares, and there were no larger cities nearby, leading some to liken it to a Bronze Age city-state (cf. Killebrew 2003). In the Shephelah, the situation is different, since the region was more significantly populated in an earlier period. But how should one connect the western areas and the developments inland and in Jerusalem? These may be separate processes occurring within the interactions between late-Canaanite culture and the Philistines, in which the Judaean Mountains would not be engaged until later (see 3.2.1.4). Even there, however, the settlements are not fortified—as in the case of Arad XII, Beer-sheba VII, and Lachish V (Khirbet Qeiyafa and possibly Beth-shemesh are notable exceptions). On their outer periphery, these localities were enclosed by the posterior sections of buildings but not walls (enclosed settlements). Fortifications were used for later settlements, such as Arad XI, Beer-sheba VI, Lachish IV, and Tel Batash IV (fortified settlements). Such settlements are probably connected to the last third of the ninth century BCE and the possible expansion of Judah into the Shephelah. At the time, Israel's influence weakened due to the activities of Aram Damascus under Hazael, who desired to enlarge his territory. It is in this same period that some researchers place the start of the Kingdom of Judah's rise under Joash, the first Davidide (Sergi 2013). In total, the developments of Israel and Judah are approximately a hundred years apart (cf. Frevel 2016; Berlejung 2010; Schipper 2020a).

Israel and Judah probably first came into contact during the rule of Ahab (871–852 BCE) and Jehoshaphat (868–847 BCE), which may be inferred from a longer section in 1 Kings 20–22. The passage discusses the conflict between Israel and the Arameans under Ben-Hadad I (ca. 900–880 BCE). Though the account is inaccurate, since the reigns of Ahab and Ben-Hadad did not overlap at all, it provides information about the constant struggle for control over disputed areas (in this case, Ramoth-gilead in Transjordan). Furthermore, the text details Jehoshaphat's loyalty to Ahab during a campaign against the Arameans, in which Judah joined forces with Israel, a stronger ally (cf. 1 Kgs 22:4), which by all accounts occupied a part of Transjordan, as proven indirectly by the Mesha stele (COS 2.23). A similar loyalty to Israel is seen during the later campaigns of Jehoram (852–841 BCE), son of Ahab, who was joined by Ahaziah (841 BCE). Both kings likely perished in another conflict with the Arameans, who grew stronger under Hazael, leading to a temporary power shift to Israel's disadvantage (see 4.1.3). The biblical account of this event paints a different image altogether, ascribing the demise of both kings to Jehu's coup d'état (see 4.2.5.1).

4.2.3 ISRAEL AND JUDAH: UNIFICATION ACCORDING TO THE NORTHERN SCENARIO

What evidence is there that supports the theory that Judah's development into a territorial state occured later than that of Israel? The first piece of evidence was provided in the preceding section (4.2.2), by briefly comparing the form and extent of the material culture with the architecture of settlements. Unlike the north, which had imposing constructions that required considerable investment and extensive adjustments, the south is typified by mostly unfortified smaller-size settlements. The same applies to material culture: finds of luxury items and artefacts in ninth-century BCE Judah are much rarer than in the north. The comparison of Jerusalem, the only important settlement in the Judean highlands, with the numerous splendid royal and administrative seats in the north is telling (Naeh 2015; Schroer 2018; Ben-Tor, Ben-Ami and Sandhaus 2012; Finkelstein and Martin 2022).

The second proof consists of ninth-century BCE epigraphic finds, which—apart from the Tel Dan stele written in Aramean (COS 2.39)—concern only Israel. It is possible that the stele mentions Ahaziah, King of Judah (see discussion below). Other texts are exclusively linked to the Omride dynasty in the north: either as the rulers in the way of Assyria's southwestern expansion, or as a kingdom expanding its own influence in Moab in Transjordan (see 4.2.5.1).

Dynastic ties are, in our view, the third piece of evidence, as well as a highly complex key to understanding the relations between Judah and Israel. The Omride dynasty used these ties to secure good political and economic relationships with its neighbours—e.g., with Sidon, by marrying Ahab to Princess Jezebel, daughter of King Ithobaal I (887-856 BCE). The point of view which claims that there were two parallel royal dynasties in Judah and Israel as of the late tenth century BCE will now be confronted with a hypothesis on the dominance of the northern dynasty or dynasties. By all accounts, it was the Omride dynasty that turned Judah into a branch kingdom by using plotted dynastic marriages, tasking members of the large royal family with administering Judah, which would have only become independent later, in the eighth century BCE.

If the United Monarchy did exist, it can be conceivably placed in the ninth and early eighth centuries BCE. This hypothesis is supported by various factors—namely, by epigraphic materials and non-written material culture, as well as by the critical reading of biblical texts. This will be the topic of the following reflections: firstly, in a more general discussion on the nature of literary tradition; and secondly, by focusing on the chronicles of Israelite and Judean kings and their genealogical connections, which make evident a strong link to Israel as the decisive power for over a century of the joint history of the north and south.

We are convinced that these links are verifiable, despite recent attempts to cast doubt on the connection between Judah and Israel in both the 9th and 8th centuries BCE (Gadot, Kleiman, A., and Uziel 2023; cf. Frevel and Čapek 2024).

4.2.4 TRADITIONS: ORIGINAL AND TRANSFORMED

When examining Israel's history and the formation of its identity, which is by no means the same, it is a great challenge to interpret the perspective offered by the most extensive textual source: the Old Testament/Hebrew Bible. Its perspective is predominantly southern, viewing events through a Judean lens, but it also features very rich traditions which originate from elsewhere. In terms of their development, there is a majority consensus: the older traditions had come from the north and had been transformed into new accounts describing a new, different, *collective* Israel (Whisenant 2008; Blum 2012b; Finkelstein 2013; Finkelstein and Römer 2014a; Finkelstein 2020; Na'aman 2020). By these accounts, Israel was born in the south and would absorb the original northern political entity bearing the name in the late eighth century BCE—i.e., the early Iron Age IIC. In this period, Israel composed a collective history going back to its very origins. How are the older, original traditions of the north, sources of "Judah's Bible," documented? And is it possible to claim that this literary ensemble still carries the original "legacy of Israel" (for both terms, see Fleming 2013)?

The above questions can be answered in two parts, which follow a temporal sequence. The first answer is that the important traditions describing the time before the putative golden era of the United Monarchy and the tenth century BCE focus on the north and Israel in matters of geography, topography, family, and cult. The second answer is a modification of the first, confirming that the traditions relating to later periods—starting with Israel's origin as a bona fide territorial state—often came from the north as well, in terms of geographical, topographical, familial, and cultic connections. As for the time of their origin and further editorial modifications, the written forms of both traditions, in their initial versions, date to the same period—i.e., the late ninth century BCE at the earliest (see 4.2.1), and especially the eighth century BCE. Subsequently, the historical context consists of the late eighth and seventh centuries BCE, when the traditions were updated and expanded upon (cf. *Fortschreibung* in German) by the successors and heirs to these traditions in Judah. This process continued through editorial amendments and the establishment of the final composition as late as the sixth century BCE and the Persian period (for further information, see chapters 6 and 7).

4.2.4.1 FROM ABRAHAM TO SAUL

Critical reading of the Hebrew Bible produces various results; among them, the discovery that events said to have occurred in the northern highlands of Israel, where they are likely to have originated, were later described as taking place in the south (i.e., Judah). Judean scribes—who may be considered editors as well as very inventive authors of new stories based on the old (Jamieson-Drake 1991; Davies 1991; Barton 1996; Toorn 2007; Carr 2011; Fleming 2013; Prudký 2015)—used subject matter from the north to form their own traditions. There are clear indications for this, since the subject matter is dominated by northern localities, linked to specific stories, tales, figures, battles, and important meetings of Israel. These literary traditions are very difficult to date, not least due to the multiple editorial changes and amendments. Views of scholars differ greatly: some attempt to determine the time in which the traditions were committed to writing; while others try to ascertain the origin of the preceding preliterary oral traditions, or to establish the dominant editing; and still others seek to identify the period in which the final form of the tradition was recorded, as preserved in the Hebrew Bible.

A northern focus is discernible in the patriarch stories, which follow the Gen. 1-11 accounts of the origins which were composed only later, in the Neo-Babylonian period at the earliest (Dozeman and Schmid 2006; Schüle 2017; Gnuse 2019; Carr 2020). Though it is preceded by later stories about Abraham and the Jacob cycle (Gen 25:19-37:1) – which is the oldest patriarchal narration—and its most original layers are particularly pertinent in showing that the north was the initial context. The purpose of these later stories is to integrate the older Jacob stories into the overall composition about the patriarchs, which is written from a Judean perspective (Blum 1984; 2012b; Finkelstein and Römer 2014a; 2014b; Na'aman 2020; Hensel 2021). Later named Israel (Gen 33:28), Jacob is a figure with geographical and cultic links to the north—specifically, the areas between Bethel and Shechem, as well as the Transjordan localities of Mizpah, Mahanaim, and Penuel. Attempts to date the cycle have yielded very disparate results. Comparing archaeological evidence, geographical connections concerning the possible total size of Israel, and biblical texts, Finkelstein (2013, 141-44) reaches the following conclusion: the original Jacob cycle was committed to writing in the first half of the eighth century BCE, at a time when the existence of developed literature may be presumed; and the earlier preliterary core dates to as early as the tenth century BCE and the Iron Age I (according to low chronology). Finkelstein rules out dating the oral tradition of Jacob to the Iron Age IIA, since there is no geographical information on the newly acquired territories in the Beth-shean and Jezreel Valley areas. Even if the proposed dating of the cycle's origin was different, and the interpretations linked to it were too (for Bethel settlement chronology, see Lipschits 2017), it is hard to cast its original northern context into doubt.

Israel's core traditions include two "founding myths", the first one is the Jacob story and the other is the Exodus from Egypt (Blum 2012a; Brett, Wöhrle 2018). Both traditions are connected to the north, especially Bethel, and probably to the rule of Jeroboam II (against this view see Na'aman 2020). This connection is evidenced by the theme of the Bethel cult of the calf that is found in 1 Kgs 12 and Exod 32. Israel leaving Egypt is mentioned in Hos 12:14, for example; while Amos 5:4-5 discusses Bethel as a central cult site, though now in a critical light (along with Beer-sheba), as an example which act as a deterrent against worship which is considered from a southern perspective to be illegitimate (for this cf. Čapek 2023). However, the beginning of this text features a positive account related to Jacob and Joseph, both of whom stand in the background of the nascent exodus tradition. The original northern context of the traditions is conclusive, though the later editorial activities of Judean authors result in passing a harsh judgment on Israel (Schart 1998; Weingart 2015).

In terms of biblical chronology, the exodus and desert wandering traditions are followed by other stories with their own backgrounds, originating, in some cases, in the north too; consequently, even these narratives are oriented towards the north. After entering Canaan, Israel moves to the city of Ai; offerings are made on Mount Ebal; a pact is struck with Gibeon, which would later become the residence of Saul. Only later do the texts focus on the south; specifically, on confrontations with the kings of Jerusalem, Hebron, Jarmuth, Lachish, and Eglon. The covenant renewal, a constitutive event for Israel, takes place in Shechem (Josh 24). Shiloh is another important location, since it houses the Tent of the Congregation with the Ark of the Covenant. Shiloh is also connected to traditions related to the prophet Samuel (1 Sam 1–3), who is linked with Mizpah, Ramah, and Bethel—i.e., the northern highlands once again. It is not until much later—for example, in the Book of Jeremiah—that Shiloh becomes an example of the judgment passed on Judah (see Jer 26:6; for more, see 5.3.3).

The tradition in the Book of Judges—understandably highly stylised, idealised, and projected into the notions of pre-monarchic Israel—is again tied to Bethel, and to Beth-shean, Taanach, Dor, Gezer, and Hazor further to the north. Deborah, one of the important figures of the book, used to sit between Ramah and Bethel. Geographically, the stories are also connected to Mount Ephraim in the Manasseh region and to Gilead in Transjordan, a site of numerous conflicts with Ammonites. All of the above, again, reflects events geographically and topographically situated in the north, in Israel. In the stories about the origins of the kingdom, there is a special and particularly ambiguous role played by the tribe of Benjamin and its traditional area (see Judg 19–21) which was likely a territory related to the Gibeon Plateau and area of Bethel (see 3.2.2). Likewise, stories about Saul, who is considered Israel's first king, are linked to the same places (Finkelstein 2022; Sergi 2023; cf. Na'aman 2023). These are depicted in a favourable light in the oldest layers, until the later pro-Davidide perspective takes over (cf. Dietrich and Münger 2003; Dietrich 2004), Saul is elected king in Mizpah (*Tell en-Nasbeh*) and dies along with his sons at Mount Gilboa above the Jezreel Valley. Here too, geographical connections to the north obviously predominate. Chapter 3 used the example of two reconstructions of Israel and Judah's origins as nascent political entities to illustrate the long-term controversy concerning the traditions related to Saul and the area of Benjamin, with the majority of scholars taking a more pro-northern stance (see 3.2.2). However, analysing the same archaeological evidence and identical biblical themes, some authors conclude that the Benjamin tradition originated in the south (see 3.2.3).

4.2.4.2 FROM DAVID TO THE END OF THE GOLDEN ERA

Earlier research on the traditions on Saul and David, as documented in Samuel and Kings, distinguished older layers which view the first king positively from newer redactions that criticise Saul instead and feature a clearly pro-Davidide line of reasoning. An imaginary dividing line was drawn between earlier, northern, and later, Judean authors—as well as between attributions of Saul to Israel in the north and David to the south, i.e., Judah and Jerusalem (for discussion see Weiser 1966; Dietrich and Münger 2003; Dietrich 2004; Veijola 1975; Rückl 2016; cf. Ber 2015).

The topic of dating involves several different approaches. Some scholars date the origins of these traditions—often in their reconstructed, preliterary phases—and place them almost concurrently with the events depicted in them (Bietenhard 1998; Vermeylen 2010; cf. Čapek 2010b). Others attempt to prove the presence of Deuteronomistic influence in the stories, which generally does not consider the existence of the northern kingdom anymore (but cf. Finkelstein 2022); consequently, the earliest point for dating these traditions is the late eighth century BCE (Kratz 2005; cf. the overview in Römer 2006). More recent research further expands upon the development and editing of these traditions, casting some previous hypotheses into doubt (Fischer 2004; Hutton 2009; Fleming 2013; Knauf and Guillaume 2016; Wright 2014; Auld 2017). The same applies to the two extensive literary compositions in the Books of Samuel and Kings: The History of David's Rise to Power (1 Sam 16:14–2 Sam 5:10) and The Succession to the Throne of David (2 Sam 9–20 and 1 Kgs 1–2). It is presumed that these are not two separate traditions (or blocks), but the results of an editorial process with multiple layers, some of which show strong pro-northern tendencies, including a surprisingly crucial role played by David, a figure usually linked to the south (Rost 1926; Fischer 2004; Adam 2007; Rückl 2016; Auld and Eynikel 2010; Hensel 2022).

David's connection to the north was elaborated on in a remarkable way by Daniel Fleming (2013), who reviewed his original claim that "the David narrative was Judean at every level, though perhaps very old at the core" (105). He reached the conclusion that the story contains "little sign of deuteronomistic handling [. . .] and political landscape unfamiliar to seventh-century Judah," while being "overwhelmingly preoccupied with David's reign over Israel" (ibid.). In this new interpretation of these biblical traditions, Fleming concludes that "from the start, David is in competition for rule over Israel, and Judah is only a footnote" (ibid., 101). The issue is that biblical texts (for possible alternatives, see 3.2.3) are the main source corroborating such a concept of David's rule over Israel, so it is necessary to identify the period which reflects the very first phases of the stories' formation.

Apart from biblical texts, the search for this period may be based on the analysis of ninth-century BCE Israel under Omride rule (see 4.2.2) and a basic notion of the development of literature throughout the region (see 4.2.1). According to Fleming, the principal texts documenting the northern origin are chapters 12 and 16 of the Book of 1 Kings; the former discusses the division of the kingdom after the death of Solomon, and the latter treats the rise of Omri. Using identically constructed lines of reasoning, both illustrate the northern origin of David-related themes, including the Absalom cycle (2 Sam 13–14; 15–20); these themes would later be incorporated into the Solomon stories (2 Sam 11–12; 1 Kgs 1–2). The most important texts for such an interpretation describe the revolts of Absalom and Sheba (2 Sam 15–20; here cf. Sergi 2023); however, some scholars date them to the seventh century BCE at the earliest and, along with other editorial amendments, to the exilic period (Kratz 2005; Römer 2005). Fleming's reconstruction presumes an earlier historical setting for these themes—to a time when Israel existed (i.e., before the fall of Samaria in 722 BCE) and David was a part of it.

Fleming is not alone in noticing that David's story has identical aspects with the texts that connect the power struggle and the rise of the Omride dynasty in the north; this northern tradition is also reflected in 1 Kgs 12. David's original connection to Israel is also corroborated by highly north-oriented geographical and topographical information, as well as by probably older traditions depicting the war between the "House of Saul" and "House of David" (2 Sam 3), which make no mention of Judah. Accompanied by Ahinoam of Jezreel and Abigail, widow of Nabal of Carmel—i.e., women with northern family ties—the latter king's connection to Hebron (cf. 2 Sam 5:1–3; esp.

David is king (2 Sam. 15–20)
- Absalom's revolt defeated
- Sheba's revolt defeated
- rule over Israel

Omri is king (1 Kings 16)
- Zimri defeated
- victory over his rival Tibni
- royal residence constructed in Samaria
- rule over Israel

Jeroboam I is king (1 Kings 12)
- conflict (with Rehoboam)
- success (Adoram killed)
- residence built in Shechem
- rule over Israel

Fig. 11. Reconstruction of the northern origin of the oldest David-related stories (based on Fleming 2013)

Fischer 2004) also points to the significance of the north. Naturally, David is linked to Judah and Jerusalem in the final form of Kings and Samuel; however, Fleming thinks that the older material "preserves plausible memories of Israelite collective politics because these memories inhere in material that knows David only as a king of Israel" (Fleming 2013, 98).

The idea of memories reflecting older historical events is admissible (Fleming, 2013; cf. Knauf and Guillaume 2016); but how far do they reach, and are they truly trustworthy and historically accurate? The geographic realities behind the Absalom cycle, one of the oldest themes of the Books of Samuel, likely overlap with the political terrain of eighth-century BCE Israel as ruled by Jeroboam II; consequently, one must pose questions about David as a king whose rule is projected into the tenth and early ninth centuries BCE. Despite the more optimistic present-day reconstructions of the origins of the "House of David," or of Judah being formed from tribal communities as early as the turn of the Iron Ages I and IIA (recently esp. Sergi 2017b; 2017c; 2023), it must be noted these are largely hypothetical attempts to harmonise later written testimonies, as well as scarce and relatively ambiguous archaeological evidence, and place these into a historical context (see, e.g., Ben-Shlomo 2019).

In our view, more solid ground is not found until the ninth century BCE, which saw the formation of Israel as a territorial state and, towards the end of the century, if not later, of Judah as well. Their traditions—first oral (but not necessarily) and later written—have more in common than expected, due to the nature of the formation of these territorial states. The key factors related to this are the characteristic dominant position of the north (as mentioned above) and the strong dynastic ties to the south, maintained by nepotism and a marriage policy (cf. Frevel 2016, 157). It is conceivable that the David traditions had genuinely originated in the north, and it was only later that they were redacted in order to function as a dynastic construct of the south promoted by the Davidides to mainly oppose Israel. Another option, suggested by Wolfgang Oswald (2009, 43), for example, is to make a historical link between the origin of the story of David's rise to power and events taking place as late as the last third of the eighth century BCE. According to him, this period, in which Judah had already been centralised during Hezekiah's rule, saw the writing of court stories that documented the structural shift during Jerusalem's transition to being the centre of a regional power for the first time, after the fall of the north.

4.2.4.3 ISRAEL'S PRESENCE IN THE TRADITIONS OF JUDAH—HOW, WHEN AND WHY?

The presence of northern traditions and authors in the background of biblical texts leads to the question of *how* and *when* these materials came to the south and *in what way* they were incorporated into the southern traditions that are included in the Hebrew Bible as the Scripture of Judah. The most common explanation is linked to the fall of Samaria in 722 BCE, when refugees brought these traditions to Jerusalem after the fall of the northern kingdom (Finkelstein 2015; but cf. Na'aman 2014). Before that, northern biblical traditions—such as the story of the exodus, the Jacob cycle, and the Book of Saviours—are thought to have been written and preserved in Iron Age IIB (eighth century BCE) Bethel (Finkelstein and Singer-Avitz 2009, 44; but cf. Na'aman 2020), most likely before the fall of the northern kingdom. These traditions were likely established and committed to writing in the late ninth and eighth centuries BCE; at that time, Aramean-Israelite relations changed in light of the campaign led by Adad-nirari III of Assyria. The influence of the Assyrians increased, as they conquered Aram Damascus, Tyre, Sidon, and Arwad; at the same time, Israel ruled by Joash (802–787 BCE) and then Jeroboam II (787–747 BCE) enjoyed economic prosperity, the development of literature (Finkelstein and Sass 2013), and the kingdom's territorial expansion reached its peak (see 4.1.3).

An explanation for the presence of northern themes in Judaean traditions is proposed by the so called *compromise model*, which is a reaction to the question of how older themes could become part of the "Bible of Judah" (Fleming 2013) which is usually critical towards Israel. The model presumes a mass influx of fugitives to Judah after the fall of Samaria in 722 BCE (cf. 1 Kings 17); in Judah, there is provable demographic growth due to the significant increase in the built-up area of Jerusalem, mainly in the area of the western hill. According to the model's champions, Israelites were an important segment of the population, which is why the "northern traditions that were cherished by what was now a significant part of the population of Judah needed to be absorbed" (Finkelstein 2013, 157; cf. Fleming 2013; Hutton 2009) and could not be ignored. Part of the compromise was the acceptance of Saulide traditions on the condition that they were made subservient to the traditions about David, who became the first of the "only legitimate rulers of all Israel and the Jerusalem Temple ... the only legitimate cult-place for all *Bene Israel*" (Finkelstein 2013, 157).

Alternatively, the political and demographic trends in the eighth century BCE may be viewed as more gradual, with the fall of Samaria not being an absolute watershed moment, but rather one of the many events, albeit important, that took place. According to this scenario, Jerusalem's growth was not necessarily a result of the mass exodus of northern Israelites, which explains the lack of unambiguous documents (what part of Jerusalem's material culture from this period is demonstrably "Israelite"?); in fact, Jerusalem's development took place earlier (Knauf and Guillaume 2016, 110; cf. Frevel 2016, 244–45). One of the scholars casting the fall of Samaria into doubt is

Na'aman (2007b), who claims that the growth of Jerusalem as an important political centre and the development of the surrounding area started as early as the ninth century BCE. In his view, this earlier growth occurred due to the expansion of Aram Damascus under Hazael (843/842-803 BCE), with Israel's influence over Judah decreasing, and Judah becoming more independent. This gradual process comprises of the construction efforts after the fall of Samaria in 722 BCE as well as the later growth of the city following the Assyrian invasion of 701 BCE. In this period, people came to the city from areas in the Shephelah conquered by the Assyrians, including Lachish (a comparison of pottery from the Broad Wall in Jerusalem with that of Lachish Stratum III led to excessive focus on Hezekiah as the only putative extender of the city).

This interpretation that claims that the fall of Samaria does not have to be the universal key to understanding the transposition of northern traditions onto Jerusalem may be further elaborated upon. It is likely that the process of passing down and disseminating literary traditions was more gradual and did not occur purely in reaction to a turning point in history. Additionally, if Judah was indeed a branch kingdom of Israel, it is probable that the northern traditions were used in the south even earlier, as dominant historiographic memories present in the royal court of Jerusalem administered by the offspring of the Omrides, who, up to a certain time, felt no need to amend them in any way. Moreover, Bethel, the presumed centre of preserved northern traditions, is located a mere twenty kilometres from Jerusalem (Samaria's distance from Bethel is double that).

The nature of the traditions—and especially their independent southern tone—is linked to the rise of Judah as an independent state. Judah seceded in the eighth century BCE, probably under Ahaz (735-716 BCE), but perhaps even sooner (see Amaziah's efforts for independence in the battle against Joash at Beth-shemesh; cf. 2 Kgs 14:8-14). At the time, a dynastic self-determination arose in the south, based on the retrospective construct of the Davidide line (contra Na'aman 2013 and Sergi 2013). However, the line is possibly rooted, and has its dynastic origins, in the north (see 4.2.5). During this period, Israel and Judah were closely linked, which is evident from the permeability of borders, cultures, and religions—even though the later transformations of biblical tradition made a conscious effort to weaken and conceal these ties by emphasising the role of borders as well as cultural and religious habits, attempting to allow Judah to shine against the backdrop of a negative depiction of Israel. The same scenario would be repeated later, in the Persian period (539-333 BCE), when Judah tried to set itself apart from its stronger sibling in the northern province of Samaria by using later literary compositions of a polemical and historiographical nature (see chapter 7).

In our view, the compromise model is also controversial in terms of biblical—albeit transformed—traditions that are highly critical of the north. It is difficult to imagine the offspring of the fugitives from Samaria reading or listening to stories that describe their original homeland as a place with no redeeming qualities, from the illegitimate cult (including the accusations of ever-present Baalism) to the corrupt political elite. The presence of Israelite traditions in the themes of the Hebrew Bible must have a different explanation. Israelites from Samaria could not be expected to accept views that were critical of the north, and this is even more likely concerning a source which intended to confront them, despite coming from the north originally.

4.2.5 THE CHRONICLES OF THE KINGS—A SPECIAL CASE

As stated above, the existence of Israel as a territorial state is fully documented at the end of the first half of the ninth century BCE, the earliest period concerning which it is possible to carry out a convincing and yet balanced synthesis of material culture, epigraphs, and biblical texts. One may step back into earlier times; however, the bigger the step, the lesser the possibility of corroborating the events of a provably later period that are referred to in biblical texts. This fact must be emphasised regardless of the undoubtedly remarkable efforts of both older and more recent scholarship to create historical reconstructions of tenth-century BCE Israel and Judah (e.g., Lemaire 1981a; Halpern 1981; Na'aman 1996b; Finkelstein 2013; Sergi 2023).

The entirely disparate theories about late eleventh- and tenth-century BCE Israel and Judah that are introduced above (see 3.2.2 and 3.2.3) prove that a high degree of hypotheticality is required to link archaeological evidence with written testimonies concerning the late Iron Age I and Iron Age IIA. Thus, contemporary research has entered a markedly wilder heuristic climate; in the past, the period was reconstructed in accordance with a simple reading of biblical texts, and could be sufficiently commented on as follows:

Nothing is more characteristic of the northern state than its extreme internal instability. Where Judah stuck with the Davidic line through the whole of her history, Israel's throne changed hands by violence thrice in the first fifty years.
(Bright 1981, 238).

To this day, the lists of kings have often been considered a reliable historical foothold, and the chronicles of kings have been interpreted as the oldest source on the early history of Israel and Judah. The lists seem to provide a trustworthy base for the critical evaluation of the description of related events. For instance, Finkelstein (2013, 65) believes that "the fact that the Hebrew Bible accurately records the order and length of reign of the northern kings does not mean that the descriptions of the events in their days are fully historical." Consequently, he proposes that "each story should be studied on its own terms according to archaeological information and text exegesis." This applies especially "in view of the strong ideology of the Judean authors, that is, the tendency to blacken and delegitimise the northern kingdom and its kings."

The first claim above on the accuracy of the order of the kings in these lists and the lengths of their reigns seems unquestionable. However, one must still consider that the chronological facts about monarchs do not have to be—and are not, as will be demonstrated later—truly accurate. The Chronicles of Israelite and Judean kings are also typified by a very casual treatment of the available facts and an emphasis on specific political and religious interests which lie in the backgrounds of the chronologies, whether they concern harmonisation, expansion, adaptation, or a vast transformation. Judean authors did not intend to provide an exact account of historically accurate events; at any rate, they probably did not even have the necessary sources to do so. The purpose of the chronicles that they introduced was to describe the way events had occurred according to their own politically and religiously charged views. This was part of efforts to harmonise the chronicles of multiple Israelite kings, whose existence was provable in an earlier historical period, with the chronicle of Judean rulers, who had entered history later but who would become more than peers of their northern counterparts.

One of the indicators of harmonisations and very inventive chronicle adaptations is the number of rulers in both kingdoms, which totals twenty in each, even though Judah existed for 140 years longer: the average length of any given king's reign is seventeen years in the south, while it is almost half that in the north. Uzziah is an exception to the rule, since the editors of the Books of Kings describe his rule as lasting for fifty-two years, albeit with him co-ruling with Jotham towards the end (see 5.3.1).

These chronicles are typified by what Graeme Auld terms *historical patterning*; their primary concern is not to provide an accurate history but to give accounts of events with emphasis on what should be considered commensurable. Commensurability is linked to a process of evaluating the actions of specific historical figures and royal dynasties as right or wrong, with the aim of setting things right. For example, one may consider the parallel reigns of Athaliah in the south and Jezebel in the north (2 Kgs 9–11). Connected to Ahab, both are pictures of depravity, characterised by wrongful actions in terms of politics and religion (murdering the competition, falling under the spell of Baalism, and eliminating the Lord's prophets). Consequently, both queens suffer violent deaths and must be succeeded by new dynasties: the Nimshide dynasty in the north and the Davidides in the south, founded by Jehu and Joash respectively (cf. Auld 2015; 2017). The more probable course of historical events, which does not correlate with the biblical account, will be discussed later (see 4.2.5.1).

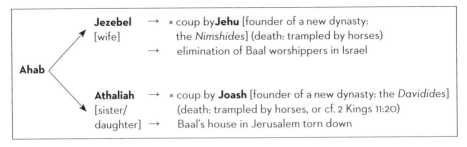

Fig. 12. Historical patterning using the examples of Jezebel, Athaliah, Jehu, and Joash

Studying the chronicles further, one cannot resist the impression that the successions of individual kings are crafted from two perspectives: either with a limited amount of information; or with a tremendous sense of the wider context (intertextuality), drama, and a more or less hidden plot, which only becomes apparent in time—all of which imbues these texts with the credibility of a "historical" account (Čapek 2016; cf. Weingart 2019). To increase the credibility of Judean kings, the chronicles, as it is well known, identify their mothers. Some interpret this phenomenon as analogous to Hittite sacrificial lists—i.e., by referring to the cultic sphere—whilst others are sceptical of this interpretation. For example, Rückl (2015) notes that the *Sitz im Leben* of the chronicles is not in the cultic sphere but must be sought in periods much later than those depicted in the texts.

Based on the above, Finkelstein's views on the reliability of the succession and rule length of individual kings included in the chronicles must be reviewed. Even seemingly accurate accounts, which might appear historically reliable, conceal specific theological and ideological interests that are expressed in two ways: by making claims as to the legitimacy or illegitimacy of a specific king's actions; and by moving the king through time and space. Even Finkelstein himself does not adhere to this claim within his reconstructions, as he shifts Israelite and Judean kings not only in accordance with low chronology but also due to a different conception of historical reconstruction to that offered by the chronicles themselves (see 3.2.2).

It is likely that the chronicles of the Israelite kings are based on older literary sources available to the authors of the Books of Kings (Lemaire and Halpern 2010). Since they have not survived, one can only speculate about their nature. These sources probably formed a basic outline, and further literary adaptations would later allow for narrative expansion, with multiple adjustments and editorial amendments containing "ideological restrictions" (cf. Hutzli 2015, 192). Efforts to reconstruct older preliterary traditions are questionable (see discussion in Otto 2001; Würthwein 2008; Robker 2012; Hasegawa 2012). The Books of Kings refer to documents termed the Chronicles of the Kings of Judah in relation to southern kings and the Chronicles of the Kings of Israel in relation to northern rulers. The existence of such chronicles cannot be ruled out; however, there is another way to view the concurrent chronological successions of Judean and Israelite kings, as documented in biblical texts. These successions betray aspects that cast a different light on the assumed authenticity of the chronologies, as well as their prior histories as described in the stories about the United Monarchy. Let us now review some of these:

- The division into the individual lines of Judean and Israelite kings depicted in a synchronous manner is preceded by a golden age of unity that comes to a dramatic end (see 1 Kings 11 for the theological reasoning and fulfilment).
- The division thesis has a formative function; without it, the individual histories of Judah and Israel would not exist.
- The origins are constructed in retrospect, using popular etymologisations of very similar names of two kingdom founders (Rehoboam means "enlarger of the people," or more loosely, "one who gives space" [in Judah]; Jeroboam means "one who contends with the people" [i.e., with Judah, but doubtlessly also with his own people in the north].
- Events are historised with the first kings' eponyms, as well as narratively: as a drama of endless conflicts between competing territorial entities and, especially, inside Israel itself. See, for example, the story of Baasha killing Nadab, son of Jeroboam I, and exterminating the entire dynasty of Jeroboam (which, in effect, should not continue at all; however, the chronicles refer to Jeroboam throughout). Baasha himself becomes the object of Jehu's prophecy that everyone from "his city" will be eaten by dogs (1 Kgs 16:4). Though Baasha still resides in Tirzah, the prophecy targets Ahab and his dynasty (see the death of Jezebel in 2 Kgs 9:11–37).
- Events and temporal settings are harmonised to emphasise important aspects and motives. Equally, the exact historical backgrounds of some events and temporal settings are defocused to underline alternative historical scenarios (for example, see Ahab's battle against Ben-Hadad in 1 Kgs 20).
- Northern kings are stigmatised, to make their wickedness apparent (more or less all of them, although some are emphasised, such as Jeroboam I, Ahab, and, later, Ahaz and especially Manasseh; for this see esp. Frevel 2019); or provisionally glorified, since their actions go against their people (Jehu being the textbook example). Furthermore, their historical importance is withheld or marginalised (Ahab and his role in the anti-Assyrian coalition; Israel's growth under Jeroboam II).
- Judean historiography treats the key figures of the northern traditions very loosely. Some are used to establish the division myth (Jeroboam I); others to foreground the deplorability of Israel's actions.

The conception of Israelite and Judean histories in biblical texts is formed in accordance with specific national self-determination based on the southern agenda. Despite the possible existence of older chronicles and other sources, these histories are mainly *standardised fiction* (cf. Frevel 2016, 177–78), including the paradigmatically ideal joint overture of the United Monarchy, which gives birth to two equal nations. According to Frevel (2016, 151), the name of Jeroboam offers a good starting point for the composition of a history which depicts the southern Kingdom of Judah as the opponent to the dominant northern Kingdom of Israel from the very beginning, turning the real course of history upside down. The king's name, denoting "one who contends with the people," was probably used in shaping the literary character of this despised founder of Israel (i.e., Jeroboam I), and a southern opponent was created who would offer his people better prospects, as the "enlarger of the people".

As for the historical reconstruction of the growth of literary traditions that relate more to these fictitious origins, it must be emphasized that the true topic is historical division, which is retrojected into the late tenth century BCE—the Iron Age IIA. Judah becomes independent in the eighth century BCE, during the rule of Jeroboam II, or later (see Na'aman 2013 and Sergi 2013 for the earlier interpretation). At the time, the southern kingdom, still with dynastic ties to the north, amended traditions that were probably shared by both kingdoms and emancipated them from the northern dynasties. It is impossible to determine exactly when this separation occurred. However, one may presume that efforts for independence were continuous, taking the form of court intrigues and attempted coups likely aided by Israel's competitors—mainly the Arameans and Assyrians. The fall of Samaria was merely the conclusion of this process.

In contrast to the compromise model, a better explanation of the reasons for, and nature of, Israel's presence in Judean traditions is that Judah took form as an independent kingdom by drawing from the older traditions of

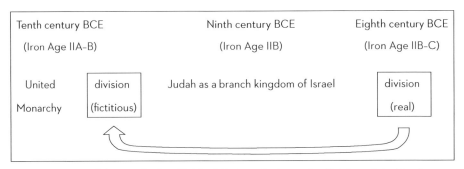

Fig. 13. Diagram of the standardised biblical fiction relating to the division of the kingdoms

the north (cf. 4.2.4.3). It seems unlikely that the fugitives from the north after the fall of Samaria would, albeit in the second or third generation, adopt a southern identity based on a radical negation of Israel. By contrast, the southern ruling class, though deriving its standing from the dominant north, could continue as a dissenting branch of the Omride dynasty, creating its own historiographic composition on the complex relations between Israel and Judah that clearly prioritised the south. Furthermore, what was the nature of migration from the north, and did the fall of Samaria itself influence events in Judah at all? Judah's gradual rise—and slow emancipation from Israel—appears a more likely scenario. The formation of Judah's own history was also enabled by the availability of the traditions in nearby Bethel (similarly, cf. Knauf and Guillaume 2016, 110).

Particularly notable in the chronicles are the great similarities between northern and southern kings in terms of names as well as the ruling periods linked to them. Scholars usually focus on synchronisms and specify the ruling periods of individual kings in accordance with either 'shorter' chronology' or 'longer' chronology (for discussion see Begrich 1929; Thiele 1944; Jepsen 1953; Hasegawa 2012; Hentschel 2014; Frevel 2016). Apart from the historical verifiability of the chronicles, which is questionable from the origins of the division to the rise of the Omride dynasty, their emphasis on genealogical continuity also performs another important function (Hasegawa 2019; Weingart 2019). In biblical texts, the genealogy of Judah is presented as equally ancient as that of Israel. Due to the visible similarity, or even correspondence, of the names of ninth-century BCE rulers, it may be assumed that this is, again, largely standardised fiction, in which historical facts are a basis for inventing a comprehensive account which details the equal histories of Israel and Judah. If there were two separate dynastic lines, what is the explanation for the identity or similarity of some names? The fiction is construed using temporal harmonisations and by doubling certain names of rulers; consequently, the chronology of Judah becomes continuous, relating to the very origins via the myth of the historical division of a once-united monarchy.

As for Israel and Judah, a strong kinship can only be assumed on the basis of literary fabrications of their origins, not on the basis of historically documentable facts. Older research traced the south's northern family ties to as early as the United Monarchy (Bright 1959; Hayes and Miller 1977; Jagersma 1982). Historically, however, family relationships are identified in a later period—the mid-ninth century BCE at the earliest. In the extended Omride dynasty, biblical texts depict Ahaziah as the son of Jehoram; however, he may also be the brother of Jehoram of the north and grandson of Ahab. Athaliah is identified as the mother of Ahaziah of Judah in 1 Kings 22:51, but according to Frevel (2016, 160), it would not be unusual for this kinship type to be a construct for legitimising a dynasty.

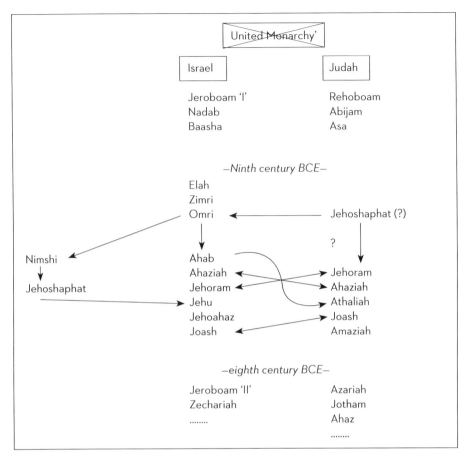

Fig. 14. Reconstruction of the relationship between the chronicles of the kings of Israel and Judah

Other aspects which support the theory that intensive chronicle-writing was a tool to legitimise the antiquity of the southern royal line include double occurrences of the same name (Čapek 2010b; 2014). This is confirmed by the fact that the names appear at roughly the same time, raising the question of whether they describe the same people (Ahaziah ↔ Ahaziah; Jehoram ↔ Jehoram; probably also Joash ↔ Joash, and maybe a similarly crafted literary "Judean" Jehoshaphat; see 4.2.5.1). The double occurrence may be simply explained by the existence of two bearers of the same name; another, more likely, explanation is that only one person existed, a member of the Omride dynasty who administered both kingdoms; while the third explanation is a combination of the two—that there were two people in the wider web of Israelite dynastic ties, which the north used to take control of Judah and Jerusalem. The view which regards this dynastic construction as historicising

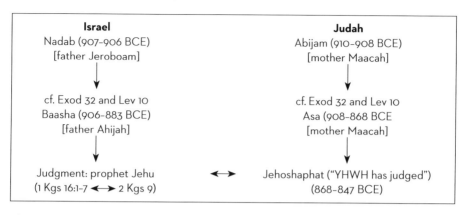

Fig. 15. Dynastic construction in 1 Kgs 15

fiction is further supported by the similarity of other names: Ahaziah and Jehoahaz are the same names written in reverse.

The ingenuity of this contrastive composition is illustrated in 1 Kgs 15; this passage mentions Abijam and Asa, two Judean kings, and Nadab and Baasha, two Israelite kings. The first pair ruled approximately in the same period, and the kings' names refer to a broader and doubtlessly intentional intertextual link in biblical historiography (see below). The names of the other two, Asa and Baasha, are almost identical (similarly in the Septuagint).

References to ancestors play an important role. The mothers of Judean kings are included to confirm the continuity of the family connection to David, the founder of the dynasty, which is why 1 Kgs 15:3 has Maacah as the mother of King Abijah, daughter of Absalom, son of David. Any possible negative evaluation of the southern kings is eventually mitigated by a positive one or a reference to David's positive heritage overall, of which the kings are part (see verses 4 and 14-15 in the same chapter). By contrast, the fathers of Israelite kings are given instead of mothers: Nadab's father is named as Jeroboam I, the embodiment of the very worst things imaginable; Ahijah is given for Baasha, who ascends to power in a revolt, killing his predecessor during conflict with the Philistines. This dynasty's continuity is intentionally weakened here, and the relations between Israel and Judah are deliberately depicted as being more or less characterised by constant war. Judah enjoys success in the conflict, arresting the expansion of its northern neighbour with the help of Ben-Hadad; by contrast, Israel meets with failure not only in confrontations with Judah, but also with the Philistines who are likely to have occupied Gibbethon.

The composition of 1 Kgs 15 features an obvious anachronism, in having Ben-Hadad, the treaty ally (v. 19), defeat Israel in areas that were, by all accounts, Aramean at the time (for this see 4.1.2. and 4.1.3.). These areas may only be considered Israelite after Hazael's retreat and the growth of the northern kingdom's power—at the turn of the ninth and eighth centuries BCE (see 4.1.3). Transitioning into the next chapter, the conclusion includes a general judgment passed on Israel through the prophet Jehu, foreshadowing the extermination of the Omride dynasty by Jehu in the second half of the ninth century BCE (again, an interesting and probably deliberate coincidence of names; cf. 1 Kgs 16:1–7; 2 Kgs 9). The section concerning this judgment evokes the name of Jehoshaphat (868–847 BCE), another Judean king of the Davidide line and son of Asa. Since his name means "YHWH is the judge," and the rule of its bearer remarkably coincides with the time of Ahab (871–852 BCE), one may assume the name was artificially created in the narratively expanded Judean chronology (see 1 Kgs 22:1–8, 41–51), to complete the royal parallel to the growing power of the Omride dynasty in the first half of the ninth century BCE.

This may also be a purposeful rearranging of the family ties of Israelite kings, so that Jehoshaphat is the father of Jehoram (and father of Jehu!). This could be the same Jehoram as was married to Athaliah, sister of Ahab (sometimes considered his daughter), who entered into marriage to strengthen the hold over the branch kingdom in the south—and this would explain her completely negative evaluation (see below). The authors of southern-edited texts undoubtedly did not like to hear of Judah being so dependent. Consequently, Athaliah becomes a contrastive figure for the rise of Joash as "a lamp for him [David] and his descendants forever" (2 Kgs 8:19), who purifies the religion, restores the temple, and starts the gradual rise of the independent dynasty of Judean kings.

Returning to the names of Nadab and Abijah, the deliberate work of the authors of the text under discussion's composition is again obvious. The pair's names allude to the narration about the sons of Aaron who behaved improperly (Lev 10). There is another intertextual link in the reference to Exod 32 and its story of the golden calf, linking Aaron to Jeroboam I, who introduces the cult of the calf in Bethel and Dan (1 Kgs 12:28–29; for the historical reconstruction, see 5.3.3). The information above may lead one to assume that these chronicles are not historically accurate. This leads Frevel, for example, to conclude that the synchronic data on the royal houses of Judah and Israel were largely based on a combinatorial construction and that they were compiled later as an idealized retrospective of the very beginnings of two concurrent royal dynasties (2016, 160; cf. Sláma 2015).

Based on the above considerations, we conclude that four stages of Israelite and Judean history can be identified, not only as they are presented in the Old Testament texts, but also as they can be hypothetically reconstructed with the help of non-biblical epigraphic and archaeological evidence:

4. THE FIRST TRUE UNIFICATION AND THE FIRST TRUE DIVISION (IRON AGE IIA-B)

> I. The paradigmatically ideal tenth century BCE and the time of the United Monarchy.
>
> II. The literary fabrication of the late tenth century BCE division in the time of Jeroboam I and Rehoboam.
>
> III. Semi-historical origins in the ninth century BCE. South-oriented historiography complements historically verifiable events and people with materials on two equal concurrent kingdoms of Israel and Judah. The latter kingdom is subordinate to Israel via elaborate dynastic ties.
>
> IV. Historically verifiable existence of the kingdoms: originally Israel's branch kingdom, Judah slowly emancipates itself from the influence of its northern neighbour, becoming fully independent. It is likely that this process was led by the influential offspring of the northern dynasties of ninth-century BCE Israel, who created their own south-oriented self-determination in Jerusalem, linked to the fictitious figure of David. The branch of the Omrides, the Nimshide dynasty, possibly originating from Tel Rehov (Mazar and Panitz-Cohen 2020; Sergi and Koch 2023; Lee-Sak 2023), reacts to the changes in the north (revolt of Jehu the Nimshide) by deposing Athaliah and using their common offspring to create a new genealogical line starting with Joash (contra Na'aman 2016b; cf. Barrick 2001; Klein 2014; Sergi 2015a), in which there could be no one from the Omride north, much less a ruler who inherits from their mother (Bench 2014).

Fig. 16. Four formation stages of the kingdoms of Judah and Israel

It must be noted that the literary and historical stages of the formation of the chronicles of the kings over Israel and Judah given above are hypothetical. This hypothesis is based on an overall analysis of the available material culture, epigraphic material (for its importance, see 4.2.5.1), and biblical texts, in which there is a clear ideological tendency (albeit one that is highly difficult to interpret) that must be taken into account. In light of what is known about the northern dynasty of Omri and their presumed Nimshidide relatives (also from the north), the sharp distinction between north and south as described in the biblical texts proves historically problematic, though more than what is understandable from a purely southern perspective. Related to this is the question of how to understand the phrase "House of David" when the relatives of the northern kings ruling in Jerusalem derived their dynastic legitimacy from it? As stated above (4.2.4.2), it is conceivable that the traditions about David had originated in the north, and it was only later that they were edited into a southern dynastic construct enforced by the new Davidide dynasty, whose main agenda was to define Judah in contrast to Israel. Should that be the case, then even the mention of "Ahaziah, son of Jehoram king of the House of David" on the Tel Dan stele (see COS 2.39) must be viewed in a different light (cf. Leonard-Fleckman 2016).

4.2.5.1 THE CASE OF JEHU AND JOASH

The biblical account of Jehu (841–814 BCE) and his grandson Joash (803–787 BCE), kings of Israel, is an example of creative rewriting (see 4.2.4). Traditionally, the two are considered part of the Jehuite period (841–750 BCE), which is preceded by the early period (922–885 BCE) and the Omride period (885–841 BCE; according to Younger 2007). Jehu is the first member of the Jehuite dynasty or the Nimshi dynasty, which seized power in the 841 BCE coup, establishing a completely new dynasty that would exist until the killing of Zechariah, the last king in this dynastic line, in 747 BCE. Such a historical reconstruction is mainly based on the biblical texts related to the period in question. However, the dynasty that succeeded the Omrides may be viewed quite differently, as will soon be discussed. Considering the Jehuites role in and continuation of the Omride dynasty, an alternative reconstruction poses two principal questions: (a) Why do biblical texts use the name "House of Ahab" to describe the "House of Omri"—i.e., why do they sideline the latter appellation, common in the ninth century BCE and used in many Assyrian texts (see 4.2.5.1.1)?; (b) Why are Jehu and Joash the only kings in the entire history of Israel with double patronymics (see 4.2.5.1.2)?

4.2.5.1.1 THE HOUSE OF AHAB AND THE HOUSE OF OMRI

The common interpretation of the Jehuite dynasty becomes less convincing when confronted with Assyrian texts; in all of them, Jehu (^{m}ia-a-ú, or ^{m}ia-ú-a) is described as the son (mār) of Omri (DUMU ^{m}ḫu-u-ri-i; refer to COS 2.113D, 2.113C, 2.113E, and 2.113F), who pays tribute (ma-da-tu) to the Assyrians. Despite the relative vagueness of the term, it must be noted that, in relation to a specific person, Assyrian texts only use it in Jehu's case. Of twenty documented references, four are linked to this ruler. The remaining texts refer to the land of Israel (KUR sir-'-la-a-a), Samaria (KUR Sa-me-ri-na-a-a), the land of Omri (KUR ḫu-u-ri-i), the city of Samaria (^{uru}Sa-me-ri-na-a), and the land of the House of Omri (^{kur}Bīt-Ḫu-um-ri-a; see the overview of occurrences in Lamb 2007). Since all other references are connected to geographical contexts, (the KUR logogram represents mātu, "a land," and the URU logogram refers to ālu, "a city"), one may assume that the meaning of the DUMU mār logogram linked to Jehu is literal and that it may be translated as "son" or, more generally, "descendant," therefore functioning as a patronymic. Assyrian historiography describes Jehu as the son of the "House of Omri" (Bīt-Ḫumrī), a ruler related to the Omride dynasty.

In biblical texts, Ahab and the Omride dynasty are the exemplary contrasts to Jehu (Würthwein 2008; cf. Frevel 2019). This king is characterised as part of a different, new dynasty and an enforcer of God's will through the killing of not just Jehoram, son of Ahab (2 Kgs 9:24), but all his descendants

(2 Kgs 10:1-17). The violent "clean-up" in Israel also included the extermination of all prophets, priests, and followers of Baal (2 Kgs 10:18-29). The literary adaptation in the Books of Kings combines these political and religious transformations. Despite the attempts to date the "original story of Jehu" (Minokami 1989)[3] to an earlier time—though it is partially based on historical memories (and very old memories at that, according to some researchers; see Lemaire and Halpern 2010, 123-53)—the depiction must be interpreted as the result of an intensive editorial effort, which started later and whose final form dates to the exilic and postexilic periods (Gugler 1996; Otto 2001; Hasegawa 2012; Robker 2012; Čapek 2010c; 2014). This is supported not only by the phraseology used and shifts of genre throughout the composition, but also by the historically inaccurate mentions of Aramean rulers (see 2 Kgs 6:24; 8:7ff.).

There is an entirely pragmatic reason for the concealment of Jehu's relation to the Omrides in biblical texts—it serves to erase the dynastic link, documented by Assyrian texts, that Jehu was a descendant of the "House of Omri." In all likelihood, that is also why there is no mention of the tribute paid by Jehu to Shalmaneser III (859-824 BCE), which would cast the Israelite king in an unfavourable light. Deuteronomistic authors writing more than two centuries later had a different agenda: their intention was to describe two completely disparate paradigmatic figures and their exemplary positive and negative behaviours (for more on the Deuteronomists, see de Pury, Römer, and Macchi 2000; Römer 2005; 2006; Rückl 2016; Lester 2024). Jehu is the first figure; the second is not Omri but Ahab (cf. 1 Kgs 16:16ff.). It is Ahab, the most influential ruler of the Omride dynasty, who is discussed in a disproportionately larger number of texts, allowing the biblical account to reshape his undisputable historical importance into a story depicting the irredeemable corruption of a ruler and his eponymous "house" (cf. Čapek 2016). It is not necessary to elaborate on the importance of Ahab as a noticeable political figure of the first half of the ninth century BCE; a reference to the rich literature on the subject should suffice (e.g., Grabbe 2008; Knauf and Guillaume 2016; Sergi 2016; Baruchi-Unna 2017).

This brings us to possibly the most important question: why does the name "House of Ahab" run as a common thread through the biblical narration, while the presumed and historically more accurate appellation of the "House of Omri" is missing? Doubtlessly, this transformation is intentional, aiming to avoid mentioning Jehu as a part of the latter "House." The first person to study the topic in more detail, David Lamb (2007), thinks that the point is to "make Jehu appear more righteous," which is why "it is reasonable that

---

3   This author considers the account of Jehu parallel to his time, reconstructing it as follows: 2 Kings 9:1-6*, 10b-12bα, 13, 16aα, 17-21bα*, 22abα, 23a, 24, 30, 35; 10:1baβ*, 2-3, 7-9, 12a*.

a connection to Omri would be left out" (ibid., 45; but also cf. as early as Cook 1908). For this reason, the well-known title "House of Omri" is replaced with "House of Ahab," and the latter name is consistently used throughout Deuteronomistic works as a negative characteristic of Israelite kings.

Remarkably, a similarly critical light is shed on two Judean kings, Jehoram (848–841 BCE) and Ahaziah (841 BCE): on the former, because "he walked in the way of the kings of Israel, as the house of Ahab had done," and because "the daughter of Ahab was his wife" (2 Kgs 8:18); and on the latter, because "he also walked in the way of the house of Ahab," and because "he was son-in-law to the house of Ahab" (2 Kgs 8:27). The biblical commentary is hardly surprising: it merely confirms the dynastic ties of Judean administrators in the early second half of the ninth century BCE to Israelite rulers, which were probably not exclusively restricted to these two kings.

This negative perspective concerning Ahab is foreshadowed and explained by an inconspicuous note at the start of the Deuteronomistic History. In the Book of Joshua, long before the establishment of the kingdom—and consequently long before the Omride dynasty and shortly before the fall of Jericho—Joshua curses those who would attempt to rebuild the city. Joshua then pronounces the oath "Cursed before the Lord be anyone who tries to build this city, Jericho! At the cost of his firstborn he shall lay its foundation, and at the cost of his youngest he shall set up its gates!" (Josh 6:26).

This seemingly inconspicuous comment plays an important role in the Deuteronomistic portrayal of history, making the text's impact far-reaching. The forbidden reconstruction of Jericho reappears in 1 Kgs 16:34, which is very precisely timed to follow the depiction of Ahab's evil acts and his improper rule. This sophisticated 'recollection' states that, in the days of Ahab, Hiel the Bethelite built Jericho; the city's foundations were laid at the cost of Abiram, his firstborn, and its gates set up at the cost of Segub, his youngest. Commentary in the text of 1 Kgs 16:34 emphasises the criticism of Ahab, who allowed the reconstruction of Jericho, even though it had been forbidden "a long time ago" in the Book of Joshua. Additionally, the city's reconstruction was aided by human sacrifice, which is, again, something unacceptable and punishable with a curse. Moreover, Hiel sacrifices both his eldest and youngest sons.

The wickedness of Ahab, during whose rule these events take place, is beyond all doubt, and the intention of the flashback is absolutely clear: it is a paradigmatic deterrent example, the king is responsible for the worst things imaginable, and Jehu plays the role of his positive counterpart. Thinking through the implications, this means that the worst things to happen since the arrival of Israel into the Promised Land occurred under Ahab. The elaborate argumentation comprises even the origins of the dynasty, mentioning the construction of Samaria under Omri ten verses earlier; his evaluation

4. THE FIRST TRUE UNIFICATION AND THE FIRST TRUE DIVISION (IRON AGE IIA–B)

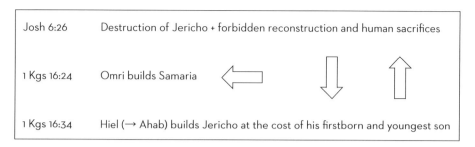

Fig. 17. Intertextual links between Josh 6:26 and 1 Kgs 16:34, with a secondary reference to 1 Kgs 16:24

is also negative, but backgrounded, since Ahab, his successor, did evil "more than all who were before him" (1 Kgs 16:30).

It is not difficult to imagine the purpose of such a depiction and the connection of the texts above: the Deuteronomistic literary composition intentionally distracts the reader from the dominant historical reality, proving to be a masterful work with numerous intertextual links, which offers its own conception of the theology of history. Faced with the suggestions that the Assyrian records were inaccurate (McCarter 1974; Sasson 1996; Na'aman 1998a), one may reiterate that Jehu was a descendant of the "House of Omri," though biblical texts attempt to conceal this relation. Possibly the first researcher to come up with such a reconstruction, Tammi Schneider (1995), believes that undoubtedly "the Assyrians knew the names of their vassals and were aware of changes in royal families," which is why, in her view, "rather than finding fault with the cuneiform, we should be critically rethinking the interpretation of the Hebrew text" (ibid., 32). Keel and Uehlinger (1994) take a similar view, considering Jehu's inclusion in the Assyrian records to be correct as well; consequently, they state that it is incorrect to consider Jehu's description as the "son of Omri" to be an indication of the fact that the great Assyrian empire did not take into account Jehu's state and the extermination of the Omride dynasty, which is the opinion of many authors. According to these authors (e.g., Dubovský 2006; Cogan and Tadmor 1988; contra Robker 2012), the Assyrians observed closely the political events in their borderlands in the ninth century BCE.

As stated previously, the Assyrians considered Jehu a member of the Omride dynasty. Some archaeologists (esp. Mazar 2016) link Nimshi, Jehu's forefather, to Tel Rehov in the Jordan Valley, where two inscriptions featuring the name Nimshi were found: the first, in Stratum V and dated to the turn of the tenth and ninth centuries BCE, states "belonging to Nimshi" (*lnmš* in Hebrew); while the second, found in Stratum IV, which is linked to massive destruction attributed to Hazael or Shalmaneser III (with a temporal connection to Megiddo VA–IVB, the destruction of Jezreel II, and Beth-shean S-1a), speaks of a probably high-ranking official serving Nimshi (*lšqy nmš* in Hebrew). The first inscription may relate directly to the founder of the dynasty; the second is proof of its continuation in the early second half of the ninth century BCE, the time to which the Tel Rehov IV stratum is dated as well. Others (e.g., Na'aman 2016a) place the original seat of the Nimshides to Jezreel and, more generally, to the Beth-shean area (cf. Sergi and Koch 2023).

The following section will examine whether or not (and in which context) these dynastic links are discernible in biblical stories. If Jehu was partly a member of the Omride dynasty, who were his direct predecessors and what was their probable genealogy?

4.2.5.1.2 THE DOUBLE PATRONYMIC

The second key to the reconstruction of Jehu and Joash's link to the Omride dynasty is, in our view, the double patronymic given for both rulers. In 2 Kgs 9 (verses 2 and 14), Jehu is titled the "son of Jehoshaphat son of Nimshi". Such a combination is uncommon, and, apart from Joash in 2 Kgs 14:8, it is the only occasion where the forefather of an Israelite king is mentioned; only the father is given for the other Israelite kings. This is certainly not a coincidence.

If we further compare the depiction of the dynastic connections of the rulers in the north and south, both fathers and mothers are given for Judaean kings, underlining another link to ancestors up to David (see 4.2.5); while for Zimri and Omri—both described as usurpers to the Israelite throne—not even the father is mentioned (1 Kgs 16:16–22). Again, this is certainly no coincidence. Biblical texts provide both Jehu's father, Jehoshaphat (cf. 1 Kgs 22:41-51), as well as his putative ancestor, Nimshi (cf. 1 Kgs 19:16, where Nimshi is the only one mentioned), and two intentions may be deduced from this double patronymic.

The first aim was to extract the king from his original wider family and thus to remove Jehu and his direct descendants from a heritage (i.e., Ahab and his family) that was condemned to oblivion in biblical texts. In Schneider's view (1996, 101), the royal connection between Jehu and Omri, documented by Assyrian texts, explains why only the Ahabides were exterminated. However, since Jehu was also part of the "House of Omri," the second aim was to create at least a covert connection between the two; this is achieved by withholding the link to Ahab, by emphasising Jehu himself, and by outlining the genealogical perspective of his own dynasty. This is clear from 2 Kgs 10:30, where Jehu is promised to rule for four generations. The historical developments confirm this: Jehoahaz (814–803 BCE), Joash (803–787 BCE), Jeroboam II (787-747 BCE), and Zechariah (747 BCE) form an important dynasty in Israel's history. By contrast, Ahab is stigmatised, and his existence in history comes to a violent end.

4. THE FIRST TRUE UNIFICATION AND THE FIRST TRUE DIVISION (IRON AGE IIA–B)

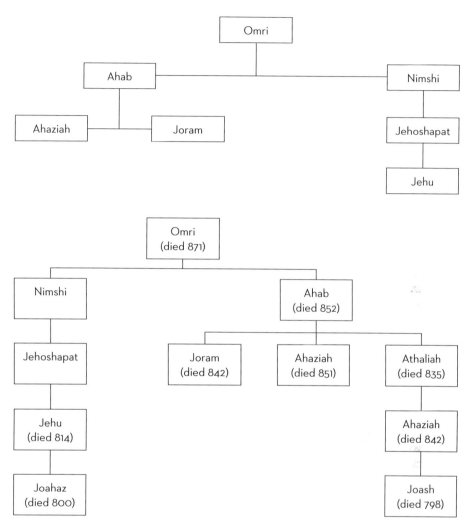

Fig. 18. The Nimshide dynasty as part of the wider Omride family (according to Lamb 2007 and Baruchi-Unna 2017)

Critical analysis of biblical texts suggests that it is both likely and provable that Omri had several sons, of whom at least two are known: Ahab and Nimshi (furthermore, Athaliah may be considered a sister). This was not necessarily a polygamous family (e.g., Lamb 2007, 41), but the siblings, who were possibly born to different wives, may have been rivals and certainly competed for power (Schneider 1995, 33). Let us include more arguments supporting Jehu's putative blood relation to the Omrides:

1. Similarity of the names Omri and Nimshi: The names are very similar and sound similar too; both lack theophoric aspects (Lamb 2007, 45).

2. Jehu's important position at the royal court: Jehu was the leader of Jehoram's army (see 2 Kgs 9:5). Abner, the cousin of Saul, and Joab, the nephew of David, held similar positions (cf. Čapek 2010b).
3. Hostility to Ahab and his descendants: Jehu competed with Jehoram and Ahaziah, sons of Ahab. The discussion as to whether Jehu indeed killed them will be left aside; still, it is more likely that the person linked to their deaths was Hazael of Aram (see discussion in Lamb 2007; Sasson 1996; Schneider 1995; Schniedewind 1996; Čapek 2010b; Baruchi-Unna 2017; Quine 2020).
4. Use of the double patronymic for Joash: The manner of describing Jehu's relation to Omri is adopted for Joash, his grandson, who is also introduced using a double patronymic: "Joash, son of Jehoahaz, son of Jehu" (2 Kgs 14:8). The message is conveyed in this way to emphasise the genealogy of a dynasty that seemingly starts with Nimshi and enjoys success due to its military competence. Withholding Omri is logical, since he is also the father of Ahab and forefather of Jehoram and Ahaziah—all rivals to Jehu and interests of his competing dynasty. There is speculation about the role of the double patronymic in the 2 Kgs 14:8 story (although cf. 2 Kgs 13:10, where it is not present). It may be a warning for Amaziah (796–782 BCE) to avoid conflict with Joash, descendant of Jehu, who is stronger and was able to destroy the family branch of Ahab, the influential son of Omri (see chapter 5), while emphasizing that Jehu is the founder of a new dynasty.
5. Assyrian texts: In the Adad-nirari III stele from Tell el-Rimah, Joash (^m^ia-'a-su) is linked to the land of Samaria (KUR *Sa-me-ri-na-a-a*). The document is dated to 797 BCE (see COS 2.263D); here, the name "House of Omri" is missing. Later, in Tiglath-Pileser III's Summary Inscription dated to 730 BCE, the name appears again in reference to the land of the House of Omri (^kur^ *Bīt-Hu-um-ri-a*; see COS 2.288A). Though the inscription relates to the very end of the Jehuite dynasty, Jehu and his descendants' link to the powerful Omride dynasty was clearly not forgotten.

The line of reasoning above suggests that it is not a coincidence that double patronymics were given for two kings of a dynasty. In terms of Israelite kings (for south cf. 2 Kgs 22:3; 25:22 and 25:25, where the patronymic also plays a special role; see 6.2.4.2 and 7.2.3), this rare phenomenon serves a double purpose: not only *clarification*, but also *differentiation* (cf. Lamb 2007, 28), which shows Jehu and his family's complex ties to the Omride dynasty. Due to the elaborate biblical account, Jehu is separated from his genealogy while also gaining a special position, via a comprehensive story about the destruction of a rival line of his own dynasty (i.e., Ahab and his house). Understandably, this construction goes unnoticed by Assyrian texts, an undoubtedly more reli-

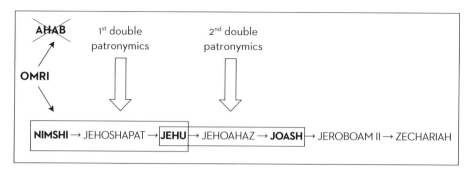

Fig. 19. Dynasty of Nimshidides/Jehuites with double patronymics in the Books of Kings

able and historically almost synchronous source. Historically, the separation of Jehuites or Nimshides from the Omride dynasty was more complex than, and different from, the biblical account. Jehu and his direct descendants—Jehoahaz, Joash, Jeroboam II, and Zechariah—are an extension of the same dynasty. Consequently, it is important to examine the reasons for modifying the historical context and the purpose of a historiographic account composed in such a manner.

4.2.5.1.3 INVENTING UNITY, CREATING DISUNITY

From the above, it is far from surprising that the biblical texts adapt the historical events of the ninth century BCE to suit the needs of their authors; they play a decisive role, and their perspective is crucial. Historically speaking, it is likely that the influential Omride dynasty controlled not only Israel but—by means of consanguineous marriages—also Judah, which would only become independent later (see chapter 5). This reconstruction is refuted by some researchers, since they consider Israel and Judah to be two equal states with their own genealogical lines from the beginning (Na'aman 2013; 2016a), or they place the origins of Judah and the first Davidides into the last third of the ninth century BCE (Sergi 2013; but cf. Sergi 2023).

The analysis of biblical traditions and comparison with non-biblical textual evidence makes it clear that Jehu and his branch of the Omride dynasty are used to express Judean interests in a very deliberate manner. It is quite conceivable that two traditions meet in the Books of Kings—and especially in the key composition of 2 Kgs 8:26-10:18—which may be separated, albeit at the cost of hypotheticality. Older and likely of a northern origin, the former depicts the political changes in the "House of Omri." The latter, which would later be edited several times, uses the older tradition to express its own political and religious interests, which are intrinsic to the south (cf. Otto 2001; Na'aman 2006; Würthwein 2008; Hasegawa 2012; Robker 2012; Ghantous 2014). This later tradition is pro-Judean, aimed against Israel, which serves as a negative counterpart. That is also why the topic of Israelite succession itself is deliberately discussed in a negative light. Equally, it is understandable why Jehu's tribute to the Assyrians is withheld and why the name "House of Omri," albeit well documented in Assyrian texts, is backgrounded and replaced by the purposely confrontational title "House of Ahab." Firstly, this replacement decentralises Jehu's powerful ancestors; and secondly, it generally weakens the significance of the northern dynasty in comparison with Judah, which benefits from everything depicted in the Books of Kings.

In the biblical account, Jehu is shown as a temporarily good king, which is only due to Judean interests and to Israel's disadvantage. "Temporarily" because his eventual fate would be sealed by the account of the abandonment of the law of YHWH and the rise of Hazael, who begins to oppress Israel (2 Kgs 10:31–33). There is an even more drastic message in the prophetic Book of Hosea, which passes judgment on the house of Jehu over the blood spilled in Jezreel. Originally well received, the punishment exacted upon the "House of Ahab" is transformed into a statement on the punishment meted out on all of Israel, whose fate would be no different to that of the kings Jehoram and Ahaziah in Jezreel (Hos 1:4–5). It is unclear if the Jehu-initiated coup was also linked to religion and, specifically, to the reform aimed at countering the worship of Baal, as depicted in biblical texts (this is refuted by Würthwein 2008; Na'aman 2007a views the link as artificial; while Albertz 2007 considers it historically reliable; for further study see Stahl 2021).

Perhaps surprisingly, it is biblical texts that provide the most conclusive evidence to suggest that Jehu was a member of the extended Omride dynasty. Critical analysis may propose a scenario in which he was a part of the royal genealogy starting with Omri. This interpretation is based on four features: determining exact tensions in the overall literary composition; observing genre shifts (the prophetic, historical, and narrative discourses); using polarising patterns (good or bad kings according to their pro-Yahweh or pro-Baal cultic practices); and comprehending the role of double patronymics.

When explaining the dynastic construction of concurrent genealogies of Israelite and Judean kings, it is crucial to examine its place in history—i.e., the time in which it probably originated (let us leave its later editorial history aside for now). In Frevel's view, with which we concur, the construction was formed in the first half of the eighth century BCE. In that time, Judah asserted its independence from Israel and projected Jeroboam II, its competitor, back to the late tenth century BCE, into the founding myth describing the origins of the separate kingdoms (see 1 Kgs 12). In our view, the study of the historical contexts, the analysis of material culture and the critical reading of biblical texts confirm this hypothesis. More and more, current research is veering towards this thesis of dynastic construction, though scholars find different explanations for its nature, diverging in their views on the proportion of its historical and fictitious sections, as well as in dating its editorial history (Pakkala 2013; Sergi 2016a; Frevel 2016; Römer 2017b; 2020a).

4.2.6 NINTH-CENTURY BCE JERUSALEM

Judah's strong and visible ties to the north in the ninth century BCE might also be confirmed by the newest findings of archaeological research carried out in Jerusalem. The proposed thesis about dynastic links connecting the north and the south, which were expressed on an architectural level as well, is supported by the revised dating of the walls and tower of the Gihon spring in the eastern part of the City of David. Until recently, it was assumed that the size of ninth-century BCE Jerusalem had been moderate and more of local relevance. The city is described as a rather minor settlement with numerous small buildings and no monumental architecture (cf. Ben-Ami 2013), and its growth was usually linked to the eighth century BCE. Latest data from Areas C, H, and E provide a different perspective on the late Iron Age IIA and the late ninth century BCE. The consensus on the fortifications of the City of David and especially the Gihon Spring Tower, dated to the Middle Bronze Age (Shiloh 1984; de Groot, Bernick-Greenberg 2012; Reich and Shukron 2008; 2010), was supplemented with a new interpretation, proposing that the modifications of the tower and the adjoining walls should be newly dated to the late ninth century BCE, or viewed as buildings from the same period (Uziel and Szanton 2015; Gadot and Uziel 2017; Ussishkin 2016). This interpretation is based on the analysis of C14 samples procured in 2014 from two distant profiles under Wall 104 (Regev et al. 2017). Though the newly proposed dating was immediately contested (Finkelstein in Haaretz, January 27, 2018; Maeir 2017; Reich 2018), the volume of material analyzed (23 sediments and 26 envelopes containing carbonised material) and the painstaking method used for collecting the samples lend some credence to the newly determined time horizon.

If the dating above is correct, which is confirmed by further chronological and stratigraphical analysis performed by Uziel and Gadot (a total of five sets of "stratigraphic anchors"; see Gadot and Uziel 2017, 124-37), new features of ninth-century BCE Jerusalem come to light (cf. also Mazar 2007). Constructed using "cyclopean stones" up to two metres in size, the monumental tower with a floor plan of 16 by 16 metres that protects the Gihon spring and the adjoining fortification walls (along with the possibility that they are extended by the town walls from the same period in Areas D and E) may serve as evidence of the growing socioeconomic potential of the early Kingdom of Judah. Despite recent criticism that the presumed connection of the south to the north is too much predetermined by biblical texts without taking into account material culture, which does not seem to support this (Gadot, Kleiman A., and Uziel 2023; cf. Frevel and Čapek 2024), it is possible that the growth of the city is related to close political ties to the stronger north. Jerusalem's rise was not sudden (see 4.2.4.3), triggered by a single historical event such as the fall of Samaria in 722 BCE, but had begun at an earlier point (Gadot, Bocher, Freud and Shalev 2023). Consequently, as the only explanation for the movement of originally northern literary traditions to the south (see 4.2.4.3), the compromise model must be reviewed. Judah was previously a branch kingdom of Israel and its elites, who ruled from Jerusalem, evidently had strong dynastic ties to the north and so the transition and adoption of northern traditions seems to have occurred earlier than previously thought.

4.3 SUMMARY

The late Iron Age IIA and early Iron Age IIB are possibly the most complex historical periods in which to seek the very origins of Israel and Judah as territorial states. This is mainly due to the relations between the two entities. For the "difficult" tenth century BCE (see chapter 3), there are theories urgently seeking to discover these entities which use rather scarce information, limited archaeological evidence, and far-reaching reconstructions of historical scenarios in biblical texts; by contrast, one is on firmer ground in the ninth century BCE. As time passed, a dynamically developing Israel with institutional foundations emerged in the north, constructing well-fortified cities and imposing buildings, amassing an army, and expanding its territory at the appropriate time. Israel also fostered trade relations with neighbouring states (especially Aram Damascus and Phoenicia) and formed pragmatic political coalitions. Similar developments later occurred in Judah, which gradually became independent of the influence of Israel and the Omrides, both of which used an elaborate marriage policy to turn Jerusalem into their branch kingdom. Judah's close ties to Israel hinder the identification of the origins of the relevant literary traditions, the nature of religious practices, as well as the birth of Judah as a political entity independent of the north.

Research heavily focuses on what caused the changes in Judah that would eventually lead to the establishment of an independent kingdom, and numerous hypotheses have been proposed. According to some scholars, the changes were triggered by dynastic transference, as the northern coup under Jehu's rule in 841 BCE had been followed by the Nimshides taking control over the south as well. Interpreting these dynastic developments independently, others point to the Omrides' connection to local rulers in the south. In their view, Jerusalem grew stronger with the marriage of Athaliah to Jehoram and became the first territorial state to expand not just into the southern highlands, but also the Shephelah (Beer-sheba V, Lachish IV, Arad XI, and Beth-shemesh 3 are given as proof of this). This expansion is often connected to Hazael, who put Israel, his southern neighbour, in dire straits, whilst also defeating the Philistine city-state of Gath, which facilitated Judah's growth on its western border (Sergi 2013; cf. Čapek 2015; 2018). Others underline Judah's own dynamic evolution (Na'aman 2013); and a combination of all factors is also a possible explanation. However, it is necessary to exercise caution when interpreting "Hazael's gambit", which is essentially linked to any destruction in the region, including the Shephelah, and is especially popular among archaeologists and historians; it seems an attractive explanation, but it is controversial because it suggests that the Arameans alone were responsible, which is unsupported by specific evidence (see Maeir 2016). The key text for such a focused interpretation of the events of 2 Kgs 10:32 concerns the north, and the crucial question is how reliable is the picture that it paints of the history of the south (cf. Mazar 2016; Frevel 2016).

This chapter proposes that the histories of Judah and Israel are very closely connected. If there ever was a "United Monarchy", it existed in the late ninth century BCE and the first half of the eighth century BCE. Apart from material culture and epigraphic evidence, biblical texts constitute the primary source of information (for a different view Gadot, Kleiman A., and Uziel 2023). Critical reading—mainly by analyzing the chronicles of the kings of Judah and Israel and related narrative units—reveals a strong link to Israel as a state with a decisive role in the joint history of the north and south for over a hundred years, but which according to the later Judean perspective should not be observable or considered (see Frevel and Čapek 2024). The first unification is a matter of the ninth century BCE; whilst at the end of the century, certain processes took place that led to the separation and establishment of an independent Judah in the eighth century BCE (the Iron Age IIB), which will be the subject of the next chapter.

5. FIRST INDEPENDENCE (IRON AGE IIB–C)

*It is known that history is always constructed;
the only difference is if it is constructed rightly or wrongly.*
—Julius Wellhausen

The previous chapter proposed that the histories of Judah and Israel were more closely linked than has been generally assumed, and that northern royal dynasties were the source of this connection. The interconnection of Judah and Israel is proven not only by material culture and, to a limited degree, epigraphy, but also—and especially—by the critical reading of biblical texts; specifically, by analyzing the chronicles of the kings of Israel and Judah and related material. If there ever was a United Monarchy, it did not exist in the tenth century BCE and the Iron Age IIA, but in the second half of the ninth century BCE, and possibly also in the first half of the eighth century BCE (see especially 5.2; for a similar proposal see recently Finkelstein 2022). The first unification is a matter of the ninth century BCE; whilst at its end, certain processes took place that led to the separation and establishment of an independent Judah in the eighth century BCE (the Iron Age IIB). There is a scholarly discussion as to the exact time when Judah became an independent territorial state, which will be introduced and expanded on below.

5.1 ANCIENT DOMINOES

Even the turn of the ninth and eighth centuries BCE is typified by constantly shifting power relations between Assyria, Aram Damascus, and Israel. During this period, the Neo-Assyrian Empire is the most important political entity, with its presence or absence and specific political activities having far-reaching consequences for events in the southern Levant. In a domino effect, the actions of this entity also had an impact on Judah and other political entities in the south, such as Edom, Moab, and Philistine cities on the Coastal Plain and in the western Shephelah. The hegemony of Aram Damascus under Hazael's rule (ca. 843–803 BCE) in the interim period, in which Assyrian influence beyond the Euphrates weakened, started to affect the south especially after 837 BCE, and impacted Israel as well. Specifically, Samaria grew weaker, creating the opportunity for the Nimshides from the Omride dynasty (see 4.2.5) to stage the coup led by Jehu (842/841–814 BCE) which was possibly supported by the Arameans. At that time, the royal competitors were eliminated: Jehoram, Ahaziah, and later also Athaliah in Jerusalem. The changes occurring in Israel, in turn, had consequences for Judah, whose independence grew — according to some, at the cost of greater dependence on Hazael and paying tribute (according to 2 Kgs 12:18; for possible reconstructions, see Schneider 1995; Schniedewind 1996; Lamb 2007; Čapek 2010b; Baruchi-Unna 2017).

The dominance of Aram Damascus was interrupted by the campaigns of Adad-nirari III (811–783 BCE); apart from Damascus, the Assyrians also conquered Tyre, Sidon, and Arwad. Having had its ambition limited by the Arameans in the preceding period, Israel took advantage of the situation. Samaria's resistance against Hazael may have begun as early as the rule of Jehoahaz (818–802 BCE), who, according to 2 Kgs 13, had fought against Hazael and Ben-Hadad without success until the Assyrians entered the power struggle. Named the king of the land of Samaria by the Tell el-Rimah stele (KUR *Sa-me-ri-na-a-a*), the successor of Jehoahaz and grandson of Jehu, Joash (802–787 BCE) had to pay tribute to Adad-nirari III from 796 BCE, which shows the extent of Assyrian influence. Due to deliberate Assyrian policies under Shalmaneser IV, Ashur-Dan III, and Ashur-nirari V (ruling from 783–754 BCE), Israelite rulers maintained their independence, extending the Assyrian sphere of influence further to the south. Consequently, it was under Joash and later Jeroboam II (787–747 BCE) that their territorial expansion reached a peak, with Israel acquiring a part of Transjordan and Galilee, including the north up to Tel Dan (Stratum II), to the detriment of Aram Damascus; Israel also fortified Kinneret II, Hazor VI/IVA, Yokneam XIII, and Jibleam X (for discussion Arie 2008; Sergi, Oeming, and de Hulster 2016; Sergi and Kleiman A. 2018; Kleiman A. 2019; Zwickel 2019).

Israelite influence extending far south is proven by epigraphic findings from Kuntillet 'Ajrud, a site by the Arab trade route of Darb el-Ghazza in the Negev, where inscriptions have been found including the phrases "Yahweh of Samaria" and "Yahweh of Teman" (COS 2.47; see also Singer-Avitz 2006; Finkelstein 2016), and a wall painting possibly depicting Jeroboam II (Ornan 2016; cf. Meshel 2012, who dates the site to ca. 800 BCE, during the rule of Joash). Though under Assyrian patronage, Israel enjoyed forty years of economic prosperity, with international trade on the rise, a developing body of literature (e.g., Samaria ostraca; for discussion see Hall 2022), and the cult undergoing gradual centralisation (Finkelstein 2013, Kleiman A. et al. 2017; cf. Hall 2020).

Three successive events are crucial to the history of Judah, Israel, and the entire area of the southern Levant in the second half of the eighth century BCE. The first is the accession of Tiglath-Pileser III (745–727 BCE) to the throne. It was during his rule that Assyria—after an interim period of weakness caused by the pressure of Urartu to the northeast of the empire—expanded into most of the Levant and conquered Babylonia. Assyrian interests were enforced through violent means: by exerting pressure on states to submit to vassalage, annexations, and deportations. Tiglath-Pileser III's western campaigns are dated to 742, 741, 740, 738, 734, 732, and 731 BCE (Younger 2007; Kuan 2016).

Linked to the first, the second event came in 747 BCE, with the death of Jeroboam II. Israel's political situation underwent a radical change. Jeroboam was briefly succeeded by Zechariah, who was, however, murdered at the behest of Rezin of Damascus (754–732 BCE). After a half-century, the northern kingdom again fell under the influence of Aram Damascus; King Pekah (735–732 BCE) enlisted the help of Aram and Hiram II of Tyre (739–730 BCE) to attempt, in vain, to stop Assyrian expansion. Zechariah was the last scion of the Nimshide dynasty (see 4.2.5), which controlled the power dynamics in Jerusalem from the north. In Judah, Jotham (750–736 BCE) was the last king following Samarian orders.

During Pekahiah's brief rule in Israel (737–736 BCE), Ahaz became King of Judah; he had previously co-ruled with Jotham in 741–736 BCE, and after being king in 736–725 BCE he would again co-rule, with his son Hezekiah, from 725 BCE. Ahaz is the very first Judean ruler documented in non-biblical textual sources—leaving aside the historically ambiguous mention of Ahaziah from the "House of David" (*Bytdwd* in Aramaic), marked on the eighth line of the Tel Dan stele dated to 841 BCE (half the name is reconstructed and Jehoram, the king of Israel, is supplemented entirely; for different dating, see Athas 2005; 2006). Ahaz is recorded in the vassal list of Tiglath-Pileser III, where he is referred to in full form as Jehoahaz of Judah (^{m}Ia-$ú$-ha-zi ^{kur}Ia-u-da-a). Tiglath-Pileser III attacked Gaza in 734 BCE to secure the empire's southern border with Egypt, and thereafter Ahaz submitted to Assyria, as did the rulers of Ashkelon, Ammon, Moab, and Edom. Similarly, from 738 BCE tribute was imposed upon King Menahem of Israel, who was allowed to continue ruling in exchange for this tribute (cf. 2 Kings 15:19–20).

According to Frevel (2016, 239), Ahaz was aware that paying tribute created an opportunity for his own political activities in the protective shadow of Assyrian power. Consequently, he resisted the pressure to join a nascent anti-Assyrian coalition and dared to take a step in the opposite direction. Ahaz became a vassal of Tiglath-Pileser III, joining a system that would later be termed *Pax Assyriaca* (cf. 2 Kgs 16:7–20). On one hand, this decision involved Jerusalem in the Syro-Ephraimite War (736–732 BCE) and exposed it to the Philistines and Edom, both of whom took advantage of the situation; and on the other, Judah grew more powerful as an independent state, whose fate was decided by the Assyrians based on the loyalty shown to them.

The following decades of Judean history under Hezekiah (728–687 BCE) and Manasseh (687–642 BCE) serve as clear evidence that the prudence demonstrated by the governors of this satellite state was key to its economic prosperity and relative political independence. Judah joined the Neo-Assyrian Empire for pragmatic reasons, since it had had a harrowing experience of confrontation with its power: possibly as early as under Tiglath-Pileser III, Tell Beit Mirsim, Lachish, Tel 'Eton, Tel Khalif, and maybe Tel Burna were all annexed or destroyed (Shai 2016; Aster and Faust 2018). Assyrian expansion in Judah resulted in demographic changes and the displacement of its population, which are apparent from the extent of Jerusalem's populated area during this period. As mentioned earlier (see 4.2.4.3), the exact nature of this undoubtedly growing capital and the dating of the individual phases in the eighth century BCE remain the subjects of discussion (Geva 2006; Na'aman 2007b; Faust 2014; Ben-Ami 2014; Finkelstein 2015; Gadot and Uziel 2017, Gadot 2022).

The third and final formative event of the Kingdom of Judah was the fall of Israel in 722 BCE. Though the road to independence had begun earlier (for more detail, see 5.2), this was the point when the reduced influence—and later two centuries of absence—of a stronger neighbour gave the impulse to create a new look at history, which would comprise of Israel as well. Writing began to develop in Jerusalem (Whisenant 2008; Finkelstein and Sass 2017; Rollston 2017; Na'aman 2020; Sergi 2023), and some degree of cult centralisation seems to be documented in the late eighth-century BCE (see chapter 6). Probably preserved in Bethel, Israel's oral and literary traditions had earlier reached the south due to the close links between both kingdoms, alongside other cultural and economic influences. However, the fall of Samaria constituted another turning point in historical reflections, as shown in the efforts that led to the composition of an independent Judean historiography. This featured a far-reaching transformation of past events, which allowed the heirs to Israel's legacy—now living in Judah—to view the past as something continual, whole, understandable, and, especially, as something created in Judah, the place where this history originates (see 4.2.4.2).

5.2 TRANSFORMATIONS IN JUDAH—THE FIRST HALF OF THE EIGHTH CENTURY BCE

This introduction to the late ninth- and eighth-century BCE historical context has so far deliberately omitted Judah in the first half of the eighth century BCE. This is an important period in terms of Jerusalem's development and its gaining of independence from Israel, for which there are numerous archaeological findings, in addition to frequent descriptions in biblical texts. On the other hand, both sources of information are complex and ambiguous to interpret. The following section attempts to understand this epoch, which played a formative role in shaping Judah but is also difficult to grasp.

There are various explanations for the gradual economic growth of Judah. Most frequently, references are made to Judah's close link with Israel, on which it relied and which made the changes in the south possible. As early as the ninth century BCE, Israel had already been a dynamically developing state with well-fortified cities, imposing buildings, and a strong army, which is mentioned in Assyrian texts (see the Kurkh stele; COS 2.113A). Israel had also fostered active trade relations with neighbour states (mainly Aram Damascus and Phoenicia) and formed pragmatic political coalitions. Sometime later, Judah took a similar path as a territorial state that may have been politically dependent on the north until the mid-eighth century BCE. This was due to enforced dynastic marriages with northern rulers, some of whom were instated as governors of the branch kingdom in Jerusalem (see below for an in-depth perspective).

Some interpretations connect the first signs of Judean independence to 841 BCE and Jehu's coup in Israel which led to the Nimshides assuming control over the south. In their view, Judah grew stronger with the marriage of Athaliah to Jehoram and, for the first time, became a territorial state which expanded not only into the southern highlands, but also the Shephelah (Beersheba V, Lachish IV, Arad XI, and Beth-shemesh 3 are given as evidence for this). This expansion is sometimes linked to Hazael, who put his southern neighbour, Israel, into dire straits and defeated Gath. As some assume, the developments on the western border of Judah would have been inconceivable without the defeat of the powerful Philistine city-state at the hands of the Arameans (for discussion see Sergi 2013; Na'aman 2016a; 2016b).

The newest archaeological research findings in the southeastern and eastern parts of the City of David in Jerusalem prove the existence of monumental architecture in the late ninth century BCE, which—until recently—was viewed exclusively as a Middle Bronze Age construction effort, or as partial modifications carried out in the eighth century BCE. The new dating of the construction phases of certain walls, fortifications, and the Gihon Spring tower paints a picture of Jerusalem as being something other than a provincial town (Gadot and Uziel 2017; Uziel and Szanton 2015; Ussishkin 2016; and esp. Regev et al. 2017; contra Reich 2018, cf. Sergi 2023; Schipper 2020a).

The possible explanations for this include the strong link to Israel and the state's support for the growing centre of the branch kingdom in the sout (see 4.2.6). In the eighth century BCE, Jerusalem's western part continued to grow, but this development phase is—similar to most of the discovered epigraphic material (bullae from the area of the Gihon Spring and Ophel ostraca)—dated to the second half of the eighth century BCE (see discussion in Frevel 2016, 235-38). Over the past two decades, the opinions on the transformations of the Judean centre have changed, and numerous scholars (cf. Na'aman 2007b; 2014; Guillaume 2008; but Finkelstein 2015; Gadot and Uziel 2017) do not now consider the fall of Samaria to be the universal key to comprehending Jerusalem's growth; it is merely one phase of a development which had started earlier (cf. also Gadot, Kleiman, A., and Uziel 2023).

5.3 JUDAH IN THE FIRST HALF OF THE EIGHTH CENTURY BCE AND BIBLICAL TEXTS

The Kingdom of Judah in the first half of the eighth century BCE is discussed in biblical texts, albeit not to the same extent as Israel in the mid-ninth century BCE and the rest of the following century. This imbalance is not random; there is a reason for it, which will be expanded upon later (see 5.3.1 and 5.3.2). The abrupt shift in dynastic relations, which play a crucial role in understanding the histories of both kingdoms, was foreshadowed by the year 841 BCE. According to 2 Kgs 9-10, that was the year when Jehu killed Ahaziah of Judah and Jehoram of Israel (see discussion in Schneider 1995; Schniedewind 1996; Athas 2006; Lamb 2007; Čapek 2010b; Hasegawa 2012; Baruchi-Unna 2017; Quine 2020) and completely eliminated Ahab's descendants. Ahaziah's mother, Athaliah, reacted by murdering royal offspring in Jerusalem. There is a key question here, which the biblical text does not make entirely clear, who exactly were they and what dynastic line did they came from? Essentially mirrored in the north, where, however, no member of Ahab's family survived (2 Kgs 10:16), this palace purge left a survivor: the boy Joash, who remained in hiding for six years until the queen herself died during a coup led by the priest Jehoiada.

The new king's accession (ca. 835 BCE) was marked by an anti-Baal cult purge (an account is given in 2 Kgs 10:18-27), and during Joash's rule, Jerusalem also bought itself out of being threatened by Hazael (2 Kgs 12:18-19). The king was later assassinated by his servants—Jozabad, son of Shimeath, and Jehozabad, son of Shomer (see 5.3.1)—and succeeded by his son Amaziah (801-773 BCE), who eliminated his father's killers and, after a successful campaign against Edom (2 Kgs 14:7, 10), entered into a military conflict with Joash of Samaria that concluded with a humiliating defeat at Beth-shemesh. The Judean king was captured, Jerusalem was besieged and eventually conquered, the walls were breached, and the temple treasures and hostages were taken to Samaria. This political fiasco resulted in a revolt against Amaziah in Jerusalem; the king escaped to Lachish, only to be murdered by people sent from the capital. Amaziah was succeeded by his sixteen-year-old son Azariah (787-736 BCE), who would go on to rule Jerusalem for fifty-two years

(2 Kgs 15:2). In 756 BCE, the king started to suffer from leprosy which forced him to live in a separate house until the end of his life and his son Jotham (756–741 BCE) became the ruler of Judah. Towards the end of Jotham's rule, Judah was pressured by Aram Damascus and Pekah of Samaria, with this situation lasting until the rule of Ahaz, son of Jotham, who made a pragmatic change of political direction by becoming a vassal of Assyria ensured his country's relative autonomy (see 5.1 and 6.2.1).

5.3.1 JUDAH IN THE FIRST HALF OF THE EIGHTH CENTURY BCE—CRITICAL READING

When reading biblical texts, the first question that comes to mind is how the events in Judah are linked to the north. There are several conspicuous aspects to the biblical account of the late ninth century BCE and first half of the eighth century BCE; firstly, there is an emphasis on separation from the north by referring to the independent dynastic context of Judah (by highlighting the Davidide line and listing the names and Judean origins of the mothers of succeeding monarchs); secondly, the account underlines religious differences (Judah as the place where the cult practice is proper—or with reservations, if that is not the case; Israel as the land constantly betraying YHWH and serving Baal); and thirdly, it contains close links to political events in Israel.

The reason for this tension stems from the intentions of the authors of these texts. On one hand, there is a need to introduce the history of Judah as an ancient and glorious territorial entity in a wider geopolitical context, in which the existence of its closest significant neighbour, Israel, cannot be concealed; yet on the other hand, it is also necessary to push Judah's northern neighbour into the background. This dual objective and dual nature of Old Testament materials is noticeable during a critical reading of these texts, and identifying them allows one to reconstruct specific historical events (even if only as hypotheses).

As has already been noted, there is a hypothesis which claims that, historically, it was the Omrides and later the Nimshides, one of the related dynasties, who were likely originally seated in Tel Rehov. Rulers from these dynasties subjugated Judah as a branch kingdom in the ninth century BCE

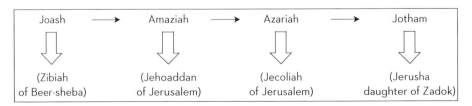

Fig. 20. Judean kings and their mothers, according to the Books of Kings

and the first half of the following century, using plotted dynastic marriages and tasking family members with ruling the south (see 4.2.3; see discussion in Würthwein 2008; Robker 2012; Hasegawa 2012; Bolen 2013; Ghantous 2014). Consequently, the south was not ruled by Judean kings, whether based on geography or genealogy (this is also why both areas are emphasised in the chronicles; see the diagram above), but by northern royal houses between whom bloody clashes subsequently broke out. The murder of Athaliah constituted a change in the Omride dynasty, as the Nimshides (or Jehuites; see 4.2.5.1 and below) took control of Jerusalem. There were further rulers in this line until the first half of the eighth century BCE.

Reconstructing the history of specific southern kings and their reigns is very complicated, since the synchronisms used in Kings are not mere anchors in history, and historical facts are often deliberately obscured (see 4.2.5). The chronologies of the kings of Israel and Judah treat the facts available to the authors and editors of the Books of Kings very loosely. There is an emphasis on specific political and religious interests, and the tools used include harmonisation, expansion, adaptation, withholding, and vast transformations of concrete historical events; including the creation of narratives that are relatively free from history (cf. Čech 2002). The aim is not to provide a faithful account of specific events in history, but to describe the way that events happened from the Judean perspective.

Among the indicators of harmonisation efforts, we may again mention very inventive chronicle adaptations in terms of the total number of rulers in the two kingdoms: the number given for both is twenty, though Judah existed for an additional 140 years (the average reign therefore lasted approximately seventeen years in the south, while in the north, the length is almost half that). As mentioned above, *historical patterning* is another typical feature (cf. Auld 2015; 2017). This literary technique details events in a certain manner, with emphasis on what should be seen as commensurate, and therefore plausible, to the readers or listeners. The commensurability is linked to the evaluation of specific figures and royal dynasties and whether their actions are right or wrong; the aforementioned concurrent reigns of Athaliah in the south and Jezebel in the north (2 Kgs 9–11) may serve as an example. Since both are connected to Ahab, the avatar of depravity, their actions are improper on a political as well as a religious level (murdering the competition, sinking into Baalism, and eliminating the prophets of YHWH). Consequently, both queens meet the same violent end (but cf. 2 Kgs 11:20) and must be succeeded by new dynasties: the Nimshides in the north and the Davidides in the south, founded by Jehu and Joash respectively, who behave similarly in many respects to further underline this historical patterning. Jehu purges both the northern royal house, by murdering the offspring of Ahab, and the cult, by eliminating all worshippers of Baal, in a story with almost sarcastic undertones (2 Kgs 18-28; cf. Elijah in 1 Kgs 18). Since Joash is only a child, he does not carry out a purge of the cult in Jerusalem—the priest Jehoiada does; still, it would be on his initiative in the twenty-third year of his rule that the temple would be repaired, having been neglected by the priests' laxness (2 Kgs 12:5-17). The above makes it clear that, where necessary, the authors of biblical texts used *standardised fiction* (Frevel 2016), which appears to provide historiographic accounts that document historical facts faithfully (see the overview diagram earlier in this section).

Events in Judah may be reconstructed using biblical texts by comparison with Assyrian and Aramean epigraphic material and the material culture of the corresponding period. This synthesis shows that Israel enforced its interests in the south over a long period, even providing economic support to Jerusalem (see 4.2.6). This took place through an elaborate marriage policy enacted by the Omrides until the mid-ninth century BCE and later, in the late ninth century BCE and the first half of the following century, by the Nimshides, who were a part of the Omride dynasty, and whose original seat was probably Tel Rehov in the Jordan Valley (see 4.2.5.1.1). This reconstruction is supported by frequent double occurrences of king names, such as Ahaziah, Jehoram, and Joash (cf. Čapek 2010b; 2016). In Jehoram's case, it is possible that he was the same man Athaliah married to strengthen her influence over the branch kingdom in the south.

A completely opposite interpretation was proposed some time ago by John Strange (1975); in his view, Jehoram of Israel is a ruler deliberately invented by an unidentified Deuteronomist. Jehoram is considered a "ghost" without historical basis, contrasting with the eponymous southern king who did exist. This interpretation stems from 2 Kgs 3:2, where Jehoram removes the sacred pillar of Baal, thereby betraying that his origins are from somewhere other than Samaria. According to Strange, it was Jehoram who helped Jehu eliminate Ahab's offspring, weakening Israel while allowing Judah to gain the upper hand. If there was truly only one Jehoram, and from the south no less—which is contested by the available epigraphic evidence (see the Mesha stele; COS 2.23)—why is Jehoram of Israel featured in the Books of Kings at all? Strange offers two explanations: the first is the Deuteronomist's possible misuse of a source, as he was working with data over two centuries old; the second—and more likely according to Strange—is that the Deuteronomist used "every ambiguity in his sources and created a 'ghost' in Israel. He did so to avoid that any of the descendants of David should have had any part in the apostate and abominable kingdom of Israel" (Strange 1975, 201).

Returning to the interpretations stemming from the north's dominance, it may be assumed that the southern branch of the Omrides reacted independently to changes in the north—especially Jehu's coup—removing Athaliah and using the common offspring of both dynasties to form a new genealogical line starting with Joash (cf. Baruchi-Unna 2017). The death of the king would also confirm the existence of unrest in late ninth-century BCE Jerusalem, since he also was murdered, and his successor Amaziah also met the same end. Ancient historiography often utilises conflict, unrest, and palace coups as tools to highlight important changes that are to be disclosed or concealed.

A more complex interpretation of these circumstances, but along the same lines, is offered by Frevel (2016, 223–226). He is surprised at Joash's murder and, given the king's very positive appraisal in 2 Kgs 11-12 (a long rule lasting forty years; temple reconstruction; the symbolism of accession at seven years of age; proper worship overall, led by the priest Jehoiada), considers it literary fiction intended to obscure the true nature of events occurring in Jerusalem. There is an important role in the fiction played by the popular etymologisation of the killers' names—Jozabad and Jehozabad, meaning "YHWH has bestowed" - which are practically identical, and are entirely identical in the Czech Ecumenical Translation. One killer is the son of Shimeath (meaning "message"); the other is the son of Shomer ("guardian"). According to Frevel, Joash is one and the same person: the Nimshide Joash of Samaria (802–787 BCE), who succeeded Jehoahaz (818–802 BCE) and consequently—contrary to the biblical account—was not murdered. A son or grandson of Jehu, the king was sent to Jerusalem in his early childhood, and after entering into an agreement with the local nobility, which wished to retain power, he dethroned Athaliah, the last member of the Omride dynasty. In biblical historiography, Joash is de facto doubled, and another Joash is created from the Nimshides of Samaria (or Tel Rehov), linked to the Davidides via dynastic fiction.

Joash later also made use of the political skills he acquired in the south in Samaria, while under pressure by Aram Damascus. Gradually gaining control over Hazael and his successor, Ben-Hadad, Joash also regained lost lands in the Transjordan and north of the Jezreel Valley, as far as Upper Galilee. According to Frevel (2016, 226), the king utilised his political skill in Judah too, where he had to fight Amaziah, a likely usurper of power in Jerusalem and a ruler controlled by the Arameans—that is, not a ruler in the Davidide line, and without a notable lineage (cf. also similarities with Hazael in 1 Kgs 8).

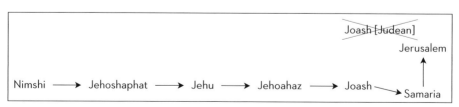

Fig. 21. Joash of the Nimshide dynasty as the ruler of Jerusalem and Samaria (according to Frevel 2016)

The tension that could indirectly confirm this interpretation may be seen in 2 Kgs 14. The chronistic introduction is similar to that of other rulers (synchronism with Joash, mother's name, rule length), as is the theological evaluation claiming that the king did "what was right in the sight of the Lord," but "not like his ancestor David" (a standard explanation is provided as well). The introduction is followed by a longer story about the king's pride and fall; firstly, it mentions Amaziah's success in conflicts with the Edomites; then, an invitation to fight Joash; and afterwards, the northern king's answers in the form of a parable. The next section depicts Amaziah's defeat at Beth-shemesh, which is only the start of his political downfall (for a more detailed view, including the prophetic expansion, see 2 Chr 25). Next comes the sacking of Jerusalem, imposing of tribute, escape to Lachish, and murder. Azariah, the ascending ruler, is described as the son of Amaziah in the Davidide line; he could also be another Nimshide prince crowned king in the south. According to Frevel (2016, 227), this restores the previous status quo, and Samaria rules Jerusalem with clientelism-based politics.

The depiction of the battle at Beth-shemesh and its result make it obvious that Israel had the upper hand over Judah and made the decisions in Jerusalem in the late ninth century BCE and the first half of the eighth century BCE. This confirms that, in that period, Judah was still more or less a branch kingdom of Israel, controlled from Samaria by the Nimshides, a family line of the Omride dynasty. This interpretation may also be supported by the biblical text of 2 Kgs 13:5, in which Jehoahaz is promised a saviour—i.e., Joash, the next acceding member of the Nimshide dynasty, who helps the former escape the Aramean thrall and recaptures lands lost earlier (v. 25). Surprisingly benevolent towards the north and, by all accounts, with a real historical background, these statements have a theological frame. All of Israel's successes are derived from God's grace enjoyed by the northern rulers (who ruled the south as well), though they still "did not depart from the sins of the house of Jeroboam [...] the sacred pole also remained in Samaria" (2 Kgs 13:6). A similar pattern, in which the synchronistic listing of Judean and Israelite kings is followed by a mixture of negative theological evaluations and political success statements, is found in the description of another Nimshide, Jeroboam, in 2 Kgs 14:24–27. Regarding the king, it is here stated that,

> 24 He did what was evil in the sight of the Lord; he did not depart from all the sins of Jeroboam son of Nebat that he caused Israel to sin. 25 He restored the border of Israel from Lebo-hamath as far as the Sea of the Arabah, according to the word of the Lord, the God of Israel ... 26 For the Lord saw that the distress of Israel was very bitter; there was no one left, bond or free, and no one to help Israel. 27 But the Lord had not said that he would blot out the name of Israel from under heaven, so he saved them by the hand of Jeroboam son of Joash.

The phrase about blotting out the name of Israel from history carries several meanings: the first one is political, involving the Nimshide dynasty, which ascends to power with Jehu and rules the north—and, to a great extent, the south as well—for four generations. This stage of history ends with Zechariah (see 2 Kgs 15:11) whose reign is followed by a rapid decline which ended in the defeat of Samaria. It is not a coincidence that, save for a single verse (2 Kgs 17:2), the evaluation of the remaining Israelite kings—Shallum, Menahem, Pekahiah, Pekah, and Hoshea—is entirely negative. The theological explanation for the fulfilment of God's promise to Jehu in 2 Kgs 10:30—that if not for the violent coup in the house of Ahab, Jehu's sons of the fourth generation would sit on the throne of Samaria—should be anchored in real history.

It may be assumed that the message has a pragmatic political background with a theological frame. As rulers of the north and probably, to a great extent, Judah as well, the Nimshides became part of the southern traditions after the end of the dynasty in 747 BCE. The name *Israel* is maintained through the gradual transmission of heritage, carefully separated from Ahab and his dynasty (see 6.2.5.1.1), to Jerusalem, which becomes a co-successor to the legacy of Samaria probably long before 722 BCE. Outwardly, Judean historiography must proclaim its distinction and separation from the history of the north; at the same time, however, the former must stay in contact with the latter, since both are connected on a historical, religious, and political level. The ambivalence of Judah's relation to the north is a result of two realities mentioned earlier—the dual objective and dual nature of pro-Judean biblical texts.

The nature of the succession of three Judean kings—Azariah and Jotham in the first half of the eighth century BCE, and Ahaz in the early second half of the same century—is no less complex. According to 2 Kgs 15, Azariah acceded at sixteen years of age and went on to rule Jerusalem for fifty-two years (see 5.2). In 756 BCE, the king started to suffer from leprosy, forcing him to live in a separate house until the end of his life, and Jotham, his son, became the ruler of Judah (756–741 BCE).

The length of Azariah's rule is astounding, and it is likely that his reign contained several co-rulers. Especially in the prophetic tradition, Azariah is

---

Azariah (787–736 BCE; co-ruling with Jotham from 756 BCE)

Jotham (756–741 BCE; co-ruling with Ahaz from 741 BCE)

Ahaz (741–725 BCE; ruling independently from 736 BCE)

Fig. 22. Judean kings in the first half and early second half of the eighth century BCE

listed as Uzziah (in the introductions to Isaiah, Hosea, and Amos; see 5.3.2), and the same applies to four instances in 1 Kgs 15 (verses 13, 30, 32, and 34), as well as the entire 2 Book of Chronicles. It is worth noting here, the priest who stands against the king and exhorts him that he must not offer incense to YHWH bears the same name, namely Azariah (see 2 Chr 26: 17–21).

King Uzziah could be related to some Hebrew signets and seals. One of these artifacts bears the name of the king's servant, named Shebanyaw (see COS 2.70R). Though the material is from an unsecured source (now stored in the Louvre and the National Library in Paris), its link to the king appears likely (see Avigad and Sass 1997; Mykytiuk 2004). Since it features the *-yaw* aspect, which, again, might prove the connection of the king and his officials to Samaria, the name is typically Israelite (similarly to another name Abiyaw, again the servant of Uzziyaw; COS 2.70R), and not Judean (which commonly include the theophoric aspects *-yeho-*, *-yahu-*, and *-yah*; but cf. Fleming 2013; Hualong 2024; Čapek and Frevel 2024).

Jotham was likely the last Judean king controlled by the Nimshides from the north. He became the ruler of Jerusalem sometime around 756 BCE, succeeding Azariah. The biblical text provides theological reasons for the takeover—i.e., the leprosy with which the Lord "struck the king" (2 Kgs 15:5). Frevel (2016, 228), on the other hand—although admitting it is a hypothesis—considers the change to be due to the dissatisfaction of Samaria, which led to Israel planting Jotham, another trustworthy Nimshide. His more general claim—that the fifty-two years of Azariah's rule may be understood as a sort of parenthesis, in which Jerusalem's emancipation from Samaria started or even finished—seems to be convincing.

5.3.2 BIBLICAL TEXTS—THE EIGHTH CENTURY BCE AND THE PROPHETIC TRADITIONS

Initiation of the process of Judah's emancipation may be identified in certain prophetic texts relating to the rule of Judean and Israelite kings in the first and early second half of the eighth century BCE. Though these texts were composed gradually and mostly after the time they refer to (see chapter 1), their relation to specific historical events and figures of the period under discussion is evident, as shown in the overview below. The same texts and entire prophetic books were further amended, edited, and their current final forms are dated to a far later time—in biblical studies, both are self-evident, recognised facts (Berges 1998; Schart 1998; Wöhrle 2008; Hoblík 2009; Albertz et al. 2012; Williamson 2019; Nissinen 2019; Mackerle 2019).

Although prophetic texts are very often focused on Israel, their target audience was in Judah. Prophetic criticisms are levelled at Israel as represented by Ephraim and Samaria, but the educational intent is aimed at Jerusalem.

5. FIRST INDEPENDENCE (IRON AGE IIB-C)

Fig. 23. Prophetic books referring to the eighth century BCE

Hosea, the oldest written prophet, claims that "like a stubborn heifer, Israel is stubborn" (Hos 4:16). Such a harsh statement is intended to paint the north as a deterrent example for the south, which does not escape criticism either; hence, the south is the addressee, as the successor to the north. The reason for the frequent presence of Israel is that much of the tradition originated in the north (see 4.2.4). The criticism of Samaria spans all areas of life: cult practices are denounced as abandoning the Lord, dissolving YHWH's marriage to his people, and adultery is described in the same manner. Neither priests nor leaders perform their duties properly, since they lead the people astray. All this is explained against the backdrop of Israel's actions, which serve as a damning testimony on the overall "Baalisation" of the northern state and its departure from the Yahwistic cult.

The history depicted by Hosea, one of the principal witnesses to the northern tradition (Hoffman 1989; Dozeman 2000; Kató 2019; Nissinen 2019), focuses on paradigmatic events that are described with refined poetics: on one hand, the exodus from Egypt and the acquiring of the land form a good beginning of identity formation; however on the other, the defection to Baal and the establishing of a monarchy in general (in a narrower context, this involves Israel, however), is expressed as YHWH's people losing their dignity. As Hosea emphasises, Israel stands trial due to God's righteous anger. The oldest historical reference in Hos 1:4 is linked to Jehu, who is promised punishment (cf. 2 Kgs 9–10!)—i.e., that the kingdom of Israel will meet its end for the "blood of Jezreel." The punishment is then meted out with the kingdom's downfall after the death of Jeroboam II (787–747 BCE; cf. Hos 11:15). Though the other facts included in this prophetic book are of a later date, the original parts of the text, along with the prophetic traditions of the Elijah cycle, can be considered northern, though adapted and reflected from a Judean perspective, with Israel possibly still existing, in the second half of the eighth century BCE (cf. Fleming 2013; Oeming 2016; Na'aman 2020).

Another prophetic tradition, Amos, is situated at the time of the Judean king Uzziah (Azariah) and the acceding Jeroboam II of Israel. Here too, scathing criticism of the north occupies most of the text; however, the main and target addressee is Jerusalem and the new Israel, which Judah gradually becomes in its self-conception, possibly even prior to the fall of Samaria (see 5.3; cf. Čapek 2023).

Isaiah, the most extensive prophetic book, mainly discusses the relation of Israel—which may still have existed then, in the early second half of the eighth century BCE (cf. Williamson 2019)—to Judah in its first section, called Proto-Isaiah (Isa 1–39). Considered among the most authentic passages (Berges 1998; contra Becker 1997), verses 6:1–8:18 treat the relationship between the north and the south as that of two connected houses. The first house, Israel (further specified as Ephraim, Samaria, and Jacob), serves as a warning for the second house, Judah (Jerusalem, Zion), and an example of what not to do. The text unfolds against the historical backdrop of the Syro-Ephraimite War (736–732 BCE) and the threat posed to Judah by Rezin of Aram and Pekah of Israel (Isa 7:1). Gradually, this danger is dissolved in the text, transforming into a lesson for the younger of the two houses, since Assyria becomes the new threat (see Isa 7:9 and 8:4), probably as early as the end of the rule of Ahaz. Isaiah preserves the memory of Israel as "two houses of Israel", which are tied by their respective histories as well as their fates. According to Kristin Weingart (2014; 2015; 2016)—who centred her dissertation upon the name of Israel and dedicated numerous other studies to the same topic—the kingdoms of Israel and Judah were linked by a collective concept of identity, based on more or less presumed mutual ancestors.

These examples from three prophetic traditions further corroborate the close ties between Judah and Israel, be they founded on the stories of patriarchs, tribes, ancestors, or—as proposed by this book—on dynastically related rulers, whose origins must be sought in the north.

5.3.3 BIBLICAL TEXTS—THE EIGHTH CENTURY BCE AND BETHEL

Located twenty kilometres north of Jerusalem, the site of Bethel (*Beitin*) is a subject of intense discussion in contemporary research. As is relatively predictable, earlier dating of the settlement was mainly based on a plain reading of the biblical text which describes the separation of the kingdom and the establishment of the cult under Jeroboam I (933–911 BCE). Having led archaeological expeditions in the area in 1954, 1957, and 1960 (and prior to that, in 1934, with William Albright), James Kelso interpreted the material culture in accordance with biblical texts; consequently, he was in no doubt that the site had been settled in the Iron Age IIA. The excavators did not work stratigraphically, and so "it is Albright's knowledge of the pottery and observation of ceramic changes that redeem" the very unclear stratigraphy of the locality (Gomes 2006, 4). More recent Palestinian-Japanese research, led by Keio University in 2011-13, focused on other features at Bethel; specifically, it examined the Byzantine period water reservoir, the Ottoman period tower, and the necropolis with shaft tombs, where a small amount of Iron Age I pottery was found.

The recently proposed dating of the stratigraphy of Bethel stems from a revision of older excavation reports and especially from detailed pottery analysis (Herzog and Singer-Avitz 2006; Finkelstein and Singer-Avitz 2009; Finkelstein 2013). According to this interpretation, the area was more significantly populated in the Iron Age IIB, and only very sporadically in the Iron Age IIA. If this is the correct conclusion (see discussion in Blenkinsopp 2003; Lipschits 2017 and especially Tavger 2015; 2021), the site was a key Israelite centre during the reigns of Joash (802-787 BCE) and Jeroboam II (787-747 BCE); in this period, Assyrian patronage and the easing off of pressure from Aram Damascus facilitated the growth of Israel, whose territorial expansion reached its peak (see 4.2.2). The influence of the kingdom probably extended far to the south, as the epigraphic finds at Kuntillet 'Ajrud seem to prove. The north's upper hand over the south is acknowledged in biblical texts too (see 5.2.1). From the late ninth century BCE, forty years of economic prosperity were accompanied by the flourishing of literature and also cult centralisation (Na'aman 2002a; Finkelstein 2017; but cf. Na'aman 2020).

According to some scholars, it was in Bethel—the heart of Israel's national, religious, and political identity (Finkelstein and Singer-Avitz 2009, 59)—that such core traditions as the stories about the exodus from Egypt and desert wandering were written or preserved (for a detailed reconstruction, see Finkelstein 2013, 145-51; cf. Blum 2012; but cf. Koenen 2003). Both traditions are likely linked to the time of Jeroboam II, and this connection is indirectly confirmed by a later, pro-southern theological confrontation with the cult of the calf, practised in Bethel, according to biblical texts (see 1 Kgs 12; cf. also Exod 32!). The exodus tradition linked with Moses heading north is, for example, discussed in Hos 12:14; Amos 5:4-5 deals with Bethel as a cult centre; and the same place is referred to in the Jacob cycle and its central legend of a sanctuary being established in Gen 28 (cf. Hos 12:4), as a halfway point between Beer-sheba and Haran (cf. Finkelstein and Römer 2014a).

The northern context of these traditions is demonstrable, which is why it is appropriate to ask how they became part of Judean traditions. According to the *compromise model* (see 4.2.4.3), these literary materials were preserved there in the late Iron Age IIB (the eighth century BCE), and they probably reached the south even prior to the fall of the northern kingdom (Finkelstein

2015; 2017). Alternatively, the events of the late ninth and eighth centuries BCE may be viewed as a gradual development, in which the fall of Samaria and that which immediately preceded it do not constitute a dramatic turn, but are part of a series of events, however important they may have been. The rise of Jerusalem is not necessarily a result of the mass exodus of Israelites from the north—which de facto lacks clearer archaeological evidence—but likely happened earlier than that (Knauf and Guillaume 2016, 110; cf. Frevel 2016, 244-45). The year 722 BCE does not have to be—and by all accounts is not—a universal key to understanding the transmission of northern traditions to Jerusalem; instead, it is more of a scholarly myth *sui generis*, which is slowly and repeatedly reevaluated.

The opinion presented in this book is that the process of transmission and dissemination of biblical traditions was probably gradual and did not occur merely as a reaction to a seminal moment in history. Moreover, if Judah was indeed a branch kingdom of Israel, it is likely that northern traditions had been used in the south even earlier. These were, then, dominant historiographic memories present in the Jerusalem royal court administered by the Nimshides and their descendants, who felt no need to amend them—up to a certain time. Later, in hindsight, the north is viewed through a different and markedly more critical lens (e.g., see the evaluation of Jehu in 2 Kgs 10:28-29). Finally, it should also be noted that the Bethel sanctuary is located a mere twenty kilometres from Jerusalem (Samaria is twice the distance from Bethel).

The peculiar and distinctive southern touch used to rewrite, reform, and update northern traditions is linked to the rise of Judah as an independent state. Judah became independent from Israel in the eighth century BCE under the rule of Ahaz (735-716 BCE), or possibly even before this (see Amaziah's emancipation efforts in the battle against Joash at Beth-shemesh; cf. 2 Kgs 14:8-14). At the time, there was opposition to, as well as the creative adaptation of, northern traditions, which occurred during the formation of a dynastic self-determination that was based on the retrospective construct of the Davidide line (see 4.2.5). During this period, Israel and Judah were still closely linked, a situation that was typified by permeable borders, cultures, and religions (cf. Berlejung 2017, 158-81). Pro-Judean biblical traditions make a conscious effort to weaken and obscure these ties by emphasising borders and underlining cultural and religious habits and differences, aiming to put Judah in the spotlight against the backdrop of a negative depiction of Israel; the latter state is described as a place of violence perpetrated on both an international and domestic level (see Hosea), as well as being a place of social injustice (Amos) and idolatry.

As shown in biblical texts and other sources, the worship of YHWH was part of a cult that became centralised into several sanctuaries in the early eighth century BCE at the latest (Wazana 2016; Hall 2020; but cf. Stahl 2021). Originally northern and redacted in the south, the prophetic tradition attempted to counter this fact by claiming that the north was incapable of honoring its religious commitments and that it was gradually abandoning YHWH to serve Baal, and this process is said to have started at the very beginning of the monarchy, during the time of Jeroboam I. Consequently, several political catastrophes occurred in succession (violent coups, subjugation by Aram Damascus, Assyria, and, finally, a complete demise), which are theologised as punishment for idolatry.

A longer narrative section in 1 Kgs 12-13 is a textbook example of rewriting northern history via religious criticism of Bethel and, by extension, all of Israel. Apart from multiple levels of editorial amendment, this section especially shows the struggle over the legacy of the true "Israel." Judah and the exemplary king Josiah (639-609 BCE) emerge victorious due to the prophecy confirmed in 2 Kgs 23:15-20; Bethel is rejected, since that is where Jeroboam I instituted the cult of the calf (in the north, there is a similar situation in Dan); but through an intertextual connection, even Shiloh, a more ancient sanctuary, is condemned in 1 Sam 2:27-36, along with the local clergy. The mention of Josiah in 1 Kgs 13:2 is one of the reasons that the final composition date is set to as late as the exilic-postexilic period (some date the end of the composition process to the second century BCE; see Knauf 2016; cf. Čapek 2021). The facts identifiable in and beyond the text relate to an earlier period: firstly, to the fictitious conflict in the late tenth century BCE under the "first" Jeroboam; and secondly, to his historically verifiable namesake ruling two centuries later.

In the text mentioned above, the criticism of the Bethel cult focused on the time of Jeroboam I, a period in which the site had not yet been populated, according to the newest interpretations (cf. Römer 2017b; 2020a); therefore, this is likely an elaborate, standardised fiction (Frevel 2016; see 4.2.5). The real, historical, and archaeologically more verifiable setting is the rule of Jeroboam II, when the sanctuary became a border point of the northern kingdom, similarly to Dan. Here, the cult was according to some a state cult, and its centralisation supported inner political stability and ruler legitimacy (Koenen 2003). From a Judean perspective, the site's illegitimacy is underlined by a description in 1 Kings 12 of the establishment of the cult of the calf, which "became a sin" (v. 30), with priests appointed from "among all the people" (v. 31). The calf idolatry may be considered a literary construct, as proposed by some scholars, such as Juha Pakkala (2008; but cf. Berlejung 2009), who thinks the purpose of this idea was to accentuate the sinfulness of Jeroboam I and to ridicule him as the dynastic founder of Israel. As with other researchers (Römer 2017b; Knauf 2017; cf. Sláma 2015), Pakkala speaks of Jeroboam II in the eighth century BCE, who is transformed into the eponymous, and largely historically unverifiable, late tenth-century BCE figure (for more detail, see 4.2.5).

Biblical texts involving Bethel refer to the history of Israel and a specific important place therein in the first half of the eighth century BCE, even though they are projected into the literary construct of the conflict that ostensibly occurred after the division of the United Monarchy, in the late tenth century BCE and the Iron Age IIA. Their confrontational tone, identical to that of prophetic books, may be interpreted as an expression of a wish to exist separately, to differentiate, and to define the borders of a new state—a completely independent Judah. The same literary traditions were further edited and updated, always in accordance with the message that ought to be emphasised in any given historical context.

For example, the ongoing updates are seen in the later commentary on northern religious practices after the fall of Israel in 2 Kgs 17:24–33, albeit situated to the late eighth century BCE. According to the text, the Assyrian king had to send a priest back to Bethel from exile to teach the people "the law of the god of the land" (v. 27). Those who were taught had come from different places and built their shrines on the high places which were previously used by the "Samaritans" or "people of Samaria" (*Šōmrōnîm* in Hebrew; the only occurrence of the name in the Old Testament). The text seems to be a much later polemic reflecting the Persian period and using the myth of the empty land, but this time without the Israelites (see Magen, Misgav, Tsafia et al.; Knoppers 2006; Dušek 2007; 2014; Hensel 2016; cf. 7.2.6).

5.4 SUMMARY

From the available evidence, it is impossible to determine the exact moment when Judah became a fully independent state; yet the terminology concerning this topic is of particular importance (cf. 3.3). As with Israel (see chapter 4), it is necessary to define the meaning and context of independence. Independence is a status in which the existence of a territorial entity—a full-blown state with solid institutional and organisational foundations—is clearly documented. Such a state features a bureaucracy, an army, a justice system, systematic tax collection, as well as construction and the financing of large facilities for use in the economy, such as canals and tunnels (see chapter 6). Other characteristic aspects include social stratification, centralised religion, and contemporary epigraphic and iconographic materials. All of the above is documented for Judah no sooner than the mid-eighth century BCE (see chapter 6).

Having evaluated material culture as well as biblical and non-biblical texts, some researchers consider an independent Judah to date from the second half of the ninth century BCE, or from the end of that century (Sergi 2013; 2015c; 2023; Na'aman 2013; 2016a). However, the present publication proposes that Judah became independent at a later date. The reasoning for this is based on an analysis of the dynastic relations between Israelite and Judean rulers, showing Jerusalem's lasting dependence on Samaria, which used planned marriages to enforce its interests on the south, possibly up until the mid-eighth century BCE (see especially 4.2.5 and 5.2). Judah may have met the above criteria for a developed state even earlier, but it would only become independent later. Placing Judah's independence within this historical context is supported by the shifts in power relations on the small and large maps of the Levant and the role Judah played in them. The following successive events are particularly important:

1. The end of the dominance of Aram Damascus in the late ninth century BCE: Possibly as early as under Jehoahaz (818–802 BCE), Israel resisted Hazael (cf. 2 Kgs 13), and there was no significant change until the Assyrians entered the power struggle, with Adad-nirari III (811–783 BCE) conquering Damascus. King of the land of Samaria (KUR *Sa-me-ri-na-a-a*), Joash (802–787 BCE) of the Nimshide dynasty related to the Omri dynasty paid tribute to Assyria in 796 BCE. A period of calm followed and the Israelite kings—a more acceptable political entity to the Assyrians than the more powerful Aram Damascus—enjoyed relatively significant independence. This expanded Assyrian influence in the south. Under Joash and Jeroboam II (787–747 BCE), Israel expanded or became influential in both the north and south (see for instance the Kuntillet 'Ajrud epigraphic findings) and, under Assyrian patronage, enjoyed forty years of economic prosperity, with flourishing international trade, the development of literature, and cult centralisation.

2. Jeroboam II's death in 747 BCE: After this period of consolidation, the calm political situation ended; Zechariah, the last Nimshide ruler, was killed during the incipient Aramean revolt against Assyria, and Israel's economic prosperity ground to a halt.

3. The accession of Tiglath-Pileser III in 745 BCE: The acceding, mighty Assyrian king transformed the southern Levant with his offensive politics. Aram Damascus and other states came under pressure; Rezin of Damascus had Zechariah murdered, weakening the northern kingdom, and he, with Pekah of Israel (735–732 BCE) and Hiram II (739–730 BCE), established a coalition that intended to prevent Assyrian expansion (see Kuan 2016).

4. Judah joining Assyria: Ahaz, king of Judah, became a vassal of Assyria at the cost of conflict with his northern neighbours in the Syro-Ephraimite War (ca. 736–732 BCE). This pragmatic decision enabled Ahaz to resist a military intervention from the north in 735 BCE and to increase the in-

fluence of Judah (cf. 2 Kgs 16:5–9). The Assyrian vassal list from 734 BCE names him "Jehoahaz of Judah" (^{m}*Ia-ú-ha-zi* ^{kur}*Ia-u-da-a*), making him the very first Judean ruler to be unequivocally documented in non-biblical texts (also see 5.1).
5. The gradual defeat of Aram Damascus and Israel: The changes in the political landscape of the Southern Levant showed in the establishment of numerous Assyrian provinces and vassal states. Damascus was finally defeated in 732 BCE, becoming a province of Assyria, like the northern part of Israel (the province of Magidû). The highlands met a similar fate ten years later, turning into the province of Samarina (Becking 1992; Kahn 2019, Levin 2019; Radner 2019; Tappy 2019) after the fall of Samaria. As Israel's successor state sui generis, Judah formulated its origins in a specifically designed historiography based on northern traditions, which underwent far-reaching reform and were rewritten; however, Israel as such remained present in its concept of history.

When considering the origins of specific states, one has to bear in mind that the written documents—especially biblical texts in Israel and Judah's case—describe the moment of a political entity's conception in retrospect. This is not an uncommon phenomenon, as proven by the emergence process of Czech statehood, for example: Czech statehood is born retrospectively, centuries later, using more or less verifiable historical facts, mythical themes, and traditions, which aim to document its very origins first, and only then to focus on the periods that follow (see Třeštík 1997; 1999; 2003; Charvát 2007; 2011; Wihoda 2015; Lutovský 2006, Sommer, Třeštík a Žemlička 2009). Origins are often depicted in great detail (for a demonstration, see 1 Kgs 11–13), to emphasise the turning point and the moment of conception. Such a description ought to be subjected to critical analysis, so that the reconstruction is informed by historically verifiable facts rather than events portrayed in a paradigmatically ideal manner. There is no doubt that the latter are crucial to subsequent identity formation, but they must be assigned to a specific verifiable place in history—i.e., we must examine their provenance and what they mean to convey with their retrospective view. In literary compositions, it is necessary to differentiate between standardised historical fiction and accounts of actual historical events.

Judah was still a branch kingdom of Israel in the late ninth and early eighth centuries. Compared to the impressive depiction of its mythical origins, Judah's journey to independence is much less conspicuous, beginning at the time of Israel's final flourishing before that state entered a period of slow decay and ended completely with the fall of Samaria in 722 BCE. Either detailing the events of the first half of the eighth century BCE directly or making more or less veiled references to these, several prophetic (esp. Hosea and Amos) and historiographic texts have a polemical tone that testifies to this subtle and long birth of Judean independence. With this, the Kingdom of Judah entered a new historical period, as well as a time during which it created its own form of memory, thereby establishing its own independent identity, whilst being heavily influenced by the traditions and legacy of the north, from which it largely originated.

6. THE LAST LONG CENTURY (IRON AGE IIC)

> *Tendencies in biblical studies sometimes appear to overshadow objectivity of interpretation, and the fundamentalist approach has also had its impact. On such background some major mistakes were made in the interpretation of archaeological discoveries.*
> —Amihai Mazar

The Iron Age IIC—defined as the last third of the eighth century BCE to the early sixth century BCE in modified conventional chronology—may be termed a long century in the history of Judah (Čapek—Lipschits 2019), starting with transformations in the Southern Levant, which include the fall of Damascus in 732 BCE and the collapse of Israel ten years later (Lipschits 2019). The end of this period is foreshadowed by the events of 605 BCE: due to the battles of Carchemish and then Hamath, in which the remnants of the Egyptian army were defeated, the status quo in the Near East was shattered (cf. ABC 5). Led by Nebuchadnezzar II (605–562 BCE), the Neo-Babylonian Empire became the new hegemon, defeating Assyria and restricting the 26th Dynasty's influence over the Southern Levant. The very end of the Kingdom of Judah came in 587/586 BCE: after Neo-Babylonian interventions and the deportation of a part of the Judean population, Jerusalem was fully conquered, the walls were torn down, the temple and other important buildings burned down, and another section of the populace was taken captive. This marked the end of the time termed the *pre-exilic*, or the First Temple period in the history of ancient Israel.

In the period under discussion, traditions adopted from the north were continuously edited in Judah, and a monumental historiography conceived from a Judean perspective was gradually composed which resulted in the Deuteronomistic History. According to Martin Noth, the author of the comprehensive theory about the work's existence, it featured biblical books from Deuteronomy to the Second Book of Kings and started to be composed during the reign of Josiah, yet was only finished after 562 BCE (see esp. Noth 1943). The theory of a Deuteronomistic History has been further developed and, despite all the criticisms, changes, additions and extensive reformulations, it is still one of the fundamental pillars and key historiographical concepts that are applied to the Old Testament (Prudký 2011; Rückl 2016; Römer 2020b).

6.1 ANCIENT DOMINOES

Similar to the first half of the eighth century BCE, the majority of the long last century in the history of the Kingdom of Judah is characterised by the dominance of Assyria, which, starting in the first half of the seventh century BCE, was increasingly pressured by Egypt and, eventually, the Neo-Babylonian Empire as well. In the first half of the eighth century BCE, Assyrian rulers allowed states in the southern Levant to remain largely independent for pragmatic reasons, only restricting the political activities of the most influential among them, Aram Damascus; however, Assyria changed its policies drastically with the accession of Tiglath-Pileser III (745–727 BCE). The ruler led several campaigns beyond the Euphrates, with the 734 BCE (Younger 2007; Kuan 2016) campaign carrying particular importance for Judah. With the rule of Pekahiah of Israel (737–736 BCE) coming to an end, Ahaz (736–725 BCE), King of Judah, became an Assyrian vassal and the first Judean ruler clearly documented in a non-biblical text. Listed in the Assyrian text by the longer name of Jehoahaz of Judah (ᵐIa-ú-ha-zi ᵏᵘʳIa-u-da-a), Ahaz joined the rulers of Ashkelon, Ammon, Moab, and Edom in paying tribute, which provided the kingdom with an opportunity to establish a political existence of its own. This pragmatic decision came at the cost of exposing Judah to the threat posed by the anti-Assyrian coalition in the Syro-Ephraimite War (736–732 BCE) but Assyria stood up for its Judean vassal and thereby secured its loyalty.

Gradually, those polities which actively resisted Assyria were defeated, and the conquered kingdoms were transformed into provinces. Damascus met this fate in 732 BCE, and so did Samaria under the last Israelite king, Hoshea (732–723 BCE), who chose to form a new anti-Assyrian coalition with Osorkon IV (730–713 BCE), pharaoh of the 22nd Dynasty. However, this orientation towards Egypt did not pay off for Israel. Hoshea was captured, Israel occupied, and Samaria conquered, either by Shalmaneser V (727–722 BCE) or Sargon II (722–705 BCE). Contrary to the idea of the total destruction of Israel, as depicted in biblical texts, the available archaeological evidence suggests that the Assyrians merely paralysed the administrative and strategic centres—such as Dan, Bethsaida, Tel Hadar, En Gev, Dor, Dothan, Tirzah, and Beth-shean—while other localities—Taanach, Jezreel, Tel Qiri, and Bethel—were left untouched, as proven by the settlement continuity therein. It is also likely that the nature of these deportations were different to the traditional account: by all accounts, the number of people deported and, consequently, of those that were brought into the northern highlands and Samaria from Mesopotamia may have been lower than the figure included in biblical texts (cf. 2 Kgs 17:5–6.24–28). These events did take place, but the proportions were not the same. A similar development occurred in Judah later (see chapter 7), with an almost identical literary depiction, which amplifies historical events—including the conquest, relocation, and deportation—with historicising myths about utter destruction, a completely empty land, and the people that must return to this empty land (Barstad 1996; cf. Lipschits 2005; Moore and Kelle 2011; Stöckl and Waerzeggers 2015; cf. Ntozakhe and Leepo 2020).

The reign of Ahaz (741–725 BCE) provided Judah with calm and economic prosperity, which affected numerous areas of life, but only on the condition that the vassalage to Assyria be honoured. The cultural influence of Assyria gradually became more and more evident in the Judean cult, architecture, economy, land administration, and small material culture (see 6.2.1). The last third of the eighth century BCE saw the growth of Jerusalem and its surroundings, but also other cities in the Beer-sheba Valley and the Shephelah. It is possible to assume that the Assyrians had everything under control until 706 BCE, when Hezekiah, son of Ahaz, became the leader of another line of anti-Assyrian resistance. Consequently, the construction efforts in Judah (canals, forts, walls, terraces, and gardens), which are still often seen in biblical studies as well as archaeology as activities that should be linked to subsequent resistance (e.g., Berlejung 2017), must be reevaluated. In terms of material culture, the change in political orientation cannot be clearly identified on an archaeological basis within such a small time frame, a matter of a few years, apart from its unintended final consequences—i.e., unmistakable traces of destruction. Absolute dating may be possible in this particular case, but alone it provides no clear clues to describing life in Judah during the preceding period and therefore no understanding of any possible transformations of that life (see 6.2.1).

At the start of his rule, Hezekiah (725–697 BCE) was a loyal vassal of Assyria. According to the annals of Sargon II (722–705 BCE), it seems unlikely that Hezekiah participated in the uprising joined by Hanunu of Gaza and Ilubidi of Hamath in 720 BCE (Frevel 2016, 253). Seven years later, in 713 BCE, growing support for Egypt—which was rising in power—was documented among rulers throughout the Coastal Plain. Having conspired with the local aristocracy to depose the pro-Assyrian ruler, Ahimit, Yaman of Ashdod attempted to form an anti-Assyrian coalition with Egypt, Moab, Edom, and Judah. In response, Sargon II led a campaign against Ashdod and Gath and formed a province in southern Philistia. According to Assyrian annals, Ashdod was sacked and Yaman fled the city, only to be captured by the pharaoh Shabaka (715–700 BCE) and handed in chains to Sargon II (COS 2.118J).

The beginning of Hezekiah's active resistance against the Assyrians dates to 706–705 BCE. In the latter year, Sargon II was succeeded by his son Sennacherib (705–681 BCE), who then led his first western campaign in the fourth year of his rule (see an overview of the campaigns in Elayi 2018). At the time, there was more unrest in the Levant, stirred up by Ekron, Arwad,

Sidon, Byblos, Ashkelon, the Transjordanian states, and Hezekiah's Judah. The rebels refused to pay tribute and tried to get Shabaka of Egypt to ally with their cause; Hezekiah was considered the guiding spirit of the uprising (first mentioned in Donner 1987; later also in, e.g., Schipper 1999; Frevel 2016). On the other hand, other polities refused to join the anti-Assyrian league—for example, Padi of Ekron, who remained loyal to Assyria and was consequently deposed, with Judah's assistance. The revolt against the Assyrians was ended by Sennacherib's belated third campaign into the southern Levant in 701 BCE, which had been delayed by the construction of a new residence in Nineveh and then by conflicts with Babylonia. Assyrian armies gradually reconquered Sidon, forcing King Luli to escape to Cyprus and they replaced him with the loyal ruler Tub'alu. Similar situations played out elsewhere too, as tribute was again paid by Arwad, Byblos, the Philistine states, and the rulers from the Transjordan and Edom. After stabilising matters in Ashkelon by replacing its ruler, Sennacherib moved to Ekron to restore order there as well. Ekron's governors sought Egypt's help against the threat of Assyrian intervention. An important—and the only—battle took place at Eltekeh, north of the Philistine city, where the Assyrian army defeated the Kushite forces of the King of Nubia, restoring the original ruler, Padi of Ekron, to his seat.

After the victory at Eltekeh, the Assyrian military campaign continued south in the Shephelah, leading to the capture of the strategic Judean forts of Lachish and Azekah. These strategically placed cities had protected access routes from the Coastal Plain to Judah, which is why they were destroyed, to paralyse the country's military, allowing Assyria to restore its hegemony. The downfall of Lachish is documented on the monumental Lachish relief (COS 2.119C) discovered in Nineveh. The Azekah inscription (COS 2.119D) refers in detail to the latter area, describing the destruction of the Judean city as follows:

> 3 [..... Assur, my lord, encouraged] me and [I marched] against Ju[dah. In] the course of the campaign [I recieved] the tribute [of all] the k[ings of Amurru] 4 by the po]wer of Assur, my lord, [I overwhelmed] a district [of Hezeki]ah of Judah as [with a bird-snare] 5 [.....] Azekah, his supply city, which between my territory and Judah [.....] 6 [.....] situated [on] a mountaintop like countless sharp blades of i[ro]n reaching the sky (while) [its] foundations reach the center of the netherworld]. 7 [Its walls] were extremely strong and competed with high mountains, at the lo[ok] of the eyes as if from the sky [..........] 8 [The building of sie]ge ramps, drawing battering-rams up close, the powerful work of the "b[ig fl]y" (?), the hand-to-hand combat of infantry [.....] 9 They saw [the storming] of my [hors]es, heard the battle cry of the proud hosts of Assur (and) they became afraid [.....] 10 [Azekah I besieged], conquered (and) plundered, and I destroyed (it) completely [..........].
>
> (Mayer 2003, 199)

Dating Sennacherib's campaign and the destruction of the Judean cities to 701 BCE is chronologically secure (cf. Frahm 1997; Galil 1995). Assyrian records state that Sennacherib besieged forty-six cities and forts in total. However, the available archaeological evidence makes it obvious that numerous places—especially in the central parts of Judah—were not damaged by the Assyrian campaign. This applies to Jerusalem as well, which may have been besieged (possibly more than once; see Becking 2003) by smaller Assyrian units, or cut off from strategic access routes; but no attempt was made to seize it (cf. 2 Kgs 19), since it was unnecessary.

The aim of the Assyrian campaign was not destruction; instead, it was meant to restore order and secure the southern border. By subjugating the rebels, a buffer zone with Egypt was formed, stretching from the Transjordan below the Beer-sheba Valley to the Mediterranean Sea. Sennacherib's campaign allowed him to ensure the safety of trade routes in the Negev—through which caravans passed carrying copper, spice, and other wares from the Arabah to Mediterranean ports—and to gain control over maritime trade by the Via Maris. Vassal states were expected to pay tribute in commodities that they produced (mainly olive oil, wine, and corn). The famous quote about the imprisonment of Hezekiah "like a bird in a cage," on the Rassam cylinder (COS 2.119B), is a poetic depiction of the efficiency and ruthlessness of Assyrian policies in the south. The same expression is used earlier by Tiglath-Pileser III, when he imprisoned Rezin in Damascus in 733 BCE (see COS 2.117A); a similar turn of phrase is featured in Amarna correspondence even prior to that, in the fourteenth century BCE (see EA 74 and 81).

Judah was punished for its resistance, by losing lands in the fertile parts of the seaside area, the western Shephelah, and the south. Hezekiah's kingdom was bordered and enclosed by Assyrian provinces in the north and the Transjordan in the east. Its western border was formed by Philistine cities, loyal vassals to Nineveh as well. Owing to Sennacherib's 701 BCE campaign, "the land below the border of Assyria's Palestinian provinces, now a viable glacis, was secured, as were important routes and lines of communication on the coastal plain. This together with the young king's gained experience and new familiarity with the region were valuable preventive measures against future military conflicts" (Mayer 2003, 185). According to Frevel (2016, 259), throughout this entire scenario Judah was more of a means to an end, not the purpose of the campaign.

According to Assyrian records, under the next Judean king, Manasseh (696–642 BCE),—who may have been installed as Hezekiah's co-ruler by pro-Assyrian powers as early as 701 BCE—Judah was a loyal vassal of Esarhaddon (681–669 BCE) and Ashurbanipal (669–631 BCE). During Manasseh's rule, the kingdom enjoyed a new period of prosperity, linked to the economic growth of the Neo-Assyrian Empire, whose territorial expansion reached its peak.

In 671 BCE, Esarhaddon led a campaign into Memphis and declared himself King of Egypt; four years later, Ashurbanipal conquered Thebes as well. Under Manasseh, Jerusalem continued to grow, which may have also been due to an influx of population from the lands that were lost under Hezekiah and which were gradually repopulated (Tel 'Eton, Lachish, Tell Beit Mirsim, and Tel Khalif; for more on the dating of resettled lands, see 6.2.3).

The son of Manasseh, Amon (641-640 BCE), only ruled Judah briefly before being murdered. Some believe his elimination was a result of a power struggle in Jerusalem between the supporters of pro- and anti-Assyrian groups (cf. Frevel 2016), but this interpretation cannot be substantiated further, even though such inner political tensions are to be expected (cf. 6.2.4). According to the biblical text, Amon was murdered by his servants (2 Kgs 21:23), and the people of the land took it upon themselves to avenge the murder and enthrone Amon's son, Josiah (639-609 BCE; the enthroning of Jehoahaz in 609 BCE is described in a similar manner). Thus, the throne was ascended by one of the most important kings in Judean history, who is linked mainly to religious reform and the rise of monotheism, but for whom there is no substantial evidence apart from the biblical account, despite the length of his rule (for more detail, see 6.2.6).

Josiah's rule saw an irreversible decline in Assyrian influence after more than two centuries; this took place towards the end of the rule of Ashurbanipal (669-631 BCE), Ashur-etil-ilani (631-627 BCE), and other kings. The southern Levant gradually came under the influence of the 26th Dynasty of Egypt, under Psamtik I (664-610 BCE) and Necho II (610-595 BCE). Currently, the period between Assyria's retreat and the arrival of Egypt can be only approximated. Though, it is clear that Egypt assumed control over Judah no later than 610 BCE (Schipper 2011, Wimmer 2008a; 2008b). Older research interpreted these power shifts as resulting in the formation of a *Machtvakuum*, which Judah took advantage of to expand its territory into the Coastal Plain, or even as far as the Mediterranean Sea, and far north into lands that had originally belonged to Israel (Aharoni 1978, 348; cf. Mazar 1992, 405). By contrast, the uncovering of more abundant material evidence now makes it clear that there was an essentially seamless transition from Assyrian presence in the region to Egyptian influence, and that the 26th Dynasty used the existing administration, merely adapting it to suit its needs (Lipschits 2005; Keel 2007).

Egyptian presence in the area administered by Judah, according to the map outlined by biblical texts, is documented by material culture, especially a large number of scarabs and imported Greek pottery linked to Greek mercenaries serving Egypt, who resided in military bases guarding the Via Maris. Such was the reasoning behind the construction, circa 615 BCE, of the Egyptian fort near Ashdod, named Mesad Hashavyahu (for the possible Judean origin of the locality, see Wenning 1989). There were other posts manned by soldiers, such as Ashkelon and Dor, and inland these included Ekron, Arad, and Tel Batash. Though it was integral to the cultural, trade, and religious interactions in the region, Judah had neither the time nor the power to take control over the putatively empty space vacated by the Assyrians (cf. Čapek 2019a). The Assyrians, and, later, Egypt and Philistine cities, held power over important processes in Judah, which is why Jerusalem was not the tax collector but a contributor—it was not in, but under control, remaining a vassal state on the periphery of the empire (cf. Na'aman 1991). Judean fiscal seals and an ostracon from the Moussaief Collection, both dated to the time of Josiah, prove that Judah became part of the Egyptian tax collection system soon after the Assyrian tribute had ended (Wimmer 2008a; Schipper 2010).

The end of Josiah's rule is connected to another power shift that took place in the north, in Syria, but which struck Judah with full force. The king headed to Megiddo to help Necho II, during the joint campaign of Assyria and Egypt to the Euphrates against the rising Neo-Babylonian Empire, but he was killed for unknown reasons in 609 BCE. One can only speculate as to what caused Josiah's violent demise. The most likely clue might be in the change within the 26th Dynasty, with the accession of Necho II in the preceding year (610 BCE). Josiah might have been summoned to Megiddo, since Judah had shirked its vassal obligations, and received punishment there as a warning (cf. Na'aman 1991; Talshir 1996; Blenkinsopp 2013; Delamarter 2004). The draconian punishment would match the tension which was undoubtedly mounting in Egypt and Assyria due to the rise of new competition in the form of the Neo-Babylonians.

According to the biblical account, in 609 BCE Josiah was succeeded by Jehoahaz, who was enthroned by the "people of the land" (2 Kgs 23:30; cf. 2 Kgs 21:24). However, after a mere three months, he was deposed by Necho II and deported to Egypt. Eliakim (608–598 BCE) became the new king supported by Egypt, with the pharaoh renaming him Jehoiakim and imposing heavy tribute requirements upon him. After the Battle of Carchemish in 605 BCE, Egypt's situation took a turn for the worse. The influence of the new hegemon, the Neo-Babylonian Empire under Nebuchadnezzar II (605–562 BCE), rose even in the region west of the Euphrates and to the south. Like many former vassals of Egypt, Judah voluntarily submitted to Babylonia in 604 BCE. Three years later, there was a battle on the Egyptian border with an indecisive outcome, but in which the Neo-Babylonian army sustained substantial losses. Despite different opinions advising him against it—as evidenced from biblical texts (cf. Jer 36)—Jehoiakim was tempted by Egypt's temporary rise to bet on the southern card again, and this decision backfired on Judah four years later. In 597 BCE (according to 2 Kgs 24:12, it was in 596 BCE), Nebuchadnezzar II led a campaign against Jerusalem and conquered it for the first time; this occurred under Jehoiachin (598–597 BCE), since the preceding Judean king met a violent or peaceful end in the meantime (see 2 Kgs 24:6; 2 Chr 36:6; Jer 22:18). According to Flavius Josephus (Ant. 10:96–98), Jehoiakim was killed by the Babylonian king himself, and his body was left unburied outside the city walls.

Jehoiakim's rule is usually interpreted in accordance with biblical texts as a period that constrasts with the time of Josiah. The younger king is seen as godless, weak, and an oppressor of his own people (2 Kgs 23:37; 24:4; Jer 36), while his predecessor is described as a paragon of piety, who built and expanded the territory of the Kingdom of Judah. Bernd Schipper (2010) offers a different perspective of Jehoiakim: a ruler who achieved the best he could, in that he was able to "consolidate his territory" with the help of Greek mercenaries whom he kept in his service even after changing vassalage. It follows that "from the perspective of foreign policy Jehoiakim was the more significant, and apparently the more skillful king of Judah on the eve of the exile—even if he ultimately could not stop the developments that led to the conquest of Jerusalem and the collapse of the Kingdom of Judah" (ibid., 221). This more positive depiction may be indirectly confirmed by rosette stamp impressions from the western Shephelah, especially the Tel Batash Stratum II, if they were taken as proof of Judean economic administration still functioning on the western border. Jane Cahill (1995) champions another interpretation: the rosettes prove Jehoiakim's efforts to foster trade with the Philistine city of Ekron, strengthening local ties against the growing influence of the Neo-Babylonian Empire (cf. Cahill 1997; 2000; 2003; and furthermore, Koch and Lipschits 2013).

The first conquest of Jerusalem and the first deportation in 597 BCE are well documented in the Babylonian Chronicles (ABC 5) and biblical texts. The capital was symbolically despoiled and robbed of its splendour rather than sacked: all treasures were taken from the temple and the royal palace and brought to Babylon, and all gold articles were cut up (2 Kgs 24:13; the bronze items are not moved away until the second deportation; see 2 Kgs 25:13–18). It is likely that only a minority of the population was led away to Babylonia, while the rest remained in place (cf. a different account in 2 Kgs 24:14); and it is possible that Jehoiachin's surrender was voluntary (cf. 2 Kgs 24:12). Nebuchadnezzar took him hostage and led him away to Babylon, along with the king's family and attendants. Mattaniah—Jehoiachin's uncle, also named Zedekiah—was then installed as king. Biblical texts follow the deported king's fate until the accession of Amel-Marduk (562–560 BCE), who released him and his sons in 561 BCE, after thirty-seven years of captivity (according to 2 Kgs 25:27).

The very end of the Kingdom of Judah occurred with the second conquest of Jerusalem under Zedekiah (598/597–587/586 BCE), the third son of Josiah. The king was a loyal vassal of the Neo-Babylonian Empire until 594 BCE, when Egypt grew stronger in the southern Levant, again under Psamtik II (595–589 BCE). The strengthening of Egypt's position was probably due to an uprising in Babylon, which Nebuchadnezzar needed to resolve. Siding with Apries (589–570 BCE), son of Psamtik, who continued his father's policy of expansion, Zedekiah renounced his vassalage to Babylon. As stated by some prophetic biblical traditions in hindsight—especially Jeremiah—this decision again turned out to be a grave error in foreign policy (cf. Frevel 2016, 274), soon leading to grave consequences. Led by Nebuzaraddan, the Babylonian army besieged Jerusalem, although the siege was temporarily lifted to allow military forces to be moved northwest to protect the Via Maris (this political and tactical interpretation must be applied to the text of Jer. 37:5, which is confirmed by verse 8), where Apries had taken advantage of the Babylonian army's concentration in Judah to attack Phoenician coastal cities. Judah's situation was made worse by pressure exerted in the south by the attempts of the Edomites to take control over the southern Shephelah. This may be corroborated by Arad ostraca 24 and 40 (COS 3.43K and COS 3.43L); in the latter ostracon, the commander of the southern stronghold of Tel Ira asks for reinforcements (see discussion in Guillaume 2013). According to some researchers, the Edomites were also involved in the siege of Jerusalem, which is reflected in their poor reputation in numerous biblical texts (see the overview in Frevel 2016, 277).

Nebuzaraddan renewed the siege of Jerusalem in the late summer of 588 BCE and breached the walls approximately a year later, on 29 July 587 BCE. The biblical account depicts the army entering the city and Zedekiah attempting to escape to Jericho, before being arrested and dragged away to Riblah, Syria, where Nebuchadnezzar had set up his headquarters. The text also describes the murder of the king's sons, the blinding of the king, and his eventual departure to Babylon. A month after the king's imprisonment, Nebuzaraddan ordered that Jerusalem be destroyed completely: the temple was burned down, as was the palace and all significant buildings, and the walls were demolished; plus, there is a detailed description of the temple being despoiled and the inventory being taken away (2 Kgs 25:9–10). Meanwhile, representatives, priests, and other important Judean officials linked to the administration of the city and the temple were systematically eliminated in Riblah. According to the depiction, there was no one left in the city or probably even its surroundings, apart from peasants, vineyard workers, and farmers (2 Kgs 25:12). Consequently, "Judah went into exile out of its land" (v. 21; however, cf. the very next verses, 22–26), and the reader is faced with a picture of utter destruction, which carries a political, as well as an ideological, message (see below, and especially chapter 7).

The end of this long century, which finished with the fall of Jerusalem, was a major turn in the history of Judah, which was also the bearer of northern traditions. Having been dispersed into several areas and in several waves, the Judeans—as well as those who remained in the land—looked for a way to explain the defeat and to justify why they had "acted the way they did." They depicted the shifting political landscape of the southern Levant under Assyria, Egypt, and the Neo-Babylonian Empire in a very distinct manner. The Hebrew Bible offers numerous often competing or even contradictory answers, which are influenced by two main factors: firstly, the various different literary stages of individual textual testimonies, from the time of their original composition to their later forms after any editorial amendments; and secondly, the authors, who did not form a single, clearly defined group, since they came from various spheres. This explains the diverse trains of thought present throughout biblical texts, which cannot be attributed to a single common denominator; the only denominator is the conviction that the year 587/586 BCE was not merely an end but was also—and especially—a new beginning. This conviction is expressed in a far-reaching reflection on history, including its very beginnings; it is even present within historiographies that focus on the exilic and postexilic periods and give new interpretations of the past.

6.2 HISTORICAL CROSSROADS, INTERSECTIONS, AND CUL-DE-SACS

The preceding section described the Kingdom of Judah in the Iron Age IIC and its history vis-à-vis other nations and empires (cf. Lipschits 2021). The independent Judah's last long—and only whole—century is a series of dramatic events, which are reflected in distinctive biblical historiographies that were composed in a remarkable manner. Their aim is to depict history as a continuum that reaches back to the origins of the kingdom, which are traced back as far as the Iron Age I and the late eleventh century BCE—to its very dawn under Saul and to also include what happened beforehand as well (see chapter 2). In this history, important events are emphasised and elaborated into longer literary compositions, while those that do not fit the authors' intentions are backgrounded, creatively rewritten, and transformed—such as via extensive narrative compositions that are imbued with negative undertones (see the stories of Jeroboam I and Ahab). One can best comprehend these historiographies through a *theology of history*, which has a specific intention and is expressed in the text in a way that does not necessarily overlap with history as reconstructed using material culture and non-biblical textual evidence.

The sections below discuss the individual kings according to the order in which they ruled Judah in the Iron Age IIC, essentially following two basic lines of interpretation. The first line focuses on the way biblical historiography authors use and transform historical facts in order to form a particular view of the identity of ancient Israel, whose legitimate successor Judah claims to be; whilst the second line deals with the results of the most recent archaeological research and engages this in critical confrontation with the first.

6.2.1 AHAZ: CONSOLIDATION, REFORMS, AND CONSTRUCTION EFFORTS UNDER ASSYRIAN SUPERVISION

Ahaz (736–725 BCE)—the first king of the territorial state of Judah (cf. 5.1) to be clearly documented in a non-biblical text – recognised the power of Assyria and made the pragmatic decision to become its loyal vassal in 734 BCE, ruling from the safety of the hegemon's shadow. The period is subject to some moderate criticism in Kings (2 Kgs 16) and is portrayed in a very negative light in Chronicles (2 Chr 28) and also some prophetic traditions; in terms of Judean history, the king is depicted as entirely capitulating to the will of Tiglath-Pileser III (747–727 BCE). This view is further emphasised by the entirely contrasting, highly positive evaluation of Hezekiah, the king's successor, and his revolt in 701 BCE. Though the uprising ended in bitter defeat, the destruction of many key areas of Judah, and a more severe subjugation than Ahaz suffered, the Judean king is described as a ruler who aimed to enforce national interests, which brings him into the same idealogical milieu as David, an idealised politician and "founding father" of the kingdom, and also King Josiah, who ruled in the second half of the seventh century BCE and is also regarded positively. The biblical account paints Hezekiah's reign as a crucial period, which makes it all too easy for scholars to harmonise this with the closest period that contains significant material culture, which, in turn, corroborates the same account. When faced with such a presentation of Hezekiah and his time, one cannot resist the impression that this is a case of circular reasoning.

Determined mainly by the biblical perspective for decades, this view is based on a logic which considers that if something new happened, it did not occur during the rule of Ahaz—a ruler portrayed negatively in biblical texts—but later. Consequently, all significant administrative measures, construction efforts, and territorial gains are attributed to Hezekiah, who resisted the might of Assyria and engaged in intense building activities, preparing Judah to fight for political independence (Keimer 2011; cf. Ein-Mor 2013, Ein-Mor and Ron 2016, Gadot and Uziel 2017). As proven by a more detailed investigation and critical reading of biblical texts, this is one of several possible interpretations, and a different historical reconstruction will be proposed here.

The previous chapter showed that Judah had started its journey to independence in the first half of the eighth century BCE, and that this process had likely finished under Ahaz. Owing to his prudent policies—which were, however, seen by some in retrospect as minimalistic—Judah maintained its status as a vassal kingdom and was not transformed into a province, unlike numerous other states in the area. Certainly, the advantageous geographical location of Judah and strategic decisions made by the decisive figures on the great map of the Near East played a part in that as well. Ahaz accepted Assyrian superiority and paid tribute, allowing Judah to enjoy a period of peace and economic prosperity. Concurrently, cultural influences were also adopted, which involved the nature of the cult (see the analysis of 2 Kgs 16 below), architecture, and the character of small material culture items. At this juncture, we will avoid discussing the Assyrianisation of Judah and content ourselves with the following: if such a process ever took place, it entailed individual cultures in the southern Levant blending and enriching each other gradually and in multiple directions, and it was not the violent development that some think (see 6.2.3).

It appears necessary to reevaluate scholarly opinion regarding building efforts in Judah—which included the construction of water supply tunnels, irrigation canals, fortifications, walls, strongholds, and terraces—and to not merely link them to the thesis about the resistance prepared by Hezekiah (cf. Keimer 2011; Berlejung 2010), which did not start until 706 BCE (see 6.1). Without contemporary texts that provide an accurate description of the change in political orientation, and given that archaeological findings cannot be dated to within a decade or two, it is impossible to hypothesise a single initiator of the change. The Assyrian texts that refer to the revolt itself, i.e. to the very end of the 8th century BCE, are reliable sources, but they do not in any way describe the internal political events in Judea as such. The biblical preference for Hezekiah, placing Ahaz into history's shadow, is, at the very least, ambiguous in terms of its historical value to scholarly reconstructions of events in the southern kingdom. When attempting to render the developments in Judah in the second half of the eighth century BCE as precisely as possible, there are interpretive tools other than biblical texts. The latter were committed to writing only later, but are often—and almost superficially—interlinked with analyses of archaeological findings.

There is a highly efficient and exact method to observe the history of the Kingdom of Judah in the Iron Age IIC—the analysis of stamp impressions on jars. With a capacity of 40–50 litres and four massive handles, these vessels were used to gather and transport agricultural produce. Until the early 2000s, Hezekiah's preparations to confront the Assyrians were thought to be proven by lemelekh seals and eponymous vessels (in Hebrew, *lmlk* means "belonging to the king," in the sense that the contents of the jar—such as oil, corn, or olives—are demanded by the king as tax). Under their symbols, seals adorned with a winged scarab, sun disc, or the emblem of a flying scroll with two wings usually featured the name of one of four Judean places (Hebron, Sokho, Ziph, and Mamshit) that served as administrative centres either for the manufacture of the jars or the collection of agricultural commodities. The two former localities have been identified; for the latter two, numerous localities have been proposed, including Jerusalem and Ramat Rahel, an area close to the capital (see below). As proven by petrographic analysis and geographical context, the second place, Sokho, is the most likely hub for the production of these vessels (Goren 2016).

Until recently, the seals were dated mainly using the stratigraphy of Lachish submitted by David Ussishkin (2004a) and a very detailed typology of these artefacts by André Lemaire (1981b). Many impressions found in Stratum III (dated to 701 BCE, the time of Sennacherib's campaign) and a clear differentiation from Stratum II, linked to another conquest of the city by the Neo-Babylonian army in 587/586 BCE, allowed these findings to be connected to Hezekiah's economic measures before the Assyrian invasion (Ussishkin 2004a; 2004b; Vaughn 1999; Keimer 2011). This modified the notion proposed by older research that the seals were dated to a later period, in the time of Josiah (Albright 1943; 1958; Cross 1969).

Due to the growing number of impressions discovered (over 2,000 in total, of which 1,400 are from a clear context), an even more in-depth typology of stamp impressions was proposed in the early 2010s, which also analysed the morphology of the jars based on 3D scanning as well as petrography. Owing to both tools, the areas of clay mining and vessel production were determined with high precision, and a jar distribution map was established. This documented a more complex and longer development of the *lmlk* impressions and vessels, including their functions, which modifies the history linked to them (Lipschits, Sergi, and Koch 2010; 2011; Sergi et al. 2012; Koch and Lipschits 2013; Lipschits 2018a; 2018b; 2021).

The authors of this new typology primarily point to a longer jar development process, which started in Judah as early as the ninth century BCE (Shai and Maeir 2003; cf. also the discussion in 3.2.1.4). Furthermore, they claim that the *lmlk* impressions are not a short-term phenomenon, but are in fact based on several developmental phases in the context of long-term socioeconomic relations (first in Ji 2001; then Grena 2004). Moreover, on a critical note, they state that, until recently, the overall historical reconstruction was quite unilaterally based on Lachish, and Stratum III therein, as a terminus post quem (contra Na'aman 1979; 1986). This conclusion is said to have shown no regard for the events in the Kingdom of Judah as a whole, including the developments after the Assyrian invasion, when numerous places—especially in the Judaean Mountains—remained untouched which can serve as good evidence for the continual usage of these seals. Consequently, Oded Lipschits (2018b, 342), the main proponent of this new interpretation, claims that "concluding that 701 BCE is the terminus ad quem of the entire *lmlk* system . . . , without carefully examining the typology of the actual finds, can only be considered a general, untidy and poorly based assumption."

Current archaeological research confirms the newly proposed theory, and the impressions discovered in various Judean areas—not only Lachish, where most have been found so far (more than 400 in total)—have been classified into three basic types, with numerous subtypes (Lipschits, Sergi, and Koch 2010; 2011; Lipschits 2018; 2021). Firstly, there are pre-701 BCE impressions secured by the Lachish III stratigraphic horizon; secondly, there are findings dated to post-701 BCE; and thirdly, there are late *lmlk* impressions from the early seventh century BCE. It follows that this seal-based administrative system was no ad hoc matter, but a longer-term economic and administrative tool created in the time when Judah became a vassal of Assyria (Lipschits, Sergi, and Koch 2011).

Ahaz (741–725 BCE) is a historically plausible candidate for the introduction of the *lmlk* seal system—specifically, in the second part of his rule, when he became an Assyrian vassal in 734 BCE. Lipschits proposes that the system was introduced shortly after 732 BCE, but, for now, it is impossible to determine the exact date, due to the lack of archaeological evidence. Most impressions were found in Lachish, the earliest important area in which agricultural commodities had been gathered to be exchanged for the gold and silver that was used to pay tax. Later, after 701 BCE, when Judah had lost a section of the western Shephelah, the administrative centre in Ramat Rahel became the collection point.

Situated in a strategic spot, elevated above the road connecting Hebron to Jerusalem at an altitude of 818 metres above sea level, this locality was identified by some scholars as Beit Hakerem, following the biblical text of Jer 3:1 (as early as Aharoni 1954; similarly, Lipschits et al. 2017). A total of 224 lemelekh *lmlk* impressions were found there, placing the site third in terms of quantity, after Lachish and Jerusalem (where some 300 impressions were discovered; Gibeon, Mizpah, Beth-shemesh, Moreshet-Gath, Azekah, and Gezer are the other localities with high numbers of impressions). Like Lachish, Ramat Rahel was a Judean administrative centre under Assyrian patronage, and the design of the complex reflects that, since its second construction phase (Stratum Va) imitates an Assyrian palace surrounded by gardens with several water tanks, which underline the importance of the residence (Langgut et al. 2013; Lipschits et al. 2017; cf. Na'aman 2001; Reich 2003).

The line of reasoning above provides an important conclusion: even if it was not Ahaz who initiated the impression system, this method of economic administration existed long before, during, and after Hezekiah's revolt, even though the *lmlk* emblem was first replaced by concentric circles and then by rosette stamp impressions (see 6.1 and below). Assyria administered the Southern Levant, including Judah, both to minimise security risks and maximise economic profit: it was not an oppressor state wreaking havoc, but one which made a systematic effort to allow the subjugated kingdoms and provinces to exist under its supervision (cf. Lipschits 2018a; contra Aster and Faust 2018). Consequently, some established notions of the events in Judah in the last third of the eighth century BCE must be reevaluated, and the nature of the administrative system must be reinterpreted (for a defence of the original interpretation of the seals and the chronology linked to them, see Ussishkin 2011; Kreimer 2011; Vaughn 2016).

One of the crucial changes entailed by the newly proposed interpretation is the fact that it is not necessary to view the construction activities in the Kingdom of Judah as a rising wave of national consciousness and as preparation for a conflict with Assyria, which fully erupted after 705 BCE. Strongholds, fortifications, water supply tunnels, and canals were mostly built with the knowledge and support of Assyria. Fortifying Jerusalem was a logical step, as was constructing a network of strongholds which would raise the defensive capabilities of the capital as well as well as those of its surroundings in the event of an attack (see, for example, other Iron Age IIC strongholds in Giv'at Shapira, Gilo, Pisgat Ze'ev, and possibly Beitar Illit; see Barkay, Fantalkin, and Tal 2002). Dated to the second half of the eighth century BCE, the "broad wall" in the western hill area of Jerusalem therefore need not be considered a consequence of the city's growth after the influx of refugees from the north in 722 BCE (Finkelstein 2015), nor a fortification intended for defence against Assyria sometime later. Conceivably, this activity served to strengthen the defence capacity of a vassal state of the Assyrian Empire on its southern border, where a confrontation with Egypt, bolstered again by the rise of the 26th Dynasty, would commence a mere few decades later. Strongholds and massive walls were built in the Negev area as well, due to the more immediate danger of invasion from the south. This too was a measure serving Assyria, rather than one aimed against it (cf. Gadot 2022).

The Siloam Tunnel is another example of construction activity carried out at the time, securing the water supply from the Gihon spring to the southern part of the City of David in Jerusalem. Based on biblical texts (2 Kgs 20:20; 2 Chr 32:30), it is traditionally called Hezekiah's Tunnel, but there is controversy regarding its dating, since it could also have been built earlier: either in the last years of the rule of Ahaz—during his co-rule with his son, Hezekiah—or later, under Manasseh (see, e.g., Knauf 2001; Sneh, Weinberger, and Shalev 2010). Now stored in the Istanbul Archaeological Museum, the text discovered in the tunnel is technical in nature (COS 2.28) and, consequently, it is impossible to determine its exact time of origin, due to the absence of clear historical references therein. Paleographic analysis of the text allows only relative dating, which specifies the decade at most, and so it is necessary to consider several candidates who may have built the tunnel. Even if it was Hezekiah, the start of construction does not have to be linked to the resistance against Assyria, but instead to economic growth and the usage of increasingly sophisticated technological procedures—and that, again, with the knowledge and support of the Mesopotamian authorities.

More underground water supply systems have been documented in the Judaean Mountains, and especially near Jerusalem, from the second half of the eighth century BCE. These ingeniously designed springs drained into aqueducts that distributed water to terrace fields—such as the tunnel in Suba or Nabi Samuel (for more, see Angelakis et al. 2016). Discovered as early as 1983, but better mapped only recently, the 233.2-metre-long tunnel under the village of Walaja, on the left bank side of the Valley of Rephaim, deserves particular attention. Draining the Joweizeh spring, the aqueduct has a Proto-Ionian capital by the entrance (Ein-Mor 2013; Ein-Mor and Ron 2016). This imposing architectural element found in situ suggests that intensive agricultural cultivation of the land took place in the area, requiring developed state administration, skilled craftsmen, and especially sufficient funds. The capitals discovered in Judah are dated to the turn of the eighth and seventh centuries BCE. They are therefore later than similar capitals from the north (here, a total of twenty-five findings have been documented in Hazor, Megiddo, Samaria, and Tel Dan), from where they spread south, starting in the second half of the ninth century BCE—another piece of evidence that corroborates the strong ties between Israel and the Kingdom of Judah (see 4.2.2).

Ramat Rahel is the closest administrative centre with possible links to the Walaja aqueduct (cf. Ein-Mor 2013, who instead proposes a place that is closer but is yet undiscovered). A total of thirteen Proto-Ionian capitals have been found there, with four perfectly preserved (only two fragments have been found in Jerusalem so far). Convincing evidence of monumental architecture, the capitals as well as the large number of *lmlk* impressions add importance to the area, which is confirmed by its strategic placement on the highest point south of Jerusalem, by the routes leading to Beth-shemesh, Hebron, and Beer-sheba and close to the Valley of Rephaim, Jerusalem's granary. Further evidence of the developed administration of Judah is the site of Arnona, uncovered between Ramat Rahel and Jerusalem. Here, a large number of *lmlk* impressions have been found since 2020, as well as Proto-Ionian capital and installations (apparently a toilet) indicating the importance of the site (cf. Langgut 2022), according to excavators, in time of Hezekiah and Menasseh (Sapir-Hen, Ben-Ari, Freud and Lipschits 2022).

In our view, the above considerations imply that that the view determined mainly by the biblical perspective and the analysis of material culture based upon it must be reconsidered. Ahaz played a crucial role in the history of Judah: by accepting Assyrian dominance (and from its shadow and with its support), he led the kingdom to relative independence—naturally contingent on loyalty to Assyria—and to economic prosperity. Important political and economic events are linked to Ahaz and Hezekiah, his son, who spent most of his rule continuing his father's policies as a loyal vassal. The last third of the eighth century BCE cannot be reduced to a mere thesis which states that every important construction occurred during the Judean resistance (only in 706-701 BCE). As proven by the *lmlk* seal system on the level of small material culture, the events of the time were continuous and proceeded in a similar manner—and under the same hegemon—even after the crucial year of 701 BCE.

6.2.2 HEZEKIAH: REFORMS AND UNWISE POLITICS ENDING WELL

In biblical texts, the Judean king Hezekiah (725-697 BCE) is described as a positive figure, in stark contrast to Ahaz. Despite various obstacles, including a serious illness (2 Kgs 20), the king is presented as an example to his people when the small nation of Judah is threatened by the powerful Neo-Assyrian Empire (cf. Chalupa 2013). The acceding ruler and his predecessor are separated by an extensive depiction of the end of Israel (2 Kgs 17) which emphasises the fact that Judah is the only tribe left. Hezekiah's rule over Judah is linked to territorial expansion, religious reform, and resistance against Assyria, as is evidenced in his construction efforts which were intended to end the vassalage of Judah and win it independence. The last of these phenomena has already been discussed in the historical context (see 6.2.1), and so the following section will focus on the topics of territorial expansion and religious reform.

Territorial expansion under Hezekiah is described in 2 Kgs 18:7-8; there, the king is said to have been successful in all his efforts, even revolting against the Assyrian king and refusing to serve him. Furthermore, the same passage claims that "he attacked the Philistines as far as Gaza and its territory, from watchtower to fortified city." The introductory overview on the power relations in the southern Levant provided in this chapter paints a rather different picture of Judean territory at the turn of the eighth and seventh centuries BCE, demonstrating that, until the conflict with Sennacherib, Hezekiah's kingdom remained the same as under Ahaz. At most, one may presume small, temporary territorial gains in the western Shephelah after 711 BCE, when Sargon II (722-705 BCE) led a campaign against Ashdod and Gath, conquering them and transforming Philistia into an Assyrian province. It is conceivable that, at the time, Judah used the weakness of the borderland areas—especially Gath and Ekron—to acquire temporary influence therein (cf. Lipschits and Maeir 2017).

By contrast, it is undisputable that Judah lost an important part of its territory after 701 BCE. The Assyrian army destroyed numerous places (Lachish,

Tel Batash, Beth-shemesh, Tel Arad, Tel Khalif, Tel Ira, Tel Azekah, Tell en-Nasbeh, possibly Tel Burna, and others); according to some estimates, up to 75% of the Shephelah and the areas south of it, fertile and strategic parts of Judah, were abandoned temporarily and then repopulated either in the first or the second half of the seventh century BCE (see the discussion on dating in 6.2.3). The westernmost section of the Shephelah came under the influence of Philistine cities, and strategic spots were occupied by Assyrian forces (Lachish, Tel Haror, Tel Sera, Tell Beit Mirsim, and others), strengthening the hegemon's influence and control over Judah, which, however, still remained a kingdom. Consequently, Hezekiah's territorial successes are inconclusive, to say the least; while in contrast, the fact that, after 701 BCE, Jerusalem was de facto the only city left (cf. Frevel 2016, 261), provides a very persuasive account of Judah's political situation.

Determining exactly why the king is so positively evaluated in the historiography of the biblical texts is more difficult than it might seem at first glance. If Hezekiah did not expand Judean territory, and his rule probably did not see such extensive construction efforts as deduced by a simple reading of the biblical text, what is the motivation of such a positive depiction? Is it due to his religious reform? When examining the perspective provided in the Books of Kings, the answer is clear and further corroborated by the text's elaborate composition. Hezekiah reached the Mediterranean coast as far south as Gaza after he "removed the high places, broke down the pillars, and cut down the sacred pole. He broke in pieces the bronze serpent" (2 Kgs 18:4) that Moses had made and to which "the people of Israel had made offerings" (ibid.). In biblical historiography, as the text quoted above makes clear, political success is inextricably linked to religious contexts.

The same historiography features Hezekiah's predecessor, Ahaz, in an extensive text that depicts him as a ruler who follows wrong cultic practices, even offering up his own son (the phrase used states he "made his son pass through fire"). This act is always linked to the least exemplary biblical figures (see Josh 6:26 during the destruction of Jericho, and especially 1 Kgs 16:34 in connection with Ahab's accession, and also Manasseh in 2 Kgs 21:6). Ahaz also adopted cultic customs from Damascus, where he had travelled to petition for the help of Tiglath-Pileser III. An unusually long passage describing the construction of the bronze altar, built according to plans Ahaz acquired in Damascus, raises numerous questions as to the historicity of the event and its nature. One may speculate that the text serves as a contrasting religious background for subsequent events under Hezekiah, the true reformer; but that is merely one of many possibilities.

As pointed out by Nili Wazana (2016), it is noteworthy that 2 Kgs 16 features no criticism of the cultic changes in Jerusalem per se, and that even Hezekiah's reform does not remove the altar; consequently, it is possible that the altar was not destroyed under Josiah either (however, cf. 2 Kgs 23:11–12, which depicts the removal of altars made by Judean kings and Manasseh). According to Wazana, one may assume that "Ahaz's religious innovations remained intact till the destruction of the first Temple" (ibid., 386), which could be confirmed by the text of the prophetic book Ezek 8:16 and especially 9:2, which mentions a bronze altar. This interpretation is indirectly supported by 2 Kgs 25, which describes in detail everything that was destroyed in, or carried away from, the temple by the Babylonians in 587/586 BCE.

After Babylonian pillaging, there was nothing left of the temple inventory: 2 Kgs 25 explicitly links items with Solomon to underline both the inevitability of the end of the Kingdom of Judah and the continuity of temple service which lasted throughout the preceding centuries. However, the same is true for other material culture that is often associated directly with the First Temple (here specifically the architecture), as none of this has yet been discovered (for discussion see Čapek 2023). Even so, later biblical tradition continues the temple theme in the detailed list of individual cultic items in Ezra 1:7–11, which elaborates that Cyrus II gave the Judeans an inventory of the house of God, so that they could use the items again in the new temple (cf. 7.2.3).

According to Wazana, the biblical leniency to Ahaz's construction efforts in modifying the altar—though the king is not evaluated positively regarding other aspects in 2 Kgs 16—comes from the fact that the altar in Damascus was Yahwistic; its "pattern" (dəmût in Hebrew; the Lucianic version of the Septuagint elaborates that the king also sent the "dimensions" of the altar) was sent to Jerusalem. The king rebuilt the Jerusalem altar based on the template adopted by the Arameans from Israel (Wazana 2016, 397; cf. Hamilton 2018). This reconstruction is in accordance with Israel's presumed strong influence on the development of Jerusalem in terms of power as well as culture and religion (cf. Grabbe 2010). It might even be the very first convincing testimony which describes the temple-linked cult in a more comprehensive manner; the prior accounts—such as the text of 2 Kgs 12, in which the Judean king Joash repairs the temple—feature heavy literary stylisation and were composed far later to support the antiquity of the Yahwistic cult in Jerusalem, but also to put in doubt the credibility of the same cult in the north under the Omride dynasty (cf. 5.3.1). To a large extent, the same applies to the literary tradition connected to Solomon's Temple.

Ascribed to Hezekiah by the biblical texts, cult centralisation can be partially mapped using archaeological evidence. However, it is necessary to exercise much caution when evaluating a possible intersection between literary testimony and material culture. Biblical texts focus on a standardised description of religious orthodoxy, as mentioned above; this description is complemented with an account that depicts the removal of the bronze snake (2 Kgs 18:3–4). Hezekiah's reform is depicted as a fact applying to Judah as a whole. In terms of the material culture linked to the cult in Judah, there are two identifiable trends supplementing this notion which paint a picture of the religious situation in the late eighth century BCE in a less unambiguous way.

The first trend is continuing syncretistic religious practice, blending the Yahwistic cult—probably adopted from Israel in the ninth century BCE (cf. Frevel 2021; and possibly also from Damascus; see Wazana 2016)—and cultic practices using a variety of religious artifacts. These include figurines, both anthropomorphic (especially Judean pillar figurines, abbreviated to JPF; Ben-Shlomo and Darby 2014; Briffa 2019; Sugimoto 2014) and zoomorphic (e.g., a rider on horseback likely representing a solar deity or a protective spirit; see Moulis 2017). And it is not just syncretistic religious practice of that kind, but also on the level of specific known deities such as Baal or El, who are competitors to YHWH (Stahl 2021) who apparently came to prominence only at the very end of the Iron Age IIC or even later after 586 BCE (Berlejung 2010; Čapek 2019a).

The second, concurrent trend promotes cult centralisation, which is an important aspect of a full-blown territorial state. Such a state has institutional and organisational backing secured by the bureaucracy, army, justice system, and effective tax collection to finance buildings and economic facilities (see 6.2.1), but also by centralising religion (for the same phenomenon earlier in the north see Finkelstein 2013; Kleiman A. et al 2017; cf. Hall 2022). It is likely that the process had begun as early as the rule of Ahaz, a loyal vassal of Assyria, possibly with innovative features adopted from the north—these were left uncriticised in 2 Kgs 16 (!), unlike the king's other cultic misbehaviours—and was eventually completed under Hezekiah.

Despite the claims of some scholars who state that Hezekiah's programmatic reform of the cult can be neither established nor refuted based on archaeology (cf. Frevel 2016, 252), there is some evidence for transformations, which seem to corroborate the centralisation. In the second half of the eighth century BCE, cultic changes are traceable in several areas of the Kingdom of Judah. In Tel Arad, older research identified a shrine in Stratum XI (dated by the authors to the tenth century BCE), assigning its downfall to Arad VIII (cult centralisation under Hezekiah) and Arad VII (the time of Josiah), when it had been completely closed, according to Aharoni (1968). More recent revision of this research by Ze'ev Herzog (2001; 2002; 2010) has proved that the temple could not be documented in Stratum XI but only in Stratum X. At the time, there was a fire, followed by the restoration and enlargement of the shrine in Stratum IX. The last horizon mentioned is one of the cult centralisation phases under Hezekiah, which Herzog claims started around 715 BCE. Towards the end of this phase, most of the temple was dismantled, and individual cultic items were covered by a layer of earth (see also the overview of different interpretations in Moulis 2017; 2019).

Tab. 6. Original and revised stratigraphies of Tel Arad (according to Aharoni 1981 and Herzog 2002)

Stratum	Dating (Aharoni)	Dating (Herzog)
XII	11th cent. BCE	second half of 10th cent.—first half of 9th cent. BCE
XI	10th cent. BCE (before 920 BCE)	second half of 9th cent.—first half of 8th cent. BCE
X	9th cent. BCE	first half of 8th cent. BCE
IX	8th cent. BCE (till 734 BCE)	second half of 8th cent. BCE
VIII	end of 8th cent. BCE (after 715 BCE)	late 8th cent. BCE
VII	7th cent. BCE (till 609 BCE)	7th cent. BCE
VI	605–595 BCE	late 7th—beginning of 6th cent. BCE

Beginning in the second half of the 8th century BCE, cultic changes with centralising aspects seem to have occurred in some other places of Judah as well. Although no sanctuary has been unequivocally discovered at Lachish, the second most important city of the kingdom, some of the areas there deserve attention. This is true first of all for the so-called Cultic Room 49, which Aharoni identified as a small shrine (Aharoni 1975b) because a number of cultic items (limestone altar, clay incense burners, chalices, lamps, juglets, jugs etc.) were found there as well as a raised platform (*bamah*) and benches. A completely different view was later proposed by Ussishkin. He interprets Cultic Room 49 as a site of deliberate preservation dated to stratum Lachish V (c. 760 BC), but not as a sanctuary (Ussishkin 2004). According to him, the site of the sanctuary is unknown.

In 2016, the most recent discovery in the area documented is according to some a small sanctuary in one of the chambers of the inner gate of the city (Ganor and Kreimerman 2017). Here, specifically in Chamber 3, oil lamps, bowls, pedestals, and two small altars presumably with traces of horn removal were found. Placed higher in the same chamber, the toilet discovered in the same site is interpreted—somewhat bafflingly, since in most other spots, and Lachish too, cultic artefacts are preserved with due respect—as part of Hezekiah's supposed religious reform (Ngo 2017; for criticism see Kleiman S. 2020; 2023, cf. also Čapek 2023). In 2018, Liraz interprets the opposite chamber of the gate in a similar way, i.e. the sanctuary, which is desacralized at the end of the 8th century BCE (Liraz 2018).

In Beer-sheba, another important city of Judah located further to the south, a dismantled monumental sacrificial altar was found in Stratum III in 1973. Stones from the altar were reused in Stratum II. As for the time of use of the altar and its decommissioning, Aharoni dated its dismantling straight to the reign of Hezekiah (Aharoni 1974b) and connected its demolition with the Neo-Assyrian campaign in 701 BCE. Herzog assumes that the installation "could have been in use in Stratum III" (Herzog 2016b, 1477) but the intentional decommissioning of the cult leaves a broader time frame that is not limited only to Hezekiah, and he assumes that this ruler is the best candidate for the reform which manifested itself in the voluntary closure of local shrines stating "indeed, nothing in the archaeological record proves that the cultic reform at Tel Beer-sheba was carried out during Hezekiah's days... However, even without biblical data, the shift from Stratum III to II at Tel Beer-sheba must have occurred during the second half of the 8th century BCE" (Herzog 2010, 195).

Perhaps similarly abandoned to Tel Arad, another temple was discovered in 2013 at Tel Moza, just seven kilometres west of Jerusalem. Here, too, the late eighth century BCE is considered by campaign directors Kisilevitz and Lipschits to be a time horizon in which cultic practices were restricted (Kisilevitz, Lipschits 2020a; 2020b and esp. Kisilevitz 2022), probably as a result of centralization or changes brought about by other factors, including, of course, the site's close proximity to Jerusalem. What exactly caused the end of worship in the temple and to which deity it was actually dedicated is still intensely debated (Garfinkel 2020; Kisilevitz et al. 2020; 2022; Čapek 2023).

By contrast, at the time of the presumably ongoing centralisation, cultic activities resumed in Tell Halif, located south of Lachish—where, in 1992, a cultic space was uncovered, featuring two *masseboth*, a fenestrated stand, and the head of a pillar figure. Other artefacts found in Tell Halif include an oil lamp, a fragment of a zoomorphic jar, and two small incense altars made of limestone, one of which is engraved with figures of animals and a human (Borowski 2017, 110–11). The end to the occupation of this locality is clearly determined by the Assyrian invasion and destruction in Stratum VIB, dated to 701 BCE. Explaining the area's continuing religious life in the preceding decades of the eighth century BCE, Borowski (1995) states that it was not a state sanctuary, but a place outside of Jerusalem's jurisdiction. A more plausible explanation is proposed by Moulis (2017): Tell Halif did not host any more significant sacrifices (animals sacrificed on the altar) but merely used incense instead; consequently, the sanctuary was less important in terms of cult and it avoided the changes linked to centralisation.

The many evaluations of Hezekiah's rule, based either on archaeology or biblical texts, differ in numerous aspects. The biblical evaluation stems from national interests, from which the theme of the cult is derived, and it is under Hezekiah that the cult must be purified, reformed, and centralised. In connection to this, territory is acquired as an almost essential bonus. The logic of this view is corroborated by the very negative evaluation of Ahaz, though he probably also supported the cult in Jerusalem and its pivotal role—he may have even been the first ruler to do so, inspired by the north (cf. 6.2.1). The negative depiction of the king in biblical historiography is due to his political loyalty to Assyria. Quite conceivably, both rulers enforced the same policies, but the evaluation of the latter was elaborated in the literature against the backdrop of a crucial theme: the eighth century BCE national revolt, which would later be remembered and glorified in Judah. In actual fact, the revolt brought Judah temporary stagnation at least, if not a short-term decline and, according to some, led to a so-called *de facto* centralization, whereby the concentration of the cult in the center of the kingdom of Judah was the result of a socio-economic transformations and the constitution of a new form of a kind of "state" religion (cf. Kleiman 2023). Despite evidence of very similar material culture in their respective periods, Ahaz and Hezekiah are pictured as two particularly distinct figures in biblical texts: the former king is criticised due to his pro-Assyrian orientation, while the latter is extolled owing to his pro-Judaean and anti-Assyrian inclinations.

When examining the broad archaeological evidence relevant to the possibility of ongoing cult centralisation as an important feature of a full-blown territorial state, a question comes to mind: is it necessary to link some areas and their conservation to Hezekiah and not to the earlier rule of Ahaz (especially Lachish, possibly Tel Moza, and maybe also Beer-sheba)? Unlike biblical texts, archaeology does not offer a clear distinction between the reigns and cultic practices of the kings. Since a similarly unequivocal view later appears in the descriptions of Manasseh and Josiah, this aspect of interpretation must be considered when reconstructing history, which may not be a mere paraphrase of biblical testimony.

Contained mainly in Kings, the first more extensive historiographic compositions were presumably committed to writing after Assyria had lost influence over Judah—i.e., in the last third of the seventh century BCE, with the rise of the 26th Dynasty of Egypt (Čapek 2019a; Lipschits 2018). Some authors date these compositions to earlier periods (cf. Bietenhard 1998; Vermeylen 2000; Lemaire and Halpern 2010; Sergi 2013; Finkelstein 2013). Texts referring to the kings of the last long century feature understandable criticism of Assyria: the Kingdom of Judah was a vassal state, and though the subjugation undoubtedly brought various economic and cultural advantages, it was viewed negatively in conservative nationalist spheres that would give birth to the early Deuteronomistic movement. Later, retrospective reflections reinforce this trend in the literature, using historical patterning and evaluating the rulers based on criteria that strongly theologise historical facts (cf. 4.2.5 and 5.3.1). Ahaz and Hezekiah are the first pair, with another directly following them (see 6.2.3 and 6.2.4).

6.2.3 MANASSEH: BAD REPUTATION, BAD KING?

Manasseh (696–642 BCE) was the longest ruling king of Judah—according to 2 Kings 21:1 he ruled for fifty-five years. Moreover, if he truly was installed as Hezekiah's co-ruler immediately after the 701 BCE revolt, as some assume, his rule would be even further ahead of the second-longest ruling king, Azariah/Uzziah (787–738 BCE; he ruled Jerusalem for fifty-two years, but from 756 BCE he was deputised by Jotham and later Ahaz). As documented in the Assyrian annals, Manasseh was a vassal of Esarhaddon (681–669 BCE) and Ashurbanipal (669–631 BCE; cf. Grabbe 2007b). Similar to twenty-one other rulers in the southern Levant, this Judean king had to serve the Assyrians. The Esarhaddon Prism B notes that these leaders supplied construction material for Esarhaddon's palace—large logs, long beams, and thin cedar and pine planks from Mount Sirara and Lebanon, as well as stones, doorstones, limestone slabs, and other material from their quarries (see ANET 290).

During Manasseh's long rule, Judah recovered from the consequences of misjudged and overestimated ambitions that were nurtured under Hezekiah. Owing to cooperation with Assyria, which had reached its territorial peak and temporarily subjugated Egypt, Judah again flourished during the reigns of Ahaz and Hezekiah, prior to the Assyrian invasion. Under Manasseh, Jerusalem's population grew once more, with people arriving from areas conquered and destroyed by Assyria; such places would later be gradually repopulated, possibly still during the king's rule (e.g., Tel 'Eton, Lachish, Tell Beit Mirsim, Tel Khalif, Azekah). Most frequently attributed to Hezekiah, the construction efforts may be equally well sought in the early seventh century BCE, proving ongoing post-701 BCE reconstruction of a partially destroyed land (see below for the biblical account in 2 Chr 33:14). Some scholars think the Siloam Tunnel is the work of Manasseh (Knauf 2001; Sneh, Weinberger, and Shalev 2010; cf. Gadot 2022), as well as the palace at Ramat Rahel in the Va construction phase (Na'aman 2001 and Reich 2003; contra Lipschits et al. 2017, who date the phase to the earlier rule of Hezekiah). The same may apply to the aqueducts mentioned above (see 6.2.1 and 6.2.2), and a stele fragment which refers to an unspecified water structure found in Jerusalem and is dated to the first half of the seventh century BCE (see Naveh 1982).

Judah's economic continuity as a vassal state of Assyria is documented by an administrative system that was introduced earlier which used seals that mark jars containing commodities which were collected in royal administrative centres. As has been demonstrated, *lmlk* impressions are not Hezekiah's one-time measure that was adopted as part of preparations for the Assyrian invasion (see 6.2.2), but a long-term instrument for collecting agricultural produce; this is also the likely reason why the Hebrew inscription "belonging to the king" features no specific name. The seal emblems change in the seventh century BCE, and the late *lmlk* type impressions, documented even after 701 BCE, are followed by the symbol of two concentric circles. Both impressions have been found on the same jar, proving that there was a transitional period (Lipschits et al. 2017; Lipschits 2021).

During the existence of the Kingdom of Judah, rosette stamp impressions were the last type featured in this system, dated by some scholars to the second half or last third of the seventh century BCE—i.e., probably at the time of Josiah (Koch and Lipschits 2013). Other researchers suggest an earlier temporal setting—the first half of the seventh century BCE (Finkelstein 1994; 2012b)—as proof that the influence of the Kingdom of Judah again stretched even into the Shephelah, where others do not identify economic growth until later. The difference in dating involves one decade, or two decades at most; it is difficult to make a more precise determination in this part of the seventh century BCE. In both periods proposed, the pottery has the same typology, and due to peaceful political developments, there are no layers of destruction that would allow one to determine absolute chronology. Stretching from Jericho to Ein Gedi, newly populated spaces in what used to be barren, semi-dry areas may play a key role in this. Similarly, the populated zone expanded into the Beer-sheba Valley, which may have served as an agricultural production area (mainly for grain) under Manasseh, replacing the loss of the western Shephelah, which would slowly be repopulated (cf. discussion in Frevel 2016, 262–63).

Viewed as a prudent, long-ruling, and politically successful king elsewhere, Manasseh is evaluated differently in biblical historiography, and his depiction is essentially twofold, depending on which literary source is used as the starting point. In the Books of Kings, Manasseh is linked to the worst behaviour imaginable; by his list of misdeeds, resembling a catalogue in its length, the king surpasses all his predecessors. While in many respects akin to Jeroboam I and Ahab—two other prototypes of depravity—Manasseh is described as being even worse, with his rule characterised by severe improprieties. He builds sacred hilltops and altars to Baal, as well as a sacred pole (as did Ahab), bowing to the host of heaven and dedicating altars to them in the house of God, where he also places an idol of Asherah; the king makes his son pass through fire, and sheds a great deal of innocent blood (see 2 Kgs 21:1–18). Consequently, the final comment on his rule claims that he was buried with his ancestors, but "in the garden of his house, in the garden of Uzza" (cf. 2 Chr 33:20, where he is said to have been buried "in his house"). Without needing to search for the real grave, this ambiguous note describes a figure that has to suffer a different fate to other Judean kings even after death, due to the evils committed during his life. The authors of Kings show Manasseh as an accumulation of all of Israel's sins. The text of 2 Kgs 21:15 states his actions are a sum of all evil "since the day their ancestors [i.e., Israel] came out of

Egypt even to this day." This entire line of reasoning results in a programmatic historical outlook that suggests that Manasseh would eventually be held responsible for the fall of the Kingdom of Judah as well.

The second source of Judean historiography, Chronicles, also depicts Manasseh as a bad king, who is dragged away in chains to Babylon by Assyrian soldiers as a cruel punishment for the collective disobedience of his people. Terminologically, the king's capture corresponds to the fate met by Jehoiachin in 597 BCE (see 2 Chr 36:6). In captivity, Manasseh begs God for help and is freed; the king is allowed to return to Jerusalem, where he purifies the cult of the Lord and builds a high "outer wall for the city of David west of Gihon, in the valley, reaching the entrance at the Fish Gate; he carried it around Ophel" (2 Chr 33:14). The note on construction efforts is a good demonstration of how the king's evaluation is reflected in a statement on his specific activities; knowing this, caution should be exhibited when working with often stylised literary accounts in ancient historiographies, if there is no archaeological evidence for what they describe (see also the historically (un)verifiable construction activities of Hezekiah).

Both biblical historiographies have clear intentions in their depictions of Manasseh: the Books of Kings continue the process of historical patterning, identifying the king as a counterfigure to Josiah and as the one responsible for the fall of the Kingdom of Judah. The punishment that is administered is severe and definitive for the king (separation from the Judean kings after death) as well as later for Judah (the fall in 587/586 BCE). There is a clear anti-Assyrian tone in the text, and the logic of the reasoning is no different to that used for Ahaz and Hezekiah. The Kingdom of Judah was a vassal of Assyria, and though it was under Manasseh that this subjugation brought about a long period of peace and economic stability, it was viewed in a negative light by nationalist and religious groups. Conceivably, the first written commentaries likely appeared as early as during his rule or shortly afterwards, but more extensive sections of the historiography were committed to writing later, using this primary and contemporary interpretive context for other purposes as well. The circles linked to these compositions may be identified with the milieu which would create the Deuteronomic movement that promoted the exclusivity of the Yahwistic cult. This movement is responsible for the editing and growth of the most comprehensive Judean historiography rendered in the Deuteronomistic History, which, as a whole, is dated to a far later time (de Pury, Römer, and Machi 2000; Rückl 2016; Römer 2005; 2006; 2020b).

Manasseh's historiographic depiction in Chronicles (Carr 2011; but cf. Auld 1994), offers a different view of Judaean history in the first half of the seventh century BCE. Having had access to the older account of Manasseh, the authors show the king as a person capable of change, receiving forgiveness, and stabilising the situation temporarily. In the text, the Judaean king symbolises the punishment, repentance, restoration, and new blessing of Israel in the postexilic period (Cielontko 2019).

In both historiographies, as rendered in Kings and Chronicles, the central theme is that of religious apostasy from the Yahwistic cult. Older research (e.g., Donner 1987) considered the biblical account a more or less reliable historical description of Israelite religious phenomena, resulting in a claim about an Assyrian crisis in Israelite religion during the first half of the seventh century BCE which was precipitated by the Mesopotamian hegemon and demanded by Manasseh (cf. also Hensel 2022). According to this notion, the Assyrian cult was adapted in Judah and Israel—i.e., an area in which the Yahwistic cult had been practised—to replace YHWH and to centre on worshipping Baal, Asherah, and the host of heaven as transformed forms of Assyrian deities.

This conception has been modified by newer research. Indeed, Assyrian and Aramean influences gradually permeated the iconography of Judah, but the trend is not enforced; instead, it is a result of long-term cultural influence to which Judah was exposed, much like other vassals of Assyria (Koch 2019). Consequently, the local gods YHWH and Asherah are transposed into contemporary categories (cf. Berlejung 2017) and likened to Asshur and Ishtar in terms of their typology, actions, and attributes, even though these names are not featured in biblical texts (cf. Anthonioz 2014; Sugimoto 2014a). However, there was no such thing as a programmatic Assyrisation of the Judean cult which took place in Iron Age IIB Judah, not even under Manasseh, who is heavily criticised mainly for political reasons, though the grounds for his denouncement are especially evident in the literary account describing the complete abandonment of the Yahwistic cult (for details see Frevel 2016).

The negative evaluation of Manasseh is a conglomerate of several factors which resulted in his criticism and which served as the basis for the gradual creation of a more extensive literary composition that was oriented historiographically. It is difficult to identify these and determine their exact relationships due to the nature of the accounts of Manasseh's rule in Kings and Chronicles. Conceivably, the first criticism of the king was contemporary and mainly political. The Kingdom of Judah was a vassal of Assyria for a long time, and a part of Judean society took a particularly dim view of the situation. This discontent was then transferred to a primarily religious context and elaborated into an extensive, dark tale of a ruler who was responsible for the political catastrophes to come. As with Ahaz and Hezekiah, the deterrent example of Manasseh evidently needed be perfected through the retrospective identification of a counterfigure who showed that there is an alternative way of life. The counterfigure chosen was Manasseh's grandson, Josiah.

6.2.4 JOSIAH: *DAVID REDIVIVUS*, MONOTHEISM, AND POLICIES

Josiah (639-609 BCE) succeeded Amon (641-640 BCE), son of Manasseh, who was killed shortly after ascending the throne. The rapid developments in Jerusalem around this time are sometimes attributed to the tension generated by the political situation changing in the Southern Levant, as Assyria retreated and the area of the Coastal Plain gradually came under the control of Psamtik I (664-610 BCE) and then Necho II (610-595 BCE). Amon may have been removed by groups who preferred either the continuity of Assyrian vassalage or instead by those who viewed the rising 26th Dynasty in Egypt as the better option; conceivably, the responsibility might have also lain with nationalist circles who desired absolute independence. It is impossible to find any more exact information in the biblical account other than that Josiah was enthroned by the "people of the land" (see 2 Kgs 21:24; cf. Schipper 2011; for overview of the term's usage and shifts see Fried 2006). Frevel (2016, 265) identifies Josiah's supporters with the aristocratic group of the Shaphanides, who wished to use the young king to gain influence in Jerusalem and to preserve Judah's vassalage to Assyria, ensuring that Judah would continue to profit from the empire's economic prosperity in the region. It is clear that Josiah's rule saw Assyrian as well as Egyptian dominance and, indirectly, the rise to power of the Neo-Babylonian Empire. To stop Neo-Babylonian expansion, the king was most likely forced to participate in the joint campaign of Egypt and Assyria, which would have fatal consequences for him.

Surprisingly, there is no contemporary written record of the thirty years of Josiah's rule, unlike Ahaz, Hezekiah, and Manasseh, all of whom were mentioned in the Assyrian annals. Even popular treatises unencumbered by religious agenda confirm that Josiah is known only from biblical texts; there is no mention of him in Egyptian or Babylonian texts; and there is no clear archaeological evidence, such as an inscription containing his name (cf. Alpert and Alpert 2012, 74). Possible explanations for this disproportion include the rapid developments in the region: no temporary hegemon managed to seize control over the area for a longer period of time, and so no record was made. Undoubtedly, Josiah is a historical figure, and his rule may be reconstructed using material culture and via the critical reading of biblical texts.

In the last third of the seventh century BCE, Judah was still a vassal of Assyria and, towards the end of the century, of Egypt. Regarding its economic situation, the kingdom continued to enjoy the long decades of stability which were brought about by Manasseh after Hezekiah's revolt against Assyria at the very end of the eighth century BCE. Mentioned several times already and later replaced by the concentric circle emblem, the role of *lmlk* impressions in the administrative system of tax and agricultural commodity collection was at this time supplanted by the rosette motif, which has been documented by several hundred findings in various areas of Judah. This dominant emblem type from the period of the Kingdom of Judah is linked either to Manasseh or to the last third of the seventh century BCE and Josiah (see discussion in 6.2.3). Its continuation is documentable as late as the rule of Jehoiakim, whether or not disputed locations such as Stratum II in Tel Batash fell under Judean jurisdiction (see 6.1). Clearly, the seal-marking system was tried and tested as well as adaptable in later years too (for other iconographic and emblematic types in the later periods, see Lipschits and Vanderhooft 2011; Lipschits 2021). The usage of the rosette motif, which has an iconographical connection to the goddess Ishtar, is another proof of Assyrian cultural influence in Judah (Koch 2019).

6.2.4.1 THE EXTENT OF THE TERRITORY

The total area of the Kingdom of Judah under Josiah in the Iron Age IIC is difficult to determine, considering the uncertain identification of the territory itself. Older research often harmonised biblical texts with the material culture and vice versa; an example of this is the Mesad Hashavyahu stronghold on the Coastal Plain, where an ostracon written in Hebrew has been found (COS 3.14; see Naveh 1960; Aharoni 1979; Mazar 1992). This text was formerly used to prove the Judean origin of the fort as well as influence stretching to the sea, since the following is written about the inherited portion of the Judah tribe in the Book of Joshua 15:20–62: verses 46–47 state that the territory extended from Ekron to the sea, Ashdod, Gaza, the Wadi of Egypt (i.e. Wadi el-Arish), and the coastline of the Mediterranean Sea. According to other biblical texts, Judah expanded to Jericho in the east and to the Bethel area in the north (cf. 2 Kgs 23:15–20). Optimistic reconstructions include a larger section of what used to be the Kingdom of Israel into the Kingdom of Josiah, based on a mention of Megiddo, where the king went to meet the pharaoh Necho and where, during the prior cult purification, "removed all the shrines of the high places that were in the towns of Samaria" (2 Kgs 23:19).

Newer research reconstructs a far more modest map of the Kingdom of Judah. The coast never escaped the influence of the hegemons, since Judah had neither the time nor the power to fill the putatively empty space (Čapek 2019a; for details see 6.1). The evidence of rosette stamp distribution and diffusion makes it clear that the total area was far smaller under Josiah, comprising centres in the Judaean Mountains (especially Jerusalem, Ramat Rahel, and the Valley of Rephaim), the western Shephelah (the Gezer-Tel Batash-Azekah-Lachish axis), the northern Negev (including Arad and up to Tel Ira), and the western area of the Dead Sea. The northernmost locations where rosette stamps have been documented are Tell en-Nasbeh and Gibeon (Koch and Lipschits 2013); however, none have been found further north in Bethel.

Regarding the supposed total area of the Kingdom of Judah, a similar conclusion may be drawn from the analysis of other small material culture items proposed by Raz Kletter (1996; 1998), who examined JPFs as well as inscribed Judean weights. Though we certainly need to be mindful of the fact that mixed archaeological artefacts cannot serve to determine borders, but—at most—may describe temporary rule over areas where they were found (cf. Grabbe 2007b, 204-7), the evidence presented above is quite persuasive.

Regarding the total area of the Kingdom of Judah, it is still unclear how to read the biblical text of Josh 15 and the geographic references made in relation to the king and the land controlled by him in general. The best option available is that Josh 15:20-62 depicts the paradigmatically ideal borders of an ideal ruler where the author is merely describing the Kingdom of Judah as it

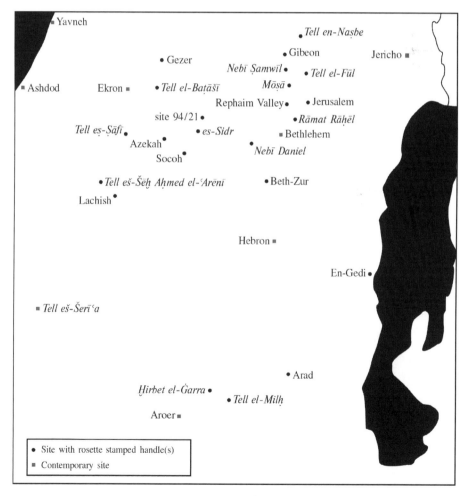

Fig. 24. Rosette stamped handles distribution map (according to Koch and Lipschits 2013)

should have been, according to his later perspective. Consequently, the genre of the text is neither a geographical account, nor an effort to reconstruct the total area as faithfully as possible, but fictionalised geography, in which the king's importance also stems from the area under his control. Similar descriptions are linked to several paradigmatic rulers: David (2 Sam 7), Solomon (1 Kgs 5), and Hezekiah (2 Kgs 17). The significance of Josiah's rule is also underlined by another literary aspect—the depiction of religious reform, which may or may not overlap with reality. In 2 Kgs 23:15–20, there is a clue to a possible historical context, in which a broader literary composition on Josiah might have been written: the section refers to Bethel, which was not included in the kingdom in the late seventh century BCE and would only become a part of it in the time of the Persian province of Yehud (see 7.2.6).

6.2.4.2 RELIGIOUS REFORM AND DEATH

As outlined in the Books of Samuel and Kings, the basic historiographic framework presumes an ideal king in the early history of Israel as a kingdom as well as at its end, when Judah assumed the role of the new "Israel." The Books of Kings depict Josiah as this model successor of the Davidide line who "walked in all the way of his father David" (2 Kgs 22:2), and as a reformer, in whose time the "Book of the Law" is found during the reconstruction of the temple; the book then serves as the source document for Judah as a national and religious community carrying the legacy of ancient Israel. In a way, Josiah is *David redivivus*. Using biblical chronology, it is possible to find the origin of this reform described in the Old Testament which is traditionally linked to 622 BCE (see 2 Kgs 22:1–3). This cult transformation in Judah was far-reaching and connected to another of Josiah's exploits: territorial expansion (see 6.2.4.1).

The story providing information on Josiah's reform, perceived as synonymous with the final establishment of monotheism not only in the Kingdom of Judah but also Israel as a whole (see 2 Kgs 23:19), is one of the most distinct messages of the Old Testament. At the same time, it programmatically foreshadows cultic practices in the exilic and postexilic periods, during the birth of Judaism. Since the inception of critical biblical studies, there have been discussions as to the nature of the book discovered during the temple reconstruction (see the overview of older research in Kraus 1982). As formulated by Wilhelm M. L. de Wette (1780–1849) in the early nineteenth century, the most common interpretation claims that the book was either the Book of Deuteronomy or its oldest sections which share numerous features with 2 Kgs 22–23; consequently, it may be assumed that the reform was based on this book in particular. The connection between the reform and the Book of Deuteronomy, which was not merely ideological but also terminological, gave rise to the theory of the Deuteronomistic history. In the late preexilic, but mainly exilic and postexilic periods, these authors and editors gradually wrote, amended, and updated the literary corpus which has come to be designated the Deuteronomistic History. Starting with the Book of Deuteronomy and ending with the Second Book of Kings, according to the canonical order of the Hebrew Bible (Deuteronomy—Joshua—Judges—Samuel—Kings), this extensive biblical literary unit was first identified and, in 1943, described by Martin Noth.

The central text on Josiah's reform in 2 Kgs 22–23 mainly describes a religious programme with clear theological emphases and an elaborate accompanying strategy based on an imagined idealized past. The new, supposedly binding record of history, is introduced into the past—in this case, the seventh century BCE—to gain authority for the present, be it exilic or postexilic. The reason for this is obvious: it is impossible to stake any authoritative claims in the present as such, since there can be no aspirations to validity or importance without antiquity. Berlejung expresses this differently, stating that modernisation operates under the cover of restoration (see Berlejung 2010). Consequently, the Book of the Law/Deuteronomy, which is, factually, a religious document created during or after the Babylonian exile, is "discovered" under Josiah and passed off as even older. In short, this strategy can be described as follows: present claims to authority do not provide satisfactory justification for religious modernisation or consolidation, and so it is necessary to refer to the past which will authenticate these claims and justify the new norms as both effective and binding for everybody.

In this case, which parts of Josiah's religious reform are verifiable? The exact developments involving the cult during Manasseh's long rule are subject to speculation, but the small material culture findings, including religious artefacts, do not suggest any radical turn (cf. Grabbe 2007b). As mentioned before, the criticism levelled at Manasseh is a conglomerate of many factors, one of which is the negative historical patterning of the king—especially in the Books of Kings—to allow his successor to shine even brighter in contrast (see 6.2.3) and to determine a guilty party for the fall of the Kingdom of Judah.

Paradoxically, the archaeological findings offer no unequivocal support for Josiah's reform, in contrast to the centralization of the cult under Hezekiah, which material culture seems to more readily reflect. Older interpretations suggesting, for example, that the restoration of the Tel Arad shrine was a work of Josiah have been revised, with the changes dated to the late eighth

---

Book of the Law → Josiah → exilic/postexilic time

Book of the Law ← Josiah ← exilic/postexilic time & Book of the Law

Fig. 25. Fictitious and real (retroactive) timelines of Josiah's reform

century BCE (Herzog 2001; 2002; Moulis 2017; for discussion see also Münnich 2004; Zevit 2001; Edelman 2008; Moulis 2019; Kleiman, S. 2023). The artefacts of a religious nature from the seventh century BCE document the ongoing practices of a domestic syncretistic cult. In Jerusalem and other centres of the Kingdom of Judah, a large quantity of anthropomorphic and zoomorphic figurines has been found, mainly JPF figurines likely to represent Asherah or another female deity (cf. Sugimoto 2014b; Ben-Shlomo and Darby 2014; Darby 2014) and fertility in general (for discussion see esp. Briffa 2019; Moulis 2021), and a rider on horseback, who may have been a representation of a solar deity or a protective spirit. The absence of such religious items only relates to the sixth century BCE, a time when, apart from cult centralisation, monolatrisation and monotheisation started to become enforced in Judah as well.

The nature of the reform linked to Josiah may be reconstructed using biblical texts especially, but it is necessary to examine their character and their time of origin. In research, mention is made of searching for a well-grounded biblical foundation. That is, one which is found after the text has been critically examined (Uehlinger 1994); even here, the situation is ambiguous, since the reform is not documented in the contemporary prophetic traditions of Zephaniah, Nahum, and Jeremiah, and so it might have been merely an episode (cf. Berlejung 2010). Moreover, it must be emphasised that the biblical account of the reform is highly stylised, which is one of the reasons it is difficult to reconstruct the specific political and religious tendencies and tensions which are described in the biblical texts. Some scholars think that there is no anti-Assyrian tone in the texts whatsoever (Frevel 2016). By contrast, Angelika Berlejung (2010) suggests that the reform itself is a reaction to the fall of Assyria and an effort to strengthen Judah. According to this author, the advisors of Josiah, the fathers of the later Deuteronomists, elaborated a religion modeled on the Assyrian god Ashur, and the king emancipated Jerusalem and Judah from Assyrian influence and expanded it. He then went on to invade Assyrian-controlled territory in the province of Samaria, and may have adopted the religious traditions of Bethel (Hosea, Amos—if they did not reach Jerusalem with the refugees in 722/1), thus clearly claiming the legacy of northern Israel.

Two objections to this notion may be raised: firstly, the northern traditions had likely been present in Judah beforehand, due to the dynastic links between the kings of Judah and Israel (see chapter 4); and secondly, the text on the cult purification in Bethel (2 Kgs 23:15–20) is dated to a later period and may, in all likelihood, be ruled out from being a historical fact of the late seventh century BCE (cf. Mastin 2004; Kucová 2005; Stern 2010; Frevel 2016). As proven by the absence of rosette impressions, this locality was not included in Judah under Josiah (see 6.2.4.1), but it would be later, when Bethel was a part of the Yehud province (Lipschits 2005; 2021).

It is difficult to identify the historicity of the claim in 2 Kgs 23:11 that Josiah removed the horses which were dedicated to the sun by the kings of Judah and that he burned down the sun chariots. Possibly, the image of the quadriga driven by Helios is in the background of this description. This motif does not appear in iconography until the late sixth century BCE, which would mean that the dating of the text's origin to after the fall of Jerusalem is confirmed (cf. Keel 2007).

For almost two centuries, biblical research has been discussing who authored the account of the reform. If the Deuteronomistic History theory may still be applied, albeit not in the original sense proposed by Martin Noth in 1943, there is a follow-up question: who were the Deuteronomists (Schearing and McKenzie 1999; Römer 2005; 2006; 2020b)? These authors cannot be considered a group who operated within a single historical period. The literary depiction of this reform underwent numerous editorial amendments, and so it is not one text from a single time (synchrony), but a multi-text composition from several periods (diachrony); consequently, the existence of multiple authors must be presumed. Some researchers link the oldest literary adaptation of the reform directly to Josiah's time and to the waning influence of the Assyrian Empire; others consider it a retrospective view from the sixth and fifth centuries BCE. Due to the lack of unambiguous archaeological evidence, both on the level of architecture as well as small material culture items which are cultic in nature, it is rather difficult to determine the starting point of the reform and, therefore, of the writing of the account describing it too. Conceivably, even if the religious changes in Judah were not as visible as stated in the text, and the material culture offers no evidence of a radical turn either, there might have been small-scale purification of religion in Jerusalem, or there might at least have been ideas and plans stating that a reform was necessary.

By all accounts, these changes or plans to make them were instigated by aristocratic and priestly circles to increase Judah's independence. These intentions are mainly expressed on a religious level. Was it a group with the programmatic name of the "people of the land" (cf. Fried 2006) that enthroned Josiah (2 Kgs 21:24)? That is just as conceivable as the possibility that the same people were responsible for the murder of Amon, though this act is attributed to his servants (2 Kgs 21:23). The central figures of the text about the reform are Shaphan the scribe and Hilkiah the priest. In the biblical account, there is also the important aspect of the kinship between the Shaphanides and Gedaliah, a later Judean governor who resided in Mizpah and offered a policy of appeasement. Consequently, he was murdered by Judean nationalists led by Ishmael, who is described using a double patronymic (2 Kgs 25:25) similarly to Gedaliah (2 Kgs 2:22) and Shaphan (2 Kgs 22:3; for this see also 4.2.5.1.2) to emphasise his status as a descendant of royal blood. The ambiguous evaluation of Gedaliah and his death—intended both to sideline him and to underline the absolute abandonment of the land, which includes the descendants of the Davidides who are also exiled—prove that the texts were edited (in this case, by the third generation of exilic or postexilic Deuteronomists) to enforce a hitherto non-existent perspective with a specific time horizon and a specific group linked to it.

Ultimately, the reform, as supported by biblical texts, but not as much by the ostensibly relevant material culture, is above all a literary founding myth of postexilic Judaism. The catastrophe of the fall of Jerusalem in 587/586 BCE is reflected theologically and transformed into a thesis about monotheism as being the only legitimate articulation of Israel's religion. Its emphases and practices are retrospectively projected onto a time in which the Kingdom of Judah still existed, including its very origins, to gain importance as ancient and time-tested. The political context of Josiah's reform is backgrounded, and a religiously conscious, glorified ruler comes to the fore, to pose as a paradigmatic example. In the wider composition of Kings, this intention is emphasised in contrast to the deterrent figure of Manasseh as well as the preceding pair of Judean rulers, Ahaz and Hezekiah.

When examining the entire long century of the Kingdom of Judah, politically motivated cult centralisation—which was by all accounts inspired by Assyria (cf. Koch 2019)—clearly started as early as the mid-eighth century BCE. Biblical historiography focused on a more complex agenda than the simple progression of macro- and micro-history, and had limited resources to do so. This historiography reflects time-based conceptions that clearly show the longer growth of biblical materials and their compositions (cf. Rückl 2016). The central subjects include the following:

1. coming to terms with Assyrian hegemony in a critical manner
2. cult centralisation (also painted as cult purification with a monotheising direction as part of Judean king patterning)
3. explaining the fall of Jerusalem in 587/586 BCE by retrospectively introducing a historicising tale of King Manasseh, an unexemplary figure in terms of religion, into the seventh century BCE
4. using the founding myth of cult reform under Josiah, which encompassed all of Israel including the north, to provide the reasoning for monotheism as a formative fact of the Kingdom of Judah as well as Israel

The account of Josiah's reform and rule in 2 Kgs 22–23 mixes proclamations and ideals with historical reality. According to its extensive depiction in Kings, the religious purification programme was comprehensive, and the summarising commentary, which describes the king as a ruler like no other before or after him, could be read as a good end for an exemplary ruler in the Davidide line (2 Kgs 23:25). However, in terms of the time of narration, the

Books of Kings and those who authored them must explain the imminent end of the Kingdom of Judah in advance, and so they return to Manasseh as the cause of the coming disaster (2 Kgs 23:26–27; cf. 2 Kgs 21:10–16). This task is completed using historical patterning (see the accompanying table).

Tab.7. Historical patterning of Judean kings in the eighth and seventh centuries BCE

Ahaz (741–725 BCE)	Hezekiah (725–697 BCE)	Manasseh (697–642 BCE)	Josiah (639–609 BCE)
cult changes under Assyrian influence (centralisation?)	cult centralisation ("followed completely the ways of David")	Yahwistic cult abandoned	cult reform ("followed completely the ways of David")
makes his son pass through fire	purification of the cult	**makes his son pass through fire**	purification of the cult
high places	territorial expansion (unproven)	Asherah and Baal worshipped	territorial expansion (unproven)
stabilised kingdom	revolt against Assyria with catastrophic consequences	kingdom re-stabilised	kingdom stabilised (later conflict with Egypt)
loyal vassal of Assyria		loyal vassal of Assyria	

The Books of Kings provide no comprehensive explanation as to Josiah's death in Megiddo, only mentioning the place where it happened (see 6.1 for the possible historical reconstructions). The later account in Chronicles elaborates the pharaoh's meeting with the king into an epic tale about Josiah's stubbornness, which leads to his death, though God orders the pharaoh to warn the king against engaging in conflict (2 Chr 35:20–26). In this story—which is a marvellously composed compilation of other biblical texts that describe war conflicts (for more detail, see Japhet 2003)—Josiah's intransigence and desire for battle prevent Necho II from quick progress northwards to aid the Assyrian armies against the rising Neo-Babylonian Empire. Consequently, Josiah becomes both a paradigmatic (in Kings) and a tragic figure of the imminent end of Judean independence (in Chronicles).

6.2.5 JEHOIAKIM AND HIS SUCCESSORS ACCORDING TO BIBLICAL TEXTS

The final part of the last long century in Judean history begins with the death of Josiah in 609 BCE and with four significant and long-ruling kings, succeeded by four kings who rule for only slightly longer than a total of two decades. Whilst in the preceding period Judah was a long-term vassal of Assyria (734–615 BCE), the city now came under the dominance of the 26th Dynasty of Egypt and, later, the inexorably expanding Neo-Babylonian Empire. The history of the region until the fall of Jerusalem in 587/586 BCE has already been discussed, including the theory which positively evaluates Jehoiakim (608–598 BCE). Schipper (2010), for example, considers him to be a more astute politician than Josiah—one who consolidated the complex political situation in his land as far as it was possible (see 6.1), while his predecessor had gone on an ill-advised adventure to Megiddo (see 6.2.4.2; cf. Čapek 2019a).

The end of the long century is discussed in the last two chapters of Kings (2 Kgs 24–25), whilst Chronicles describe it more briefly, in only one chapter (2 Chr 36). Both biblical historiographies depict Jehoiakim in contrast to Josiah as a deterrent example and a godless ruler; apart from this, the older account also recalls Manasseh as the one responsible for the imminent disaster (2 Kgs 24:4).

The Book of Jeremiah is an important and comprehensive testimony on the events in Judah at the turn of the seventh and sixth centuries BCE. On one hand, it describes the gradual decline of Jerusalem concurrently with 2 Kgs 24–25 (Jer 37–39); and on the other, it offers a more detailed perspective on the events in Judah from Josiah's time until the Babylonian captivity. The book was written gradually and edited several times before it became a complete work, with much of it dating from a later period; nevertheless, its text is highly valuable for reconstructing the events and relationships at the end of Judean independence. Formulated as prophecies, Jeremiah's texts betray a considerable internal tension in Jerusalem vis-à-vis the power shifts in the Southern Levant. Influential groups lead a debate as to which hegemon is more appropriate for Judah: while some see hope in Egypt under the 26th Dynasty and rail against dependence on Babylonia, others use the opposite reasoning; and yet others warn against both (see, e.g., Jer 20:1–6; 21:1–10; 22:10–30; 27:4–20; 42:1–43:13).

The main participants in the debate include people close to the royal court, priests, an prophetic groups (see 6.2.4.2 as well). In chapter 36, Jeremiah has the scribe Baruch write his words passing judgment on Jerusalem due to its godlessness, bringing them first to Jehoiakim (and probably also to Jehoiachin; cf. Jer 37:1) and later to Zedekiah, both of whom reject them. In some respects, the introduction of the scroll dictated to Baruch by the prophet as well as other circumstances (the reading, the audience, etc.) resemble the declaration of Josiah's reform. The prologue of Jeremiah links the work to the author of the reform, and the word of YHWH comes to the prophet during Josiah's rule (see Jer 1:2); consequently, one may assume that the scroll of the book is an appendix of sorts, expressing some criticism of Josiah as well, even though the brunt of this is levelled at Jehoiakim, which shows that the reform was not an unmitigated success and that Judah still has a long journey ahead to practicing monotheism.

Texts included in Jeremiah treat the end of the last long century in Judah's history against the backdrop of a generally formulated theology of punishment and repentance (manifesting in the return to YHWH), bearing typical Deuteronomistic features (see discussion in Römer 2016). Undoubtedly, these texts are written from exilic and postexilic perspectives, as indicated by the idealised notion of a fictitious future king (Jer 23:1-7) and by the favourable attitude towards the Judeans in the Babylonian diaspora (Jer 24:1-14; 29:1-23; 38:1-28).

6.3 SUMMARY

The period of the Iron Age IIC, which comprised the dramatic long century of the Kingdom of Judah, saw ancient Israel further establish its self-determination. However, Judah only entered the Iron Age IIC after the fall of Samaria in 722 BCE, becoming the heir to the northern traditions due to its strong dynastic ties to the Israelite kings in the ninth and eighth centuries BCE (see 4.2.4.3). The process was a gradual one, and so it is not necessary to assume that "it was only the fall of the northern kingdom and the move of a large number of Israelites to Judah that brought about the rise of pan-Israelite ideology in the south" (Finkelstein 2013, 163; see also Finkelstein 2015 and 2020b; Na'aman 2014). What was a branch kingdom in the second half of the ninth and early eighth centuries BCE became an independent state no later than the rule of Ahaz, in the mid-eighth century BCE. Its survival was then determined by the astute policies of Judean kings, who became vassals to Assyria, Egypt, and the Neo-Babylonian Empire successively.

A confrontation between material culture, epigraphy, and biblical texts reveals that the Old Testament account frequently differs from the other two sources of information. As depicted in the biblical historiographies in Kings, Chronicles, and prophetic texts, this history has a different focus than merely describing "what happened": its purpose is to emphasise its own version of events. This history testifies to the exceptionality of a nation that may be small, located away from the most crucial action, subjugated by great powers and stronger neighbours most of the time, and which was eventually defeated in dramatic circumstances, but which despite all this is a nation with good prospects, since it views its own past as a chain of logically interconnected events (see below).

The new and substantial aspect of the biblical account is that it levels heavier criticism even at Judean kings after the fall of Samaria. They too are subjected to historical patterning that does not tally with facts about the history of Judah under Ahaz, Hezekiah, Manasseh, Josiah, and Jehoiakim which may be accurately reconstructed from sources other than the biblical texts. The authors of the historiographies, whose work—and consequently, the growth of literary traditions linked to them as well—spans several generations, use the available resources with the following purposes:

a) to show the antiquity of the Kingdom of Judah and to depict the kingdom itself as a political fact no newer than Israel: this is done using the historical "overture" of the United Monarchy and the concurrent developments of both kingdoms, from the literary construct of the division (see chapter 4) to their respective falls in 722 BCE and 587/586 BCE
b) to explain the exceptional nature of paradigmatically ideal figures against the backdrop of their negative counterparts (by means of historical patterning—in this chapter, mainly the pairs of Ahaz-Hezekiah and Manasseh-Josiah) who were first responsible for the fall of Israel and later also Judah
c) to show that, even though the history of the Kingdom of Judah ended in disaster, this event was not the end but the beginning of a new Israel which existed in northern and southern traditions as a legitimate successor during both the exilic and postexilic periods

The historical—or, rather, historicising—memory formed in the long century of the Kingdom of Judah used numerous concepts to grasp the past for the purposes of the present and the future. The diverse and sometimes contradictory nature of the concepts is due to their development over a long period of time. The identity formed by biblical texts—the main point of the depiction of events preceding Jerusalem's fall in 587/586 BCE—programmatically and systematically leans on strong ideological differentiation. The authors of biblical historiographies introduce an elaborate logic into common history and use it to redraw events according to their own needs; that is why criticism is levelled at rulers that enact de facto successful policies, such as Ahaz, Manasseh, and possibly also Jehoiakim; and why Judean rulers who engaged in risky power manoeuvres with outcomes that were temporarily poor (Hezekiah) or completely tragic (Josiah) are viewed in a much more positive light.

As a whole, the criticism of unexemplary kings and the positive appraisal of their counterparts is a set of several evaluative perspectives. This is a result of the long evolution of biblical texts, and of several authors being involved in their creation who followed agendas that reflected their respective periods and own specific needs. Before the destruction of the First Temple, there was a desire for an ideal kingdom and a king who would provide his country with security, prosperity, and allow for the practising of the one-god cult in the Jerusalem Temple; in the exilic period, answers were sought as to why

6. THE LAST LONG CENTURY (IRON AGE IIC)

Jerusalem fell; and later, in the postexilic period, the issue of a new modus vivendi developed between those returning from exile and those who stayed (see chapter 7).

Biblical historiographies are politically profiled, but they also conceal their evaluations in religious language by describing the cultic practices linked to an initial paradigmatic figure: King David. Being like David, being a Davidide, is a legitimising formula of sorts, creating a religious and political link that connects a specific king and his period to the original ideal. Evaluated in this manner, such a ruler then displays exemplary religious behaviour, embarks on territorial expansion, engages in construction activities, and as a result the Kingdom of Judah flourishes during his reign (see 6.2.2 and 6.2.4). Reconstructed using the material culture and the ancient non-biblical texts, the picture of the Iron Age IIC is more ambiguous, which makes the period under discussion more dramatic. The reasons behind such different perspectives will be discussed in the following chapter—on the end, and new beginning, of Israel.

7. THE END AND A NEW BEGINNING (NEO-BABYLONIAN AND PERSIAN PERIODS)

> *Granted, the Bible is biased theological literature on one hand; on the other, this does not necessarily mean it has to be late historical fiction.*
> —Christian Frevel

The end of the Kingdom of Judah in 587/586 BCE coincided with the end of the Iron Age IIC. The new hegemon—the Neo-Babylonian Empire—introduced a dramatic change, by following the 597 BCE deportation with the outright conquest of Jerusalem. Thus, what had been a kingdom for over two centuries, albeit mostly as a vassal of Assyria and then for a short period under Egypt, was transformed into a province. In terms of historical periods, this section discusses the Neo-Babylonian (587/586–539 BCE) and Persian periods (539–333 BCE; further divided into the Persian Period I, 539–450 BCE, and the Persian Period II, until 333 BCE). In biblical studies, the Neo-Babylonian period is often also termed the exilic period; using this name entails the risk of including texts that originated over a longer period of time, i.e., even later, be it in the post-539 BCE diaspora or upon the return to Judah—and the same risk is linked to using the word "postexilic" (see discussion in Römer 2016). The year 539 BCE did not mark a clear end of the exile, since the return took multiple decades and even became a permanent and willingly accepted fact for a significant part of the diaspora (see 7.2.1).

In the Neo-Babylonian and Persian periods, the bearers of the joint traditions of the fallen kingdom of Israel and now also Judah—the latter of which survived its stronger northern brother by more than a century - wrote and edited texts and also used new literary compositions to explain their connections and links to ancient Israel, even though they were not the independent political entity and kingdom that they had been until the arrival of the Babylonian armies. Identity was further formed by explanations of Jerusalem's fall and the deportation of a part of the population to Babylonia. Consequently, in terms of the events depicted, the time of the Kingdom of Judah came back into play, with questioning and explanation of the fall of the First Temple retrospectively introduced (see especially 6.2.1 and 6.2.3).

Furthermore, the nature of the new Israel was elucidated and slowly took shape around the Second Temple which consisted of people who had gone into exile as well as those who had stayed in Judah. There is a common denominator in the conviction that the events of 587/586 BCE were not only a catastrophe but they also provided a new opportunity to confront and meaningfully interpret the past, and to learn a lesson from it for the present. Primarily, biblical texts do not offer historical or political explanations; they focus on a *theology of history*, which explains politics, history, and religious events—past or present—from a highly specific point of view, which, moreover, contrasts with some other views in the Old Testament. Consequently, there is tension not only between these texts, but also with the historical and archaeological reconstructions of the period under discussion.

7.1 ANCIENT DOMINOES

The last observable part of these "ancient dominoes"—which, in the preceding chapters, comprised of Egypt, the Assyrian Empire, and Aram Damascus, among those in power—involves two more hegemons. The first one, for a short time, is the Neo-Babylonian Empire, whose rise signified the final downfall of the Kingdom of Judah in 587/586 BCE; and the second is the Persian Empire (539–333 BCE). The Neo-Babylonians exerted considerable influence over the events in the last decades of the Kingdom of Judah. Initially, they had no direct presence in the region, but Josiah felt their steep rise to power indirectly, when he had to assist the joint campaign of Egypt and Assyria against Nabopolassar (626–605 BCE) and, for unspecified reasons, was killed in Megiddo in 609 BCE by the Egyptian pharaoh Necho II (for the possible causes of Josiah's death, see 6.1). After the Battle of Carchemish in 605 BCE, it became clear who would go on to control the Levant: Nebuchadnezzar II (605–562 BCE) slowly extended his influence further to the south, where, as early as 604 BCE, numerous former Egyptian vassals submitted to him, as did Egypt itself eventually, despite some temporary successes (for details see 6.1). Some rulers of the Kingdom of Judah felt the influence of the Neo-Babylonian Empire directly, even though—owing to the temporary power shifts between Egypt and the Neo-Babylonian Empire—they saw the minor successes of the empire on the Nile and bet on Egypt; for example, Jehoiakim (608–598 BCE) in 601 BCE and later Zedekiah (598/597–587/586 BCE). In both instances, changing the political orientation towards a presumably more advantageous hegemon proved to have devastating consequences.

The first conquest of Jerusalem and the first deportation took place in 597 BCE under Jehoiachin (598–597 BCE), and these are noted in the Babylonian Chronicles as well as Old Testament texts (ABC 5; 2 Kgs 24; 2 Chr 36; Jer 37), with the biblical text comprising of a detailed description of the fortunes of the royal family. Jehoiachin was transported into Babylon, alongside his mother, wives, and the royal court; according to the same testimony, the total number of people displaced during the first deportation amounted to eighteen thousand (but cf. Jer 52:28–30). The very end of the Kingdom of Judah came about with the second conquest of Jerusalem under Zedekiah, in 587/586 BCE, which was also a punishment for the king's decision to side with Egypt when it was administered by the pharaoh Apries (589–570 BCE). This second entry of the Neo-Babylonian army into the capital spelt the end of Judah as an independent kingdom. According to the biblical account, which will be discussed in more detail (see 7.2.3), the walls of Jerusalem were breached, the king was blinded and taken away to Babylon, and his sons were killed. A month after the conquest, the temple was burned down, and its inventory carried away (cf. 6.2.2). The palace and all the significant houses were destroyed, while the city walls were torn down. The priests and other important Judean administrators of the temple and city were eliminated; no one was left in the land apart from peasants, vineyard workers, and farmers, since "Judah went into exile out of its land" (2 Kgs 25:21).

According to biblical texts, Nebuchadnezzar II tasked Gedaliah with administering the newly formed province of Judah from Mizpah, to the north of Jerusalem. Gedaliah was subsequently murdered by Judean nationalists led by Ishmael, a scion of the royal house (2 Kgs 25:25–26; cf. Jer 40–42). Due to Gedaliah's death, more Judeans fled to Egypt, afraid of Babylonian punishment. Dated to 582 BCE, based on Jer 52:30, this third exile is depicted as a mistake in the Book of Jeremiah, serving as a powerful testimony to the very different ways of coming to terms with Babylonian supremacy (see 7.2.4).

The dominance of the Neo-Babylonian Empire continued for another half-century after the conquest of Jerusalem, under Amel-Marduk (562–560 BCE), Neriglissar (559–556 BCE), and Labashi-Marduk (556 BCE). The latter was murdered a mere nine months after ascending the throne, by a group around Belshazzar, son of Nabonidus, and the royal court aristocracy. The rule of Nabonidus (556–539 BCE), the last Chaldean dynasty ruler and a supporter of the Sîn cult, saw Persia flourish, led by Cyrus II (559–530 BCE) of the Achaemenid dynasty. The initial rise of the Persian Empire occurred when Cyrus ended its vassalage to King Astyages of Media (585–549 BCE) and gradually acquired new territories. Cyrus won a significant victory against Lydia around 550 BCE and secured Bactria in 540 BCE, an area in what is today northern Afghanistan. The end of the Neo-Babylonian Empire and its incorporation into the Persian Empire is dated to 539 BCE, when influential priests of Marduk and the people—likely in cooperation with the Persians—opened the gates of Babylon, offering no resistance. This voluntary submission is recorded in the Edict of Cyrus, discovered in Babylon in 1879. The historical accuracy of the document depicting the taking of the capital, as well as the reforms mentioned in it, are debated, but that does not diminish the fact of who was becoming the new hegemon (Kuhrt 1983; 2007; Briant 2006; Zawadzki 2010; cf. Richardson 2016; also see 7.2.5).

The fall of Babylon in 539 BCE entailed two changes for the inhabitants of Judah as well as for those who were deported. Firstly, Cyrus II continued the Babylonian system of administration, and Judah, as the province of Yehud, was included in the satrapy of Babylonia and Transeuphratia and the administrative system of the Persian Empire, which was the first to use coins in addition to seals (Lipschits and Vanderhooft 2011; Lipschits 2021). Discussions are ongoing as to whether Judah was an independent province with a governor (satrap), or if it was a part of a larger administrative unit (see the overview in Frevel 2016, 297–302). The second change was that the exiled Judean population was free to return to its land after fifty years. The people's release and return are depicted in great detail in biblical texts, which also come to terms with the fact that the land was never completely abandoned (see 7.2.1). The Persian Empire's rule of over two centuries came to an end with the Battle of Issus in 333 BCE, in which Alexander the Great (336–323 BCE) defeated Darius III (336–330 BCE).

In the Persian period, important historiographic compositions of the Old Testament were completed, including the Deuteronomistic History. With their final form established in the third century BCE, the Books of Chronicles are crucial to understanding the history of Judah at the time (Japhet 2003, Jonker 2010). In the Persian Period II, the books of Ezra and Nehemiah were finished, and both are also highly important for comprehending the identity struggle of postexilic Judean communities. These groups based their identity on their relation to the ancient kingdoms of Israel and Judah, while also defining themselves in opposition to the province of Samaria—the contemporary political and religious competition. In the second half of the fifth century BCE and the early fourth century BCE, the final forms of the five books of Moses—or the Torah/Pentateuch—were established, playing an important role for the community of the province of Yehud, but also for the northern province of Samaria and the local Yahwistic cult, with its centre in the Gerizim temple (Tov 1997; Dušek 2014, Hensel 2018; 2019; see 7.2.6).

7.2 INTELLECTUAL PROCESSING OF THE DEFEAT AND SHAPING THE NEW ISRAEL

The fall of Jerusalem in 587/586 BCE was a watershed moment in the history of ancient Israel, whose legacy was appropriated by the Kingdom of Judah especially after the conquest of Samaria in 722 BCE. In the Old Testament, this tragic end is described in many ways and using various literary genres: from simple stories and prophecies fulfilled to poetic adaptations in the Book of Psalms and the Book of Lamentations. The main message of biblical texts is the fact that Jerusalem might have fallen, but that did not signify the end of Judah and Israel per se. Quite the contrary: the fall was followed by the construction of a new temple, the restoration of Jerusalem and Judah, and the rise of a new, or re-established, national identity, through which those assuming it lodged their claim to being the same—and at the same time, transformed—Israel.

When describing the identity shaping process, Knauf and Guillaume (2016, 229) very aptly write that battles were lost but the defeats were intellectually processed, and that the Bible is a legacy of this history. The biblical texts very consistently include Israel in exilic and postexilic history as an intrinsic part of, and a synonym of sorts for, Judah. This applies, for example, to the Book of Lamentations which is dated to the Neo-Babylonian period (Dobbs-Allsopp 1998; cf. Rendtorff 2000; Assis 2009), and the Book of Ezra which was composed in the Persian Period II (Japhet 2006a; Becking 2011; Grätz 2013). In both cases, Israel is mentioned because Judah is presented as the heir to its legacy on a religious level as well as on the level of national and political self-determination.

> How the Lord in his anger has humiliated daughter Zion! He has thrown down from heaven to earth the splendor of Israel.
> (Lam 2:1)

> Thus says King Cyrus of Persia: The Lord, the God of heaven, has given me all the kingdoms of the earth, and he has charged me to build him a house at Jerusalem, which is in Judah. Let any of those among you who are of his people—may their God be with them!—go up to Jerusalem in Judah and rebuild the house of the Lord, the God of Israel; he is the God who is in Jerusalem.
> (Ezra 1:2–3)

The latter text is remarkable for the double emphases that localise Jerusalem as a place "in Judah", to make it clear where the new temple would stand. The same double emphases are linked to YHWH, the God of Israel, who is, however, God "in Jerusalem". The purpose of the detailed description in Ezra is neither to inform those unaware of where the Judeans would head from exile, nor to tell the Judeans themselves, if they, as the third or fourth generation of the deported, no longer knew where Jerusalem was located. The text is not old enough to be a record linked directly to 539 BCE and the Edict of Cyrus (see 7.2.5), and it is addressed to two groups: firstly, to the inhabitants of Judah who stayed in the land and who are not considered the true heirs of Israel; and secondly, to the northerners from the province of Samaria (be they the native population or the people who arrived there during the Assyrian deportations in the late eighth century BCE), who also practised the Yahwistic cult. However, the newly established Judean clergy of the temple rejected and opposed them (see, e.g., Ezra 4). The specific identity here is formulated by an elaborate rejection of the north, represented by Sanballat, the governor of Samaria, who initiated the construction of the temple on Mount Gerizim in 423-407 BCE (see Dušek 2008; 2012; 2014; Hensel 2016; cf. Magen 2007).

Importantly and surprisingly, external factors are not presented as the primary reason for the defeat of the Kingdom of Judah. The end mainly came from within, as was also the case in the northern kingdom. This was due to Judah's wrongdoing as a collective entity as well as a sum of individuals, since they caused the gradual coming of the empires by failing to heed the warnings of the prophets who had harshly criticised religious and social problems (see, e.g., Isa 24; Mic 1-3; Zeph 1). In the north, the kingdom does not end because of Shalmaneser V or Sargon II, but because of the Israelites themselves, and the situation is similar in the south within Judah: Nebuchadnezzar and Nebuzaraddan, his general, are merely the instruments of destruction triggered by the transgressions of Judah, its disobedience, and neglect of the Yahwistic cult. History is, therefore, masterfully wreathed in comprehensive self-reflection, which has a theological frame, but draws on history, into which justifications for the inevitable fall of the kingdom are retrospectively introduced (see chapter 6). Identifying the reasons for this fall provides the opportunity for a new beginning, since the situation is rectifiable from the inside as well—understandably, with the assistance of external factors. These include the fall of Babylon in 539 BCE and the rise of the Persian Empire; some biblical texts do not hesitate to claim that its representative, Cyrus, was a messiah, the anointed of YHWH (Is 45:1; cf. 2 Chr 36:22; Ezra 1:1).

7.2.1 MYTHS OF THE EMPTY LAND AND THE MASS RETURN

The biblical depiction of the doom of Jerusalem and the deportation of the inhabitants to Babylonia shares certain features with the description of the fall of Samaria in 722 BCE (Kahn 2019; Levin 2019; Novotny 2019). As stated before, archaeological evidence demonstrates—contrary to the notion of Israel's utter destruction—that the Assyrians only paralysed the key administrative and strategic spots, leaving other localities untouched, which is why these were continuously populated (cf. Rander 2019; see 6.1). The same applies to the extent of the deportations as depicted in biblical texts, and probably also, in reverse, to the arrival of swathes of people from Mesopotamia to the northern highlands and Samaria (see 2 Kgs 17:5-6, 24-28). These events did take place, but to a lesser extent.

The description of the fall of Jerusalem, which, however, features no arrival of a different population, uses historical patterning to make the historical events appear commensurable due to the great similarity of the literary adaptations (cf. 4.2.5). The reasoning for the end of the centres of both kingdoms, Israel and Judah, is identical: disobedience to YHWH, idolatry, and social injustice pervading all areas of life. The consequences are similar—doom and mass deportation (2 Kgs 17:6, 18; 18:11; 25:21). The end of Jerusalem's and Samaria's existence is adapted into *historicising myths* about utter destruction and complete deportation. The Judean scenario differs in the fact that the land remains empty, with no one deported into it, and the question is why this situation of "emptiness" arose.

The first answer is that "the myth of the empty land," as it is termed in research (Barstad 1996; 2003; Lipschits 2005; Weinberg 2006; Moore and Kelle 2011; contra Oded 2003), emphasises the importance of the Babylonian exile. Conceivably, the first diasporic generations did not even consider the possibility of a return (see 7.2.3). Formulated and adapted in later biblical traditions which are recorded in the books of Chronicles, Ezra, and Nehemiah, the second answer is that it is necessary for someone to come into and resettle the empty land (see 7.2.5). This brings into play the second myth, known as "the myth of the mass return." In terms of biblical historiography, these events are described as a continuum: the year 587/586 BCE is followed by the exilic period, ending with the Edict of Cyrus in 539 BCE, based on which the direct descendants of deported Judeans start to return to the land. There, after fifty years of a "demographic gap" and religious inactivity, they restore the temple, its walls, their cultic and ordinary lives, and they re-establish a community of Israel which continues in the preexilic traditions from the period of the Kingdom of Judah.

The historical reconstruction of the period is more difficult. Though the myths do have a literary connection and are linked by the chronology they depict (see the septuagintal order of the books of Chronicles—Ezra—Nehemiah, which is adopted by most modern translations of the Old Testament, though it is a translation from Hebrew—i.e., from a differently ordered canon), the textual and editorial analyses of these comprehensive compositions prove that the authors lived in different periods and environments, and that there were considerable differences even in their notions of Israel's history. The creators of the second myth had the opportunity to follow in the footsteps of the first, thereby creating a continuity that was probably unintentional. The historicising, older myth of the empty land raises two questions: firstly, was the land truly left empty and, if so, how; and secondly, if it was not empty, why was the myth created and by whom?

7.2.2 THE ARCHAEOLOGY OF JUDAH AND JERUSALEM IN THE NEO-BABYLONIAN PERIOD

For many decades, even archaeology viewed the biblical depiction of Jerusalem's utter destruction and Judah being abandoned by its population, dragged away into captivity, as a faithful description of events in Judah as a whole in the Neo-Babylonian period (587/586-539 BCE). Newer research has shown that the situation is more complex (see the overview in Lipschits and Blenkinsopp 2003; Lipschits 2005; Frevel 2016; contra Oded 2003). The findings from numerous localities which have been gradually uncovered and examined have demonstrated that apart from Jerusalem the Babylonian invasion mostly impacted the Shephelah (Lachish, Tel Batash, Beth-shemesh, Tel Azekah, and possibly Tel Burna) as well as settlements in the Beer-sheba Valley and Negev (Tel Ira, Tel Arad, Horvat Uza, Horvat Radum and Tel Malhata), while the areas to the north and south of Jerusalem remained almost untouched.

It is no coincidence that the places where there was destruction often overlap with the localities demolished by the Assyrians in the eighth century BCE: this shows the logic of the geopolitical thinking of those ruling the Levant. Both powers moved into Judah from the Coastal Plain, slowly paralysing important strategic spots, depending on the intensity of the resistance. In his 701 BCE campaign, Sennacherib was content with the destruction of strategic forts mainly in the Shephelah (Lachish, Tel Batash, Tel Burna, Tel Azekah) and the Negev (Tel Malchata), and he did not attack Jerusalem — at most, he sent a part of his army there as a warning (see 6.2.2; cf. the ambiguous record in COS 2.119B). On the other hand, due to recurring Judean resistance, Nebuchadnezzar followed the 597 BCE preventive deportation with destroying the capital completely in 587/586 BCE.

However, this does not mean that life in Judah ground to a halt. Most of the settlements were preserved so that the newly established Neo-Babylonian province could still generate an economic profit even after the exemplary destruction of Jerusalem. Therefore, a place of administration was founded in the north, in Mizpah, where, according to biblical texts, Gedaliah was made governor (2 Kgs 25:22-26), and another in the south, in Ramat Rahel (Stratum Va), a destination for agricultural produce (mainly wine and oil), as it had been in the Iron Age IIC. Neither of these settlements were damaged by the Babylonian invasion. Uninterrupted by even the conquest of Jerusalem, the continuity of the administrative system is documented by a total of seventy-seven lion stamp impressions found in Ramat Rahel (Lipschits, Gadot, Arubas and Oeming 2017), which followed after the rosette symbol (turn of the seventh and sixth centuries BCE). Subsequently, in the Persian period, the administrative system began using Yehud stamps (from the late sixth century BCE onwards).

Due to iconographic and petrographic analyses and knowledge of pottery assemblages from Tell el-Ful, Tell en-Nasbeh, Bethel, and el-Jib (Gibeon) in the Benjamin area north of Jerusalem, it is clear that ordinary life continued in Judah even after the fall of the capital, albeit to a lesser extent. This reconstruction is supported by, among other things, demographic calculations based on examining rural farm settlements, which were not destroyed either. Though the calculations differ (cf. Barstad 1996; Faust 2003; Lipschits 2005; Alstola 2020), it is obvious that Judah was not an empty land even during the time of the Babylonian exile.

In the Neo-Babylonian period, Jerusalem was only scarcely populated in the southern hill area (with an estimated 1,200 people) and had no fortifications. Still, it may be assumed that cultic life continued to some degree here, and so the texts depicting utter destruction must be viewed as stylised. Some textual testimonies (e.g., Jer 41:4) suggest that sacrificial practices were preserved, even though they were taking place in a seriously damaged and politically marginalised city (cf. Frevel 2016, 305). In the exilic period, administration of the Babylonian province in the Jerusalem area was taken over by the administrative centres in Tell en-Nasbeh and Ramat Rahel (Lipschits and Blenkinsopp 2003; cf. Zorn 2003). Therefore, in answer to the first question posed above, the Babylonian invasion did *not* leave Judah empty; and so now we turn to the second question, regarding the reasons for the claims that the land was empty and who may be the authors of the myth.

7.2.3 THREE PERSPECTIVES ON THE EXILE AND THE MYTH OF THE EMPTY LAND

The Old Testament offers several perspectives on the exile, with each following a specific, and different, agenda. Each of the authors wishes to convey to their audience that their experience of the exile is the most significant one, in order that it may be accepted by the others (cf. Knauf and Guillaume 2016, 135–42). The next section will introduce three outside perspectives—i.e., from the exile—and the subsequent one will show the view from the inside—i.e., the perspective of those who stayed in the land, as preserved by the biblical traditions linked mainly to certain parts of the Book of Jeremiah.

The first exile is linked to the 597 BCE deportation; then, Jerusalem was probably only partially despoiled, with a small number of its inhabitants led away to Babylonia. Nebuchadnezzar took Jehoiachin hostage and brought him, along with his family and courtiers, to Babylon (see ABC 5), where he took care of him and his sons, as documented by Jehoiachin's tablets discovered in Babylon, recording that the captive king and his sons received monthly oil rations (see Fant and Reddish 2008). The biblical texts connected to the second wave of exiles (see below) trace the fortunes of the king and his sons until their release under Amel-Marduk in 561 BCE (2 Kgs 25:27; Jer 52:31). Since there is no further information on Jehoiachin and his descendants, it is possible that this is literary fiction which aims to strengthen pro-Davidide circles and the hope of restoring the kingdom, whether that is in the imminent or an unspecified future. However, there is no more detailed mention of the king's return from exile (cf. Frevel 2016, 271, 282).

The perspective of the first deportation is captured in some of the texts of the book of Ezekiel; the author, belonging to the priestly circles of the Zadokites in Jerusalem, committed his views to writing in the Babylonian diaspora near the Kebar Canal probably in 592 BCE (see Ezek 1:1). Ezekiel provides readers with a utopian picture of Jerusalem and criticises the supporters of the second exile, who had angered him by taking his place in the interim. Since he had no possibility of influencing events at home, Ezekiel resorted to relentlessly castigating the nobles and leaders of the people, even including death threats (see Ezek. 11:1-21). He also incorporated visions describing an ideal restoration, which not only involves the return of a king who is in the mould of David (Ezek 34), but especially the cult (Ezek 40-48). According to the prophet Ezekiel, all of this would take place at an unspecified point in the future, since the glory of YHWH was not present due to the incompetence of the current governors of Jerusalem (cf. Ezek 43; for a similar utopian depiction of the new Jerusalem in Christian reception, see Rev 20-22).

Those who went into exile during the second deportation in 587/586 BCE are the primary authors of the myth of the empty land, and their central line of reasoning is shown in 2 Kgs 25, which, for the following reasons, should prove that there was no one left in Judah:

- The temple, palace, and all the important buildings were destroyed (v. 9).
- The walls were broken down (v. 10).
- Everyone, including the defectors to the Babylonian king (!), were deported (v. 11).
- Only some of the poor and those tending the vineyards and fields remained (v. 12).
- All temple inventory was either melted down or requisitioned and transported to Babylon (vv. 13-18; cf. Ez. 1:7-11).
- The priests, guards, and courtiers were led away to Riblah and executed (vv. 18-20).
- Consequently, "Judah went into exile out of its land" (v. 21).
- Gedaliah, the governor instated by Nebuchadnezzar in Mizpah, was also murdered after some time, so "all remaining people" left the land, this time to Egypt due to fear of Babylonian retribution (vv. 22-26; see also the third exile).

A similar account is recorded in the text of 2 Chr 36:20, which states that the rest of the people who had not been killed were deported to Babylonia and served there as slaves (2 Kgs 25 states no such thing) until the accession of Cyrus, who allowed them to return to their land (2 Kgs 25 does not record this information either). The image of a completely empty land would have appealed to the Babylonian diaspora, since it underlined its importance, including the very end of the Second Book of Kings, which depicts the absolution of Jehoiachin (undocumented by non-biblical evidence). The historicizing myth of the empty land is followed later by Ezra and Nehemiah with a similarly genre-oriented myth of the mass return, which describes the impressive homecoming to Judah (see 7.2.5). Historically, it is more likely that the return from Babylonia was gradual, taking place over several decades or even centuries. There was no mass transfer back into the land, but rather individual groups of repatriates heading back—and that did not happen immediately after the Edict of Cyrus. There are clear proofs that the exiled Judeans settled several Mesopotamian areas and did well on an economic as well as social level (Pearce 2006; Becking 2003; Alstola 2020). Biblical texts show that the exile supported Judah, even though the Judeans would stay outside their homeland for longer (cf. Ezra 6:6–9; Zech 6:9–15; cf. Schniedewind 2004). This is also confirmed by documents from the new homeland, here in particular by the Muraššu archive from the vicinity of Nippur. Here nearly nine hundred tablets dealing mainly with administrative correspondence documenting the lively economic activity of the second half of the 5th century BCE have been found. The tablets contain many West Semitic names with even theophoric elements such as *-yah, -yahu* or *-ye* (cf. Pearce and Wunsch 2014; Rom-Shiloni 2017). In addition to the Muraššu archive, texts from Bīt Našhar and al-Yahudu containing the names of the Judeans also date from around the same period, proving that the exiles continued to live in Babylonia for at least another four generations.

The most convincing proof of the exile becoming a new, permanent home (cf. Berlejung 2022), and of the fact that the mass return must be viewed as a myth sui generis, is the presence of a Jewish community in Babylonia, which ended only recently. It is a particularly bitter irony of modern history that, after more than 2,500 years, the Jews left Iraq, the place of Talmudic academies and the writing of the Babylonian Talmud, during coalition operations in the early 1990s and the start of the twenty-first century. As late as 1884, up to 30,000 Jews had lived in Baghdad; in 1900, there were as many as 50,000. After World War II, their situation began to worsen dramatically as a direct consequence of the Arab-Israeli wars (especially after 1948–49 and 1967), but the very end did not arrive until some fifteen years ago (Faraj 2021).

The third exile is connected to the period around 582 BCE, when some Judeans fled to Egypt after Gedaliah's murder (the year is calculated according to Jer 52:30, which dates Babylonian deportation to the twenty-third year of Nebuchadnezzar's rule). This was not a deportation, but an escape for fear of the Neo-Babylonians, who might have planned revenge for the death of the Judean governor they had installed in Mizpah (cf. 2 Kgs 25:26). The account describing the elimination of the pro-Babylonian governor Gedaliah, who advocated a more conciliatory policy towards Babylonia, takes aim at the tendency to stay in the land, and visibly supports the policy of exile and the myth of the empty land. The governor is murdered by Ishmael, whose special position is emphasised by the usage of the double patronymic (similarly to the northern kings Jehu and Joash; see 4.2.5.1.2) and by stating that he was "of the royal family". Apart from biblical texts (see 2 Kgs 25:22–26; Jer 42 and 43:28–30), there is no other evidence for the third exile, which, by all accounts, logically led to Egypt. Moreover, the links between the messages of these texts are unclear.

In the Book of Jeremiah, the Judeans are said to have come to Tahpanhes (Jer 43:7) and to reside in Migdol, Memphis, and the land of Pathros (Jer 44:1). The first non-biblical mentions of the Judeans—and possibly the inhabitants of Samaria too—in Egypt date to the late fifth century BCE and the Aramaic Papyri of Elephantine, a Jewish military colony. According to some scholars, a Yahwistic temple was established there as early as around 525 BCE (cf. Kratz and Schipper 2022), presumably either by the descendants of Israelites who had fled in the late eighth century BCE, or by Judean mercenaries and traders from the period of the 26th Dynasty of Egypt (for more, see 6.1 and 6.2.4; cf. Schipper 2020b).

7.2.4 THOSE WHO REMAINED . . .

Textual testimonies connected to the types of exile described above prove that, in the Neo-Babylonian period, members of individual groups outside of Judah were involved in a dispute as to the most legitimate heir to Israel's traditions. Each group legitimised its own actions while questioning the activities of the others. The first diasporic group criticised the actions of the others, who stayed in Judah until 587/586 BCE. The second exiles voiced more serious reservations about Judah, producing the thesis of the empty land, where there was no one left apart from the minimum number of people necessary to take care of farming (cf. 2 Kgs 25:12).

Since—as suggested by archaeological evidence—Judah was never an empty land (see 7.2.2), it is necessary to examine domestic literary traditions as well. Some texts in Jeremiah testify to the life of those who remained; these writings are typically more favourable to the Neo-Babylonian administration and espouse a realistic appeasement policy. It is possible that the second exiles criticised them, as the "deserters who had defected to the king of Babylon" (2 Kgs 25:11), while at the same time trying to include them in their own deportation, to ensure there would indeed be no one left in the land. However, the land was not empty even after the murder of Gedaliah, the Judean governor residing in Mizpah. Though some fled to Egypt for fear of Neo-Babylonian retribution (see the third exile), the land was still populated, and life in it went on.

Jeremiah remained in Judah and claimed that Nebuchadnezzar was representative of YHWH on earth (Jer 27:6). In retrospect, he blamed King Zedekiah for not heeding warnings and trading his vassalage to Babylon in 594 BCE for loyalty to Egypt, with this reckless shift in foreign policy later leading to catastrophic consequences. Other texts connected to the Judean group in the land claim that it tried to remain connected with the exiles. Thus, Israel may well have survived in the diaspora as well as in Judah. Jeremiah wrote a calm letter to the diaspora, suggesting that it live peacefully abroad and not influence events in Judah:

> 29 These are the words of the letter that the prophet Jeremiah sent from Jerusalem to the remaining elders among the exiles and to the priests, the prophets, and all the people whom Nebuchadnezzar had taken into exile from Jerusalem to Babylon. 2 This was after King Jeconiah and the queen mother, the court officials, the leaders of Judah and Jerusalem, the artisans, and the smiths had departed from Jerusalem. 3 The letter was sent by the hand of Elasah son of Shaphan and Gemariah son of Hilkiah, whom King Zedekiah of Judah sent to Babylon to King Nebuchadnezzar of Babylon. It said: 4 Thus says the Lord of hosts, the God of Israel, to all the exiles whom I have sent into exile from Jerusalem to Babylon: 5 Build houses and live in them; plant gardens and eat what they produce. 6 Take wives and have sons and daughters; take wives for your sons, and give your daughters in marriage, that they may bear sons and daughters; multiply there, and do not decrease. 7 But seek the welfare of the city where I have sent you into exile, and pray to the Lord on its behalf, for in its welfare you will find your welfare.
>
> (Jer 29:1–7)

The later editorial adaptations of Jeremiah include texts supporting those who remained in a further elaborated pro-diaspora discourse, which privileges the exiles over those who remained in the land (e.g., Jer 24). The overall composition of the book shows that it underwent amendments with clear Deuteronomistic and pro-exilic features (see discussion in Thiel 1981; Fischer 2007; Leuchter 2014; Najman and Schmid 2016; Mastnjak 2016; de Waard 2020). However, a critical reading of even the current version of Jeremiah may reveal the testimony of a fourth voice—of those who remained in the land, unlike the three diasporae.

7.2.5 THE MYTH OF THE MASS RETURN

The myth of the mass return is congenial with the myth of the empty land; at the same time, it is one of the central Old Testament traditions with a historiographic nature. Though the authors of the first myth probably had not anticipated the second one (see 7.2.1; but cf., e.g., Lipschits 2005), the members of the later generations returning to Judah from the diaspora followed older narratival and prophetic themes to shape a *continuous* story about the mass return of ten thousand Judeans from Babylonia. These returnees provided the "empty" land with something that had been interrupted by the fall of Jerusalem in 587/586 BCE, which secured them the right to establish new political and religious life in Judah.

Logically and given the order of biblical books—especially according the Septuagint, in which the Books of Kings are immediately followed by the Books of Chronicles, Ezra, and Nehemiah, all of which is sometimes termed the Chronistic History (for a rejection of this designation, see Japhet 2003; 2006b; cf. Auld 2017) - it appears likely that the return occurred shortly after the rise of the Persian Empire—i.e., after Cyrus II (559-530 BCE) had issued his edict in 539 BCE (cf. the identical and "connective/glue" texts of 2 Chr 36:22-23 and Ezra 1:1-4). In the canon of the Hebrew Bible, Ezra and Nehemiah as well as Chronicles are included in the Writings, and so they do not follow the Books of Kings which feature among the Former Prophets (cf. Barton 2000; 2003); consequently, it is necessary to take a cautious approach in terms of any direct links between the myths to history, considering the clues offered by the canonical order.

The historicising myth of the mass return was identified due to the critical analysis of texts and the findings of archaeological research in the 1990s, in more or less the same period as the myth of the empty land was first debated by scholarship (Grabbe 1991; cf. Becking 2006; Knoppers 2011; de Hulster 2015). Becking (1998) proposes searching for the historical origin of the myth, which answers the question of what happened after the return from the exile in the Persian period, between two opposing views. The first one is the traditional notion that the books of Ezra and Nehemiah provide a historically accurate account of events directly after the Edict of Cyrus in 539 BCE. For example, Halpern (1990) claims that the Babylonian diaspora returned en masse almost immediately following the edict, and that under Darius I (522-486 BCE) the temple began to be built in 520 BCE, to be finished five years later. Halpern considers Ezra's depiction (4:1-5) of the construction being hampered by the "people of the land" to be historically reliable, dating it to 538-520 BCE—i.e., a period prior to the commencement of the temple's construction. In accordance with the biblical text, Halpern dates the second wave of complaints about the actions of the returnees (Ezra 4:6–23) to the period of Xerxes I (486–465 BCE) and Artaxerxes I (465–424 BCE). The second extreme comes from the minimalists (for this see esp. Barr 2000; Frevel 2016; Hjelm 2017), who consider the contents of Ezra and Nehemiah to be mere fiction of late Judaism of the third and second centuries BCE (Garbini 1988; Davies 1991; cf. Becking 1998, 162–66). So, what can we learn from the texts depicting the return from exile; what happened in Judah during the Persian period; and what time horizons should we consider?

When examining the biblical historiography recorded in Ezra and Nehemiah, there is obviously considerable emphasis placed on the legitimacy and impressive nature of the return and all that followed; this mainly relates to the information provided in the list of returnees, stating that "these are the people of the province who came from those captive exiles whom King Nebuchadnezzar of Babylon had carried captive to Babylon" (Ezra 2:1; Neh 7:6). This seems to be a relatively harmless piece of information; however, it plays a distinctly ideological role. As stated by Jonathan Dyck (2000, 130), its purpose is to reproduce the ideological tensions in the postexilic community with the purpose of forming a group identity and expressing its internal hierarchy.

The picture painted by biblical texts intends to support the audiences' notion that "the return was a single event to be dated in the early years of the Persian era" (Becking 2006, 4). This myth is corroborated both by the claim that the invitation to leave the diaspora was personally issued by Cyrus, and by the comprehensive, more or less parallel texts of Ezra 2 and Neh 7, which underline that this is Israel, returnees of the "Israelite people", who number almost fifty thousand (Ezra calculates that there were 42,360 men + 7,337 slaves + 200 singers; Nehemiah offers the same numbers, with the only difference being that he counts 240 singers). Adding women and children to these calculations then makes the final totals several times higher. Numerous other texts (e.g., Ps 126) depict the return to Zion and Jerusalem as an objective fact involving all of Israel, which is, in an elaborate manner, linked intertextually (Exod 15:16; Isa 43:21, see the very rare phrase "this people", ʿām zû in Hebrew) to Israel's exodus from Egypt as a mirror event. Both depictions share the same significance and similarly inflated numbers of those departing the Babylonian and Egyptian diasporae (for more detail, see Čapek 2005, 120–22; however, cf. Becking 2018).

Egypt	⟶	The Land	⟵	Babylonia
Moses				Ezra (*Moses redivivus*)
600,000 men				some 50,000 men
Exod. 15:16 (the people– ām zû)				Isa. 43:21 (the people – ām zû)

Fig. 26. The exodus from Egypt and the return from Babylonian exile as mirror events

The description of the early mass return, as provided by biblical texts, is challenged by demographic calculations in the Yehud province; according to which, the area was continuously populated throughout the Neo-Babylonian and Persian periods (539-450 BCE), and the number of inhabitants was between twelve thousand and thirty thousand, based on these calculations and the total area of the province (see the overview in Frevel 2016, 304). Archaeological research has not yet documented any significant increase in the populated area in this period; such a rise only occurred in the Persian Period II (450-333 BCE), and it is not linked to immigration but to economic growth in the province as well as in Samaria to the north. If exiles were indeed coming back, they did so gradually, in several waves and in incomparably lower numbers than those given by Ezra 2 and Neh 7. Referring to percentage calculations of newly inhabited areas in the Persian Period I, as identified by Carter (1999), Becking (2006, 9-10) proposes that no more than four thousand people arrived.

A closer comparison between the Edict of Cyrus and its usage in 2 Chr 36:22-23 and Ezra 1:1-4 (cf. a second, more technically oriented version in Ezra 6:2-5) does not confirm a direct historical link that connects the two documents. Not only does the edict have nothing to do with Judah and the Jerusalem Temple, making no mention of either (see COS 2.124), but even the biblical references to it are highly vague, with a centripetal, pro-Judean stylisation, and must therefore be interpreted in relation to other biblical texts and their ideological intentions (especially Jer. 25:11-14; 29:10; cf. the earlier analysis of Ezra 1:1-3 in 7.2). Moreover, it is also necessary to take a critical look at the Persian document itself—not as evidence of a policy of tolerance, but as tendentious propaganda for a policy of tolerance by the priests of Marduk in Babylon, praising Cyrus II as the architect of the peace threatened by Nabonidus (556-539 BCE).

Declared not only by the Edict of Cyrus, but also by the inscription of Darius I (522-486 BCE) from Behistun/Bisutun (between 521-519 BCE; Schmitt 1991), the Persian ideological program of a harmonious world order (cf. Root 2000) was in fact by no means less cruel, humiliating, and filled with punishment. This is pointed out by Michael Roaf (2010), who interprets Achaemenid art, especially monumental scenes (e.g., from Persepolis), not as a depiction of harmony, but as an expression of real politics, which therefore has nothing to do with "an idealistic vision of the harmonious mutually supportive organisation of the relationship between the rulers and the ruled" (ibid., 140). According to Roaf, there is little doubt that the Achaimenides were "just as vicious, cruel and despotic as their Near Eastern predecessors and their successors and that they were equally feared by their subjects" (ibid., 133).

Mentioned above, the Behistun inscription clearly documents the repression meted out under Achaimenide imperial rule, depicting the punishments of subjected kings: ears and noses cut off, tongues or eyes torn out; being held in chains outside the gates so that people could watch them; and then being impaled on stakes. The supporters of the dead kings fared no better, getting beheaded or hanged (DB II, 88–91; DB III, 90–92, etc.). The same inscription also proves that Darius I was far from pursuing a policy of religious tolerance. In several places in the inscription, the rebellion against the Persian Empire is linked to a comment stating that "Auramazda was not worshipped". By contrast, the Persian ruler "worshiped Auramazda" and, by the "favour" of the deity, he defeats his opponents and treats them as is his desire (DB IV, 14–33; see also DB V 20–36). In the Persian period, the destruction of temples was another demonstration of power. It is historically attested that temples were not only rebuilt but were much more likely to be destroyed at the behest of the Persians (cf. Frevel 2016, 291). Based on the above, the characterisation of Persian kings as people of great religious tolerance (as described for instance in the commentary on Ezra 1 in the Czech Ecumenical Bible) is highly idealised.

Other "Persian" documents in the Book of Ezra (4:8–16; 4:17–22; 5:7–17; 6:6–12; 7:12–26), written in the language of the empire—Aramaic—have been analysed in detail by Lester Grabbe (2006). Regarding the texts, the author came to the following conclusions:
1. They underwent comprehensive amendment by scribes.
2. They contain elements of both older and newer language.
3. The epistolary formulae do not correspond to imperial Aramaic formulae; instead, if there are any available analogies (esp. Ezra 4–6), they are found in Early Hellenistic letters—i.e., from the third century BCE (they might have been written or only edited in this period).
4. They feature Jewish theology.
5. In various degrees, they evince aspects of propaganda.

In conclusion, Grabbe formulates a cautious claim that "the compiler of Ezra had available some original Persian documents at least part of the time, but he or a prior tradent worked these over for apologetic or theological purposes or even to support claims made by the Jewish community to the Persian administration" (ibid., 563).

7.2.6 WHO IS AND WHO IS NOT ISRAEL?

The myth of the mass return is not, as suggested by the genre used itself, a reliable imprint of historical facts; this has been proved by archaeological evidence, which considers a different history of Judah in the Neo-Babylonian and Persian periods. Still, the myth is not complete fiction, which is why the term *historicising myth* has been used consistently (Becking 2003 speaks of a *historical myth*) to denote a means of expression that draws upon history but which concurrently follows its own ideological agenda. The role of the myth was to enforce the interests of a specific group: by all accounts, those of the descendants of the Babylonian exile, who gradually returned to Judah and used the narrative of the prophecy fulfilled and the return of the deported to Sion (Jer 30-31; see Ezra 1:1) to reintroduce the prior myth of the empty land (see 7.2.3), whether it had originally been intended merely as support for the Mesopotamian diaspora or had another purpose as well.

Though the group linked to the exile was less numerous than the people of the land, its influence was undoubtedly significant. Its members were the descendants of the elites that were dragged away to Babylonia, who then continued the older traditions and, at the same time, wrote a new legitimising myth; in it, they used the historiographic accounts in Ezra and Nehemiah to form a link that argued in their favour, by guaranteeing secular (Cyrus II and his edict) as well as prophetic and divine power (see the connection between Jeremiah's prophecy and its fulfilment through YHWH, in Ezra 1:1) in support of their religious and political claims.

As proven by research in recent decades, as well as the line of reasoning presented above, the myth of the mass return is primarily a monumental literary composition with an ideological profile that originated in historical periods later than the ones it depicts. More conservative scholars date it to the sixth century BCE (Halpern 1990) and others the mid-fifth century BCE (Japhet 2006a); yet others place the beginning of the myth's usage to circa 400 BCE (Becking 2006; cf. van Seters 2015), and some to as late as the fourth century BCE (Gerstenberger 2011). Given the nature of the genre and the manner in which the return and the reconstruction of the "abandoned" Judah is described, as well as the very scant archaeological evidence, it is necessary to exercise caution when examining the dating of the restoration of Jerusalem and the construction of the temple and walls, as depicted in Ezra and Nehemiah (see discussion in Lipschits and Blenkinsopp 2003; Frevel 2016). The dating is further problematised by the Book of the Law of Moses which is described as being read outside the Water Gate in Neh 8:1. Here too, scholarly opinions differ greatly regarding the nature of the document that was read aloud and the origin and dating of the Pentateuch itself. While some think that Ezra held a complete Pentateuch, which had been finalised earlier, no later than the end of the Neo-Babylonian period (i.e., 539 BCE), numerous researchers place the final edition of the composition to the Persian Period II (see the overview in Römer 2013).

The purpose of the myth was to strengthen the identity of the Judeans linked to the Babylonian exile, who were an elite that were slowly returning to the land and intending to govern it as its own. To that end, it creates a complex system of legitimising or, conversely, delegitimising aspects, which de-

termine who should lead the postexilic community in the Persian period and who should not. Such features include the following:
- creating a link between the prophecy about the return and the exilic community through which this return takes place
- proving the corresponding genealogical ties (especially concerning paternal lines and the people's Israelite origin)
- excluding those without such ties from the opportunity to govern the Judean community
- The same applies to the priestly order (see, e.g., Ezra 1:59-62).
- The Law and the gradual restoration of temple service are placed at the centre of community life.
- There is strong editorial connection between the First and Second Temples (see 2 Kgs 25:13–18; Ezra 1:7–11).
- Ezra becomes the guarantor of change as *Moses redivivus*.
- The Law (Ezra 8) is used as a tool for the purification of Israel (esp. Neh 13:1).
- Mixed marriages are refused (Ezra 10).

As demonstrated (see 7.2), the myth's message is aimed in two principal directions: to Judah, where the people of the land are made aware of who has the claim to lead the Judean community; and to the province of Samaria in the north, which rivals Jerusalem with its Yahwistic temple on Mount Gerizim. Unmentioned as yet, the third addressee is the diasporic community itself. Here too, great tension and a more or less concealed power struggle can be seen in the biblical texts.

Upon closer examination, the texts of Ezra 2 and Neh 7 show the imposing nature of the return of ten thousand exiles into "their" land (cf. 7.2.5), but also the rejection (!) of those among them who would be unable to hold the priestly office in Judah, since they could prove neither the paternal line nor the tracing of their genealogy back to Israel (see Ezra 1:59–62; Neh 7:61–65). Rather than considering the texts as a description of contemporary events, it is more appropriate to view them as a later, highly stylised, retrospective literary construct, intended to support the claim of a specific contemporary group, which comes into conflict with another one (cf. Dyck 2000; Laird 2016).

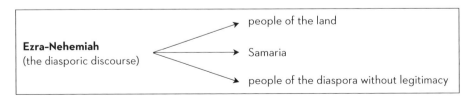

Fig. 27. The triple conflict of the Babylonian diaspora upon its return to Judah

Garry Knoppers (2005; 2006; 2013; 2011; 2015) points to less polemic relations between the diaspora and the domestic scene, as well as those in Samaria. In his view, the tension in Ezra and Nehemiah must be considered a rhetorical proclamation which defends the writers of the texts themselves. According to Knoppers, it is far more likely that the communities in Judah and the diaspora lived in mutual dependence. The exiles maintained their bond with their ancestral land, historical city, temple, and people. They were dependent on the other community, since everything in the land (the people, leaders, temple, priests, Levites, and ground) was also a life-giving part of themselves. On the other hand, the people in Judah relied on their—by all accounts—economically better-situated close friends and relatives in the diaspora, who did well for themselves in their new environment.

The existing and presumably good relations between Judah and Samaria are proven by the fifth century BCE papyri of Elephantine, Egypt; according to these, when the Jewish diaspora in Egypt planned to rebuild the temple destroyed in 410 BCE, it turned to both Jerusalem and Samaria for assistance (TAD A.4.3; Porten 1996, 130-32; Schipper 2020; Kratz and Schipper 2022). This evidences the ongoing ties between the governors of the Yehud province and Samaria. Equally, the text of Neh 13:28 may be read as proof of mixed marriages existing, though they are condemned (possibly only later and on an ideological level). In all likelihood, the reason why this strong stance was committed to writing is that Jerusalem elites were faced with a stronger and more populated neighbour that also had more long-term prosperity (Frevel 2016). In terms of redaction criticism, which analyses the growth and interconnectedness as well as the diversity of literary traditions, it is no coincidence, therefore, that the Persian period saw the return of several themes in biblical literature that was produced or redacted during this time: the origins of the kingdom; the division under Rehoboam and Jeroboam I; the reasons for the fall of Israel; and the polemic involving the cult in Samaria and Bethel as competitors to Jerusalem (see, for example, the later editorial amendments in the texts of 2 Kgs 17 or 23; for more, see Kucová 2005). Judah and Samaria had more in common than they had differences, and so Jerusalem aimed to find a new self-designation to set itself apart (cf. Hensel 2016; 2019). If there was a temple on Mount Gerizim (Dušek 2014) as early as the second half of the fifth century BCE, "this would only have added further impetus for Jerusalem Temple scribes to authenticate the distinctive positions of their city and shrine" (Knoppers 2006, 279).

Apart from the Persian period literary traditions that are based on themes of differentiation and exclusiveness, the same era—probably in reaction to their sharp tone—sees the creation of texts which describe Israel as an open community that is not averse to change. Such texts include the Book of Ruth, some later parts of Isaiah, and the Book of Jonah (however, cf. Rendtorff

2000)—i.e., newer literature that continued to take shape even in the Hellenistic period (Römer, Macchi and Nihan 2013; Schmid 2021).

7.3 SUMMARY

The end of the Kingdom of Judah in 587/586 BCE, in the late Iron Age IIC, constituted a turning point in the history of this small state. In the Neo-Babylonian (586–539 BCE) and Persian (539–333 BCE) periods, a new Judah slowly arose from the Babylonian diaspora and the ashes of the destruction that mainly engulfed Jerusalem and strategic areas in the access points to the Judaean Mountains—but not every place (see 6.2.2), meaning that the land was not empty. Judah was no longer a vassal kingdom, but a province belonging to the new hegemon, the Persian Empire. The newly written and older (edited) literary traditions made a joint effort to explain this province's link to the southern kingdom as well as to Israel, whose heritage was continued by the preexilic Kingdom of Judah.

The main task for the authors of these literary traditions was to explain why Jerusalem fell, as well as to clarify that the fall was not the end of history of Judah. The paradigmatically ideal origins of the kingdom in the late eleventh century BCE, and the time from the sixth to fourth century BCE, were linked in multifaceted ways, which were mainly based on the retrospectively projected notion of Judah's continuous existence that started from the late Iron Age I and continued down even to the present in the Persian Period II. The defeat in 587/586 BCE was intellectually processed (cf. Knauf and Guillaume 2016) and the reasons for it were introduced into this history as the result of the neglect of the Yahwistic cult. Despite the main culprits being identified (see 6.2.4.2), the guilt was considered to be collective and thus so were the consequences, with the Neo-Babylonian army wreaking havoc on the entire populace. A significant section of the Judean society—especially the elite—was deported to Babylonia, where extensive portions of what would become the Old Testament were created.

There was another assignment for the same authors and their successors, whether they remained in the diaspora or were back in Judah: they had to explain the importance of the exile. Consequently, two constitutive, historicising myths were born which described the repopulation of the empty land after the Edict of Cyrus in 539 BCE as due to the return of the Judeans from Babylonia. Utter destruction and total deportation gave way to the mass return of the deported, who viewed themselves as the true descendants of Israel, and at whose heart stood a reconstructed Jerusalem, the temple, and the service held in it, all of which was determined by the Law (Torah). However, biblical texts do not include only this monumental conception of history, intended to set the true heirs apart from the competition—the people of the land, those who remained, and the Yahwistic cult in the province of Samaria—but they also feature other voices which react to this conception of history in a deliberately more conciliatory manner.

Using archaeological evidence, this chapter has demonstrated that biblical texts are indeed tendentious theological literature, but that they are not merely late historical fiction. These texts relate to past events, drawing on and processing them, so that a specific lesson may be learned by reflecting upon them. History serves as a means of self-reflection, framed theologically but based on history—i.e., it is a *theology of history*, into which justifications are introduced retrospectively to explain the reasons for the fall of the kingdom, as well as the rebirth of Judah in the late Neo-Babylonian and Persian periods.

8. CONCLUSIONS

> *History becomes historically relevant not through tradition per se,*
> *but through interpretation; not through mere discovery of facts, but through*
> *comprehension of past events, which reified into, and fossilised in facts.*
> —Ernst Käsemann

Piece by piece, the seven chapters of this book have observed how and when the kingdoms of Israel and Judah appeared on the map of the ancient Near East. Rather than setting a fixed date, the analysis of archaeological evidence and biblical and non-biblical textual sources revealed possible historical coordinates which show the periods in which these political entities could have conceivably existed. As documented throughout, the desire to determine an exact time is a noble aim. However, the modest starting point of uncertainty is a recognised necessity of critical science which must keep to working hypotheses rather than proposing simple and unfounded conclusions.

The pre-historic origins of Israel and Judah are determined by geopolitical developments in the Late Bronze Age and Iron Age I; at the time, the Canaanite city-state system underwent changes that resulted in its eventual collapse. The important factors include Egypt's retreat from southern Canaan and the rise of the Philistines, whose economic influence and growing power presented a challenge to the late-Canaanite population mainly in the area of the Shephelah in the south, but not only. It has been stated that the developments in the southern and northern highlands differed. The Israel mentioned in the late thirteenth century BCE is not a clearly identifiable entity in terms of politics or geography; moreover, it cannot be directly connected to the establishing processes of the northern Kingdom of Israel in the ninth century BCE. This link is a later construct and must be analysed as such—critically and using all the scientific instruments available. The gap between Merneptah and Israel, or Judah in the tenth century BCE, has not been bridged by this book.

In modified conventional chronology, the late Iron Age I and the early Iron Age IIA especially overlap with the tenth century BCE, which has been termed a "difficult" century. It is in this century that the late-Canaanite substratum gave birth to new political entities in the northern highlands as well as the

Shephelah, and probably also in the southern highlands around Jerusalem. Since these were merely embryos of future states, it is impossible to discuss Israel and Judah as demonstrably existing, developed polities in this period either. Such a discussion would lack evidence as to their institutional and organisational foundations, the existence of bureaucracy, an army, the ability to levy taxes, and the construction of public and monumental buildings. In terms of identifying possible political entities, the archaeological evidence is ambiguous, which is also reflected in the often radically different reconstructions of the origins of Judah and Israel; these are strongly influenced by the usage of biblical texts written much later (by entire centuries!). Epigraphic material from the period is also scarce, especially in the highlands, into which Phoenician script, the precursor to Hebrew, began to spread no sooner than the turn of the tenth and ninth centuries BCE.

Discussing the Iron Ages IIA–B, chapter IV states that it was not until this period that a process, which had begun earlier, concluded with the formation of two kingdoms. The existence of Israel, in the north, is provable just before the mid-ninth century BCE; while Judah, which is slightly younger and was dependent on the former due to strong dynastic ties, became independent no sooner than the end of the same century, but more probably, as late as the first half of the eighth century BCE. The perspective provided by biblical texts is different, since it describes the period using a later historiography with a strong literary stylisation, which originated no sooner than the eighth century BCE and mostly in the seventh century BCE. Biblical texts depict the golden age of the United Monarchy in the tenth century BCE, which, in a power struggle, gives rise to two equal independent political units, Israel and Judah, with the former existing until 722 BCE and the latter until the end brought about by the fall of Jerusalem in 587/586 BCE. The historical reconstruction proposed by this book comes to another conclusion: that the original unification cannot be proven historically—it is a status quo lasting throughout the concurrent existences of Israel and Judah, but under the direction of the Omrides and their closely related successor dynasty, the Nimshides, who governed the south as a branch kingdom via enthroning family members until the first half of the eighth century BCE. The one who decided and set the rules of the game was in our view the north, although the biblical texts see the situation differently and create a separate Davidide dynasty in the south.

The independence of the Kingdom of Judah is not fully provable until later—i.e., the late Iron Age IIB—when Judah emancipated itself from Israel, which—after enjoying a period of growth under Joash (802–787 BCE) and Jeroboam II (787–747 BCE)—gradually lost power due to increasing pressure from the Neo-Assyrian Empire. No later than 734 BCE, the same hegemon allowed the Kingdom of Judah to become a fully visible political entity with all aspects of a full-blown state, including the existence of writing documented by epigraphic and iconographic material, centralised tax collection, the construction of fortifications and large economic facilities (e.g., water canals and tunnels), and centralised religion. The only caveat to Judah's full independence was its vassalage to Assyria, which, however, provided Jerusalem with political security as well as involvement in wider and now stable economic relations, bringing prosperity and progress even into a remote kingdom on the periphery of the southern Levant.

The road to independence for the Kingdom of Judah is also depicted in biblical texts. The polemical tone of numerous prophetic and historiographic texts, which either describe the events of the first half of the eighth century BCE directly or make more or less overt references to them, testifies to the subtle and gradual birth of the new state. In this period, Judah started to exist in history on its own, and entered a time in which it formed a cultural memory. Simultaneously, an independent identity was created, strongly influenced by the traditions and heritage of the north, from which Judah largely originated. If the theory about the strong dynastic ties of both kingdoms holds true, the adoption of Israelite traditions was neither a singular event (i.e., the fall of Samaria in 722 BCE) nor a compromise from the same period (see 4.2.4.3), but a longer process, which had begun earlier and was concluded by the transfer of the name of Israel to be borne by the Kingdom of Judah. Thus, Old Testament texts preserve two houses of Israel with interconnected histories as well as fortunes. The kingdoms of Israel and Judah are linked by the notion of a collective identity based on their common ancestors (cf. Weingart 2014; 2015; 2016)—the originally northern dynasties of the Omrides and Nimshides, whose fate is now in the hands of Jerusalem-based scribes composing their own, pro-Davidide historiography, with which they rewrite past events in favour of the south.

The last long century of the independent Kingdom of Judah overlapped with the Iron Age IIC. Jerusalem's very existence in this period depended on the shrewd politics of Judean kings who successively became vassals to Assyria, Egypt, and the Neo-Babylonian Empire. The time of peace and prosperity contingent on loyalty to the Assyrian hegemon was interrupted by Hezekiah's uprising against Nineveh, which was quelled in 701 BCE. Judah recovered from the defeat during the long rule of Manasseh, again a loyal vassal of Assyria. Under Josiah, his successor, the kingdom fell under the influence of Egypt, and later the Neo-Babylonian Empire, which ended Judah's existence.

The comparisons of material culture, epigraphy, and biblical texts throughout this book have revealed that the information provided by the first two sources often differs from that of the third. This is due to the fact that biblical historiographies offer their own interpretations of events with emphases that support a version of history in which one nation is extraordinary. Granted, the nation is a small one, on the geographical periphery, most of the time a subject to ancient hegemons and stronger neighbours, and eventually defeated in dramatic circumstances; however, it also has good prospects for the future, since it views its past as a chain of logically interconnected events, and more or less systematically depicts it in its memory as such.

In this historicising concept of memory, the Kingdom of Judah is described as a political entity that is, at the very least, as old as Israel, alongside which it lives through much of history, later becoming the only heir to the joint traditions of both. Historical patterning plays a specific role in this idea of memory, criticising provably successful Judean rulers (especially Ahaz and Manasseh), much like earlier Israelite kings (e.g., Jeroboam and Ahab), due to their putative neglect of the Yahwistic cult. By contrast, their counterparts, Hezekiah and Josiah, enjoy success in construction activities and territorial expansion due to their loyalty to the same cult. The real reasons for criticising some figures and extolling others is difficult to determine unambiguously; it is a peculiar conglomerate of a longer retrospective, created gradually as well as in several editions, and a perspective that transfers political and national issues and encodes them into a religious language, which readers of this history or its audience should understand as the main key to its comprehension.

Dedicated to the Neo-Babylonian and Persian periods, this final chapter no longer discusses the Kingdom of Judah as an independent political entity but instead focuses on Jerusalem as the exilic and postexilic heir to the traditions of both kingdoms. For authors of the biblical text, this heir is the true Israel, reborn from the ashes. The tensions in some biblical texts make it evident that this heir was not the only one, with competition arising in the province of Samaria in the north—the territory of the historical Kingdom of Israel—in the form of the Yahwistic cult practised on Mount Gerizim. In the period examined, the defeat is intellectually processed as the consequence of religious guilt, which is at the same time collective and concentrated on the examples of deplorable individuals, upon whom the entire burden is placed in representation (especially Manasseh). The retrospectively traced history is mainly a comprehensive self-reflection with a theological framing; thus, justifications are introduced into the history to explain why Jerusalem had to fall.

The rebirth of Judah as Israel is depicted in two impressive historicising myths: the myth of the empty land, after 587/586 BCE; and the myth of the mass return, linked to the Edict of Cyrus and the year 539 BCE. These myths have been introduced, analysed, and compared with archaeological evidence and some biblical and non-biblical texts that paint a different picture. This comparison shows an alternative view of Judah in the Neo-Babylonian and Persian periods: that the land was never completely empty, and that no early mass return from the diaspora ever took place. Equally, it has been proven that the myths—as suggested by the genre used—are not and did not wish to be a mere description of historical facts. Still, they are not pure fiction, but a means of expression drawing on history while also following its own ideological agenda. The role of the myth of the mass return is to enforce the interests of a particular group, by all accounts the Judean elites and the descendants of the Babylonian exile; they gradually came back to Judah, or already were there for some time, using the story of the "prophecy fulfilled" and the return of the deported to Sion to revive the myth of the empty land, and so to confirm their importance to the land they were trying to reclaim.

In the Persian period, and mainly its second part (450–333 BCE), older traditions (the Deuteronomistic History) were completed, elaborated upon, and updated, while new traditions (mainly Ezra, Nehemiah, and Chronicles) were committed to writing, with the aim of creating an understandable and compelling connection between the origins and the present. Memories and stories were included in the present to become a common cultural memory (Rogerson 2010; cf. Assmann 2001). A multifaceted link was interposed between the paradigmatically ideal origins, even of humankind itself (see the introduction to 1 Chr 1:1 and the first chapters of Genesis), the time of the patriarchs, judges, and the historically stylised creation of the kingdom in the late eleventh century BCE and the sixth to fourth century BCE. This link is mainly based on a retrospectively projected notion of Judah's continuous existence as a fact present throughout history, as far back as humans can perceive it.

According to this reconstruction of history using archaeology and ancient literary sources, biblical texts are indeed tendentious theological literature, but they are not merely late historical fiction, since they include themes featuring material of historical importance. There continues a lively debate about how much biblical texts preserve a faithful imprint of events that did take place and how much vague memories conceal facts from as early as the city-state collapse in the Late Bronze Age and the subsequent Iron Age I (see 3.2.2.1 and 3.2.1.4.5). In the Old Testament, history is a tool of self-reflection, which is why it acquires an entirely specific form according to the "portfolio" of argumentation chosen.

The Old Testament is a book focusing on religion, and so the self-reflection included in it is designed accordingly, intended to be mainly a *theology of history*, into which reasons are introduced for the creation of Israel, the fall of Samaria and then Jerusalem, and for Judah itself becoming Israel. The notion of identity that comes to the fore in biblical texts is multifaceted and multitiered, since it was formed in different historical contexts. The cultural memory of ancient Israel relates to the very origins and what followed, in order to establish a continuous link between the past and present.

However, the search for a link to the past is not only tied to the Old Testament, but can draw on other, even older, sources to form diverse "identity" constructions with biblical texts. Therefore, the identity with which the ancient person and other people throughout history may connected themselves with is based upon Israel under Merneptah, Israel of the northern kingdom, Israel of the adopted northern traditions in Judah, Israel formulated against the backdrop of the exilic and postexilic communities, and its other, later forms, up to the present day. The power of such a religious, political, and cultural self-determination is obvious and is time-tested, but at the same time this power may threaten others and lead to conflict since the land, a subject of constant and continuous dispute in modern history even up to the very present, was never truly empty; consequently, even the "filling" of the land creates controversy and pain. Ancient historicising myths have a certain audience even today, which to various extents identifies itself with their conceptions of history.

This book has explored and utilised three main methods which may serve to trace the formation of the identity of ancient Israel. Using the analysis of material culture, archaeology, and non-biblical textual evidence provides results that allow the greatest possible accuracy when reconstructing history viewed through a specific and biased lens in biblical texts. Selected and systematically justified, this method allows biblical texts to be something other than the historically accurate records of events that they are often considered to be. Recognition of the division of competences may result in the confirmation of the opening motto of this book: that biblical interpretation, historical investigations, and archaeological research can successfully dialogue even in the absence of consensus about the "facts."

Arad—view of the Judean fortress (David R. Moulis)

Arad—sacrificial altar (David R. Moulis)

Beth-shean—testimony to the presence of Egypt (Filip Čapek)

Lachish—view of the Judaean Mountains (Filip Čapek)

Gath—one of the Philistine Pentapolis cities (David R. Moulis)

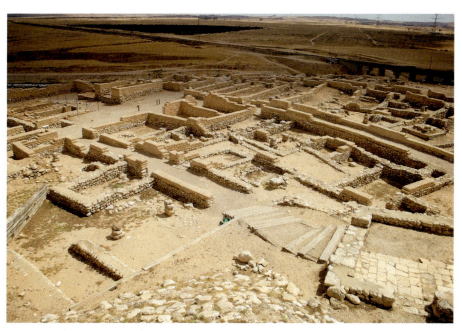

Beer-sheba (David R. Moulis)

Khirbet Qeiyafa—aerial view (courtesy of Khirbet Qeiyafa Excavations)

Tel Rehov with a view of Transjordan (Filip Čapek)

Hazor (David R. Moulis)

Bethel—historical photo from the 1954 research

Khirbet Qeiyafa—Gate in Area B with a view of Tel Azekah (David R. Moulis)

Gezer—six-chambered gate (David R. Moulis)

Azekah—uncovering Iron Age destruction (David R. Moulis)

Azekah—Late Bronze Age destruction (David R. Moulis)

Khirbet Qeiyafa—Ashdod Ware style (courtesy of Khirbet Qeiyafa Excavations)

Khirbet Qeiyafa—baking tray (courtesy of Khirbet Qeiyafa Excavations)

Khirbet Qeiyafa—storage jars (courtesy of Khirbet Qeiyafa Excavations)

Khirbet Qeiyafa—thumbed handles (courtesy of Khirbet Qeiyafa Excavations)

Azekah—Bronze Age assemblage (courtesy of The Lautenschläger Azekah Expedition)

Azekah—Iron Age storage jars (courtesy of The Lautenschläger Azekah Expedition)

Development overview of Judean impressed storage jars (courtesy of Institute of Archaeology, Tel Aviv University)

Storage jar with the *lmlk* impression (turn of the eighth and seventh centuries BCE)

Storage jar with the rosette impression (turn of the seventh and sixth centuries BCE)

Storage jar with the Yehud impression (fifth and fourth centuries BCE)

Examples of impressions on storage jars (courtesy of Institute of Archaeology, Tel Aviv University, David R. Moulis)

Lmlk impression (late eighth and early seventh century BCE)

Lmlk and concentric circles impressions (turn of the eighth and seventh centuries BCE)

Concentric circles impression (first half of the seventh century BCE)

Rosette impression (turn of the seventh and sixth centuries BCE)

Lion impression (587–539 BCE)

Karnak—record of Pharaoh Shoshenq I's campaign

Judean pillar figurines (David R. Moulis)

Horse and rider figurine (David R. Moulis)

Ramat Rahel—Proto-Ionian capital (Courtesy of Ramat Rahel Excavations)

Ramat Rahel—seventh-century BCE palace reconstruction (Courtesy of Ramat Rahel Excavations)

Broad Wall in Jerusalem (David R. Moulis)

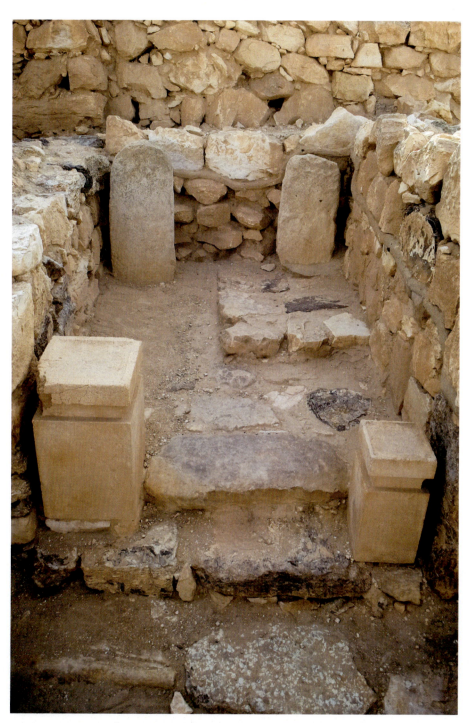
Arad—Judean shrine (David R. Moulis)

BIBLIOGRAPHY

Adam, K.-P. 2007. *Saul and David in der judäischen Geschichtsschreibung.* FAT 51. Tübingen: Mohr Siebeck.
Adams, D. L. 2009. "Between Socoh and Azekah: The Role of the Elah Valley in Biblical History and the Identification of Khirbet Qeiyafa." In *Excavation Report 2007-2008.* Vol. 1 of *Khirbet Qeiyafa,* ed. Y. Garfinkel and S. Ganor, 47-66. Jerusalem: Printiv.
Aharoni, Y. 1954. "Excavations at Ramat Rahel: Preliminary Report." *IEJ* 6:102-111 and 137-157.
———. 1968. "Arad: Its Inscriptions and Temple." *The Biblical Archaeologist* 31 (1): 2-32.
———. 1972. "Excavations at Tel Beer-sheba." *The Biblical Archaeologist* 35 (4): 111-127.
———. 1974a. "Excavations at Tel Beer-sheba: Preliminary Report of the Fourth Season, 1972." *TA* 1:34-42.
———. 1974b. "The Horned Altar of Beer-sheba." *The Biblical Archaeologist* 37 (1): 2-6.
———. 1975a. "Excavations at Tel Beer-sheba: Preliminary Report of the Fifth and Sixth Seasons, 1973-1974." *TA* 2:146-168.
———. 1975b. *Lachish V: Investigation in Lachish; The Sanctuary and the Residency.* Tel Aviv: Gateway Publisher.
———. 1979. *The Land of the Bible.* Philadelphia, PA: Westminster Press.
———. 1981. *Arad Inscriptions.* Jerusalem: The Israel Exploration Society.
Ahlström, G. 1993. *The History of Ancient Palestine from the Palaeolithic Period to Alexander's Conquest.* Sheffield: Sheffield Academic Press; Minneapolis: Fortress.
Albertz, R. 2007. "Social History of Ancient Israel." In *Understanding the History of Ancient Israel,* ed. H. G. M. Williamson, 347-368. Oxford: Oxford University Press.
Albertz, R., Nogalski, J., Wöhrle, J., ed. 2012. *Perspectives on the Formation of the Book of Twelve: Methodological Foundations - Redactional Processes - Historical Insights.* Berlin: de Gruyter.
Albright, W. F. 1943. *The Excavation of Tell Beit Mirsim III: The Iron Age.* AASOR 21/22. New Haven, CT: American Schools of Oriental Research.
Alpert, P., Alpert, F. 2012. *Archaeology and the Biblical Record.* New York: Hamilton Books.
Alstola, T. 2020. *Judeans in Babylonia: A Study of Deportees in the Sixth and Fifth Centuries BCE.* CHANE 19. Leiden: Brill.
Angelakis, A. N., Chiotis, E., Eslamian, S., Weingartner, H., ed. 2016. *Underground Aqueducts Handbook.* Boca Raton, FL: CRC Press.
Anthonioz, S. 2014. "Astarte in the Bible and her Relation to Asherah." In *Tranformation of a Goddess: Ishtar - Astarte - Aphrodite,* ed. D. T. Sugimoto, 125-140. OBO 263. Fribourg: Academic Press; Göttingen: Vandenhoeck & Ruprecht.
Arav, R. 2013. "Geshur: The Southwesternmost Aramean Kingdom." In *Arameans, Chaldeans, and Arabs in Babylonia and Palestine in the First Millennium B.C.,* ed. A. Berlejung, M. P. Streck, 1-29. Wiesbaden: Harrassowitz Verlag.
Arie, E. 2008. "Reconstructing the Iron Age II Strata at Tel Dan: Archaeological and Historical Implications." *TA* 35 (1): 6-64.
Assis, E. 2009. "The Unity of the Book of Lamentations." *CBQ* 71:306-329.
Assmann, J. 1992. *Das kulturelle Gedächtnis: Schrift, Erinnerung und politische Identität in frühen Hochkulturen.* Munich: C. H. Beck.
———. 2000. *Religion und kulturelles Gedächtnis.* Munich: C. H. Beck.

———. 2003. *Die Mosaische Unterscheidung oder der Preis des Monotheismus*. Berlin: Carl Hanser Verlag.
Aster, S. Z., Faust, A., ed. 2018. *The Southern Levant under Assyrian Domination*. University Park, PA: Eisenbrauns.
Athas, G. 2005. *The Tel Dan Inscription: A Reappraisal and a New Interpretation*. JSOTSup 360. Copenhagen International Seminar 12. New York: T&T Clark.
———. 2006. "Setting the Record Straight: What are We Saying about the Tel Dan Inscription?." *JSS* 51 (2): 241-255.
Auld, G. A. 1994. *Kings Without Privilege: David and Moses in the Story of the Bible's Kings*. Edinburgh: T&T Clark.
———. 2015. "Righting Israel's Kings." In *A King like All the Nations? Kingdoms of Israel and Judah in the Bible and History*, ed. M. Oeming, P. Sláma, 147-158. BVB 28. Berlin: LIT Verlag.
———. 2017. *Life in Kings: Reshaping the Royal Story in the Hebrew Bible*. AIL Series. Atlanta, GA: SBL Press.
Auld, G., Eynikel, E., ed. 2010. *For and Against David: Story and History in the Books of Samuel*. BETL 232. Leuven: Peeters.
Avigad, N., Sass, B. 1997. *Corpus of West Semitic Stamp Seals*. Jerusalem: The Israel Academy of Sciences and Humanities.
Barkay, G., Fantalkin, A., Tal, O. 2002. "A Late Iron Age Fortress North of Jerusalem." *BASOR* 328:49-71.
Barrick, W. B. 2001. "Another Shaking of Jehoshapat's Family Tree: Jehoram and Ahaziah Once Again." *VT* 51 (1): 9-25.
Barr, J. 1974. "Etymology and the Old Testament." In *Language and Meaning: Studies in Hebrew and Biblical Exegesis*, ed. A. S. Van der Woude, OTS 19, 1-28. Leiden: Brill.
———. 1995. "The Synchronic, the Diachronic and the Historical. A Triangular Relationship?" In *Synchronic or Diachronic: A Debate on Method in Old Testament Exegesis*, ed. Johannes de Moor, OTS 35, 1-14. Boston: Brill.
Barstad, H. M. 1996. *The Myth of the Empty Land: A Study in the History and Archaeology of Judah during the "Exilic" Period*. Symbolae Osloensis Fasc. Suppl. 28. Oslo: Scandinavian University Press.
———. 2003. "After the "Myth of the Empty Land": Major Challenges in the Study of Neo-Babylonian Judah." In *Judah and the Judeans in the Neo-Babylonian Period*, ed. O. Lipschits and J. Blenkinsopp, 3-20. Winona Lake, IN: Eisenbrauns.
Bárta, M., Kovář, M. et al. 2013. *Civilizace a dějiny: Historie světa pohledem dvaceti českých vědců*. Prague: Academia.
Barton, J. 1996. *Reading the Old Testament: Method in Biblical Study*. Louisville: John Knox Press.
———. 2000. "Canons of the Old Testament." In *Text in Context: Essays by Members of the Society for Old Testament Study*, ed. A. D. H. Mayes, 200-222. Oxford: Oxford University Press.
———. 2003. "Unity and Diversity in the Biblical Canon." In *Die Einheit der Schrift und die Vielfalt des Kanons - The Unity of Scripture and the Diversity of the Canon*, ed. J. Barton and M. Wolter, 11-26. Berlin: de Gruyter.
Baruchi-Unna, A. 2017. "Jehuites, Ahabites, and Omrides: Blood Kinship and Bloodshed." *JSOT* 42 (1): 3-21.
Becker, U. 1997. *Jesaja - von der Botschaft zum Buch*. FRLANT 178. Göttingen: Vandenhoeck & Ruprecht.
Becking, B. 1992. *The Fall of Samaria: An Historical and Archaeological Study*. SHCANE 2. Leiden: Brill.
———. 1998. "Ezra on the Move: Trends and Perspectives on the Character and his Book." In *Perspectives in the Study of the Old Testament & Early Judaism: A Symposium in Honour of Adam S. van der Woude on the Occasion of His 70th Birthday*, ed. G. Martínez and E. Noort, 154-179. Leiden: Brill.

———. 2003. "Chronology: A Skeleton without Flesh? Sennacherib's Campaign as a Case-Study." In *Like a Bird in a Cage: The Invasion of Sennacherib in 701 BCE*, ed. L. L. Grabbe, 46-72. JSOTSup 363. London: Sheffield Academic Press.

———. 2006. "'We All Returned as One!': Critical Notes on the Myth of the Mass Return." In *Judah and the Judeans in the Persian Period*, ed. O. Lipschits and M. Oeming, 3-18. Winona Lake, IN: Eisenbrauns.

———. 2011. *Ezra, Nehemiah, and the Construction of Early Jewish Identity*. FAT 80. Tübingen: Mohr Siebeck.

———. 2018. "Does Ezra Present the Return from Exile as a Second Exodus?" *BN* 177:65-73.

———. 2020. "More Than One God? Three Models for Construing the Relations Between YHWH and the Other Gods." In *Divine Doppelgängers: YHWH's Ancient Look-Alikes*, ed. C. Cornell, 60-76. University Park: Eisenbrauns.

Begrich, J. 1929. *Die Chronologie der Könige von Israel und Juda und die Quellen des Rahmens der Königsbücher*. Tübingen: Mohr.

Beit-Arieh, I., Freud, L. 2015. *Tel Malḥata. A Central City in the Biblical Negev*. 2 vols. Winona Lake, IN: Eisenbrauns.

Ben-Ami, D. 2001. "The Iron Age I at Tel Hazor in Light of the Renewed Excavations." *IEJ* 51:48-170.

———. 2013. *Jerusalem: Excavations in the Tyropoeon Valley (Givati Parking Lot)*. Vol. 1. IAA Report 52. Jerusalem: Israel Antiquities Authority.

———. 2014. "Notes on the Iron IIA Settlement in Jerusalem in Light of Excavations in the Northwest of the City of David." *TA* 41 (1): 3-19.

Ben Dor Evian, S. 2011. "Egypt and the Levant in the Iron Age I-IIA: The Ceramic Evidence." *TA* 38 (1): 94-119.

———. 2017. "Egypt and Israel: The Never-Ending Story." *NEA* 80 (1): 30-39.

Ben-Shlomo, D. 2019. "New Evidence of the Fortifications at Hebron." In *The Last Century in the History of the Kingdom of Judah – The 7th Century BCE in Archaeological, Historical and Biblical Perspective*, ed. O. Lipschits and F. Čapek, 63-88. AIL 37. Atlanta, GA: SBL Press.

Ben-Shlomo, D., Darby, E. D. 2014. "A Study of the Production of Iron Age Clay Figurines from Jerusalem." *TA* 41 (2): 180-204.

Ben-Tor, A. 2000. "Hazor and the Chronology of Northern Israel: A Reply to Israel Finkelstein." *BASOR* 317:9-15.

Ben-Tor, A., Ben-Ami, D. 1998. "Hazor and Archaeology of the Tenth Century B.C.E." *IEJ* 48:1-37.

Ben-Tor, A., Ben-Ami, D., Sandhaus, D., ed. 2012. *Hazor VI. The Selz Foundation Hazor Excavations in Memory of Yigael Yadin. The 1990-2009 Excavations. The Iron Age*. Jerusalem: Israel Exploration Society.

Ben-Yosef, E., Thomas, Z. 2023. "Complexity Without Monumentality in Biblical Times." *JAR* 2023 (online).

Ben Zvi, E. 1994. "On the Reading "bytdwd" in the Aramaic Stele from Tel Dan." *JSOT* 19 (64): 25-32.

Bench, C. H. 2014. "The Coup of Jehoiada and the Fall of Athaliah: The Discourses and Textual Productions of 2 Kings 11." Ph.D. thesis. University of Alberta, Edmonton.

Ber, V. 2015. "The Census and the Priestly King." In *A King like All the Nations? Kingdoms of Israel and Judah in the Bible and History*, ed. M. Oeming, P. Sláma, 113-146. BVB 28. Berlin: LIT Verlag.

Berges, U. 1998. *Das Buch Jesaja: Komposition und Endgestalt*. HBS 16. Freiburg: Herder.

Berlejung, A. 2009. "Twisting Traditions: Programmatic Absence-Theology for the Northern Kingdom in 1 Kgs 12:26-33* (The "Sin of Jeroboam")." *JNSL* 35 (2): 1-42.

———. 2010. "Geschichte und Religionsgeschichte des antiken Israels." In *Grundinformation Altes Testament*, ed. Gerz, J. Ch., 59-192. Göttingen: Vandenhoeck & Ruprecht (Czech Translation in 2017).

Berlejung, A., Maeir, A. M., Schüle, A., ed. 2017. *Wandering Arameans: Arameans Outside Syria. Textual and Archaeological Perspective*. LAS 5. Wiesbaden: Harrassowitz Verlag.

Berlejung, A., Maeir, A. M., ed. 2019. *Research on Israel and Aram. Autonomy, Independence and Related Issues. Proceedings of the First Annual RIAB Center Conference, Leipzig, June 2016*. Tübingen: Mohr Siebeck.

Bietenhard, K. S. 1998. *Des Königs General: Die Heerführertraditionen in der vorstaatlichen und frühen staatlichen Zeit und die Joabgestalt in 2 Sam 2-20; 1 Kön 1-2*. OBO 163. Freiburg: Universitätsverlag; Göttingen: Vandenhoeck & Ruprecht.

Biran, A. 1994. *Biblical Dan*. Jerusalem: Israel Exploration Society.

Biran, A., Naveh, J. 1995. "The Tel Dan Inscription: A New Fragment." *IEJ* 45:1-18.

Blenkinsopp, J. 2003. "Bethel in the Neo-Babylonian period." In *Judah and the Judeans in the Neo-Babylonian Period*, ed. O. Lipschits and J. Blenkinsopp, 93-107. Winona Lake, IN: Eisenbrauns.

———. 2013. "Remembering Josiah." In *Remembering Biblical Figures in the Late Persian and Early Hellenistic Period—Social Memory and Imagination*, ed. Diana V. Edelman and Ehud Ben Zvi, 236-256. Oxford: OUP.

Blum, E. 1984. *Die Komposition der Vätergeschichte*. WMANT 57. Neukirchen-Vluyn: Neukirchener Verlag.

———. 2012a. "Der historische Mose und die Frühgeschichte Israels." *HeBAI* 1 (1): 37-63.

———. 2012b. "The Jacob Tradition." In *The Book of Genesis: Composition, Reception, and Interpretation*, ed. C. A. Evans, J. N. Lohr and D. L. Petersen, 181-212. Leiden: Brill.

———. 2016a. "Die altaramäischen Wandinschriften vom Tell Deir 'Allā und ihr institutioneller Kontext." In *Metatexte*, ed. F.-E. Focken and M. R. Ott, 21-52. Berlin: de Gruyter.

———. 2016b. "The Relations between Aram and Israel in the 9th and 8th Centuries BCE: Textual Evidence." In *In Search of Aram and Israel: Politics, Culture and the Question of Identity*, ed. O. Sergi, M. Oeming, and I. de Hulster, 37-56. ORA 20. Tübingen: Mohr Siebeck.

Boaretto, E. et al. 2019. "The Chronology of the Late Bronze (LB)-Iron Age (IA) Transition in the Southern Levant: A Response to Finkelstein's Critique." *Radiocarbon* 61:1-11.

Bolen, T. 2013. "The Aramean Oppression of Israel in the Reign of Jehu." Ph.D. thesis. Dallas Theological Seminary, Dallas.

Borowski, O. 1995. "Hezekiah's Reforms and the Revolt Against Assyria." *BA* 58:148-155.

———. 2017. "Tell Halif in the Late Bronze and Iron Age." In *The Shephelah during the Iron Age: Recent Archaeological Studies*, ed. O. Lipschits and A. M. Maeir, 103-114. Winona Lake, IN: Eisenbrauns.

Brett, M. G., Wöhrle, J., ed. 2018. *The Politics of the Ancestors*. FAT 124. Mohr Siebeck: Tübingen.

Briant, P. 2006. *From Cyrus to Alexander: A History of the Persian Empire*. Winona Lake, IN: Eisenbrauns.

Briffa, J. M. 2019. "'Through a Glass Darkly': Figurines as a Window on the Past." In *The Last Century in the History of the Kingdom of Judah - The 7th Century BCE in Archaeological, Historical and Biblical Perspective*, ed. O. Lipschits and F. Čapek, 181-199. AIL 37. Atlanta, GA: SBL Press.

Bright, J. 1981. *A History of Israel*. 3rd ed. (1st ed. 1959). London: SCM Press.

Brooks, S. S. 2005. *Saul and the Monarchy: A New Look*. Aldershot: Ashgate.

Bruins, H. J., Plicht, J. van der, Mazar, A. 2003. "^{14}C Dates from Tel Rehov: Iron-Age Chronology, Pharaohs, and Hebrew Kings." *Science* 300 (5617): 315-318.

Bunimovitz, S., Lederman, Z. 1997. "Beth Shemesh: Culture Conflict on Judah's Frontier." *BAR* 23 (1): 42-47 and 75-77.

———. 2016. *Tel Beth-Shemesh: A Border Community in Judah. Renewed Excavations 1990-2000: The Iron Age*. 2 vols. Winona Lake, IN: Eisenbrauns.

———. 2017. "Swinging on the "Sorek Seesaw"." In *The Shephelah during the Iron Age: Recent Archaeological Studies*, ed. O. Lipschits and A. M. Maeir, 27-44. Winona Lake, IN: Eisenbrauns.

Bunnens, G. 2016. "Confrontation, Emulation and Ethno-genesis of the Aramaeans in Iron Age Syria." In *In Search of Aram and Israel: Politics, Culture and the Question of Identity*, ed. O. Sergi, M. Oeming, and I. de Hulster, 253-280. ORA 20. Tübingen: Mohr Siebeck.

Cahill, J. M. 1995. "Rosette Stamp Seal Impression from Ancient Judah." *IEJ* 45:230-252.

———. 1997. "Royal Rosettes Fit for a King." *BAR* 23 (5): 48-57 and 68-69.

———. 2000. "Rosette-Stamped Handles." In *Inscriptions*. Vol. 6 of *Excavations at the City of David 1978-1985 Directed by Yigal Shiloh*, ed. D. T. Ariel et al., 85-108. Qedem 41. Jerusalem: Institute of Archaeology, Hebrew University of Jerusalem.

———. 2003a. "Rosette Stamp Seal Impressions." In *The Finds from Areas A, W and X-2*. Vol. 2 of *The Finds from Areas A, W and X-2 Jewish Quarter Excavations in the Old City of Jerusalem*, ed. H. Geva, 85-98. Jerusalem: Israel Exploration Society.

———. 2003b. "Jerusalem at the Time of the United Monarchy: The Archaeological Evidence." In *Jerusalem in Bible and Archaeology: The First Temple Period*, ed. A. G. Vaughn and A. E. Killebrew, 13-80. SBL Symposium Series 18. Atlanta, GA: SBL.

Campbell, E. F., Wright, G. R. H. 2002. *Shechem III: The Stratigraphy and Architecture of Shechem/ Tell Balâtah*. 2 vols. Boston, MA: American Schools of Oriental Research.

Carr, D. M. 2011. *The Formation of the Hebrew Bible. A New Reconstruction*. Oxford: Oxford University Press.

———. 2020. *The Formation of Genesis 1-11: Biblical and Other Precursors*. Oxford: Oxford University Press.

Carter, C. E. 1999. *The Emergence of Yehud in the Persian Period: A Social and Demographic Study*. JSOTSup 294. Sheffield: Sheffield Academic Press.

Cezula, N. S., Modise, L. 2020. "The "Empty Land" Myth: A Biblical and Socio-historical Exploration." *Studia Historiae Ecclesiasticae* 46 (2) (online). doi.org/10.25159/2412-4265/6827.

Chalupa, P. 2013. "Chizkijášova nemoc a uzdravení (2Kr 20,1-11)." In *Obtížné oddíly Předních proroků*, ed. M. Prudky and J. Heller, 361-366. Kostelní Vydří: Karmelitánské nakladatelství.

Charvát, P. 2007. *Zrod českého státu: 568-1055*. Prague: Vyšehrad.

———. 2011. *Václav, kníže Čechů*. Prague: Vyšehrad.

———. 2013. "K úvahám o prvotním a raném státu: Go and catch a falling star." *Marginalia Historica* 2:109-128.

Charvát, P., Maříková Vlčková, P., eds. 2010. *Who Was the King, Who Was not King. Proceedings of Colloquium*. Prague: Institute of Archaeology of the Academy of Sciences.

Cielontko, D. 2019. "Two Faces of Manasseh: The Reception of Manasseh in the Literature of Early Judaism." In *The Last Century in the History of the Kingdom of Judah - The 7th Century BCE in Archaeological, Historical and Biblical Perspective*, ed. O. Lipschits and F. Čapek, 239-260. AIL 37. Atlanta, GA: SBL Press.

Cline, E. H. 2014. *1177 B.C.: The Year Civilization Collapsed*. Princeton: Princeton University Press (Czech translation 2019).

Cline, E. H. 2024. *After 1177 B.C.: The Survival of Civilizations*. Princeton: Princeton University Press 2024 (Czech translation planned 2024/2025).

Cogan, M., Tadmor, H. 1988. *II Kings: A New Translation with Introduction and Commentary*. The Anchor Bible. Vol. 11. Garden City, NY: Doubleday.

Cohen-Weinberger, A., Szanton, N., Uziel, J. 2017. "Ethnofabrics: Petrographic Analysis as a Tool for Illuminating Cultural Interactions and Trade Relations between Judah and Philistia during the Iron Age II." *BASOR* 377:1-20.

Cook, S. A. 1908. "Notes on the Dynasties of Omri and Jehu." *JQR* 20:597-630.

Cross, F. M. 1969. "Judean Stamps." *EI* 9:20-27.

———. 1973. *Caananite Myth and Hebrew Epic: Essays in the History of Religion of Israel*. Cambridge, MA: Harvard University Press.

Čapek, F. 2005. *Hebrejská Bible, její kánon a možnosti výkladu: Kánon jako interpretační možnost rozvedená na pozadí díla B. S. Childse a J. A. Sanderse*. Jihlava: Mlýn.

———. 2010a. "David's Ambiguous Testament: The Role of Joab in 1 Kings 2:1-12." *CV* 52 (1): 4-26.

———. 2010b. "Jehu, the King Who Repaid and Paid: Last King of "Omride" Dynasty According to Biblical, Neo-Assyrian and Aramean Historiography." In *Who Was the King, Who Was not King. Proceedings of Colloquium*, ed. P. Charvát and M. Vlčková, 95-112. Prague: Institute of Archaeology of the Academy of Sciences.

———. 2012. "Shephelah in the Iron Age I and IIA: New Survey on Emergence of the Early Kingdom in Judah." *ArOr* 80:475-504.

———. 2014. "Jehu and Joash in Ancient Near East Texts - Critical Reassessment." *CV* 56 (1): 23-34.

———. 2015. "United Monarchy as Theological Construct in Light of the Contemporary Archaeological Research on Iron Age IIA." In *A King like All the Nations? Kingdoms of Israel and Judah in the Bible and History*, ed. M. Oeming and P. Sláma, 9-20. BVB 28. Berlin: LIT Verlag.

———. 2016. "Theological Reshaping of one (Hi)story: Israel in the Second Half of 9th Century BCE." *CV* 58 (1): 5-18.

———. 2019a. "King Josiah Between Eclipse and Rebirth - Judah of the 7th Century BCE in History and Literature." In *The Last Century in the History of the Kingdom of Judah - The 7th Century BCE in Archaeological, Historical and Biblical Perspective*, ed. O. Lipschits and F. Čapek, 45-62. AIL 37. Atlanta, GA: SBL.

———. 2019b. "Judah in Transition Between Iron Age I and IIA: Chronologies and Biblical Texts Reviewed." In *Das Alte Testament im Rahmen der antiken Religionen und Kulturen*, ed. M. Oeming. BVB 39. Münster: LIT Verlag.

———. 2020. Good Things Come Only Retrospectively: Search for Historical and Theological Topoi of the Phrase שמו יאשיהו נולד לבית־דוד הנה־בן in Kings 13:2. In: *And God Saw That It Was Good (Gen 1:12) The Concept of Quality in Archaeology, Philology and Theology*, ed. Čapek F, and Sláma, P., 234-223. BVB 42. Münster: LIT Verlag.

———. 2023. *Temples in Transformation Iron Age Interactions and Continuity in Material Culture and in Textual Traditions*. BVB 47. Münster: LIT Verlag.

Čech, P. 2002. "Königlisten und ihre (Ir)relevanz für die Geschichtsforschung." *UF* 34:39-44.

Dagan, Y. 1992. "The Shephelah during the Period of the Monarchy in Light of Archaeological Excavations and Survey." In Hebrew. M. A. thesis. Tel Aviv University, Tel Aviv.

Darby, E. 2014. *Interpreting Judean Pillar Figurines. Gender and Empire in Judean Apotropaic Ritual*. FAT 69. Tübingen: Mohr Siebeck.

Davies, P. R. 1991 (1994²). *In Search of "Ancient Israel"*. JSOTSup. Sheffield: Sheffield Academic Press.

Davies, P. R. 1998. *Scribes and Schools: The Canonization of the Hebrew Scriptures*. Louisville: Westminster John Knox Press.

Davies, G. I. et al. 1991. *Ancient Hebrew Inscriptions - Corpus and Concordance*. Cambridge et al.: Cambridge University Press.

de Pury, A., Römer, T., Macchi, J.-D. (ed.) 2000. *Israel Constructs Its History: Deuteronomistic Historiography in Recent Research*. JSOTSup 306. Sheffield: Sheffield Academic Press.

Delamarter, S. 2004. "The Death of Josiah in Scripture and Tradition: Wrestling with the Problem of the Evil?" *VT* 54 (1): 29-60.

Demsky, B. I. 1995. "On Reading Ancient Inscriptions: The Monumental Aramaic Stele Fragment from Tel Dan." *JANES* 23:29-35.

Dever, W. G. 1990. "Commentary: Of Myths and Methods." *BASOR* 277 (8): 121-130.

———. 1995. "Ceramics, Ethnicity, and the Question of Israel's Origins." *BA* 58:200-213.

———. 2001. *What Did the Biblical Writers Know, and When Did They Know It? What Archaeology Can Tell Us about the Reality of Ancient Israel*. Grand Rapids, MI—Cambridge: Eerdmans.

———. 2003. *Who Were the Early Israelites and Where Did They Come From?* Grand Rapids, MI: Eerdmans (Czech translation in 2010)

———. 2017. *Beyond the Texts: An Archaeological Portrait of Ancient Israel and Judah*. Atlanta, GA: SBL.

———. 2019. "Archaeology and Folk and Family Religion in Ancient Israel." *Religions* 10 (12): 667.

———. 2020. *Has Archaeology Buried the Bible?*. Grand Rapids, MI: Eerdmans.

Dever, W. G., Burke, A. 2014. "Divided Kingdom, United Critics: Two archaeologists independently review Israel Finkelstein's The Forgotten Kingdom." *BAR* 40 (4).

Dietrich, W., ed., 2004. *David und Saul im Widerstreit—Diachronie und Synchronie im Wettstreit*. OBO 2006. Fribourg—Göttingen: Academic Press—Vandenhoeck & Ruprecht.

Dietrich, W., Münger S. 2003. "Die Herrschaft Sauls und der Norden Israel." In *Saxa Loquentur: Studien zu Archäologie Palästinas/Israels. Festschrift für Volkmar Fritz zum 65. Geburtstag*, ed. C. G. den Hertog, U. Hübner and S. Münger, 39-60. AOAT 302. Münster: Ugarit-Verlag.

Dietrich, W., Naumann, T. 2000. "The David-Saul Narrative." In *Reconsidering Israel and Judah. Recent Studies on the Deuteronomistic History*, ed. N. G. Knoppers and J. G. McConville, 276-318. Winona Lake, IN: Eisenbrauns.

Doak, B. R. 2020. "The Arameans." In B. R. Doak, *Ancient Israel's Neighbors*, 51-73. Oxford: Oxford University Press.

Dobbs-Allsopp, F. W. 1998. "Linguistic Evidence for the Date of Lamentations." *JANES* 26:1-36.

Donner, H. 1987 (1995²). *Geschichte des Volkes Israel und seiner Nachbarn in Grundzüge*. 2 vols. Göttingen: Vandenhoeck & Ruprecht.

Dozeman, T. B., Schmid, K., ed. 2006. *A Farewell to the Yahwist? The Composition of the Pentateuch in Recent European Interpretation*. SBLSymp 34. Atlanta, GA: SBL.

Dubovský, P. 2006. *Hezekiah and the Assyrian Spies: Reconstruction of the Neo-Assyrian Intelligence Services and its Signicance for 2 Kings 18-19*. BibOr 49. Rome: Pontificio Istituto Biblico.

Dušek. J. 2007. *Les manuscrits araméens du Wadi Daliyeh et la Samarie vers 450-332 av. J.-C.* Leiden: Brill.

———. 2012. "Archaeology and Texts in the Persian Period: Focus on Sanballat." In *Congress Volume Helsinki 2010*, ed. M. Nissinen, 117-132. VTSup 148. Leiden: Brill.

———. 2014. "Mt. Gerizim Sanctuary, Its History and Enigma of Origin." *HeBAI* 3 (1): 111-133.

Dušek, J., Mynářová, J., ed. 2019. *Aramaean Borders: Defining Aramaean Territories in the 10th-8th Centuries B.C.E.* Leiden: Brill.

Dyck, J. 2000. "Ezra 2 in Ideological Critical Perspective." In *Rethinking Contexts, Rereading Texts - Contributions from The Social Sciences to Biblical Interpretation*, ed. D. M. R. Carroll, 129-145. JSOTSup 299. Sheffield: Sheffield Academic Press.

Ebeling, J. et al., ed. 2017. *The Old Testament in Archaeology and History*. Waco, TX: Baylor University Press.

Edelman, D. 2008. "Hezekiah's Alleged Cultic Centralization." *JSOT* 32:395-434.

Ein-Mor, D. 2013. "Walaje ('Ain Joweizeh)." *Hadashot Arkheologiyot* 125 (online), 16. 6. 2013.

Ein-Mor, D., Ron, Z. 2016. "'Ain Joweizeh: An Iron Age Royal Rock-Cut Spring System in the Nahal Repha'im Valley, near Jerusalem." *TA* 43 (2): 131-150.

Elayi, J. 2018. *Sennacherib, King of Assyria*. Atlanta, GA: SBL Press.

Fant, C. E., Reddish, M. G. 2008. *Lost Treasures of the Bible: Understanding the Bible Through Archaeological Artifacts in World Museums*. Grand Rapids: Eerdmans.

Fantalkin, A. 2008. "The Appearance of Rock-Cut Bench Tombs in Iron Age Judah as a Reflection of State Formation." In *Bene Israel: Studies in the Archaeology and the Levant during the Bronze and Iron Ages in Honour of Israel Finkelstein*, ed. A. Fantalkin and A. Yasur-Landau, 17-54. Leiden: Brill.

Faraj, S., Benhaida, S. 2021. "On Passover 2021, Iraq's Jewish Community Swindles to Fewer than Five." *Times of Israel* (online), 28. 3. 2021.

Farber, Z. I. and Wright, J. L., ed. 2018. *Archaeology and History of Eight-Century Judah*. Ancient Near East Monographs 23. ANEM 23. Atlanta, GA: SBL Press.

Faust, A. 2003. "Judah in the Sixth Century B.C.E.: A Rural Perspective." *PEQ* 135:37-53.

———. 2012. *The Archaeology of Israelite Society in the Iron Age II*. Winona Lake, IN: Eisenbrauns.

———. 2014. "On Jerusalem's Expansion during the Iron Age II." In *Exploring the Narrative: Jerusalem and Jordan in the Bronze and Iron Ages*, ed. E. van der Steen et al., 256-285. London: T&T Clark.

———. 2017a. "The Bounded Landscape: Archaeology, Language, Texts, and the Israelite Perception of Space." *Journal of Mediterranean Archaeology* 30:3-32.

———. 2017b. "An All-Israelite Identity: Historical Reality or Biblical Myth?" In *The Wide Lens in Archaeology: Honoring Brian Hesse's Contributions to Anthropological Archaeology*, ed. J. Lev-Tov, P. Wapnish, and A. Gilbert, 169-190. Atlanta, GA: Lockwood Press.

Faust, A. et al. 2017. "The Birth, Life and Death of an Iron Age House at Tel 'Eton, Israel." *Levant* 49 (2): 136-173.

Faust, A., Katz, H. 2017. "The Archaeology of Purity and Impurity: A Case-Study from Tel 'Eton, Israel." *Cambridge Archaeological Journal* 27:1-27.

Faust, A., Lev-Tov, J. 2011. "The Constitution of Philistine Identity: Ethnic Dynamics in Twelve to Tenth Century Philistia." *OJA* 30 (1): 13-31.

Ferguson, Y. H., Mansbach, R. W. 1996. *Polities: Authority, Identities, and Change*. Columbia: University of South Carolina Press.

Finkelstein, I. 1988. *The Archaeology of the Israelite Settlement*. Jerusalem: Israel Exploration Society.

———. 1990. "On Archaeological Methods and Historical Considerations: Iron Age II Gezer and Samaria." *BASOR* 277/278:109-119.

———. 1994. "The Archaeology of the Days of Manasseh." In *Scripture and Other Artifacts. Essays on the Bible and Archaeology in Honor of Philip J. King*, ed. Michael D. Coogan, J. Cheryl Exum, and Lawrence E. Stager, 169-187. Louisville, KY: Westminster John Knox Press.

———. 1996. "The Territorio-Political System of Canaan in the Late Bronze Age." *UF* 28:221-255.

———. 1998. "Bible Archaeology or Archaeology of Palestine in the Iron Age? A Rejoinder." *Levant* 30:167-174.

———. 1999a. "Hazor and the North in the Iron Age: A Low Chronology Perspective." *BASOR* 314: 55-70.

———. 1999b. "State Formation in Israel and Judah: A Contrast in Context, A Contrast in Trajectory." *NEA* 62:35-52.

———. 2000a. "Hazor XII-XI. With an Addendum on Ben-Tor's Dating of HazorX-VII." *TA* 27 (2): 231-247.

———. 2000b. "Omride Architecture." *ZDPV* 116:114-138.

———. 2006. "The Last Labayu: King Saul and the Expansion of the First North Israelite Entity." In *Essays on Ancient Israel in Its Near Eastern Context: A Tribute to Nadav Na'aman*, ed. Y. Amit, E. Ben Zvi, I. Finkelstein, and O. Lipschits, 171-188. Winona Lake, IN: Eisenbrauns.

———. 2010. "A Great United Monarchy? Archaeological and Historical Perspectives." In *One God - One Cult - One Nation*, ed. R. Kratz and H. Spieckermann, 3-28. BZAW 405. Berlin: de Gruyter.

———. 2011a. "Saul, Benjamin and the Emergence of "Biblical Israel": An Alternative View." *ZAW* 123:348-367.

———. 2011b. "The "Large Stone Structure" in Jerusalem: Reality versus Yearning." *ZDPV* 127:1-10.

———. 2012a. "The Great Wall of Tell en-Nasbeh (Mizpah), The First Fortifications in Judah, and 1 Kings 15:16-22." *VT* 62:14-28.

———. 2012b. "Comments on the Date of the Late-Monarchic Judahite Seal Impressions." *TA* 39 (2): 203-211.

— 2013. *The Forgotten Kingdom. The Archaeology and History of Northern Israel*. Atlanta, GA: SBL (French original *Le Royaume biblique oublié*. Paris: Odile Jacob, 2013; Czech translation in 2016).

———. 2015. "Migration of Israelites into Judah after 720 BCE: An Answer and an Update." *ZAW* 127:188-206.

———. 2016b. "Israel and Aram: Reflections on their Border." In *In Search of Aram and Israel: Politics, Culture and the Question of Identity*, ed. O. Sergi, M. Oeming, and I. de Hulster, 17-36. ORA 20. Tübingen: Mohr Siebeck.

———. 2017. "A Corpus of North Israelite Texts in the Days of Jeroboam II?" *HeBAI* 3: 262-289.

———. 2020a. "Saul and Highlands of Benjamin Update." In *Saul, Benjamin, and the Emergence of Monarchy in Israel*, ed. J. J. Krause, O. Sergi and K. Weingart, 33-56. AIL 40. Atlanta, GA: SBL.

———. 2020b. "Northern Royal Traditions in the Bible and the Ideology of a "United Monarchy" Ruled from Samaria." In *Stones, Tablets, and Scrolls. Periods of the Formation of the Bible*, ed. P. Dubovský and F. Giuntoli, 113-126. Tübingen: Mohr Siebeck.

———. 2020c. "Jeroboam II's Temples." *ZAW* 132: 250-265.
Finkelstein, I., Bunimovitz, S., Lederman, Z., ed. 1993. *Shiloh: The Archaeology of a Biblical Site*. Monograph Series of the Sonia and Marco Nadler Institute of Archaeology 10. Tel Aviv: Tel Aviv University.
Finkelstein, I., Fantalkin, A. 2012. "Khirbet Qeiyafa: An Unsensational Archaeological and Historical Interpretation." *TA* 39 (2): 38-63.
Finkelstein, I., Herzog, Z., Singer-Avitz, L., Ussishkin, D. 2007. "Has KingDavid's Palace in Jerusalem Been Found?." *TA* 34 (2): 142-164.
Finkelstein, I., Koch, I., Lipschits, O. 2011. "The Mound on the Mount: A Possible Solution of the "Problem with Jerusalem"." *JHS* 11:2-24.
Finkelstein, I., Lipschits, O. 2010. "Omride Architecture in Moab: Jahaz and Ataroth." *ZDPV* 126:29-42.
Finkelstein, I., Martin, M. A. S. 2022. *Megiddo VI. The 2010-2014 Seasons*. Vol. 2 and 3. Monograph Series of the Sonia and Marco Nadler Institute of Archaeology 41. Tel Aviv: Tel Aviv University.
Finkelstein, I., Mazar, A., Schmidt, B. B. 2007. *The Quest for the Historical Israel*. Atlanta, GA: SBL Press.
Finkelstein, I., Piasetzky, E. 2003. "Comment on [14]C Dates from Tel Rehov: Iron-Age Chronology, Pharaohs, and Hebrew Kings." *Science* 302:568.
———. 2007a. "Radiocarbon Dating and the Late-Iron I in Northern Canaan: A New Proposal." *UF* 39:247-260.
———. 2007b. "Radiocarbon, Iron IIa Destructions and the Israel: Aram Damascus Conflicts in the 9th Century BCE." *UF* 39:261-276.
———. 2010. "The Iron I/IIA Transition in the Levant: A Reply to Mazar and Bronk Ramsey and a New Perspective." *Radiocarbon* 52:1667-1680.
———. 2015. "Radiocarbon Dating Khirbet Qeiyafa and the Iron I-IIA Phases in the Shephelah: Methodological Comments and a Bayesian Model." *Radiocarbon* 57:891-907.
Finkelstein, I., Römer, T. 2014a. "Comments on the Historical Background of the Jacob Narrative in Genesis." *ZAW* 26:317-338.
———. 2014b. "Comments on the Historical Background of the Abraham Narrative: Between "Realia" and "Exegetica"." *HeBAI* 3 (1): 3-23.
Finkelstein, I., Sass, B. 2013. "The West Semitic Alphabetic Inscriptions, Late Bronze II to Iron IIA: Archaeological Context, Distribution and Chronology." *HeBAI* 2:149-220.
———. 2017. "Epigraphic Evidence from Jerusalem and Its Environs at the Dawn of Biblical History: Facts First." *NSAJR* 11:21-26.
Finkelstein, I., Silberman, N. 2001. *The Bible Unearthed: Archaeology's New Vision of Ancient Israel and the Origin of Its Sacred Texts*. New York et al.: Touchstone (Czech translation in 2007).
———. 2007. *David and Solomon: In Search of the Bible's Sacred Kings and the Roots of the Western Tradition*. New York: Free Press (Czech translation in 2010).
Finkelstein, I., Singer-Avitz, L. 2009. "Reevaluating Bethel." *ZDPV* 125:33-48.
Finkelstein, I., Ussishkin, D., Halpern, B., ed. 2006. *Megiddo IV: The Seasons 1998-2002*. Tel Aviv: Emery and Claire Yass Publications in Archaeology.
Fischer, A. A. 2004. *Von Hebron nach Jerusalem: Eine redaktionsgeschichtliche Studie zur Erzählung von König David in II Sam 1-5*. BZAW 335. Berlin: de Gruyter.
Fischer, G. 2007. *Jeremia: Der Stand der theologischen Diskussion*. Darmstadt: Wissenschaftliche Buchgesellschaft.
Fleming, D. E. 2013. *The Legacy of Israel in Judah's Bible: History, Politics, and the Reinscribing of Traditions*. Cambridge: Cambridge University Press.
Frahm, E. 1997. *Einleitung in die Sanherib-Inschriften*. AfO Beiheft 26. Vienna: Berger & Söhne.
Franklin, N. 2003. "The Tombs of the Kings of Israel: Two Recently Identified 9th Century Tombs from Omride Samaria." *ZDPV* 119:1-11.
Franklin, N. 2004. "Samaria: From the Bedrock to the Omride Palace." *Levant* 36:189-202.

Franklin, N. 2008. "Trademarks of the Omride Builders?." In *Bene Israel: Studies in the Archaeology and the Levant during the Bronze and Iron Ages in Honour of Israel Finkelstein*, ed. A. Fantalkin and A. Yasur-Landau, 45-54. Leiden: Brill.

Fredericks, D. C. 1996. "A North Israelite Dialect in the Hebrew Bible? Questions of Methodology." *HS* 37:7-20.

Freud, L. 2019. "Production and Widespread Use of Holemouth Vessels in Jerusalem and its Environs in the Iron Age II: Typology, Chronology and Distribution." In *The Last Century in the History of the Kingdom of Judah - The 7th Century BCE in Archaeological, Historical and Biblical Perspective*, ed. O. Lipschits and F. Čapek, 119-152. AIL 37. Atlanta, GA: SBL Press.

Frevel, Ch. 2016. *Geschichte Israels*. Stuttgart: Kohlhammer.

Frevel, Ch. 2019. "Wicked Usurpers and the Doom of Samaria." In *The Last Days of the Kingdom of Israel*, ed. S. Hasegawa, Ch. Levin, K. Radner, 303-334. BZAW 511. Berlin: de Gruyter.

Frevel, Ch. 2021. "When and from Where did YHWH Emerge? Some Reflections on Early Yahwism in Israel and Judah." *Entangled Religions* 12 (2) (online), 30. 3. 2021.

Frevel, Ch., Čapek, F. 2024. "The Connections between Samaria and Jerusalem in the Ninth to Eighth Centuries BCE - What Can We Expect from Archaeology?" In *Gegenwart und Wirksamkeit des transzendenten Gottes in der Geschichte* (Festschrift zum Gedenken an Axel Graupner) BVB 53, ed. M. Oeming. Münster: LIT Verlag (forthcoming).

Fried, L. S. 2006. "The 'am hā'areṣ in Ezra 4:4 and Persian Imperial Administration." In *Judah and the Judeans in the Persian Period*, ed. O. Lipschits and M. Oeming, 123-145. Winona Lake, IN: Eisenbrauns.

Fritz, V., Davies, P. R., ed. 1996. *The Origins of the Ancient Israelite States*. JSOTSup. 228. Sheffield: Sheffield Academic Press.

Gadot, Y. 2017. "The Iron Age I in the Samaria Highlands: A Nomad Settlement Wave or Urban Expansion?." In *Rethinking Israel: Studies in the History and Archaeology of Ancient Israel in Honor of Israel Finkelstein*, ed. O. Lipschits, Y. Gadot, and J. M. Adams, 103-114. Winona Lake, IN: Eisenbrauns.

———. 2022. "Jerusalem, the Reign of Manasseh and the Assyrian World Order." In *Jerusalem and Coastal Plain in the Iron Age and Persian Periods: New Studies on Jerusalem's Relations with the Southern Plain of Israel/Palestina (c. 1200-300 BCE)*, ed. F. Hagemeyer, 145-161. RIABT IV, ORA 46. Tübingen: Mohr Siebeck.

Gadot, Y., Bocher, E., Freud, L., Shalev, Y. 2023. "An Early Iron Age Moat in Jerusalem between the Ophel and the Southeastern Ridge/City of David." *TA* 50 (2): 147-170.

Gadot, Y., Lipschits, O., Gross, B. 2014. "A Rare Cypriot Krater of the White Slip II Style from Azekah." *IEJ* 64 (1): 1-8.

Gadot, Y., Kleiman, S., Lipschits, O. 2018. "A Tale of Two Cities: Tel Azekah and Tel es-Safi/Gat during the Late Bronze Age." In *Tell it in Gath: Studies in the History and Archaeology of Israel Essays in Honor of Aren M. Maeir on the Occasion of his Sixtieth Birthday*, ed. I. Shai et al., 206-221. Ägypten und Altes Testament 90. Münster: Zaphon.

Gadot, Y., Uziel, J. 2017. "The Monumentality of Iron Age Jerusalem Prior to the 8th Century BCE." *TA* 44 (2): 123-140.

Gadot, Y., Uziel, J., Kleiman, A. 2023. "The Interconnections Between Jerusalem and Samaria in the Ninth to Eighth Centuries BCE: Material Culture, Connectivity and Politics." In *"And in Length of Days Understanding" (Job 12:12): Essays on Archaeology in the Eastern Mediterranean and Beyond in Honor of Thomas E. Levy*, ed. E. Ben-Yosef and I. W. N. Jones, 771-786. Cham: Springer International.

Galil, G. 1995. "A New Look at the "Azekah Inscription"." *RB* 102:327-328.

———. 1996. *The Chronology of the Kings of Israel and Judah*. Leiden: Brill.

———. 2009. "The Hebrew Inscription from Khirbet Qeiyafa / Neta'im." *UF* 41:193-242.

Ganor, S., Kreimerman, I. 2017. "Going to the Bathroom in Lachish." *BAR* 43 (6): 56-60.

Garbini, G. 1988. *History and Ideology in Ancient Israel*. London: SCM Press.

Garfinkel, Y. 2017. "Khirbet Qeiyafa in the Shephelah: Data and Interpretations." In *Khirbet Qeiyafa in the Shephelah*, ed. S. Schroer and S. Münger, 5-59. OBO 282. Fribourg: Academic Press.

Garfinkel, Y. 2020. "The Face of Yahweh?" *BAR* 46 (4): 30-33.
Garfinkel, Y., Ganor, S. 2009, ed. *Excavation Report 2007-8*. Vol. 1 of *Khirbet Qeiyafa*. Jerusalem: Israel Exploration Society—Institute of Archaeology.
———. 2010. "Khirbet Qeiyafa in Survey and in Excavations: A Response to Y. Dagan." *TA* 37 (1): 67-78.
Garfinkel, Y., Ganor, S., Hasel, M. G. 2014. *Excavation Report 2009-2013: Stratigraphy and Architecture (Areas B, C, D, E)*. Vol. 2 of *Khirbet Qeiyafa*. Jerusalem: Israel Exploration Society.
Garfinkel, Y., Streit, K., Ganor, S., Reimer, P. J. 2015. "King David's City at Khirbet Qeiyafa: Results of the Second Radiocarbon Dating Project." *Radiocarbon* 57:881-890.
Garfinkel, Y., Kang, H.-G. 2011. "The Relative and Absolute Chronology of Khirbet Qeiyafa: Very Late Iron Age I or Very Early Iron Age IIA?" *IEJ* 61 (2): 171-183.
Garfinkel, Y., Kreimerman, I., Zilberg, P. 2016. *Debating Khirbet Qeiyafa: A Fortified City in Judah from the Time of King David*. Jerusalem: Israel Exploration Society.
Garfinkel, Y., Streit, K., Ganor, S., Hasel, M. G. 2012. "State Formation in Judah - Biblical Tradition, Modern Historical Theories, and Radiometric Dates at Khirbet Qeiyafa." *Radiocarbon* 54:359-369.
Garsiel, M. 2011. "David's Elite Warriors and Their Exploits in the Books of Samuel and Chronicles." *JHS* 11, Article 5 (online), 22. 8. 2011.
Gerstenberger, E. S. 2011. *Israel in the Persian Period: The Fifth and Fourth Centuries B. C. E.* Atlanta, GA: SBL Press.
Geva, H. 2006. "The Settlement of the Southwestern Hill of Jerusalem at the End of the Iron Age." *ZDPV* 122:140-150.
Ghantous, H. 2014. *The Elisha - Hazael Paradigm and the Kingdom of Israel: The Politics of God in Ancient Syria-Palestine*. Abingdon: Routledge.
Gitin, S., Wright, J. E., Dessel, J. P., ed. 2006. *Confronting the Past: Archaeological and Historical Essays on Ancient Israel in Honor of William G. Dever*. Winona Lake, IN: Eisenbrauns.
Gitin, S. 2015a. "Iron Age IIA-B: Philistia." In *The Ancient Pottery of Israel and Its Neighbors*. Vol. 1, ed. S. Gitin, 257-280. Jerusalem: Israel Exploration Society, W. F. Albright Institute of Archaeological Research, Israel Antiquities Authority and American Schools of Oriental Research.
———. 2015b. "Iron Age IIC: Philistia." In *The Ancient Pottery of Israel and its Neighbors*. Vol. 1, ed. S. Gitin, 383-418. Jerusalem: Israel Exploration Society, W. F. Albright Institute of Archaeological Research, Israel Antiquities Authority and American Schools of Oriental Research.
Gnuse, R. 2019. "Similarities between the Primeval History in Genesis 1-11 and the Greek Historiographers, Hecataeus of Miletus and Herodotos of Halicarnassus." *IJRHSC* 6 (1): 20-25.
Gomes, J. F. 2006. *The Sanctuary of Bethel and the Configuration of Israelite Identity*. BZAW 368. Berlin: de Gruyter.
Goren, Y. 2016. Excurses: "Petrographic Analysis of lmlk and Official Sealed Jars Handles from the Renewed Excavations." In *Tel Beth-Shemesh: A Border Community in Judah. Renewed Excavations 1990-2000: The Iron Age*, vol. 2, ed. S. Bunimovitz and Z. Lederman, 502-504. Winona Lake, IN: Eisenbrauns.
Görg, M. 2001. "Israel in Hieroglyphen." *BN* 106:21-27.
Grabbe, L. L. 1991. "Reconstructing History from the Book of Ezra." In *Second Temple Studies: 1. Persian Period*, ed. P. R. Davies. JSOTSup 117. Sheffield: Sheffield Academic Press.
———, ed. 2003. *Like a Bird in a Cage. The Invasion of Sennacherib in 701 BCE*. JSOTSup 363. Sheffield: Shefield Academic Press.
———. 2006. "The Persian Documents in the Book of Ezra: Are They Authentic?" In *Judah and the Judaeans in the Persian Period*, ed. O. Lipschits and M. Oeming, 531-570. Winona Lake, IN: Eisenbrauns.
———, ed. 2007a. *Ahab Agonistes: The Rise and Fall of the Omri Dynasty*. London: T&T Clark.
———. 2007b. *Ancient Israel: What Do We Know and How Do We Know It?* New York: T&T Clark.
———. 2010. "'Many Nations Will Be Joined to YHWH in That Day': The Question of YHWH Outside Judah." In *Religious Diversity in Ancient Israel and Judah*, ed. F. Stavrakopoulou and J. Barton, 175-187. New York: T&T Clark.

Grätz, S. 2013. "The Adversaries in Ezra/Nehemiah—Fictitious or Real? A Case Study in Creating Identity in Later Persian and Hellenistic Time." In *Between Cooperation and Hostility: Multiple Identities in Ancient Judaism and the Interaction with Foreign Powers*, ed. R. Albertz and J. Wöhrle, 73-87. JAJSup 11. Göttingen: Vandenhoeck & Ruprecht.

Grayson, A. K. 2000. *Assyrian and Babylonian Chronicles*. Winona Lake, IN: Eisenbrauns.

Greer, J. S. 2013. *Dinner at Dan: Biblical and Archaeological Evidence for Sacred Feasts at Iron Age II Tel Dan and Their Significance*. Leiden: Brill.

Greer, J. S. 2017. "The Cult at Tel Dan: Aramean or Israelite?" In *Wandering Arameans: Arameans Outside Syria. Textual and Archaeological Perspective*, ed. A. Berlejung, A. M. Maeir and A. Schüle, 3-18. LAS 5. Wiesbaden: Harrassowitz Verlag.

Grena, G. M. 2004. *LMLK-A Mystery Belonging to the King*. Vol. 1. Relondo Beach, CA: 4000 Years of Writing History.

Groot, A. de, Bernick-Greenberg, H. 2012. *Excavations at the City of David 1978-1985 Directed by Yigal Shiloh*. Vol. 7A: *Area E: Stratigraphy and Architecture*. Qedem 53. Jerusalem: Institute of Archaeology, Hebrew University of Jerusalem.

Gugler, W. 1996. *Jehu und seine Revolution: Voraussetzungen, Verlauf, Folgen*. Kampen: Pharos.

Guillaume, P. 2008. "Jerusalem 720-705 BCE." *SJOT* 22:195-201.

———. 2013. "The Myth of the Edomite Threat. Arad Letters # 24 and 40." *KUSATU* 15:78-108.

Hall, E. 2020. "The Archaeology of Cult in the Northern Kingdom of Israel." Ph.D. thesis. Tel Aviv University, Tel Aviv. Unpublished.

Hall, E. 2022. Agency, Kinship and the Case of the Northern Kingdom of Israel, *PEQ* (online), 11. 11. 2022.

Hallo, W. W., Younger Jr., K. L. 2003. *The Context of Scripture*. Vol. II: *Monumental Inscriptions from the Biblical World*. Leiden: Brill.

Halpern, B. 1981. "The Constitution of Monarchy in Israel." Ph.D. thesis. Harvard University, Cambridge, MA.

———. 1990. *A Historiographic Commentary on Ezra 1-6: Achronological Narrative and Dual Chronology in Israelite Historiography*. Winona Lake, IN: Eisenbrauns.

———. 1994. "The Stele from Tel Dan: Epigraphic and Historical Considerations." *BASOR* 296:63-80.

Hamilton, M. W. 2018. *A Kingdom for a Stage: Political and Theological Reflection in the Hebrew Bible*. FAT 116. Tübingen: Mohr Siebeck.

Handy, K. L., ed. 1997. *The Age of Solomon: Scholarship at the Turn of Millennium*. Leiden: Brill.

Haran, B. 1993. Archives, Libraries, and the Order of the Biblical Books. *JANES* 22:51-61.

Hasegawa, S. 2012. *Aram and Israel During Jehuite Dynasty*. BZAW 434. Berlin: de Gruyter.

———. 2018. "Use of Archaeological Data for Investigating Itineraries of Assyrian Military Campaigns." In *Neo Assyrian Sources in Context: Thematic Studies on Texts, History, and Culture*, ed. S. Yamada, 239-251. SAAS 28. Helsinki: The Neo-Assyrian Text Corpus Project.

———. 2019. "The Qualifications in Evaluations of the Kings of Israel and Judah in the Book of Kings." In *Story and History: The Kings of Israel and Judah in Context*, ed. J. U. Ro, 31-51. Forschung zum Alten Testament, 2. Reihe, 105. Tübingen: Mohr Siebeck.

Hasegawa, S., Levin, Ch., Radner, K., ed. 2019. *The Last Days of the Kingdom of Israel*. BZAW 511. Berlin: de Gruyter.

Hasel, M. G. 1994. "Israel in the Merneptah Stela." *BASOR* 296:45-61.

———. 2003. "Merenptah's Inscription and Reliefs and the Origin of Israel." In *The Near East in the Southwest: Essays in Honor of William G. Dever*, ed. B. Alpert Nakhai, 19-44. AASOR 58. Boston, MA: American Schools of Oriental Research.

Hayes, J. H., Miller, J. M., ed. 1977. *Israelite and Judaean History*. London: SCM Press.

Heiser, M. 2008. "Monotheism, Polytheism, Monolatry, or Henotheism? Toward an Assessment of Divine Plurality in the Hebrew Bible." *BBR* 18/1:1-30.

Hensel, B. 2016. *Juda und Samaria—Zum Verhältnis zweier nach-exilischer Jahwismen*. FAT 110. Tübingen: Mohr Siebeck.

———. 2019a. "Dtn 12,13-19: Zur Lokalisierung des einen Maqom." *Biblische Notizen* 182:9-43.

———. 2019b. "On the Relationship of Judah and Samaria in Post-Exilic Times: A Farewell to the Conflict Paradigm." *JSOT* 44 (1): 19-42.

———, ed. 2021. *The History of Jacob Cycle (Genesis 25-35): Recent Research on the Compilation, the Redaction and the Reception of the Biblical Narrative and Its Historical and Cultural Contexts.* Tübingen: Mohr Siebeck.

———. 2022. "The Ark Narrative(s) of 1 Sam *4:1b-7:1/2 Sam 6* between Philistia, Jerusalem, and Assyria. A New Approach for a Historical Contextualization and Literary Historical Classification." In *Jerusalem and Coastal Plain in the Iron Age and Persian Periods: New Studies on Jerusalem's Relations with the Southern Plain of Israel/Palestina (c. 1200-300 BCE)*, ed. F. Hagemeyer, 163-191. RIABT IV, ORA 46. Tübingen: Mohr Siebeck.

Hentschel, G. 2014. "Alter und Herkunft der Synchronismen in den Königebüchern." In *Nichts Neues unter der Sonne? Zeitvorstellungen im Alten Testament. Festschrift für Ernst-Joachim Waschke zum 65. Geburtstag*, ed. J. Kotjako-Reeb, B. Ziemer and S. Schorch, 171-185. BZAW 450. Berlin: de Gruyter.

Herzog, Z. 1999. "Deconstructing the Walls of Jericho." *Ha'aretz* (29. 10. 1999).

———. 2001. "The Date of the Temple at Arad: Reassessment of the Stratigraphy and the Implications for the History of Religion in Judah." In *Studies in the Archaeology of the Iron Age in Israel and Jordan*, ed. A. Mazar, 151-178. Sheffield: Sheffield Academic Press.

———. 2002. "The Fortress Mound at Tel Arad: An Interim Report." *TA* 29 (1): 3-109.

———. 2010. "Perspectives on Southern Israel's Cult Centralization: Arad and Beer-sheba." In *One God, One Cult, One Nation: Archaeological and Biblical Perspectives*, ed. R. G. Kratz and H. Spieckermann, 169-199. BZAW 405. Berlin: de Gruyter.

Herzog, Z., Singer-Avitz, L. 2004. "Redefining the Centre: The Emergence of State in Judah." *TA* 31 (2): 209-244.

———. 2006. "Sub-dividing the Iron Age IIA in Northern Israel: A Suggested Solution to the Chronological Debate." *TA* 33 (2): 163-195.

———. 2015. "Iron Age IIA-B: Judah and the Negev." In *The Ancient Pottery of Israel and its Neighbors*, vol. 1, ed. S. Gitin, 213-255. Jerusalem: Israel Exploration Society, W. F. Albright Institute of Archaeological Research, Israel Antiquities Authority and American Schools of Oriental Research.

Hesse, B. 1990. "Pig Lovers and Pig Haters: Patterns of Palestinian Pork Production." *Journal of Ethnobiology* 10 (2): 195-225.

Hesse, B., Brown, E., Griffith, T. 2016. "Animal Husbandry in the Early Iron Age at Tel Beth-Shemesh." In *Tel Beth-Shemesh: A Border Community in Judah. Renewed Excavations 1990-2000: The Iron Age*, vol. 1, ed. S. Bunimovitz and Z. Lederman, 257-265. Winona Lake, IN: Eisenbrauns.

Hesse, B., Wapnish, P. 1997. "Can Pig Remains be Used for Ethnic Diagnosis in the Ancient Near East?." In *The Archaeology of Israel*, ed. N. A. Silberman and D. B. Small, 238-270. JSOTSup 237. Sheffield: Sheffield Academic Press.

Hjelm, I. 2017. "Maximalist and/or Minimalist Approaches in Recent Representations of Ancient Israel and Judaean History." In *History, Politics and the Bible from the Iron Age to the Media Age: Essays in Honour of Keith W. Whitelam*, ed. J. G. Crossley and J. West, 1-18. LHBOTS 651. London: T&T Clark.

Hrůša, I. 2015. *Náboženství staré Mezopotámie: bohové, chrámy, obřady a lidé*. Prague: Vyšehrad.

Hoblík, J. 2009. *Proroci, jejich slova a jejich svět*. Prague: Vyšehrad.

Hoffmeier, J. K. 2007. "What is the Biblical Date for the Exodus? A Response to Bryant Wood." *JETS* 50 (2): 225-247.

Hulster, I. de 2015. "The Myth of the Reborn Nation." In *Open-Mindedness in the Bible and Beyond: A Volume of Studies in Honour of Bob Becking*, ed. M. C. A. Korpel and L. L. Grabbe, 123-138. London: T&T Clark; New York: Bloomsbury.

Hualong, M. 2024. *Nation and Empire as Two Trends of Political Organization in the Iron Age Levant*. CHANE 136. Leiden: Brill.

Hutton, J. M. 2009. *The Transjordanian Palimpsest: The Overwritten Texts of Personal Exile and Transformation in the Deuteronomistic History*. BZAW 396. Berlin: de Gruyter.

———. 2011. "Of David's Actions and the Davidic Redaction. Review of: Fischer, A. A. Von Hebron nach Jerusalem: Eine redaktionsgeschichtliche Studie zur Erzählung von König David in II Sam 1–5. BZAW 335. Berlin / New York: de Gruyter, 2004." *JHS* 11 (online), 22. 2. 2012.

Hutzli, J. 2015. "Observations and Considerations on the Epilogue Formulae in the Books of Kings." In *A King like All the Nations? Kingdoms of Israel and Judah in the Bible and History*, ed. M. Oeming and P. Sláma, 9–20. Berlin: LIT Verlag.

Isser, S. 2003. *The Sword of Goliath: David in Heroic Literature*. Atlanta, GA: SBL.

Itach, G. 2018. "The Kingdom of Israel in the Eight Century: From a Regional Power to Assyrian Provinces." In *Archaeology and History of Eight-Century Judah*, ed. Z. I. Farber and J. L. Wright, 57–77. ANEM 23, SBL Press: Atlanta 2018.

Jagersma, H. 1982. *A History of Israel to Bar Kochba*. London: SCM Press.

James, P., Veen, P. van der, ed. 2015. *Solomon and Shishak: Current Perspectives from Archaeology, Epigraphy, History and Chronology*. Proceedings of the Third BICANE Colloquium held at Sidney Sussex College, Cambridge 26–27 March, 2011. Oxford: Archaeopress.

Jamieson-Drake, D. W. 1991. *Scribes and Schools in Monarchic Judah: A Socio-Archaeological Approach*. JSOTSup 109. Sheffield: Phoenix Press.

Japhet, S. 2002. *1 Chronik*. HThKAT. Vienna: Verlag Herder.

———. 2003. *2 Chronik*. HthKAT. Vienna: Verlag Herder.

———. 2006a. "Periodization between History and Ideology II: Chronology and Ideology in Ezra-Nehemiah." In *Judah and the Judaeans in the Persian Period*, ed. O. Lipschits and M. Oeming, 265–289. Winona Lake, IN: Eisenbrauns.

———. 2006b. *From the Rivers of Babylon to the Highlands of Judah*. Winona Lake, IN: Eisenbrauns.

Jepsen, A. 1956. *Die Quellen des Königsbuches*. Halle: Niemeyer Verlag.

Ji, C.-H. 2001. "Judean Jar Handles Bearing Concentric Circles." *NEASB* 46:11–24.

Jonker, L. C., ed. 2010. *Historiography and Identity (Re)formulation in Second Temple Historiographical Literature*. LHBOTS 543. London: T&T Clark.

Kaiser, O. 2010. "Der historische und der biblische König Saul (Teil I)." *ZAW* 122:520–545.

———. 2011. "Der historische und der biblische König Saul (Teil II)." *ZAW* 123:1–14.

Kahn, D. 2019. "The Fall of Samaria: An Analysis of the Biblical Sources." In *The Last Days of the Kingdom of Israel*, ed. S. Hasegawa, Ch. Levin, K. Radner, 229–250. BZAW 511. Berlin: de Gruyter.

Kang, H.-G., Garfinkel, Y. 2015. "Finger-Impressed Jar Handles at Khirbet Qeiyafa: New Light on Administration in the Kingdom of Judah." *Levant* 47 (2): 186–205.

Keel, O. 2007. *Die Geschichte Jerusalems und die Entstehung des Monoteismus*. Göttingen: Vandenhoeck & Ruprecht.

Keel, O., Uehlinger, C. 1994. "Der Assyrerkönig Salmanassar III. und Jehu von Israel auf dem Schwarzen Obelisken aus Nimrud." *ZKT* 116:391–420.

Kehati, R. 2009. "Faunal Assemblage." In *Excavation Report 2007–8*. Vol. 1 of *Khirbet Qeiyafa*, ed. Y. Garfinkel and S. Ganor, 201–208. Jerusalem: Israel Exploration Society—Institute of Archaeology.

Keimer, H. K. 2011. "The Socioeconomic Impact of Hezekiah's Preparations for Rebellion." Ph.D. thesis. University of California, Los Angeles.

Kelm, L. G., Mazar, A. 1982. "Three Seasons of Excavations at Tel Batash – Biblical Timnah." *BASOR* 248:1–36.

Kenyon, K. M. 1974. *Digging Up Jerusalem*. London: Benn.

Killebrew, A. E. 2003. "Biblical Jerusalem: An Archaeological Assessment." In *Jerusalem in Bible and Archaeology: The First Temple Period*, ed. A. G. Vaughn and A. E. Killebrew, 329–345. Boston, MA: Brill.

Kitchen, A. K. 2001. "How We Know When Solomon Ruled." *BAR* 27 (5): 32–37 and 57.

Kisilevitz, S. 2015. "The Iron IIA Judahite Temple at Tel Moza." *Tel Aviv* 42 (2): 147-164.

———. 2022. "Cult in Iron IIA Judah: The Development of the Cultic Precinct at Tel Moẓa as a Case Study." Ph.D. thesis. Tel Aviv University, Tel Aviv.

Kisilevitz, S., Koch, I., Gdolter, N., Agnon, A., Lipschits, O. 2022. "The Image of God or the Image of the Governor? Iron Age IIa Stone Relief from the Moza Temple." *NSAJR* 15:35-47 [Hebrew].

Kisilevitz, S., Koch, I., Lipschits, O., Vanderhooft, D. S. 2020. "Facing the Facts about the "Face of God" — A Critical Response to Yosef Garfinkel." *BAR* 46 (5): 38-45.

Kisilevitz, S., Lipschits, O. 2020a. "Another Temple in Judah: The Tale of Tel Moẓa." *BAR* 46 (1): 40-49.

———. 2020b. "Tel Moẓa: An Economic and Cultic Center from the Iron Age II (First Temple Period)." In *The Mega Project at Motza (Moẓa): The Neolithic and Later Occupations up to the 20th Century*, ed. H. Khalaily, A. Re'em, J. Vardi and I. Milevski, 295-312. NSAJRSup. Jerusalem: Israel Antiquities Authority.

Kleiman, A. 2015. "A Late Iron IIA Destruction Layer at Tel Aphek in the Sharon Plain." *Tel Aviv* 42 (2): 177-232.

———. 2019. "Invisible Kingdoms? Settlement Oscillations in the Northern Jordan Valley and State Formation in Southwestern Syria." In *Research on Israel and Aram. Autonomy, Independence and Related Issues. Proceedings of the First Annual RIAB Center Conference, Leipzig, June 2016*, ed. A. Berlejung and A. M. Maeir, 293-314. Tübingen: Mohr Siebeck.

———. 2022. *Beyond Israel and Aram: The Archaeology and History of Iron Age Communities in the Central Levant*. ORA 49. Tübingen: Mohr Siebeck.

Kleiman, A. et al. 2017. "Cult Activity at Megiddo in Iron Age: New Evidence and Long-Term Perspective." *ZDPV* 133 (2017): 24-52.

Kleiman, A., Kaplan, A., Finkelstein, I. 2016. "Building 338 in Megiddo: New Evidence from the Field." *IEJ* 66:161-176.

Kleiman, A., Finkelstein, I. 2017. "The Date of Building 338 at Megiddo: Eppur Si Muove!." *IEJ* 68:50-55.

Kleiman, S. 2023. "The End of Cult Places in 8th Century Judah: Cult Reform or de facto Centralization?." In *Sacred Architecture in Ancient Palestine from the Bronze Age to Medieval Times*, ed. J. Kamlah and M. Witte, 249-266. ATSAT 49. Wiesbaden: Harrassowitz Verlag.

Klein, R. C. 2014. "Queen Athaliah: The Daughter of Ahab or Omri?" *JBQ* 42:11-20.

Kletter, R. 1996. *The Judean Pillar-Figurines and the Archaeology of Asherah*. BAR International Series 636. Oxford: Tempus Reparatum.

———. 1998. *Economic Keystones: The Weight System in the Kingdom of Judah*. JSOTSup. 276. Sheffield: Sheffield Academic Press.

———. 2004. "Chronology and United Monarchy: A Methodological Review." *ZDPV* 120:13-54.

———. 2006. *Just Past? The Making of Israeli Archaeology*. London: Equinox.

———. 2016. "Anthropomorphic and Zoomorphic Figurines and Hollow Vessels." In *Tel Beth-Shemesh: A Border Community in Judah. Renewed Excavations 1990-2000: The Iron Age*, vol. 2, ed. S. Bunimovitz and Z. Lederman, 507-559. Tel Aviv—Winona Lake, IN: Yass Publications—Eisenbrauns.

Kloner, A. 2000-2003. *Survey of Jerusalem. The Southern Sector; The Northeastern Sector; Northwestern Sector. Introduction and Indices*. 3 vols. Jerusalem: Israel Antiquities Authority.

Knauf, E. A. 2000. "The "Low Chronology" and How Not to Deal with It." *BN* 101:56-63.

———. 2001. "Hezekiah or Manasseh? A Reconsideration of the Siloam Tunnel and Inscription." *Tel Aviv* 28 (2): 281-287.

———. 2006. "Bethel: The Israelite Impact on Judean Language and Literature." In *Judah and the Judaeans in the Persian Period*, ed. O. Lipschits and M. Oeming, 291-349. Winona Lake, IN: Eisenbrauns.

———. 2016. *1 Könige 1-14*. HthKAT. Vienna: Herder.

———. 2017. "Jeroboam ben Nimshi: The Biblical Evidence." *HeBAI* 3:290-307.

Knauf, E. A., Guillaume, Ph. 2016. *A History of Biblical Israel: The Fate of Tribes and Kingdoms from Merenptah to Bar Kochba*. Sheffield: Equinox.

Knoppers, G. N. 2005. "Mt. Gerizim and Mt. Zion: A study in the early history of the Samaritians and Jews." *SR* 34 (3-4): 309-338.
———. 2006. "Revisting the Samarian Question in the Persian Period." In *Judah and the Judaeans in the Persian Period*, ed. O. Lipschits and M. Oeming, 265-289. Winona Lake, IN: Eisenbrauns.
———. 2011. "Exile, Return and Diaspora: Expatriates and Repatriates in Late Biblical Literature." In *Texts, Contexts and Readings in Postexilic Literature: Explorations into Historiography and Identity Negotiation in Hebrew Bible and Related Texts*, ed. L. Jonker, 29-61. FAT 2/53. Tübingen: Mohr Siebeck.
———. 2013. *Jews and Samaritans: The Origins and History of Their Early Relations*. Oxford: Oxford University Press.
———. 2015. "The Construction of Judean Diasporic Identity in Ezra-Nehemiah." *JHS* 15, Article 3 (online), 1. 1. 2015.
Koch, I. 2012. "The Geopolitical Organization of the Judean Shephelah during Iron Age I-IIA." *Qathedra* 143:45-64 [Hebrew].
———. 2017a. "Revisiting the Fosse Temple at Tel Lachish." *JANER* 17:64-75.
———. 2017b. "Settlements and Interactions in the Shephelah during the Late Second through Early First Millennia BCE." In *The Shephelah during the Iron Age: Recent Archaeological Studies*, ed. O. Lipschits and A. M. Maeir, 181-207. Winona Lake, IN: Eisenbrauns.
———. 2019. "Pictorial Novelties in Context: Assyrian Iconography in Judah." In *The Last Century in the History of the Kingdom of Judah - The 7th Century BCE in Archaeological, Historical and Biblical Perspective*, ed. O. Lipschits and F. Čapek, 153-166. AIL 37. Atlanta, GA: SBL Press.
———. 2020a. "On Philistines and Early Israelite Kings." In *Saul, Benjamin, and the Emergence of Monarchy in Israel*, ed. J. J. Krause, O. Sergi and K. Weingart, 7-31. AIL 40. Atlanta, GA: SBL Press.
———. 2020b. "Southern Levantine Temples during the Iron Age II: Towards a Multivocal Narrative." *Ancient Judaism* 8:325-344.
———. 2021. *Colonial Encounters in Southwest Canaan during the Late Bronze Age and the Early Iron Age*. Leiden: Brill.
———. 2022. "Israel and Assyria, Judah and Assyria." In *The Ancient Israelite World*, ed. K. H. Keimer and G. A. Pierce, 693-712. London: Routledge.
Koch, I., Lipschits, O. 2013. "The Rosette Stamped Jar Handle System and the Kingdom of Judah at the End of the First Temple Period." *ZDPV* 129:55-76.
Koch, I., Sergi, O. 2023. *Studies in the History and Archaeology of Ancient Israel and Judah*. Tübingen: Mohr Siebeck.
Koenen, K. 2003. *Bethel: Geschichte, Kult und Theologie*. OBO 192. Freiburg: Universitätsverlag; Göttingen: Vandenhoeck & Ruprecht.
Köhlmoos, A. 2006. *Bet-El - Erinnerungen an eine Stadt. Perspektiven der alttestamentlichen Bet-El-Überlieferung*. FAT 49. Tübingen: Mohr Siebeck.
Kratz, R. G., Schipper, B. U., ed. 2022. *Elephantine in Context. Studies in History, Religion and Literature of the Judeans in Persian Period Egypt*. FAT 155. Tübingen: Mohr Siebeck.
Kraus, H.-J. 1982. *Geschichte der historisch-kritischen Erforschung des Alten Testaments*, 3rd edition. Neukirchener Verlag: Neukirchen-Vluyn.
Kreuzer, S. 1996. "Die Religion der Aramäer auf dem Hintergrund der frühen aramäischen Staaten." In *Religionsgeschichte Syriens von der Frühzeit bis zur Gegenwart*, ed. P. W. Haider, M. Hutter, and S. Kreuzer, 101-115. Stuttgart: Kohlhammer.
———. 2006. "Saul - Not Always - at War: A New Perspective on the Rise of Kingship in Israel." In *Saul in Story and Tradition*, ed. C. S. Ehrlich and M. C. White, 39-58. Tübingen: Mohr Siebeck.
Kuan, J. K. 2016. *Neo-Assyrian Historical Inscriptions and Syria-Palestine: Israelite/Judean-Tyrian-Damascene Political and Commercial Relations in the Ninth-Eighth Century BCE*. Eugene, OR: Wimp & Stock.
Kucová, L. 2005. "Common Source Theory and Composition of the Story of the Divided Monarchy in Kings with Special Emphasis on the Account of Josiah's Reform." Ph.D. thesis. University of Edinburgh, Edinburgh.

Kuhrt, A. 1983. *The Cyrus Cylinder and Achaemenid Imperial Policy*. JSOTSup 25. Sheffield: Sheffield Academic Press.

———. 2007. "Cyrus the Great of Persia: Images and Realities." In *Representations of Political Power: Case Histories from Times of Change and Dissolving Order in the Ancient Near East*, ed. M. Marlies and M. H. Feldman, 169-192. Winona Lake, IN: Eisenbrauns.

Laird, D. 2016. *Negotiating Power in Ezra-Nehemiah*. AIL 26. Atlanta, GA: SBL Press.

Lamb, D. T. 2007. *Righteous Jehu and His Evil Heir: The Deuteronomist's Negative Perspecive on Dynastic Succession*. Oxford: Oxford University Press.

Lambert, W. G. 1994. "When Did Jehu Pay Tribute?." In *Crossing the Boundaries: Essays in Biblical Interpretation in Honour of M. D. Goulder*, ed. S. E. Porter et al., 51-56. Leiden: Brill.

Langgut, D. 2022. "Mid-7th century BC human parasite remains from Jerusalem." *International Journal of Paleopathology* 36:1-6.

Langgut, D., Finkelstein, I., Litt, T., Neumann, H. F., Stein, M. 2015. "Vegetation and Climate Changes during the Bronze and Iron Ages (~3600-600 BCE) in the Southern Levant Based on Palynological Records." *Radiocarbon* 57:217-235.

Langgut, D., Gadot, Y., Porat, N., Lipschits, O. 2013. "Trapped Pollen Reveals the Secrets of Royal Persian Garden at Ramat Rahel (Jerusalem)." *Palinology* 37 (1): 115-129.

Lederman, Z., Bunimovitz, S. 2014. "Canaanites, "Shephelites" and Those Who Will Become Judahites." *NSAJR* 8:61-71 [Hebrew].

Lee-Sak, Y. 2023. "The Solomonic Districts and the Nimshide Dynasty Administrative System in the Southern Levant." *Religions* 14:598.

Lehmann, G. 2003. "The United Monarchy in the Countryside: Judah and the Shephelah during the 10th Century BCE." In *Jerusalem in Bible and Archaeology: The First Temple Period*, ed. A. G. Vaughn and A. E. Killebrew, 117-162. SBL Symposium Series 18. Atlanta, GA: SBL.

Lemaire, A. 1981a. *Les écoles et la formation de la Bible dans l'Ancient Israël*. Fribourg: Universitätsverlag; Göttingen: Vandenhoeck & Ruprecht.

———. 1981b. "Classification des estampilles royales Juéennes." *EI* 15:54*-59*.

———. 1998. "The Tel Dan Stela as a Piece of Royal Historiography." *JSOT* 81:3-14.

Lemaire, A., Halpern, B. 2010. *The Book of Kings: Source, Composition, Historiography and Reception*. Leiden: Brill.

Leonard-Fleckman, M. 2016. *The House of David: Between Political Formation and Literary Revision*. Minneapolis: Fortress Press.

Lester M. 2024. *Deuteronomy and the Material Transmission of Tradition*. VTSup 198. Leiden: Brill.

Leuchter, M. 2014. "The Medium and Message, or, what is »Deuteronomistic« about the Book of Jeremiah." *ZAW* 126:208-227.

Lev-Tov, J., Hesse, P., Gilbert, A. 2017. *The Wide Lens in Archaeology: Honoring Brian Hesse's Contributions to Anthropological Archaeology*. London: Lockwood Press.

Levin, Y. 2012. "The Identification of Khirbet Qeiyafa: A New Suggestion." *BASOR* 367:73-86.

Levin, Ch. 2019. "In Search of the Original Biblical Record of the Assyrian Conquest of Samaria." In *The Last Days of the Kingdom of Israel*, ed. S. Hasegawa, Ch. Levin, K. Radner, 251-264. BZAW 511. Berlin: de Gruyter.

Levy, T. E., ed. 1998. *The Archaeology of Society in the Holy Land*. London: Bloomsbury Academic.

Linville, J. R. 1998. *Israel in the Book of Kings—The Past as a Project of Social Identity*. JSOTSup 272. Sheffield: Sheffield Academic Press.

Lipiński, E. 2000. *The Aramaeans: Their Ancient History, Culture, Religion*. Leuven: Peeters.

———. 2006. *On the Skirts of Canaan in the Iron Age*. OLA 153. Leuven: Peeters.

Lipschits, O. 2005. *The Fall and Rise of Jerusalem: Judah under Babylonian Rule*. Winona Lake, IN: Eisenbrauns.

———. 2011. "The Origin and Date of the Volute Capitals from the Levant." In *The Fire Signals of Lachish: Studies in the Archaeology and History of Israel in the Late Bronze Age, Iron Age, and Persian Period in Honor of David Ussishkin*, ed. I. Finkelstein and N. Na'aman, 203-226. Winona Lake, IN: Eisenbrauns.

———. 2017. "Bethel Revisited." In *Rethinking Israel: Studies in the History and Archaeology of Ancient Israel in Honor of Israel Finkelstein*, ed. O. Lipschits, Y. Gadot, and J. M. Adams, 233–246. Winona Lake, IN: Eisenbrauns.

———. 2018a. "The Changing Faces of Kingship in Judah under Assyrian and Babylonian Rule." In *Changing Faces of Kingship in Syria-Palestine 1500–500 BCE*, ed. P. Dubovský and A. Gianto, 116–138. AOAT 459. Münster: Ugarit-Verlag.

———. 2018b. "Judah under Assyrian Rule and the Early Phase of Stamping Jar Handles." In *Archaeology and History of Eighth Century Judah*, ed. J. Wright and Z. Farber, 337–356. Atlanta: SBL.

Lipschits, O., Blenkinsopp, J., 2003. *Judah and the Judeans in the Neo-Babylonian Period*. Winona Lake, IN: Eisenbrauns.

Lipschits, O., Čapek, F., ed. 2019. *The Last Century in the History of the Kingdom of Judah – The 7th Century BCE in Archaeological, Historical and Biblical Perspective*. AIL 37. Atlanta, GA: SBL Press.

Lipschits, O., Gadot, Y., Arubas, B., Oeming, M., ed. 2017. *What Are the Stones Whispering? Ramat Rahel: 3000 Years of Forgotten History*. Winona Lake, IN: Eisenbrauns.

Lipschits, O., Maeir, A. M., ed. 2017. *The Shephelah during the Iron Age: Recent Archaeological Studies*. Winona Lake, IN: Eisenbrauns.

Lipschits, O., Oeming, M., ed. 2006. *Judah and the Judeans in the Persian Period*. Winona Lake, IN: Eisenbrauns.

Lipschits, O., Sergi, O., Koch, I. 2010. "Royal Judahite Jar Handles: Reconsidering the Chronology of the lmlk Stamp Impressions." *TA* 37 (1): 3–32.

———. 2011. "Judahite Stamped and Incised Jar Handles: A Tool for Studying the History of Later Monarchic Judah." *TA* 38 (1): 5–41.

Lipschits, O., Gadot, Y., and Oeming, M. 2017. "Tel Azekah after Four Seasons of Excavations: Expected and (especially) Unexpected Results." In *The Shephelah during the Iron Age— Recent Archaeological Studies*, ed. O. Lipschits and A. M. Maeir, 1–25. Winona Lake, IN: Eisenbrauns.

Lipschits, O., Vanderhooft, D. S. 2011. *The Yehud Stamp Impressions: A Corpus of Inscribed Impressions from the Persian and Hellenistic Periods in Judah*. Winona Lake, IN: Eisenbrauns.

Liverani, M. 2005. *Israel's History and the History of Israel*. London: Equinox.

Lutovský, M. 2006. *Po stopách prvních Přemyslovců I. Zrození státu 872-972. Od Bořivoje I. po Boleslava I.* Prague: Libri.

MacDonald, B. 2020. *A History of Ancient Moab from the Ninth to First Centuries BCE*. Atlanta, GA: SBL Press.

Mackenzie, D., Bunimovitz, S., Lederman, Z., Momigliano, N. 2016. *The Excavations of Beth Shemesh, November–December 2012*. New York: Routledge.

Mackerle, A. 2019. "Prophetic Books as a Historical Source for the Monarchic Period – The Problem of Historical Reliability." In *The Last Century in the History of the Kingdom of Judah – The 7th Century BCE in Archaeological, Historical and Biblical Perspective*, ed. O. Lipschits and F. Čapek, 203–218. AIL 37. Atlanta, GA: SBL Press.

Maeir, A. M. 2016. "The Aramaean Involvement in the Southern Levant: Case Studies for Identifying the Archaeological Evidence." In *In Search of Aram and Israel: Politics, Culture and the Question of Identity*, ed. O. Sergi, M. Oeming, and I. de Hulster, 79–88. ORA 20. Tübingen: Mohr Siebeck.

———. 2017a. "Philistine Gath after 20 Years: Regional Perspectives on the Iron Age at Tell es-Safi/Gath." In *The Shephelah during the Iron Age: Recent Archaeological Studies*, ed. O. Lipschits and A. M. Maeir, 139–154. Winona Lake, IN: Eisenbrauns.

———. 2017b. "Assessing Jerusalem in the Middle Bronze Age: A 2017 Perspective." *NSAJR* 11:64–74.

———. 2023. "Did Trade Stop in the Early Iron Age? The Evidence from Philistia and Beyond." *Diacrítica* 37 (2): 83–90.

Maeir, A. M., Hitchcock, L., Kolska Horwitz, L. 2013. "On the Constitution and Transformation of Philistine Identity." *OJA* 32 (1): 1–38.

Maeir, A. M., Shai, I. 2016. "Reassessing the Character of the Judahite Kingdom: Archaeological Evidence from Non-Centralized, Kinship-Based Components." In *From Sha'ar Hagolan to Shaaraim: Essays in Honor of Prof. Yosef Garfinkel*, ed. S. Ganor, I. Kreimerman, K. Streit, and M. Mumcuoglu, 323–340. Jerusalem: IES.

Magen, Y. 2007. "The Dating of the First Phase of the Samaritan Temple on Mount Gerizim in the Light of the Archaeological Evidence." In *Judah and Judeans in the Fourth Century B.C.E*, ed. O. Lipschits, G. Knoppers, and A. Rainer, 157–212. Winona Lake, IN: Eisenbrauns.

Magen, Y., Misgav, H., Tsafia, L. et al. 2004–2008. *Mount Gerizim Excavations*. Jerusalem: IAA.

Malamat, A. 1950. "The Last Wars of the Kingdom of Judah." *JANES* 9:218–227.

Martínez, G., Noort, E., ed. 1998. *Perspectives in the Study of the Old Testament & Early Judaism: A Symposium in Honour of Adam S. van der Woude on the Occasion of His 70th Birthday*. Leiden: Brill.

Master, D. M. 2001. "State Formation Theory and the Kingdom of Ancient Israel." *JNES* 60: 117–131.

Mastin, B. A. 2004. "Yahweh's Asherah, Inclusive Monotheism and the Question of Dating." In *In Search of Pre-Exilic Israel*, ed. J. Day, 326–351. London: T&T Clark.

Mastnjak, N. 2016. *Deuteronomy and the Emergence of Authority Jeremiah*. FAT 87/2. Tübingen: Mohr Siebeck.

Mayer, W. 2003. "Sennacherib's Campaign of 701 BCE: The Assyrian View." In *Like a Bird in a Cage. The Invasion of Sennacherib in 701 BCE*, ed. L. L. Grabbe, 168–200. JSOTSup 363. Sheffield: Sheffield Academic Press.

Mazar, A., 1992. *Archaeology of the Land of the Bible. 10,000–586 B.C.E*. New York: Doubleday.

———. 1997. "Iron Age Chronology: A Reply to I. Finkelstein." *Levant* 29:157–167.

———, ed. 2001. *Studies in the Archaeology of the Iron Age in Israel and Jordan*. Sheffield: Sheffield Academic Press.

———. 2004. "Greek and Levantine Iron Age Chronology: A Rejoinder." *IEJ* 54:24–36.

———. 2005. "The Debate over the Chronology of the Iron Age in the Southern Levant: Its History, the Current Situation, and a Suggested Solution." In *The Bible and Radiocarbon Dating: Archaeology, Text and Science*, ed. T. E. Levy and T. Higham, 15–30. London: Equinox.

———. 2006. *Excavations at Tel Beth-Shean 1989–1996*. Vol. 1. Jerusalem: IES.

———. 2007. "The Spade and the Text: The Interaction between Archaeology and Israelite History Relating to the Tenth-Ninth Centuries BCE." In *Understanding the History of Ancient Israel*, ed. H. G. M. Williamson, 143–171. Oxford: Oxford University Press.

———. 2010. "Archaeology and the Biblical Narrative: The Case of the United Monarchy." In *One God – One Cult – One Nation*, ed. R. Kratz and H. Spieckermann, 29–58. BZAW 405. Berlin: de Gruyter.

———. 2011. "The Egyptian Garrison Town at Beth-Shean." In *Egypt, Canaan and Israel: History, Imperialism, Ideology and Literature*, ed. S. Bar, D. Kahn, and J. J. Shirley, 155–189. Leiden: Brill.

———. 2014. "Archaeology and the Bible: Reflections on Historical Memory in the Deuteronomistic History." In *Congress Volume Munich 2013*, ed. C. M. Maier, 347–369. VTSup 163. Leiden: Brill.

———. 2016. "Culture, Identity and Politics Relating to Tel Rehov in the 10th–9th Centuries BCE." In *In Search of Aram and Israel: Politics, Culture and the Question of Identity*, ed. O. Sergi, M. Oeming, and I. de Hulster, 89–121. ORA 20. Tübingen: Mohr Siebeck.

Mazar, A., Panitz-Cohen, N. 2001. *Timnah (Tel Batash) II: The Finds from the First Millennium BCE*. Qedem 42. Jerusalem: Institute of Archaeology, The Hebrew University of Jerusalem.

———. 2008. "To What God? Alters and a House Shrine from Tel Rehov Puzzle Archaeologists." *BAR* 34 (4): 40–47.

———. 2020. *Tel Reḥov: A Bronze and Iron Age City in the Beth-Shean Valley, Vol. II*. Qedem 60. Jerusalem: Institute of Archaeology, The Hebrew University of Jerusalem.

Mazar, A., Ramsey, B. 2008. "14C Dates and the Iron Age Chronology of Israel: A Response." *Radiocarbon* 50:159-180.
Mazar, E. 1997. "King David's Palace." *BAR* 23:50-57 and 74.
———. 2006. "Did I Find King David's Palace?" *BAR* 32:16-27 and 70.
McCarter, P. K. 1974. "Yaw, Son of "Omri": A Philological Note on Israelite Chronology." *BASOR* 216:5-7.
McKenzie, S. L. 2019. "The Last Days of Israel: Chronological Considerations." In *The Last Days of the Kingdom of Israel*, ed. S. Hasegawa, Ch. Levin, K. Radner, 289-299. BZAW 511. Berlin: de Gruyter.
Mendel-Geberovich, A. 2023. "Judaean Glyptic Finds: An Updated Corpus of a Revision of Their Paleography." In *The Scribe in the Biblical World: A Bridge Between Scripts, Languages and Cultures*, ed. E. Eshel and M. Langlois, 115-144. BZAW 547. Berlin: de Gruyter.
Mendel-Geberovich, A., Chalaf, O., Uziel, J. 2020, "The People Behind the Stamps: A Newly-Found Group of Bullae and a Seal from the City of David, Jerusalem." *BASOR* 384:159-182.
Meshel, Z. 2012. *Kuntillet 'Ajrud (Ḥorvat Teman): An Iron Age II Religious Site on the Judah-Sinai Border*. Jerusalem: Israel Exploration Society.
Millard, A. R. 1991. "Large Numbers in the Assyrian Royal Inscriptions." In *Ah, Assyria: Studies in Assyrian History and Ancient Near Eastern Historiography Presented to H. Tadmor*, ed. I. Eph'al et al., 213-222. Jerusalem: Magnes Press.
Miller, D. R. 2004. "Identifying Earliest Israel." *BASOR* 333:55-68.
Miller, J. M. 1964. "The Omride Dynasty in the Light of Recent Literary and Archaeological Research." Ph.D. thesis. Emory University, Atlanta, GA.
Minokami, Y. 1989. *Die Revolution des Jehu*. Göttingen: Vandenhoeck & Ruprecht.
Misgav, H., Garfinkel, Y., Ganor, S. 2009. "The Ostracon." In *Excavation Report 2007-8*. Vol. 1 of *Khirbet Qeiyafa*, ed. Y. Garfinkel and S. Ganor, 243-257. Jerusalem: Israel Exploration Society—Institute of Archaeology.
Moore, M. B. 2006. *Philosophy and Practice in Writing a History of Ancient Israel*. New York: T&T Clark.
Moore, M. B., Kelle, B. E. 2011. *Biblical History and Israel's Past: The Changing Study of the Bible and History*. Grand Rapids, MI: Eerdmans.
Moran, W. L. 1992. *The Amarna Letters*. Baltimore, MD: The John Hopkins University Press.
Moulis, D. R. 2019. "Hezekiah's Cultic Reforms according to the Archaeological Evidence." In *The Last Century in the History of the Kingdom of Judah - the 7th Century BCE in Archaeological, Historical and Biblical Perspective*, ed. O. Lipschits and F. Čapek, 167-180. AIL 37. Atlanta, GA: SBL.
———. 2021. "To What Extent Did Foreign Aspects Influence the Religion of the Judahites? Sanctuaries, Altars and Terracotta Figurines." *Akta Fakulty filozofické Západočeské univerzity v Plzni* 13 (1): 1-18.
Münnich, M. M. 2004. "Hezekiah and Archaeology: The Answer for Nadav Na'aman." *UF* 36:333-346.
Muroaka, T. 1995. "Linguistic Notes on the Aramaic Inscription from Tel Dan." *IEJ* 45:19-21.
Mykytiuk, L. 2004. *Identifying Biblical Persons in Northwest Semitic Inscriptions of 1200-539 B.C.E.* SBL Academia Biblica 12. Atlanta, GA: SBL.
Mynářová, J. 2007. *Language of Amarna - Language of Diplomacy: Perspectives on the Amarna Letters*. Prague: Czech Institute of Egyptology.
Na'aman, N. 1979. "Sennacherib's Campaign to Judah and the Date of the lmlk Stamps." *VT* 29:61-86.
———. 1986. "Hezekiah's Fortified Cities and the lmlk Stamps." *BASOR* 261:5-21.
———. 1991. "The Kingdom of Judah under Josiah." *Tel Aviv* 18 (1): 3-71.
———. 1996a. "The Contribution of the Amarna Letters to the Debate on Jerusalem's Political Position in the Tenth Century B.C.E." *BASOR* 304:17-28.
———. 1996b. "Sources and Composition in the History of David." In *The Origins of the Ancient Israelite States*, ed. V. Fritz and P. R. Davies, 170-186. JSOTSup. 228. Sheffield: Sheffield Academic Press.

———. 1997a. "Historical and Literary Notes on the Excavations of Tel Jezreel." *TA* 24 (1): 122–128.
———. 1997b. "King Mesha and the Foundation of the Moabite Monarchy." *IEJ* 47:83–92.
———. 1998a. "Jehu Son of Omri: Legitimizing a Loyal Vassal by his Overlord." *IEJ* 48:236–238.
———. 1998b. "Royal Inscriptions and the Histories of Joash and Ahaz, Kings of Judah." *VT* 48:333–349.
———. 2000. "Three Notes on the Aramaic Inscription from Tel Dan." *IEJ* 50:92–104.
———. 2001. "An Assyrian Residence at Ramat Rahel?" *TA* 28 (2): 260–280.
———. 2002a. "In search of Reality behind the Account of David's Wars with Israel's Neighbours." *IEJ* 52:200–224.
———. 2002b. "The Abandonment of Cult Places in the Kingdom of Israel and Judah as Acts of Cult Reform." *UF* 33:585–602.
———. 2006. *Ancient Israel's History and Historiography: The First Temple Period*. Winona Lake, IN: Eisenbrauns.
———. 2007a. "The Northern Kingdom in the Late Tenth-Ninth Centuries BCE." In *Understanding the History of Ancient Israel*, ed. H. G. M. Williamson, 399–418. Oxford: Oxford University Press.
———. 2007b. "When and How Did Jerusalem Become a Great City? The Rise of Jerusalem as Judah's Premier City in the Eight-Seventh Centuries B.C.E." *BASOR* 347:21–56.
———. 2008a. "Naboth's Vineyard and the Foundation of Jezreel." *JSOT* 33:197–218.
———. 2008b. "Queen Mothers and Ancestors Cult in Judah in the First Temple Period." In *Berührungspunkte: Studien zur Social- und Religionsgeschichte Israels und seiner Umwelt. Festschrift für Rainer Albertz zu seinem 65. Geburtstag*, ed. I. Kottsieper, R. Schmitt, and J. Wöhrle, 479–490. AOAT 350. Münster: Ugarit-Verlag.
———. 2010. "Khirbet Qeiyafa in Context." *UF* 42:497–526.
———. 2013. "The Kingdom of Judah in the 9th Century BCE: Text Analysis versus Archaeological Research." *TA* 40 (2): 247–276.
———. 2014. "Dismissing the Myth of a Flood of Israelite Refugees in the Late Eight Century BCE." *ZAW* 126:1–14.
———. 2016a. "The Royal Dynasties of Judah and Israel." *ZABR* 22:59–74.
———. 2016b. "Queen Athaliah as a Literary-Historical Figure." *Semitica* 58:181–205.
———. 2020. "Was the Reign of Jeroboam II a Period of Literary Flourishing?" *HeBAI* 9:348–365.
———. 2023. "Saul's Story-Cycle: A North Israelite or Judahite Composition?" In *Studies in the History and Archaeology of Ancient Israel and Judah*, ed. I. Koch and O. Sergi, 125–138. Tübingen: Mohr Siebeck.
Naeh, L. 2015. "In Search of Identity: The Contribution of Recent Finds to Our Understanding of Iron Age Ivory Objects in the Material Culture of the Southern Levant." *AoF* 42 (1): 80–96.
Najman, H., Schmid, K. 2016. *Jeremiah's Scriptures: Production, Reception, Interaction, and Transformation*. JSJSup 173. Leiden: Brill.
Naveh, J. 1960. "A Hebrew Letter from the Seventh Century B.C." *IEJ* 10 (3): 129–139.
———. 1982. "A Fragment of an Ancient Hebrew Inscription from the Ophel." *IEJ* 32:195–198.
Neria, S., Ben-Ari, N., Freud, L., Lipschits, O. 2022. "History, Economy and Administration in Late Iron Age Judah in Light of the Excavations at Mordot Arnona, Jerusalem." *TA* 49 (1): 32–53.
Ngo, R. 2017. "Ancient Latrine: A Peek into the Hezekiah's Reform in the Bible?" *Biblical History Daily* (online), 13. 11. 2017. https://www.biblicalarchaeology.org/daily/biblical-artifacts/artifacts-and-the-bible/ancient-latrine-king-hezekiahs-reforms/.
Niemann, H. M. 2013. "Neighbours and Foes, Rivals and Kin: Philistines, Shepheleans, Judeans between Geography and Economy, History and Theology." In *The Philistines and Other "Sea Peoples" in Text and Archaeology*, ed. A. E. Killebrew and G. Lehmann, 243–264. Atlanta, GA: SBL Press.

Nissinen, M. 2019. "The Book of Hosea and the Last Days of the Northern Kingdom." In *The Last Days of the Kingdom of Israel*, ed. S. Hasegawa, Ch. Levin, K. Radner, 369-382. BZAW 511. Berlin: de Gruyter.

Nitsche, S., A. 1998. *David gegen Goliath: Die Geschichte der Geschichten einer Geschichte zur fächerübergreifenden Rezeption einer biblischen Story*. Münster: LIT Verlag 1998.

Noth, M. 1943 (1967³). *Überlieferungsgeschichtliche Studien: Die sammelnden und bearbeitenden Geschichtswerke im Alten Testament*. Königsberg: Niemeyer.

Novotny, J. 2019. "Contextualizing the Last Days of the Kingdom of Israel: What Can Assyrian Official Inscriptions Tell Us?" In *The Last Days of the Kingdom of Israel*, ed. S. Hasegawa, Ch. Levin, K. Radner, 35-53. BZAW 511. Berlin: de Gruyter.

Ntozakhe, S. C., Leepo, M. 2020. "The Empty Land: A Biblical and Socio-historical Exploration." *SHE* 46 (2):1-21.

Oded, B. 2003. "Where Is the "Myth of the Empty Land" To Be Found? History versus Myth." In *Judah and the Judeans in the Neo-Babylonian Period*, ed. O. Lipschits and J. Blenkinsopp, 55-74. Winona Lake, IN: Eisenbrauns.

Oeming, M. 1990. *Das wahre Israel: Die genealogische Vorhalle 1 Chr 1-9*. BWANT 128. Stuttgart: Kohlhammer.

———. 2001. *Gesamtbiblische Theologie der Gegenwart: Das Verhältnis von AT und NT in der hermeneutischen Diskussion seit Gerhard von Rad*. 3rd edition. Zürich: Pano-Verlag.

———. 2016. "'And the King of Arama Was at the War with Israel': History and Theology in the Elisha Cycle 2 Kings 2-13." In *In Search of Aram and Israel: Politics, Culture and the Question of Identity*, ed. O. Sergi, M. Oeming, and I. de Hulster, 401-409. ORA 20. Tübingen: Mohr Siebeck.

Ofer, A. 1993. "The Highland of Judah during the Biblical Period." Ph.D. thesis, Tel Aviv University, Tel Aviv [Hebrew].

Ofer, A., Langgut, D., Finkelstein, I., Litt, T. 2013. "Climate and the Late Bronze Collapse: New Evidence from the Southern Levant." *TA* 40 (2): 149-175.

Oorschot, J. van, Witte, M., eds. 2017. *The Origins of Yahwism*. BZAW 484. Berlin: de Gruyter.

Ornan, T. 2016. "Sketches and Final Works of Art: The Drawings and Wall Paintings of Kuntillet 'Ajrud Revisited." *Tel Aviv* 43 (1): 3-26.

Országh. J. 2013. "Petr Charvát: Zrození státu. Prvotní civilizace Starého světa." *Marginalia Historia* 1:109-134.

Oswald, W. 2009. *Stattstheorie im Alten Testament. Der politische Diskurs im Pentateuch und den Geschchtsbüchern des Alten Testaments*. Stuttgart: Kohlhammer.

Otto, S. 2001. *Jehu, Elia, und Elisa: Die Erzählung von der Jehu-Revolution und die Komposition der Elia-Elisa-Erzählungen*. BWANT 152. Stuttgart: Kohlhammer.

Pakkala, J. 2008. "Jeroboam without Bulls." *ZAW* 120:501-525.

———. 2013. *God's Word Omitted: Omissions in the Transmission of the Hebrew Bible*. Göttingen: Vandenhoeck & Ruprecht.

Panitz-Cohen, N., Mazar, A. 2006. *Timnah (Tel Batash) III: The Finds from the First Millenium BCE*. Qedem 45. Jerusalem: Institute of Archaeology, Hebrew University of Jerusalem.

Panitz-Cohen, N., Mullins, R. 2016. "Aram-Maacah? Aramaeans and Israelites on the Border: Excavations at Tell Abil el-Qameḥ (Abel-beth-maacah) in Northern Israel." In *In Search of Aram and Israel: Politics, Culture and the Question of Identity*, ed. O. Sergi, M. Oeming, and I. de Hulster, 139-167. ORA 20. Tübingen: Mohr Siebeck.

Pearce, L. E. 2006. "New Evidence for Judeans in Babylonia." In *Judah and the Judeans in the Persian Period*, ed. O. Lipschits and M. Oeming, 399-411. Winona Lake, IN: Eisenbrauns.

Pearce, L. E., Wunsch, C. 2014. *Documents of Judean Exiles and West Semites in Babylonia in the Collection of David Sofer*. CUSAS 28. Bethesda, MD: CDL Press.

Pfoh, E. 2009. *The Emergence of Israel in Ancient Palestine: Historical and Anthropological Perspectives*. Copenhagen International Seminar. London: Equinox.

Pienaar, D. N. 2009. "Symbolism in the Samaria Ivories and Architecture." *Acta Theologica* 28:48-68.

Pioske, D. 2014. "Review of Israel Finkelstein, The Forgotten Kingdom: The Archaeology and History of Northern Israel." *RBL* (October).

Porten, B. et al., ed. 1996. *The Elephantine Papyri in English: Three Millennia of Cross-Cultural Continuity and Change.* Leiden: Brill.

Porten, B., Yardeni, A. 1986-1999. *The Textbook of Aramaic Documents from Ancient Egypt.* 4 vols. Winona Lake, IN: Eisenbrauns.

Pritchard, J. B., ed. 1969. *Ancient Near Texts Relating to the Old Testament.* 3rd ed. Princeton: Princeton University Press.

Prosecký, J. 2015. *Když království sestoupilo z nebes – Mezopotámské kroniky od časů nejstarších až do doby perské vlády.* Prague: Academia.

Prudký, M. 2011. "Königtum in Israel aus kritischer Sicht der deuternomistischen Texten." In *Staat und Kirche. "Theologische Tage" zum 600 jährigen Bestehen der Universität Leipzig,* ed. M. Rutsatz and M. Scharzer, 11-36. Leipzig: Universität Leipzig.

———. 2015. "Abraham: The Blessed One among the Kings of the Nations. Observation on the Role of the Kings in Genesis 14." In *A King like All the Nations? Kingdoms of Israel and Judah in the Bible and History,* ed. M. Oeming and P. Sláma, 103-118. BVB 28. Berlin: LIT Verlag.

Puech, É. 2010. "L'ostracon de Khirbet Qeyafa et les débuts de la royauté en Israël." *Revue Biblique* 117 (2): 162-184.

Quine, C. 2020. "Athaliah and the Theopolitics of Royal Assassination." *Semitica* 62:111-127.

Quine, C. 2021. "Victory as Defeat: Narrative Subversion of Omride Strength in 1 Kings 20." *JTS* 72:620-633.

Rad, G. von 1947. *Deuteronomium-Studien.* Göttingen: Vandenhoeck & Ruprecht.

———. 1961. "Der Anfang der Geschichtsschreibung im alten Israel." In G. von Rad, *Gesammelte Studien zum Alten Testament,* 148-188. Munich: Chron. Kaiser.

Radner, K. 2019. "The "Lost Tribes of Israel" in the Context of the Resettlement Programme of the Assyrian Empire." In *The Last Days of the Kingdom of Israel,* ed. S. Hasegawa, Ch. Levin, K. Radner, 101-123. BZAW 511. Berlin: de Gruyter.

Rainey, A. F. 2001. "Stones for Bread: Archaeology versus History." *NEA* 64 (3): 140-149.

———. 2015. *The El-Amarna Correspondence.* 2 vols. Edited by W. M. Schniedewind and Z. Cochavi-Rainey. Leiden: Brill.

Redford, B. D. 1992. *Egypt, Canaan, and Israel in Ancient Times.* Princeton: Princeton University Press.

Regev, J., Uziel, J., Szanton, N., Boaretto, E. 2017. "Absolute Dating of the Gihon Spring Fortifications, Jerusalem." *Radiocarbon* 59:1171-1193.

Reich, R. 2003. "On Assyrian Presence at Ramat Rahel." *TA* 30 (1): 124-129.

———. 2018. "The Date of Gihon Spring Tower in Jerusalem." *TA* 45 (1): 114-119.

Reich, R., Shukron, E. 2004. "The History of the Gihon Spring." *Levant* 36:211-233.

———. 2008. "The Date of City Wall 501 in Jerusalem." *TA* 35 (1): 114-122.

———. 2010. "A New Segment of the Middle Bronze Fortification in the City of David." *Tel Aviv* 37 (2): 141-153.

Renfrew, C., Bahn, P. 2016. *Archaeology: Theories, Methods and Practice.* 7th ed. London: Thames & Hudson.

Rendtorff, R. 2001. *Theologie des Alten Testaments.* Vol. 2. Neukirchen-Vluyn: Neukirchener Verlag.

———. 2003. "Ägypten und die Mosaische Unterscheidung." In *Die Mosaische Unterscheidung oder der Preis des Monotheismus,* ed. J. Assmann, 193-207. Berlin: Carl Hanser Verlag.

Richardson, S. 2016. "The Many Falls of Babylon and the Shape of Forgetting." In *Envisioning the Past Through Memories: How Memory Shaped Ancient Near Eastern Societies,* ed. D. Nadali, 101-142. Cultural Memory and History in Antiquity 3. London: Bloomsbury.

Richelle, M. 2022. "Literacy and Scribalism in Israel During the Iron Age (ca. 1200/1150-586 BCE)." In *The Ancient Israelite World,* ed. K. H. Keimer and G. A. Pierce, 335-347. London—New York: Routledge.

Richter, W. 1966. *Traditionsgeschichtliche Untersuchungen zum Richterbuch.* Bonn: Hanstein.
Roaf, M. 2010. "The Rulers and the Ruled in Achaemenid Art." In *Who Was the King, Who Was not King. Proceedings of Colloquium*, ed. P. Charvát and P. Maříková Vlčková, 131-141. Prague: Institute of Archaeology of the Academy of Sciences.
Robker, J. M. 2012. *The Jehu Revolution: A Royal Tradition of the Northern Kingdom and its Ramifications.* BZAW 435. Berlin: de Gruyter.
Rogerson, J. 2010. *A Theology of the Old Testament: Cultural Memory, Communication, and Being Human.* London: SPCK.
Rollston, C. A. 2003. "The Rise of Monotheism in Ancient Israel: Biblical and Epigraphic Evidence." *SCJ* 6:95-115.
———. 2006. "Scribal Education in Ancient Israel: The Old Hebrew Epigraphic Evidence." *BASOR* 344:47-74.
———. 2010. *Writing and Literacy in the World of Ancient Israel: Epigraphic Evidence from the Iron Age.* Atlanta, GA: SBL Press.
———. 2011. "The Khirbet Qeiyafa Ostracon: Methodological Musings and Caveats." *TA* 38 (1): 67-82.
———. 2017. "Jerusalem and its Environs at the Dawn of Biblical History: Epigraphic Methodologies, Late Bronze, Iron I, and Iron IIA Evidence." *NSAJR* 11:7-20.
———. 2018. "Scripture and Inscriptions: Eighth-Century Israel and Judah in Writing." In *Archaeology and History of Eight-Century Judah*, ed. Z. I. Farber and J. L. Wright, 457-473. Ancient Near East Monographs 23. Atlanta: SBL Press.
Rom-Shiloni, D. M. 2017. "The Untold Stories: Al-Yahudu and or versus Hebrew Bible Babylonian Compositions." *WO* 47 (1): 124-134.
Römer, T. 2005. *The So-Called Deuteronomistic History: A Sociological, Historical and Literary Introduction.* New York: T&T Clark.
———. 2006. "Entstehungsphasen des "deuteronomistischen Geschichtswerkes"." In *Die deuteronomistischen Geschichtswerke. Redaktions- und religionsgeschichtliche Perspektiven zur Deuteronomismus – Diskussion in Tora und Vorderen Propheten*, ed. Markus Witte et al., 45-70. BZAW 365. Berlin: de Gruyter.
———. 2013. "Zwischen Urkunden, Fragmenten und Ergänzungen: Zum Stand der Pentateuchforschung." *ZAW* 125:2-24.
———. 2015. "Joschija, Moses und Abraham als Erben Davids. Der Umgang mit der davidischen Dynastie in der persischen Zeit." In *A King like All the Nations? Kingdoms of Israel and Judah in the Bible and History*, ed. M. Oeming and P. Sláma, 85-102. BVB 28. Berlin: LIT Verlag.
———. 2016. "The "Deuteronomistic" Character of the Book of Jeremiah. A Response to Christl M. Maier." In *Jeremiah's Scriptures: Production, Reception, Interaction, and Transformation*, ed. H. Najman and K. Schmid, 124-131. JSJSup 173. Leiden: Brill.
———. 2017a. Khirbet Qeiyafa: "Some Thoughts of a Biblical Scholar. Response to Yosef Garfinkel and Aren Maeir." In *Khirbet Qeiyafa in the Shephelah*, ed. S. Schroer and S. Münger, 73-86. OBO 282. Fribourg: Academic Press.
———. 2017b. "How Jeroboam II became Jeroboam I." *HeBAI* 3:372-382.
———. forthcoming. *Cultic Diversity and Cult Centralization in the Book of the so-called Deuteronomistic History.*
———. 2020a. "Jeroboam II and Invention of Northern Sanctuaries and Foundations Stories." In *Stones, Tablets, and Scrolls: Periods of the Formation of the Bible*, ed. P. Dubovský and F. Giuntoli, 127-142. Tübingen: Mohr Siebeck.
———. 2020b. "The So-called Deuteronomistic History and Its Theories and Composition." In *The Oxford Handbook of the Historical Books of the Hebrew Bible*, ed. B. E. Kelle and B. A. Strawn, 302-322. New York: Oxford University Press.
Römer, T., Macchi, J.-D., Nihan, C., ed. 2013. *Einleitung in das Alte Testament.* Zürich: TVZ.
Root, M. C. 2000. "Imperial Ideology in Achaemenid Persian Art: Transforming the Mesopotamian Legacy." *BCSMS* 35:19-27.

Rost, L. 1926. *Die Überlieferung von der Thronnachfolge Davids*. BWANT III/6. Stuttgart: Kohlhammer.
———. 1982. *The Succession to the Throne of David*. Sheffield: Bloomsbury.
Routledge, B. E. 2004. *Moab in the Iron Age: Hegemony, Polity, Archaeology*. Philadelphia, PA: University of Pennsylvania Press.
Rückl, J. 2015. "Aspects of Prologue Formulae in Kings." In *A King like All the Nations? Kingdoms of Israel and Judah in the Bible and History*, ed. M. Oeming and P. Sláma, 159–175. BVB 28. Berlin: LIT Verlag.
———. 2016. *A Sure House: Studies on the Dynastic Promise to David in the Books of Samuel and Kings*. OBO 281. Fribourg: Academic Press; Göttingen: Vandenhoeck & Ruprecht.
Sader, H. 2016. "The Formation and Decline of the Aramaean States in Iron Age Syria." In *State Formation and State Decline in the Near and Middle East*, ed. R. Kessler, W. Sommerfeld and L. Tramontini, 61–76. Wiesbaden: Harrassowitz Verlag.
Sapir-Hen, L., Meiri, M., Finkelstein, I. 2015. "Iron Age Pigs: New Evidence on Their Origin and Role in Forming Identity Boundaries." *Radiocarbon* 57:307–315.
Sasson, V. 1996. "Murders, Usurpers, or What? Hazael, Jehu and the Tell Dan Old Aramaic Inscription." *UF* 28:547–554.
———. 2005. "The Tell Dan Aramaic Inscription: The Problems of a New Minimized Reading." *JSS* 50:23–34.
Sergi, O. 2013. "Judah's Expansion in Historical Context." *Tel Aviv* 40 (2): 226–246.
———. 2015a. "Queenship in Judah Revisited: Athaliah and the Davidic Dynasty in Historical Perspective." In *Tabou et Transgressions*, ed. J.-M. Durand, M. Guichard and T. Römer, 99–112. OBO 274. Fribourg: Academic Press; Göttingen: Vandenhoeck & Ruprecht.
———. 2015b. "Die Schlacht von Ramoth-Gilead und der Niedergang der OmridenDynastie: Versuch einer historischen Rekonstruktion." In *A King like All the Nations? Kingdoms of Israel and Judah in the Bible and History*, ed. M. Oeming and P. Sláma, 33–49. BVB 28. Berlin: LIT Verlag.
———. 2015c. "State Formation, Religion and "Collective Identity" in the Southern Levant." *HeBAI* 4:56–77.
———. 2016a. "The Omride Dynasty and the Reshaping of the Judahite Historical Memory." *Biblica* 97 (4): 503–526.
———. 2016b. "The Gilead between Aram and Israel: Political Borders, Cultural Interaction and the Question of Jacob and the Israelite Identity." In *In Search of Aram and Israel: Politics, Culture and the Question of Identity*, ed. O. Sergi, M. Oeming, and I. de Hulster, 333–354. ORA 20. Tübingen: Mohr Siebeck.
———. 2017a. "The Emergence of Judah as a Political Entity between Jerusalem and Benjamin." *ZDPV* 133:1–23.
———. 2017b. "Rethinking Israel and the Kingdom of Saul." In *Rethinking Israel: Studies in the History and Archaeology of Ancient Israel in Honor of Israel Finkelstein*, ed. O. Lipschits, Y. Gadot, and J. M. Adams, 371–388. Winona Lake, IN: Eisenbrauns.
———. 2017c. "The United Monarchy and the Kindgom of Jeroboam II in the Story of Absalom and Sheba's Revolt (2Sam 15-20)." *HeBAI* 3:329–353.
Sergi, O., Gadot, Y. 2017. "Omride Palatial Architecture as Symbols in Action: Between State Formation, Obliteration and Heritage." *JNES* 76:103–111.
Sergi, O., Hulster, I. de 2016. "Some Historical and Methodological Considerations Regarding the Question of Political, Social and Cultural Interaction between Aram and Israel in the Early Iron Age." In *In Search of Aram and Israel: Politics, Culture and the Question of Identity*, ed. O. Sergi, M. Oeming, and I. de Hulster, 1–13. ORA 20. Tübingen: Mohr Siebeck.
Sergi, O., Karasik, A., Gadot, Y., Lipschits, O. 2012. "The Royal Judahite Storage Jar: A Computer-Generated Typology and Its Archaeological and Historical Implication." *TA* 39 (1): 64–92.
Sergi, O., Kleiman, A. 2018. "The Kingdom of Geshur and the Expansion of Aram Damascus into the Northern Jordan Valley: Archaeological and Historical Perspectives." *BASOR* 379:1–18.

Sergi, O., Koch, I. 2023. "The Transformative Capacities of Destructions in the Lowlands of the Kingdoms of Israel and Judah." In *Studies in the History and Archaeology of Ancient Israel and Judah*, ed. I. Koch and O. Sergi, 139-166. Tübingen: Mohr Siebeck.
Seters, J. van 2015. *The Pentateuch: A Social-Science Commentary*. 2nd ed. London: Bloomsbury.
Shai, I. 2017. "Tel Burna: A Judahite Fortified Town in the Shephelah." In *The Shephelah during the Iron Age: Recent Archaeological Studies*, ed. O. Lipschits and A. M. Maeir, 45-60. Winona Lake, IN: Eisenbrauns.
Shai, I., Maeir, A. M. 2003. "Pre-LMLK Jars: A New Class of Iron Age IIA Storage Jars." *TA* 32 (1): 108-123.
Shalom, N. 2023. "Sensitive Havoc? The Neobabylonian Campaigns to the Southern Levant and Ideological Aspects of Destruction." In *Studies in the History and Archaeology of Ancient Israel and Judah,* ed. I. Koch and O. Sergi, 167-186. Tübingen: Mohr Siebeck.
Sharon, A., Gilboa, A., Jull, T., Boaretto, T. 2007. "Report on the First Stage of the Iron Age Dating Project in Israel: Supporting a Low Chronology." *Radiocarbon* 41 (1): 11-46.
Shiloh, Y. 1984. *Excavations at the City of David I - 1978-1982: Interim Report of the First Five Seasons*. Qedem 19. Jerusalem: Institute of Archaeology, Hebrew University of Jerusalem.
Shochat, H. 2017. *Same Methods, New Ideas (or A Tale of Two Walls)*. Lecture. Tel Aviv, 2. 11. 2017.
Schart, A. 1998. *Die Entstehung des Zwölfenprophetenbuchs: Neubearbeitungen von Amos im Rahmen schriftübergreifender Redaktionsprozesse*. BZAW 260. Berlin: de Gruyter.
Schearing, L. S., McKenzie, S. L., ed. 1999. *Those Elusive Deuteronomists: The Phenomenon of Pan-Deuteronomism*. JSOTSup 268. Sheffield: Sheffield Academic Press.
Schipper, B. U. 1999. *Israel und Ägypten in der Königszeit: Die kulturellen Kontakte von Salomo bis zum Fall Jerusalmes*. OBO 170. Freiburg: Universitätsverlag; Göttingen: Vandenhoeck & Ruprecht.
———. 2010. "Egypt and the Kingdom of Judah under Josiah and Jehoiakim." *TA* 37 (2): 200-226.
———. 2011. "Egyptian Imperialism after the New Kingdom: The 26th Dynasty and the Southern Levant." In *Egypt, Canaan and Israel: History, Imperialism, Ideology and Literature*, ed. S. Bar, D. Kahn, and J. J. Shirley, 268-290. Leiden: Brill.
———. 2012. "Egypt and Israel: The Ways of Cultural Contact in the Late Bronze and Iron Age." *JAEI* 4:30-47.
———. 2020a. "Die Archäologie der Königszeit: Der neue Blick auf die Geschichte der Staaten Israel und Juda." *WUB* 96:26-33.
———. 2020b. "Die Judäer/Aramäer von Elephantine und ihre Religion." *ZAW* 132:57-83.
Schmid, K. 2013. *Gibt es Theologie im Alten Testament: Zum Theologiebegriff in der alttestamentlichen Wissenschaft*. TS(NF) 7. Zürich: Theologischer Verlag Zürich.
———. 2018. "The Biblical Writings in the Late Eight Century BCE." In *Archaeology and History of Eight-Century Judah*, ed. Z. I. Farber and J. L. Wright, 489-501. Ancient Near East Monographs 23. Atlanta, GA: SBL Press.
———. 2021. "How to Identify a Ptolemaic Period Text in the Hebrew Bible." In *Times of Transition: Judea in the Early Hellenistic Period*, ed. S. Honigman et al., 281-292. Mosaics 1. University Park: Eisenbrauns.
Schmitt, R. 1991. *The Bisitun Inscriptions of Darius the Great: Old Persian Text*. Corpus Inscriptorum Iranicarum, Part I: Inscription of Ancient Iran, vol. 1. London: School of Oriental and African Studies.
Schneider, T. 1995. "Did King Jehu Kill his Own Family?" *BAS* 21 (1): 26-33.
———. 1996. "Rethinking Jehu." *Biblica* 77:100-107.
Schniedewind, W. M. 1996. "Tel Dan Stela: New Light on Aramaic and Jehu's Revolt." *BASOR* 302:75-90.
———. 2004. *How the Bible Became a Book: The Textualization of Ancient Israel*. Cambridge: Cambridge University Press.
Schreiber, N. 2003. *The Cypro-Phoenician Pottery of the Iron Age*. Leiden: Brill.

Schroer, S. 2018. *Die Eisenzeit bis zum Beginn der achämenidischen Herrschaft.* Vol. 4 of *Die Ikonographie Palästinas/Israels und der Alte Orient: Eine Religionsgeschichte in Bildern.* Basel: Schwabe.

Schroer, S., Münger, S., ed. 2017. *Khirbet Qeiyafa in the Shephelah.* OBO 282. Fribourg: Academic Press.

Schülle, A. 2017. *Theology from the Beginning: Essays on the Primeval History and Its Canonical Context.* FAT 113. Tübingen: Mohr Siebeck.

Schulte, H. 1994. "The End of Omride Dynasty: Social-Ethical Observation on the Subject of Power and Violence." In *Ethics and Politics in the Hebrew Bible*, ed. D. A. Knight, 133–148. Atlanta, GA: SBL.

Singer-Avitz, L. 2006. "The Date of Kuntillet Ajrud." *TA* 33 (2): 196–228.

Sláma, P. 2015. "Pharaoh, the Bad King of Exodus 5, and Antimonarchical Strains in the Story of King Jeroboam (1Kgs 11–12)." In *A King Like all the Nations? Kingdoms of Israel and Judah in the Bible and History*, ed. M. Oeming, P. Sláma, 193–198. BVB 28. Berlin: LIT Verlag.

———. 2017. *New Theologies of the Old Testament and History: The Function of History in Modern Biblical Scholarship.* BVB 33. Zürich: LIT Verlag.

Smith, M. 2002. "Remembering God: Collective Memory in Israelite Religion." *CBQ* 64:631–651.

———. 2006. "In Solomon's Temple (1 Kings 6–7): Between Text and Archaeology." In *Confronting the Past: Archaeological and Historical Essays on Ancient Israel in Honor of William G. Dever*, ed. S. Gitin, J. E. Wright, and J. P. Dessel, 275–282. Winona Lake, IN: Eisenbrauns.

———. 2007. "Recent Study of Israelite Religion in Light of the Ugaritic Texts." In *Ugarit at Seventy-Five*, ed. K. L. Younger Jr., 1–25. Winona Lake, IN: Eisenbrauns.

Sneh, A., Weinberger, R., Shalev, E. 2010. "The Why, How, and When of the Siloam-Tunnel Reconsidered." *BASOR* 359:57–65.

Soja, E. W. 2008. "Putting Cities First: Remapping the Origins of Urbanism." In *A Companion to the City*, ed. G. Bridge and S. Watson, 26–34. Oxford: Blackwell.

Sommer, P., Třeštík, D., Žemlička, J. et al. 2009. *Přemyslovci: Budování českého státu.* Prague: Nakladatelství Lidové noviny.

Stager, E. L., Schloen, J. D., Master, M. D., ed. 2008. *The Leon Levy Expedition to Ashkelon: Ashkelon 1. Introduction and Overview (1985–2006).* Winona Lake, IN: Eisenbrauns.

Stahl, M. J. 2021. "God's Best "Frenemy": A New Perspective on YHWH and Baal in Ancient Israel and Judah." *Semitica* 63:45–94.

Stavrakopoulou, F., Barton, J., ed. 2010. *Religious Diversity in Ancient Israel and Judah.* London: T&T Clark.

Stern, E. 2010. "From Many Gods to the One God: The Archaeological Evidence." In *One God – One Cult – One Nation: Archaeological and Biblical Perspectives*, ed. R. G. Kratz and H. Spieckermann, 395–404. BZAW 405. Berlin: de Gruyter.

Stöckl, J., Waerzeggers C., ed. 2015. *Exile and Return.* BZAW 478. Berlin: de Gruyter.

Strange, J. 1975. "Joram, King of Israel and Judah." *VT* 25:191–201.

Sugimoto, D. T. (ed.) 2014a. *Transformation of a Goddess: Ishtar – Astarte – Aphrodite.* OBO 263. Fribourg: Academic Press; Göttingen: Vandenhoeck & Ruprecht.

———. 2014b. "The Judean Pillar Figurines and the "Queen of Heaven"." In *Transformation of a Goddess: Ishtar – Astarte – Aphrodite*, ed. D. T. Sugimoto, 141–167. OBO 263. Fribourg: Academic Press; Göttingen: Vandenhoeck & Ruprecht.

Szabolcs-Ferencz, K. 2024. "Is the Sin of Jehu the Fault of the Deuteronomist? Hosea 1* and the Deuteronomistic Redaction of the Book of the Four." *VT* 74:85–100.

Šmejda, L., Hejcman, M., Horák, J., Shai, I. 2017. "Ancient Settlements Activities as Important Source of Nutrients (P, K, S, Zn and Nu) in Eastern Mediterranean Ecosystems – The Case of Biblical Tel Burna, Israel." *Catena* 156:62–73.

Talshir, Z. 1996. "The Three Deaths and the Strata of Biblical Historiography." *VT* 46:213–236.

Tappy, R. E. 1992. *Early Iron Age through the Ninth Century B.C.E.* Vol. 1 of *The Archaeology of Israelite Samaria.* HSS 44. Atlanta, GA: Scholars Press.

———. 2019. "The Annals of Sargon II and the Archaeology of Samaria: Rhetorical Claims, Empirical Evidence." In *The Last Days of the Kingdom of Israel*, ed. S. Hasegawa, Ch. Levin, K. Radner, 147-187. BZAW 511. Berlin: de Gruyter.

Tavger, A. 2015. "E.P. 914 East of Beitin and the Location of the Ancient Cult Site of Bethel." In *the Highland's Depth* 5:49-69 [Hebrew].

———. 2021. "'And He Called the Name of that Place Bethel' (Gen 28:19): Historical-Geography and Archaeology of the Sanctuary of Bethel." In *The History of the Jakob Cycle (Genesis 25-35). Recent Research on the Compilation, the Redaction, and the Reception of the Biblical Narrative and Its Historical and Cultural Context*, ed. B. Hensel, 201-222. Tübingen: Mohr Siebeck.

Thareani, Y. 2016. "Enemy at the Gates? The Archaeological Visibility of the Aramaeans at Dan." In *In Search of Aram and Israel: Politics, Culture and the Question of Identity*, ed. O. Sergi, M. Oeming, and I. de Hulster, 169-197. ORA 20. Tübingen: Mohr Siebeck.

Thiel, W. 1981. *Die deuteronomistische Redaktion von Jeremia 26-45*. WMANT 52. Neukirchen-Vluyn: Neukirchener.

Thiele, E. R. 1944. "The Chronology of the Kings of Judah and Israel." *JNES* 3 (3): 137-186.

Thomas, Z. 2021. "On the Archaeology of 10th Century BCE Israel and The Idea of 'State'." *PEQ* 153 (3): 244-257.

Thompson, T. L. 2007. "Mesha and Questions of Historicity." *SJOT* 2:241-260.

Toorn, K. 2007. *Scribal Culture and the Making of the Hebrew Bible*. Cambridge, MA: Harvard University Press.

Tov, E. 1997. *Der Text der hebräischen Bibel: Handbuch der Textkritik*. Stuttgart: Kohlhammer.

Třeštík, D. 1997. *Počátky Přemyslovců: Vstup Čechů do dějin (530-935)*. Prague: Nakladatelství Lidové noviny.

———. 1999. *Češi: Jejich národ, stát, dějiny a pravdy v transformaci*. Brno: Doplněk.

———. 2003. *Mýty kmene Čechů (7.-10. století): Tři studie ke starým pověstem českým*. Prague: Nakladatelství Lidové noviny.

Ussishkin, D. 1995. "The Destruction of Megiddo at the End of the Late Bronze Age and its Historical Significance." *TA* 22 (2): 240-267.

———. 2004a. *The Renewed Archaeological Excavations at Lachish (1973-1994)*. Vol. 1. Tel Aviv: Emery and Claire Yass Publications in Archaeology.

———. 2004b. "A Synopsis of Stratigraphical, Chronological and Historical Issues." In D. Ussishkin, *The Renewed Archaeological Excavations at Lachish (1973-1994)*, vol. 1, 50-122. Tel Aviv: Emery and Claire Yass Publications in Archaeology.

———. 2011. "The Dating of the lmlk Storage Jars and Its Implications: Rejoinder to Lipschits, Sergi and Koch." *TA* 38 (2): 220-240.

———. 2016. "Was Jerusalem a Fortified Stronghold in the Middle Bronze Age? An Alternative View." *Levant* 48:135-151.

Ussishkin, D., Woodhead, J. 1992. "Excavations at Tel Jezreel 1990-1991: Preliminary Report." *TA* 19 (1): 3-56.

———. 1994. "Excavations at Tel Jezreel 1992-1993: Second Preliminary Report." *Levant* 26:1-71.

———. 1997. "Excavations at Tel Jezreel 1994-1996: Third Preliminary Report." *TA* 24 (1): 6-72.

Uziel, J., Szanton N. 2015. "Recent Excavations Near the Gihon Spring and Their Reflection on the Character of Iron II Jerusalem." *Tel Aviv* 42 (2): 233-250.

Vaughn, A. G. 1999. *Theology, History, and Archaeology in the Chronicler's Account of Hezekiah*. Archaeology and Biblical Studies 4. Atlanta, GA: Scholar's Press.

———. 2016. "Lmlk and Official Seal Impressions." In *Tel Beth-Shemesh: A Border Community in Judah. Renewed Excavations 1990-2000: The Iron Age*, vol. 2, ed. S. Bunimovitz and Z. Lederman, 480-501. Winona Lake, IN: Eisenbrauns.

Veen, P. van der, Theis, Ch., Görg, M. 2010. "Israel in Canaan (Long) before Pharaoh Merenptah? A Fresh Look at Berlin Statue Pedestal Relief 21687." *JAEI* 2:15-25.

Veijola, T. 1975. *Die Ewige Dynastie: David und die Entstehung seiner Dynastie nach der deuteronomistischen Darstellung*. AASF 193. Helsinki: Suomalainen Tiedeakatemia.

Velhartická, Š., ed. 2021. *100 let české staroorientalistiky. České klínopisné bádání, předovýchodní archeologie a spřízněné obory v dokumentech.* Prague: Libri.
Vermeylen, J. 2000. *La loi du plus fort: Histoire de la rédaction des récits davidiques, de 1 Samuel 8 à 1 Rois 2.* BETL 154. Leuven: Peeters.
Verner, M. 2016. *Starověký Egypt.* Prague: Ottovo nakladatelství.
Vieweger, D. 2006. *Archäologie der biblischen Welt.* Göttingen: Vandenhoeck & Ruprecht.
Waard, H. de 2020. *Jeremiah 52 in the Context of the Book of Jeremiah.* VTSup 183, Leiden: Brill 2020.
Wazana, N. 2016. "Ahaz and the Altar from Damascus (2Kings 16:10-16): Literary, Theological, and Historical-Political Considerations." In *In Search of Aram and Israel: Politics, Culture and the Question of Identity*, ed. O. Sergi, M. Oeming, and I. de Hulster, 379-400. ORA 20. Tübingen: Mohr Siebeck.
Webster, L. C., Sergi, O., Kleiman, S., Lipschits, O., Hua, Q., Jacobsen, G. E., Tristant, Y., Gadot, Y. 2017. "Preliminary Radiocarbon Results for Late Bronze Age Strata at Tel Azekah and their Implications." *Radiocarbon* 60:309-331.
Weinberg, J. 2006. "The Babylonian Conquest of Judah: Some Additional Remarks to a Scientific Consensus." *ZAW* 184:597-610.
Weinberger, A. C., Szanton, N., Uziel, J. 2017. "Ethnofabrics: Petrographic Analysis as a Tool for Illuminating Cultural Interactions and Trade Relations between Judah and Philistia during the Iron Age II." *BASOR* 377:1-20.
Weingart, K. 2014. *Stämmevolk - Staatsvolk - Gottesvolk? Studien zur Verwendung des Israel-Namens im Alten Testament.* FAT II 68. Tübingen: Mohr Siebeck.
———. 2015. "שני בתי ישראל (Isa 8:14): Concepts of Israel in the Monarchic Period." In *A King Like all the Nations? Kingdoms of Israel and Judah in the Bible and History*, ed. M. Oeming, P. Sláma, 21-32. BVB 28. Berlin: LIT Verlag.
———. 2016. "Eine zweite Chance für Israel? Gericht und Hoffnung in Hos 3,1-5." *Biblica* 97:342-359.
———. 2019. 2 Kings 15-18: "A Chronological Conundrum?" In *The Last Days of the Kingdom of Israel*, ed. S. Hasegawa, Ch. Levin, K. Radner, 267-288. BZAW 511. Berlin: de Gruyter.
Weiser, A. 1966. "Die Legitimation des Königs David: Zur Eigenart und Entstehung der sog. Geschichte von Davids Aufstieg." *VT* 16:325-354.
Wenning, R. 1989. "Meṣad Ḥašavyāhū - ein Stützpunkt des Jojakim?." In *Vom Sinai zum Horeb. Festschrift für Erich Zenger*, ed. P.-L. Hossfeld, 169-196. Würzburg: Echter.
Whisenant, J. N. 2008. "Writing, Literacy, and Textual Transmission: The Production of Literary Documents in Iron Age Judah and the Composition of the Hebrew Bible." Ph.D. thesis. University of Michigan, Ann Arbor.
Wightman, G. J. 1985. "Studies in the Stratigraphy and Chronology of Iron Age II-III in Palestine." Ph.D. thesis. University of Sydney, Sydney.
———. 1990. "The Myth of Solomon." *BASOR* 277/278:5-22.
Wihoda, M. 2015. *První česká království.* Prague: Nakladatelství Lidové noviny.
Williamson, H. G. M. 1991. "Jezreel in the Biblical Texts." *TA* 18 (1): 72-92.
———. 1996. "Tel Jezreel and the Dynasty of Omri." *PEQ* 128:41-51.
———. 2019. "Isaiah and the Fall of the Kingdom of Israel." In *The Last Days of the Kingdom of Israel*, ed. S. Hasegawa, Ch. Levin, K. Radner, 383-398. BZAW 511. Berlin: de Gruyter.
Wimmer, S. 2008a. "A New Hieratic Ostracon from Ashkelon." *TA* 35 (1): 65-72.
———. 2008b. *Palästinisches Hieratisch: Die Zahl- und Sonderzeichen der althebräischen Schrift.* Ägypten und Altes Testament 75. Wiesbaden: Harrassowitz in Kommission.
Wöhrle, J. 2008. *Der Abschluss des Zwölfprophetenbuchs: Buchübergreifende Redaktionprozesse in den späten Sammlungen.* BZAW 389. Berlin: de Gruyter.
Wood, B. G. 2005. "The Rise and Fall of the 13th-Century Exodus—Conquest Theory." *JETS* 48:475-489.
Wright, J. L. 2014. *David, King of Israel, and Caleb in Biblical Memory.* New York: Cambridge University Press.

Würthwein, E. 2008. "Die Revolution Jehus: Die Jehu-Erzählung in altisraelitischer und deuteronomistischer Sicht." *ZAW* 120:28-48.
Yamada, S. 2000. *The Construction of Assyrian Empire: A Historical Study of the Inscriptions of Shalmanaser III (859-824 B. C.) Relating to His Campaigns to the West*. Leiden: Brill.
Yardeni, A. 2009. "Further Observation on the Ostracon." In *Excavation Report 2007-8*. Vol. 1 of *Khirbet Qeiyafa*, ed. Y. Garfinkel and S. Ganor, 259-260. Jerusalem: Israel Exploration Society—Institute of Archaeology.
Yasur-Landau, A. 2012. "The Role of the Canaanite Population in the Aegean Migration to the Southern Levant in the Late Second Millennium BCE." In *Materiality and Social Practice: Transformative Capacities of Intercultural Encounters*, ed. J. Maran and P. W. Stockhammer, 191-197. Oxford: Oxbow.
Young, I. 1992. "The "Northernisms" of the Israelite Narrative in Kings." *ZAH* 8:63-70.
Younger Jr., K. L. 2007. "Neo-Assyrian and Israelite History in the Ninth Century: The Role of Shalmaneser III." In *Understanding the History of Ancient Israel*, ed. H. G. M. Williamson, 243-278. Oxford: Oxford University Press.
———. 2016. *A Political History of the Arameans. From Their Origins to the End of Their Polities*. Atlanta: SBL Press.
Zawadzki, S. 2010. "The Portrait of Nabonidus and Cyrus in Their (?) Chronicle: When and Why the Present Version Was Composed." In *Who Was the King, Who Was not King: Proceedings of Colloquium*, ed. P. Charvát and P. Maříková Vlčková, 142-154. Prague: Institute of Archaeology of the Academy of Sciences.
Zertal, A. 1986/87. "An Early Iron Age Cultic Site on Mount Ebal: Excavation Seasons 1982-1987." *TA* 13-14:105-165.
———. 1994. "'To the Land of the Perizzites and the Giants': On the Israelite Settlement in the Hill Country of Menasseh." In *From Nomadism to Monarchy*, ed. I. Finkelstein and N. Na'aman, 47-69. Jerusalem: Ben-zvi.
———. 2004. *The Shechem Syncline*. Vol. 1 of *The Manasseh Hill Country Survey*. Leiden: Brill.
———. 2007. *The Eastern Valleys and the Fringes of the Desert*. Vol. 2 of *The Manasseh Hill Country Survey*. Leiden: Brill.
———. 2016. *From Nahal 'Iron to Nahal Shechem*. Vol. 3 of *The Manasseh Hill Country Survey*. Leiden: Brill.
———. 2017. *From Nahal Bezeq to the Sartaba*. Vol. 4 of *The Manasseh Hill Country Survey*. Leiden: Brill.
Zevit, Z. 2001. *The Religions of Ancient Israel: A Synthesis of Parallactic Approaches*. London: Continuum.
Zimhoni, O. 1997a. "Clues from the Enclosure Fills: Pre-Omride Settlement at Tel Jezreel." *TA* 24:83-109.
———. 1997b. *Studies in the Iron Age Pottery of Israel: Typological, Archaeological and Chronological Aspects*. Tel Aviv: Tel Aviv University, Institute of Archaeology.
Zorn, J. 1993. *Tell en Nasbeh: A Re-evaluation of the Architecture and Stratigraphy of the Early Bronze Age, Iron Age and Later Periods*. Ph.D. thesis. University of California, Berkeley.
———. 2003. "Tell en-Nasbeh and the Problem of the Material Culture of the Sixth Century." In *Judah and the Judeans in the Neo-Babylonian Period*, ed. O. Lipschits and J. Blenkinsopp, 413-450. Winona Lake, IN: Eisenbrauns.
Zwickel, W. 2019. "Borders between Aram-Damascus and Israel: A Historical Investigation." In *Aramaean Borders: Defining Aramaean Territories in the 10th-8th Centuries B.C.E.*, ed. J. Dušek and J. Mynářová, 267-335. Leiden: Brill.

ANCIENT PERSONAL NAMES INDEX

Aaron 106
Abigail 94
Abijah 85, 105f
Abijam 104, 105
Abimelech 57, 63
Abiram 110
Abiyaw 132
Abner 114
Abraham 90f
Absalom 94f, 105
Adad-nirari III 78f, 86, 96, 114, 121, 139
Adoram 94
Ahab 35, 78f, 86, 88f, 99-101, 103f, 106,
 108-116, 125, 127f, 131, 151, 159, 166, 207
Ahaz 80, 97, 101, 104, 122, 126, 131, 133f, 136,
 139f, 143f, 152-161, 163-165, 168f, 176f, 179f,
 180, 207
Ahaziah (Israelite) 104f, 114f, 116, 121, 128
Ahaziah (Judahite) 103-105, 107, 110, 122, 125,
 128
Ahijah 105
Ahimit 144
Ahinoam of Jezreel 94
Alexander the Great 185
Amaziah 80, 97, 104, 114, 125f, 129f, 136
Amel-Marduk 149, 184, 191
Amon 147, 169, 175
Apries 150, 184
Artaxerxes I 196
Asa 36, 68f, 71, 85, 104-106
Ashurbanipal 146f, 165
Ashur-Dan III 121
Ashur-etil-ilani 147
Ashurnasirpal II 77
Ashur-nirari V 121
Astyages 184
Athaliah 79, 99f, 103f, 106f, 113, 118, 121, 124f,
 127-129
Azariah 104, 125f, 130-132, 134, 165

Baasha 68f, 71, 84f, 101, 104f
Baruch 178
Belshazzar 184

Ben-Hadad I 69, 88, 101, 105, 121, 129

Cyrus II 160, 184-188, 192, 195-197, 199, 202,
 207

Darius I 195, 197
Darius III 185
David 40, 53, 56, 60-64, 66f, 69-71, 74, 81,
 93-96, 105-107, 109, 112f, 117f, 122, 124, 128,
 130, 152, 156, 167, 169, 172, 177, 181, 191
Deborah 33, 92

Elah 84, 104
Elasah 194
Elijah 128, 133
Eliakim 148
Esarhaddon 77, 146f, 165
Ezekiel 191
Ezra 192, 195-201, 208

Gedaliah 175, 184, 189, 191-194
Gemariah 194
Goliath 62

Hanunu 144
Hazael 78f, 88, 97, 106, 111, 114, 116, 118, 120f,
 124f, 129, 139
Hezekiah 41, 85, 95, 97, 122f, 133, 144-147,
 152-165, 167-169, 172f, 176f, 180, 206f
Hezion 68
Hiel the Bethelite 110f
Hilkiah 175, 194
Hiram II 122, 139
Hosea 21, 133, 141, 174

Ilubidi 144
Ishmael 175, 184, 193
Ithobaal I 89

Jacob 59, 91f, 96, 135
Jecoliah 126
Jeconiah / Jehoiachin 194
Jehoaddan 126

242   ANCIENT PERSONAL NAMES INDEX

Jehoahaz 104f, 112, 114–115, 121, 129f, 139
Jehoahaz (of Judah) see Ahaz
Jehoiachin 148f, 167, 178, 183, 190–192
Jehoiada 125, 128f
Jehoiakim 148f, 170, 177f, 180, 183
Jehoram (of Israel) 79, 86, 88, 103, 107f, 113f, 116, 121, 125, 128
Jehoram (of Judah) 103f, 106, 110, 118, 122, 124, 128
Jehoshaphat 36, 71, 88, 104–106, 112–114, 129
Jehozabad, son of Shomer 125, 129
Jehu 79, 88, 99–101, 104, 106–116, 121, 124f, 127–129, 131, 133, 136, 193
Jehu the prophet 101, 105f
Jeremiah 178, 194
Jeroboam I 60, 64, 81, 84f, 87, 94, 101f, 104–107, 130, 134, 137, 151, 166, 201, 207
Jeroboam II 62, 79f, 84, 87, 91, 95f, 101f, 104, 112, 115–116, 121f, 130, 133–135, 137–139, 205
Jerusha 126
Jezebel 89, 99–101, 127
Joab 114
Joash (of Israel) 79, 84, 86, 96f, 104, 108, 112–115, 121, 125, 128–130, 133, 135f, 139, 205
Joash (of Judah) 79, 88, 99f, 104, 106f, 125–129, 160
Joseph 92
Joshua 110
Josiah 41, 85, 137, 142, 147–149, 152, 154, 160f, 164, 166–170, 172–178, 180, 183, 206f, 213
Jotham 80, 100, 104, 122, 126, 131–133, 165
Jozabad, son of Shimeath 125, 129

Labashi-Marduk 184
Luli 145

Maacah 105
Manasseh 92, 101, 123, 146f, 156, 159f, 164–170, 173, 176–178, 180, 206f
Mattaniah 149
Menahem 122, 131
Merneptah 24, 204, 209
Moses 135, 159, 196, 200

Nabonidus 184, 198
Nabopolassar 183
Nebuchadnezzar II 142, 148–150, 183f, 187, 189–191, 193f
Nebuzaraddan 150, 187
Nadab 101, 104–106
Nebat 130
Necho II 147f, 169f, 177, 183

Nimshi 104, 111–114, 129
Neriglissar 184

Omri 84, 86, 94, 104, 107–116
Osorkon IV 144

Padi 145
Pekah 86, 122, 126, 131, 134, 139
Pekahiah 122, 131, 143
Psamtik I 147, 169
Psamtik II 150

Ramesses II 24
Rehoboam 64–66, 81, 85, 94, 101, 104, 107, 201
Rezin 80, 122, 134, 139, 146

Samuel 92
Sanballat 187
Sargon II 143f, 158, 187
Saul 56f, 59–65, 69f, 74, 90, 92–94, 114, 151
Segub 110
Sennacherib 144–146, 154, 158, 189
Shabaka 144f
Shallum 131
Shalmaneser III 77–79, 109, 111
Shalmaneser IV 121
Shalmaneser V 77, 143, 187
Shamshi-Adad V 78
Shaphan 175, 194
Sheba 94
Shebanyaw 132
Shimeath 125, 129
Shomer 125, 129
Shoshenq I (Shishak) 35, 58–61, 63–66, 70, 72
Siamun 50
Solomon 35f, 40, 60, 64, 66, 81, 87, 94, 160, 172

Tabrimmon 68
Tibni 94
Tiglath-Pileser III 77, 80, 114, 121–123, 139, 143, 146, 159
Tub'alu 145

Uzziah 99, 132–134, 165

Xerxes I 196

Yaman 144

Zadok 126
Zechariah 80, 104, 108, 112, 115f, 122, 131, 139
Zedekiah 149f, 178, 183f, 194
Zibiah 126
Zimri 84, 94, 104, 112

HEBREW BIBLE/OLD TESTAMENT

Gen 208
1–11 91
25:19–37:1 91
28 135
33:28 91

Exod
15:16 196
32 91, 105f, 135

Lev
10 105f

Deut
6:20 20
26:5ff 20

Josh 25, 110, 173
4:6–8 20
6:26 110f, 159
15 171
15:20–62 170f
15:36 39, 41
15:57 47
19:41 45
21:16 45
24 92
24:2–15 20

Judg 32f, 59, 63, 92, 173
5:2ff 33
5:14 74
6:7–11 20
9 57
14–16 54
14 47
19–21 92
20–21 74

Ruth 201

1 Sam + 2 Sam 93, 95, 172, 173
1 Sam 16:14 – 2 Sam 5:10 93

1 Sam
1–3 92
2:27–36 137
5–6 46
9–14 69
9:1–3 62
13–14 70
17 62
17:52 39, 41
22 60
31:10 60

2 Sam
3 94
5:1–3 94
7 172
8 34
9–20 93
11–12 94
13–14 94
15–20 94
21:15–19 63

1 Kgs + 2 Kgs 85, 93, 95, 99f, 109, 114f, 126f, 128, 159, 164, 167f, 172f, 176f, 179, 195

1 Kgs
1–2 93f
5 172
8 129
9:16 35f, 50
11–13 140
11 101
12–13 137
12 91, 94, 116, 135, 137
12:21 74
12:23 74
12:28–29 106
12:30 137
12:31 137
13:2 137
14 63

14:25-28 65f, 72
15 105
15:3 105
15:4 105
15:13 132
15:14-15 105
15:30 132
15:32 132
15:34 132
15:17-22 69, 71
15:19 105
15:21 84
15:22 74
15:27 60
15:33 84
16 94
16:1-7 105f
16:4 101
16:15 60
16:16-22 112
16:16ff 109
16:17 60
16:23-24 86
16:24 35, 111
16:30 111
16:34 110f, 159
17 96
18 128
19:16 112
20-22 88
20 101
22:1-8 106
22:4 88
22:41-51 112
22:51 103

2 Kgs 142, 166, 173, 192
2:22 175
3:2 128
6:24 109
8:7ff 109
8:18 110
8:19 106
8:26-10:18 115
8:27 110
9-10 125, 133
9-11 99, 127
9 105f
9:1-6* 109
9:5 114
9:2 112
9:10b-12bα 109
9:11-37 101
9:13 109
9:14 112
9:16aα 109
9:17-21bα* 109
9:22abα 109
9:23a 109
9:24 108f
9:30 109
9:35 109
10:1-17 109
10:1bαβ* 109
10:2-3 109
10:7-9 109
10:12a* 109
10:16 125
10:18-29 109
10:18-27 125
10:28-29 136
10:30 112, 131
10:31-33 116
10:32 119
11-12 129
11:20 100, 127
12 160
12:5-17 128
12:18-19 125
12:18 121
13 121, 139
13:5 130
13:6 130
13:10 114
13:25 130
14 130
14:7 125
14:8 112-114
14:8-14 97, 136
14:10 125
14:24-27 130
15 131
15:2 126
15:5 132
15:11 131
15:19-20 122
16 152f, 159-161
16:5-9 140
16:7-20 80, 122
17 158, 172, 201
17:2 131
17:5-6.24-28 143, 187
17:6 188
17:18 188
17:24-33 138
17:27 138

18-28 128
18:3-4 160
18:4 159
18:7-8 158
18:11 188
19 146
20 158
20:20 156
21:1 165
21:1-18 166
21:6 159
21:10-16 177
21:15 166
21:23 147, 175
21:24 148, 169, 175
22-23 172f, 176
22:1-3 172
22:2 172
22:3 114, 175
23 201
23:11 175
23:11-12 160
23:15-20 137, 170, 172, 174
23:19 170, 172
23:25 176
23:26-27 177
23:30 148
23:37 149
24 183
24:4 149, 178
24:6 149
24:12 148f
24:13 149
24:14 149
24-25 178
25 160, 191f
25:9-10 150
25:9 191
25:10 191
25:11 191, 194
25:12 150, 191, 193
25:13-18 149, 191, 200
25:18-20 191
25:21 150, 184, 188, 191
25:22 114
25:22-26 150, 189, 191, 193
25:25-26 184
25:25 114, 175
25:26 193
25:27 149, 191

1 Chr + 2 Chr 167f, 177, 179, 185, 188, 195, 208

1 Chr
1:1 208
4:31-32 39

2 Chr 132
11:5-12 85
25 130
26:17-21 132
28 152
32:30 156
33:14 165, 167
33:20 166
35:20-26 177
36 178, 183
36:6 149, 167
36:20 192
36:22-23 195, 197
36:22 187

Ezra 185f, 188, 192, 195f, 198-201, 208
1 198
1:1-3 197
1:1-4 195, 197
1:1 187, 199
1:2-3 186
1:7-11 160, 191, 200
1:59-62 200
2 196f, 200
2:1 196
4-6 198
4 187
4:1-5 195
4:6-23 196
4:8-16 198
4:17-22 198
5:7-17 198
6:2-5 197
6:6-12 198
6:6-9 192
7:12-26 198
8 200
10 200

Neh 185, 188, 192, 195f, 199-201, 208
7 196f, 200
7:6 196
7:61-65 200
8:1 199
13:1 200
13:28 201

Ps 186
126 196

Isa 132, 134, 201
1–39 134
6:1–8:18 134
7:1 134
7:9 134
8:4 134
24 187
43:21 196
45:1 187
Jer 150, 174, 178f, 184, 190, 193f
1:1–3 74
1:2 178
3:1 155
17:26 74
20:1–6 178
21:1–10 178
22:10–30 178
22:18 149
23:1–7 179
24 194
24:1–14 179
25:11–14 197
26:6 92
27:4–20 178
27:6 194
29:1–23 179
29:1–7 194
29:10 197
30–31 199
32:44 74
33:13 74
36 148f, 178
37–39 178
37 183
37:1 178
37:5 150
37:8 150
38:1–28 179
40–42 184
41:4 190
42:1–43:13 178
42 193

43:7 193
43:28–30 193
44:1 193
52:28–30 184
52:30 184, 193
52:31 191

Lam 186
2:1 186

Ezek 191
1:1 191
8:16 160
9:2 160
11:1–21 191
34 191
40–48 191
43 191

Hos 21, 132f, 136, 141, 174
1:4–5 116
1:4 133
4:16 133
9:9 59
10:9 59
11:15 133
12:4 135
12:14 91, 135

Amos 132, 134, 136, 141
5:4–5 91, 135

Mic
1–3 187

Nah 174

Zeph 174
1 187

Zech
6:9–15 192

OTHER ANCIENT TEXTUAL SOURCES

ABC 5 142, 149, 183, 190
AHI 3.001ff 82
ANET 290 165
Ant. 10:96–98 149

COS 2.2.3 82
COS 2.4 82
COS 2.5 82
COS 2.6 17, 24
COS 2.23 88, 128
COS 2.28 156
COS 2.39 89, 107
COS 2.47 82, 121
COS 2.70R 132
COS 2.113A 124
COS 2.113C 108
COS 2.113D 108
COS 2.113E 108
COS 2.113F 79, 108
COS 2.117A 146
COS 2.118J 144
COS 2.119B 146, 189
COS 2.119C 145

COS 2.119D 145
COS 2.124 197
COS 2.263D 114
COS 2.288A 114
COS 3.14 170
COS 3.43K 150
COS 3.43L 150

DB II,88–91 198
DB III,90–92 198
DB IV,14–33 198
DB V,20–36 198

EA 74 146
EA 81 146
EA 254 28
EA 285–290 28
EA 289 28, 59

OIP 74 59

TAD A.4.3 201

MODERN AUTHORS INDEX

Adam, Klaus-Peter 93
Adams, David L. 63
Aharoni, Yohanan 41, 147, 155, 161–162, 170
Ahlström, Gösta W. 51
Albertz, Rainer 116
Albright, William 134–135, 154
Alpert, Bernard 169
Alpert, Fran 169
Alstola, Tero 190, 192
Arav, Rami 78
Arie, Eran 84, 86–87, 121
Arubas, Benjamin 189
Assis, Elie 186
Assmann, Jan 20–21, 208
Aster, Shawn Zelig 156
Athas, George 53, 122, 125
Auld Graeme 93, 99, 127, 167, 195
Avigad, Nachman 132

Bahn, Paul 34
Barkay, Gabriel 156
Barr, James 196
Barrick, Boyd W. 107
Barton, John 19, 90, 195,
Barstad, Hans 24, 144, 188, 190
Baruchi-Unna, Amitai 79, 109, 113, 121, 125, 129
Becker Uwe 134
Becking, Bob 19, 140, 146, 186, 192, 195–199
Begrich, Joachim 103
Ben-Ami, Doron 89, 117
Ben-Dor Evian, Shirley 31
Ben-Tor, Amnon 89
Ben-Shlomo, David 95, 161, 174
Ben-Yosef, Erez 56, 75
Bench, Clayton H. 107
Ber, Viktor 93
Berges, Ulrich 132, 134
Berlejung, Angelika 32, 85–88, 136–137, 144, 153, 161, 168, 173–174, 192
Bernick-Greenberg, Hannah 117
Bietenhard, Sofia K. 74, 93, 164
Blenkinsopp, Joseph 135, 148, 189–190, 199

Blum, Erhard 78, 90–91, 135
Boaretto, Elizabetta 22, 36
Bocher, Efrat 77, 118
Bolen, Todd 127
Brett, Mark Zvi 91
Briant, Pierre 185
Briffa, Joseph M. 161
Bright, John 98, 103
Brooks, Simcha Shalom 32
Brown, Emmett 44
Bunimovitz, Shlomo 28, 31–32, 41, 43–47, 49, 53, 61, 75
Bunnens, Guy 77
Burke, Aaron A. 64

Cahill, Jane M. 66, 149
Campbell, Edward F. 57, 84
Carr, David M. 90–91, 167
Carter, Charles E. 197
Čech, Pavel 127
Chalaf, Ortal 83
Chalupa, Petr 158
Charvát, Petr 74, 140
Cielontko, David 168
Clermont-Ganneau, Charles 47
Cline, Eric H. 33, 50–51, 60
Cogan, Mordechai 111
Cohen-Weinberger, Anat 56
Cook, Stanley A. 110

Dagan, Yehudah 34
Darby, Erin D. 161, 174
Davies, Philip R. 90, 196
Delamarter, Steve 148
Dever, William G. 18, 25, 28–29, 36, 64
Dietrich, Walter 63, 92–93
Doak, Brian R. 77
Dobbs-Allsopp, F. W. 186
Donner, Herbert 145, 168
Dozeman, Thomas B. 91, 133
Dubovský, Peter 111
Dušek, Jan 87, 138, 185, 187, 201
Dyck, Jonathan E. 196, 200

MODERN AUTHORS INDEX

Ebeling, Jennie 72
Edelman, Diana 174
Ein-Mor, Daniel 152, 157
Elayi, Josette 144
Eynikel, Erik 93

Fant, Clyde E. 190
Fantalkin Alexander 43, 56, 59-60, 156
Faraj, Salam 192
Faust, Avraham 29, 32, 41, 54-55, 123, 156, 190,
Ferguson, Yale H. 75
Finkelstein, Israel 22, 25, 28, 30, 34, 36, 42-44, 47, 51, 56-66, 69, 71, 73-74, 80, 82-93, 96, 98, 100, 117, 121, 123, 125, 135-136, 156, 161, 164, 166, 179
Fischer Alexander A. 93, 95
Fischer, Georg 194
Fleming Daniel E. 33, 53, 58, 74, 76, 83, 90, 93-96, 132, 134
Franklin, Norma 87
Fredericks, Daniel 83
Freud, Liora 117, 157
Frevel, Christian 24, 26, 28, 32-33, 35, 55, 64, 72, 74-75, 77, 79-84, 86, 88-89, 95-96, 101-103, 106, 108, 116-117, 119, 122, 125, 128-130, 132, 136-137, 144-147, 150, 159, 161, 166, 168-169, 174, 182, 185, 189-191, 196-199, 201
Fried, Lisbeth S. 169, 175

Gadot, Yuval 25, 27, 29, 34, 51, 57, 77, 81, 85, 89, 117-119, 123-125, 152
Galil, Gershon 42, 60, 82, 146
Ganor, Saar 39, 41-42, 162
Garbini, Giovanni 196
Garfinkel, Yosef 39-42, 52-53, 55, 57, 60-61, 163
Garsiel, Moshe 63
Gerstenberger, Erhard S. 199
Geva, Hillel 123
Ghantous, Hadi 115, 127
Gitin, Seymour 49
Gnuse, Robert K. 91
Gomes, Jules F. 135
Görg, Manfred 24
Grabbe, Lester L. 109, 160, 165, 171, 173, 195, 198
Grätz, Sebastian 186
Greer, Jonathan S. 86-87
Griffith, Timothy 44
Groot, Alon de 117
Gross, Boaz 27
Gugler, Werner 109

Guillaume, Philippe 33, 55, 75, 93, 95-96, 103, 109, 125, 136, 150, 186, 190, 202

Hall, Erin 75, 80, 121, 137, 161
Halpern, Baruch 32, 74, 98, 100, 109, 164, 195, 199
Hamilton, Mark W. 160
Handy, Lowell K. 35
Hasegawa, Shuichi 79, 100, 103, 109, 115, 125, 127
Hasel, Michael G. 29, 33
Hayes, John H. 103
Heiser, Michael S. 19
Hensel, Benedikt 91, 93, 138, 168, 185, 187, 201
Hentschel, Georg 103
Herzog, Zeev 19, 41, 49, 54, 61, 84, 135, 161-163, 174, 156, 165, 189
Hesse, Brian 44, 48
Hoblík, Jiří 132
Hoffman, Yair 133
Hrůša, Ivan 77
Hualong, Mei 74
Hulster, Izaak de 86, 121, 195
Hutton, Jeremy H. 93, 96
Hutzli, Jürg 100

Jagersma, Henk 103
Jamieson-Drake, David W. 72, 90
Japhet, Sara 186
Jepsen, Alfred 103

Kahn, Dan'el 81, 140, 187
Kaiser, Otto 63
Kang, Hoo-Goo 39-40, 52,
Kaplan, Jakob 47
Käsemann, Ernst 204
Kató, Szabolcs-Ferencz 133
Katz, Haya 32
Keel, Othmar 111, 147, 175
Kehati, Ron 41
Keimer, Kyle H. 152-154
Kelle, Brad E. 144, 188
Kelm, George L. 47
Kelso, James 134
Kenyon, Kathleen M. 71
Killebrew, Ann E. 87
Kitchen, Kenneth A. 50
Kleiman, Assaf 34, 78, 80-81, 86, 89, 117, 119, 121, 125, 161
Kleiman, Sabine 41, 51, 162, 164, 174
Klein, Reuven Chaim 107
Kletter, Raz 171
Kloner, Amos 68

Knauf, Ernst Axel 33, 55, 75, 83, 93, 95–96, 103, 109, 136–138, 156, 165, 186, 190, 202
Knoppers, Gary N. 138, 195, 201
Koch, Ido 30, 32, 49, 53, 55, 60, 77, 107, 112, 149, 154–155, 166, 168, 170–171, 176
Koenen, Klaus 135, 137
Kratz, Reinhard G. 93–94, 193, 201
Kraus, Hans J. 172
Kreimerman, Igor 41, 43, 52, 55, 162
Kreuzer, Siegfried 64, 77
Kuan, Jeffrey K. 122, 139, 143
Kucová, Lydie 174, 201
Kuhrt, Amelie 185

Laird, Donna 200
Lamb, David T. 79, 108–109, 113–114, 121, 125
Langgut, Dafna 25, 155, 157
Lee-Sak, Yitzhak 107
Leepo, Modise 144
Lederman, Zvi 28, 31, 41, 43–47, 49, 53, 61, 75
Lehmann, Gunnar 31
Lemaire, André 74, 98, 100, 109, 154, 164
Leonard-Fleckman, Mahri 107
Lester, Mark 109
Leuchter, Mark 194
Levin, Yigal 41, 63
Levin, Christoph 81, 140, 187
Linville, James R. 74
Lipiński, Edward 77–78
Lipschits, Oded 27, 32, 49, 51, 56, 61, 74, 77, 84–87, 91, 135, 142, 144, 147, 149, 151, 154–158, 163–166, 170–171, 174, 185, 188–190, 195, 199
Lutovský, Michal 40

MacDonald, Burton 78
Macchi, Jean-Daniel 167, 202
Mackenzie, Duncan 43
Mackerle, Adam 132
Maeir, Aren 30, 32, 49, 51–52, 55–56, 61, 74, 86–87, 117, 154, 158, 179
Magen, Yitzhak 138, 187
Malamat, Abraham 74
Mansbach, Richard W. 75
Martin, Mario A. 89
Master, Daniel M. 48
Mastin, Brian A. 19, 174
Mastnjak, Nathan 194
Mayer, Walter 145–146
Mazar, Amihai 22, 41, 47–51, 55, 57, 61, 64, 70, 75, 82, 87, 107, 111, 117, 119, 142, 147, 170
Mazar, Benjamin 47
Mazar, Eilat 66
McCarter, Kyle P. 111

McKenzie, Steven L. 175
Mendel-Geberovich, Anat 83
Miller, J. M. 103
Miller, Robert D. 29, 44
Misgav, Haggai 42, 82, 138
Moore, Megan Bishop 144, 188
Moulis, David R. 41, 161, 163, 174
Mullins, Robert 34, 78
Münger, Stefan 43, 92–93
Münnich, Maciej 174
Mykytiuk, Lawrence J. 132
Mynářová, Jana 24, 87

Na'aman, Naaman 28, 43, 59, 61, 63, 68, 74, 83, 90–92, 96–98, 102, 107, 111–112, 115–116, 118, 123–125, 134–135, 139, 148, 154–155, 165, 179
Naeh, Liat 89
Najman, Hindy 194
Naumann, Thomas 63
Naveh, Joseph 170, 165
Nihan, Christophe 202
Nissinen, Martti 132–133
Nitsche, Stefan A. 63
Noth, Martin 142, 173, 175
Ntozakhe, Simon C. 144

Oded B. 188–189
Oeming, Manfred 19, 20, 85–86, 121, 134, 189
Ofer, Avi 34
Oorschot, Jürgen van 19

Orszagh, Ján 74
Oswald, Wolfgang 95
Otto, Susanne 100, 109, 115

Pakkala, Juha 116, 137–138
Panitz-Cohen, Nava 34, 41, 47–50, 78, 83, 107
Pearce, Laurie E. 192
Pfoh, Emanuel 29, 32
Piasetzky, Eliazer 22, 51
Pienaar, Daniel N. 87
Pioske, Dan 64, 71
Porat, Naomi 25
Porten, Bezalel 201
Prudký, Martin 90, 142
Puech, Émile 82
Pury, Albert de 109, 167

Quine, Cate 79, 113, 125

Rad, Gerhard von 20–21
Radner, Karen 77, 140
Ramsey, Christopher 22, 51

MODERN AUTHORS INDEX

Reddish, Mitchell G. 190
Redford, Donald B. 29, 50
Regev, Johanna 25, 61, 74, 117, 124
Reich, Ronny 117, 124, 155, 165
Rendtorff, Rolf 20, 186, 201
Renfrew, Colin 34
Richardson, Seth 185
Richelle, Matthieu 72
Richter, Wolfgang 63
Roaf, Michael 197
Robinson, Edward 43
Robker, Jonathan M. 100, 109, 111, 115, 127
Rogerson, John 208
Rollston, Christopher A. 19, 42, 72, 80, 82–83, 123
Rom-Shiloni, Dalit M. 192
Römer, Thomas 52, 87, 91–93, 109, 117, 135, 137–138, 142, 167, 175, 179, 182, 199, 202
Ron, Zvi 152, 157
Root, Margaret C. 197
Rost, Leonhard 93
Rückl, Jan 74, 93, 100, 109, 142, 167, 176

Sader, Helene 77
Sandhaus, Deboara 89
Sapir-Hen, Lidar 45, 157
Sass, Benjamin 42, 47, 80, 96, 123, 132
Sasson, Victor 111, 114
Schart, Aaron 92, 132
Schearing, Linda S. 175
Schipper, Bernd U. 29, 81, 88, 124, 145, 147–149, 169, 178, 193, 201
Schloen, David J. 48
Schmid, Konrad 91, 194, 202
Schmitt, Rüdiger 197
Schneider, Tammi 112–114, 121, 125
Schniedewind, William M. 114, 121, 125, 192
Schreiber, Nicola 40
Schroer, Silvia 43, 89
Schüle, Andreas 87, 91
Sergi, Omer 30, 34, 55, 65–74, 78–79, 86, 88, 92, 94–95, 97–98, 102, 107, 109, 112, 115, 117, 119, 121, 123–124, 139, 154–155, 164
Shai, Itzik 42, 55–56, 74, 123, 154
Shalev, Yiftah 118, 156, 165
Sharon, Ilan 51
Shiloh, Yigal 71, 117
Shukron, Eli 117
Silberman, Neil A. 66
Singer-Avitz, Lily 54, 61, 84, 96, 121, 135
Sláma, Petr 19, 106, 138

Šmejda, Ladislav 55
Sneh, Amihai 156, 165
Sommer, Petr 140
Stager, Lawrence E. 48
Stahl, Michael J. 116, 137, 161
Stavrakopoulou, Francesca 19
Stern, Ephraim 19, 174
Stöckl, Jonathan 144
Strange, John 128
Streit, Katharina 53
Sugimoto, David T. 19, 161, 168, 174
Szanton, Nahshon 56, 117, 124

Tadmor, Hayim 111
Tal, Oren 156
Talshir, Zipora 148
Tappy, Ron 140
Tavger, Aaron 135
Thareani, Yifah 87
Theis, Christoffer 24
Thiel, Winfried 194
Thiele, Edwin R. 103
Thomas, Zachary 56, 75
Toorn, Karel van der 90
Tov, Emanuel 185
Třeštík, Dušan 140
Tsafia, Levana 138

Uehlinger, Christoph 111, 174
Ussishkin, David 35, 86, 117, 124, 154, 156, 162
Uziel, Joe 56, 81, 83, 89, 117, 119, 123–125, 152

Van Seters, John 199
Vanderhooft, David S. 170, 185
Vaughn, Andrew G. 154, 156
Veen, Pieter Gert van der 24, 60
Veijola, Timo 93
Vermeylen, Jacques 74, 93, 164
Vieweger, Dietrich 22

Waard, Henk de 194
Waerzeggers, Caroline 144
Wapnish, Paula 48
Wazana, Nili 137, 159–161
Webster, Lyndelle 30
Weinberger, Ram 156, 165
Weingart, Kristin 92, 100, 103, 134, 206
Weiser, Artur 93
Wenning, Robert 147
Wette, Wilhelm M. L. de 172

Wightman, Gregory J. 35–37
Wihoda, Martin 140
Williamson, Hugh G. M. 132, 134
Wimmer, Stefan 147–148
Witte, Markus 19
Whisenant, Jessica 90, 123
Wood, Bryant G. 24
Woodhead, John 86
Wöhrle, Jakob 91, 132
Wright, George R. 57, 84
Wright, Jacob L. 93
Wunsch, Cornelia 192
Würthwein, Ernst 100, 108, 115–116, 127

Yardeni, Ada 42, 82
Yasur-Landau, Assaf 49
Young, Ian 83
Younger, Lawson K. 77, 108, 122, 143

Zawadzki, Stefan 185
Žemlička, Josef 140
Zertal, Adam 28
Zevit, Ziony 174
Zilberg, Peter 41, 43, 52, 55
Zimhoni, Orna 49
Zorn, Jeffrey 74, 190
Zwickel, Wolfgang 87, 121

PLACE NAMES INDEX

Abel-beth-maacah 69
Adamah 59
Adorayim 85
Adullam 85
Aphek 26, 45, 78
Afghanistan 184
Ai 92
Akko 86
Al Jib (el-Jib) 17, 59, 67f, 190 (see also: Gibeon)
al-Maliha 68
al-Yahudu 192
Ammon 78, 122, 143
Arabah 146
Arabah, Sea 130
Arad (Tel Arad) 26, 39f, 49, 54, 59, 88, 118, 124, 148, 150, 159, 161-163, 170f, 173, 189
Aram (Aram Damascus) 73, 77f, 80f, 86, 88, 96f, 118, 120-122, 124, 126, 129, 135, 137, 139f, 143, 183
Aroer 171
Arpad 77
Arwad 79, 96, 121, 144f
Ashdod 26, 40, 45, 50, 56, 144, 147, 158, 170f
Ashkelon 40f, 48f, 122, 143, 145, 148
Asia Minor 82
Assyria 77-81, 86f, 89, 96f, 108f, 111f, 114f, 120-124, 126, 128, 134f, 137, 139f, 142-148, 151-159, 161, 163-165, 167-170, 174-179, 182f, 206
Ataroth 86
Ayalon 85
Azekah (Tel Azekah) 15, 26, 30, 39, 51f, 55, 58, 85, 145, 155, 159, 165, 170, 189

Babylon 149f, 167, 183-185, 187, 190f, 194, 196f
Babylonia 77, 122, 145, 148f, 178, 182, 185, 187, 190, 192f, 195f, 199, 202
Bactria 184
Baghdad 192
Beer-sheba (Tel Beer-sheba) 39, 41, 49f, 54, 88, 91, 118, 126, 135, 157, 162-164
Beer-sheba Valley 54, 62, 144, 146, 166, 189
Behistun/Bisutun 197

Beit Hakerem 155
Beit Mirsim (Tell Beit Mirsim) 26, 39, 123, 147, 159, 165
Beitar Illit 156
Benjamin 37, 62, 68f, 72, 74, 83, 92f, 190
Benjamin Plateau 68f, 71, 79f, 83
Benjamin highlands 62
Bethel (Beitin) 26, 37, 58, 67f, 70, 84, 91f, 96f, 103, 106, 123, 134-138, 143, 170, 172, 174, 190, 201 (see also: Gibeon-Bethel polity, Gibeon-Bethel Plateau)
Beth-horon 59
Bethlehem 70, 85, 171
Bethsaida 78, 143
Beth-shean 26, 28, 58-60, 70, 86, 91f, 112, 143
Beth-shemesh (Tel Beth-shemesh) 26, 37f, 41-49, 51-53, 55, 78, 88, 97, 118, 124f, 130, 136, 155, 157, 159, 189
Beth Zur 68, 85, 171
Bīt Našhar 192
Byblos 145

Canaan 19, 24-27, 29f, 32, 34, 51, 57, 65, 82, 92, 204
Carchemish 142, 148, 183
Carmel, Mount 86
City of David 56, 61, 66f, 71, 117f, 124, 156, 167
Coastal Plain 26, 30f, 34, 38, 44, 47, 82, 120, 144-147, 169f, 189
Cyprus 77, 145

Damascus 68, 78, 121f, 139f, 142f, 146, 159-161 (see also: Aram)
Dan (Tel Dan) 69f, 78, 80, 84, 86f, 89, 106f, 121f, 137, 143, 157
Darb el-Ghazza 121
Dead Sea 58
Dor (Tel Dor) 57, 86, 92, 143, 148
Dothan 143

Ebal, Mount 92
Edom 78, 80, 120, 122, 125, 130, 143-145, 150

Ephes-dammim 39
Ephraim 58, 62, 80, 122, 133f, 143
Ephraim, Mount 92
Eglon 92
Egypt 19f, 25, 28, 30f, 50f, 53, 59-62, 65f, 70, 76-78, 82, 87, 91, 122, 133, 135, 142-148, 150f, 164f, 167, 169f, 177-179, 182-184, 191-194, 196, 201, 204, 206
Ein Gedi 166, 171
Ekron (Tel Miqne) 31f, 39-42, 45, 47-51, 55, 144f, 148f, 158, 170f
el-Burj 67
el-Jib see Al Jib
Elah, Valley 30, 37-39, 42, 51, 61f
En Gev 77, 86, 143
Elephantine 193, 201
Eltekeh 145
Ephraim 58
es-Sidr 171
Etam 85
et-Tell 59, 67f, 77
Euphrates 34, 77, 120, 143, 148, 185

Galilee 28, 34, 80, 86, 121, 129
Galilee, Sea 58
Gath 31f, 39f, 42, 47, 50-52, 55, 58, 61, 78, 82, 85, 119, 124, 144, 158
Gaza 122, 144, 158f, 170
Geba 58, 69, 71
Gerizim 185, 187, 200f, 207
Geshur 77f
Gezer (Tel Gezer) 26, 30, 35f, 45, 47f, 50, 86, 92, 155, 170f
Gibbethon 105
Gibeon 17, 37, 57-62, 92, 155, 170f, 190
Gibeon-Bethel Plateau 57, 59-65, 74, 92
Gibeon-Bethel polity/territorial entity 64, 71-73, 83
Gihon 167
Gihon Spring 66f, 83, 117f, 124, 156
Gilboa, Mount 58, 60, 69, 92
Gilead 58, 62, 86, 92
Gilo 45, 67f, 74, 156
Giv'at Shapira 156
Gob 58, 63

Har Adir 86
Har Nof 67f
Hamath 77, 142, 144
Haran 135
Harod Valley 60
Hazor 26, 35f, 78, 80, 86, 92, 121, 157
Hebron 34, 85, 92, 94, 154f, 157, 171

Horvat Radum 189
Horvat Uza 189

Ijon 69
Iraq 192
Issis 216
Izbet Sartah 47
Israel 15, 17-20, 22-24, 26, 29, 32-35, 39, 43-48, 62, 64, 69, 77, 90-96, 110, 131, 134, 137, 142, 159, 168, 172, 176, 179-182, 185f, 188, 192, 196, 198, 200-202, 204, 207-209
Israel, Kingdom 17f, 27f, 32f, 36-38, 43f, 46, 49-52, 56-58, 60-65, 69-110, 112, 115, 119-128, 130-140, 142f, 147, 152, 157f, 160f, 166, 168, 170, 174, 176, 179f, 182, 185-188, 193, 200-202, 204-207, 209

Jabesh Gilead 58f
Jahaz 86
Jarmuth (Yarmuth) 30, 92
Jericho 110f, 150, 159, 166, 170f
Jerusalem 15, 17f, 28, 30f, 34, 37, 39, 42, 47, 56-62, 64-74, 78-81, 83, 87, 89, 92f, 95-97, 100, 104, 107, 116-118, 121-134, 136, 139, 142, 144, 146-150, 154-157, 159f, 163, 165, 167, 169-171, 174-176, 178, 180-191, 194-197, 199-202, 205-208
Jerusalem temple 20, 61, 63, 96, 106, 125, 128, 129, 142, 149f, 160f, 172, 180, 182, 184, 186, 188, 191, 195, 197, 199-202
Jezreel 86, 94, 112, 116, 133, 143
Jezreel Valley 28, 34, 58f, 78, 84f, 91f, 129
Jibleam 80, 121
Jordan 58f, 77f
Jordan Valley 111, 128
Joweizeh, spring 157
Judaean Mountains 17, 30f, 38, 44, 47, 56, 83, 88, 154, 157, 170, 202
Judah 70, 90, 93-96, 144-146, 152f, 156-159, 161f, 168, 170, 182, 184-186, 189-203, 207-209 (see also: Yehud)
Judah, Kingdom 17f, 27, 32, 36-40, 42f, 49-57, 60-65, 68-83, 87-90, 92f, 95, 97-99, 101-107, 115-132, 134, 136-162, 164-188, 202, 204-208

Karnak 59, 65, 72
Kebar, Canal 191
Keisan 57
Khirbat Zaquqa 67f
Khirbet Bir al-Hamam 67f
Khirbet ed-Dawwara 58, 60, 67f

Khirbet Qeiyafa 15, 30, 37-42, 45, 47, 50-53, 55f, 60-63, 82, 88
Khirbet Raddana 45, 67f
Khirbet Walaja 67f, 157
Kidron Valley 61
Kinneret (Chinneroth) 27, 57, 69, 80, 121
KTK 70
Kuntillet 'Ajrud 82, 121, 135, 139

Lachish (Tel Lachish) 25f, 30, 35, 39f, 49, 52, 85, 88, 92, 97, 118, 123-125, 130, 145, 147, 154f, 158f, 162-165, 170f, 189
Large Stone Structure 66, 73
Lebanon 34
Lebanon, Mount 165
Lebo-hamath 130
Levant 17f, 22, 59, 61, 73, 76-80, 87, 120-122, 139f, 142-145, 147, 150f, 153, 156, 158, 165, 169, 178, 183, 189, 206
Lydia 184

Magidû (province) 140
Mahanaim 58f, 91
Mamshit 154
Manaḥat 67
Manasseh 92
Maresha 52, 85
Megiddo 26, 28, 35f, 49, 57-59, 78, 83, 86, 112, 148, 157, 170, 177f, 183
Memphis 147, 193
Mesad Hashavyahu 147, 170
Mesopotamia 82, 143, 157, 168, 187, 192, 199
96, 169, 184, 197, 219
Migdol 193
Mizpah (Tell en-Nasbeh) 39, 59, 60, 67-69, 71f, 74, 91f, 155, 159, 170f, 175, 184, 189-191, 193f
Moab 63, 78, 86, 89, 120, 122, 143f
Moresheth-Gath 155
Moza (Tel Moza) 15, 67f, 163f, 171
Muraššu 192

Naphtali 69
Nebi Daniel 171
Nebi Samuel 171
Negev 43, 63, 121, 146, 156, 170, 189
Neo-Assyrian Empire 18, 76f, 86, 120, 123, 146, 163, 205 (see also: Assyria)
Neo-Babylonian Empire 20, 22, 74, 91, 142f, 148f, 151, 154, 169, 177-179, 182-184, 186, 189f, 193f, 197-199, 202f, 206f (see also: Babylonia)
New Canaan 34, 57f

New Kingdom 70
Nineveh 145f, 206
Nubia 145

Ophel 124, 167

Pathros 193
Philistia 30, 41, 45, 49-51, 55f, 78, 82, 144, 158
Philistine Pentapolis 26, 47, 87
Penuel 84, 91
Persepolis 197
Persian Empire 183-185, 187, 195, 198, 202
Phoenicia 86, 118, 124, 150
Pisgat Ze'ev 156

Qubur al-Walayda 47

Rabbah 58
Ramah 68f, 92
Ramat Rahel 15, 154f, 157, 165, 170, 189f
Ramoth-gilead 86, 88
Rehob 59
Rephaim, Valley 68, 157, 170f
Riblah 150, 191

Sam'al 77
Samaria 28, 35f, 77, 79-82, 84, 86f, 94, 96-98, 102f, 108, 110f, 114, 117, 120-123, 125f, 128-134, 136, 138-140, 143, 158, 170, 174, 179, 185-188, 193, 197, 200f, 203, 206-208
Saulide kingdom / Saul's territorial entity / polity / territory 56-62, 64f
Sidon 79, 89, 93, 96, 121, 145
Sion 199, 208
Sinai 20
Sinai Peninsula 34
Sirara, Mount 165
Sokoh (Sokho) 39, 58, 85, 154, 171
Sorek Valley 30, 37, 43f, 47f, 51
Sukkot (Tell Deir Alla) 59, 78
Syria 76f, 148, 150
Shaaraim 39, 41, 63
Sharon Plain 86
Shephelah 17, 26, 30-32, 34, 37, 43-47, 50f, 53-55, 60-63, 69, 73, 83, 87f, 97, 118f, 120, 124, 144-146, 149f, 155, 158f, 166, 170, 189, 204f
Shechem (Tell Balata) 26, 28, 57-59, 84, 91f, 94
Shiloh 28, 32, 57, 59, 63f, 73, 92, 137
Siloam tunnel 156, 165

Taanach 28, 49, 59, 92, 143
Tahpanhes 193

Tel Arad see Arad
Tel Aviv 15, 23, 35, 43, 56, 65
Tel Azekah see Azekah
Tel Batash (Timnah) 26, 30, 37–41, 43–52, 55, 88, 148f, 159, 170f, 189
Tel Beer-sheba see Beer-sheba
Tel Beth-shemesh see Beth-shemesh
Tel Burna 30, 55, 123, 159, 189
Tel Dan see Dan
Tel Dor see Dor
Tel Dover 77
Tel Erani 171
Tel ʿEton 123, 147, 165
Tel Gezer see Gezer
Tel Hadar 77, 143
Tel Harashim 86
Tel Haror 159
Tel Ira 150, 159, 170f, 189
Tel Jarmuth see Jarmuth
Tel Khalif 123, 147, 159, 165
Tel Lachish see Lachish
Tel Malchata 171, 189
Tel Masos 54
Tel Miqne see Ekron
Tel Motza see Motza
Tel Qiri 143
Tel Rehov 28, 41, 49, 57, 82, 107, 111f, 126, 128f
Tel Sera 159
Tel Zayit 26, 30, 47
Tell edh-Dhahab al-Gharbi 84
Tell el-Rimah 79, 114, 121
Tell er-Rumeith 86
Tell Balata see Shechem
Tell Beit Mirsim see Beit Mirsim
Tell el-Fûl 67f, 171, 190
Tell el-Hammah 84
Tell el-Milḥ 171
Tell en-Nasbeh see Mizpah
Tell es-Safi 31, 171
Tell esh-Sheriʾa 171
Tell Qasile 40, 45, 49, 86
Teman 121
Teqoa 85
Thebes 147
Timnah see Tel Batash
Tirzah (Tell el-Farʿah) 28, 59f, 62, 64, 69, 71, 78, 83f, 86, 101, 143
Transeuphratia 185
Transjordan 80, 86, 88, 89, 91f, 121, 129, 145f
Tyre 79, 96, 121f, 113, 142
Tyropoeon Valley 61
Tzora 85

United Monarchy 19, 34–37, 42, 56f, 61f, 74, 81, 85, 89f, 101–104, 107, 119f, 138, 180, 205
Urartu 122

Wadi El-Arish (Brook of Egypt) 170
Wadi az-Zarqa 86
Walaja see Khirbet Walaja
West Bank 28

Yarkon 45, 81
Yavne 171
Yehud, Persian province 172, 174, 185, 189, 197, 201
Yokneam 28, 49, 80, 121

Zemaraim 59
Ziph 85, 154